CATHOLIC CHRISTIANITY

PETER KREEFT

CATHOLIC CHRISTIANITY

A Complete Catechism of Catholic Beliefs

BASED ON THE

Catechism of the Catholic Church

IGNATIUS PRESS   SAN FRANCISCO

Nihil obstat   Rev. Milton T. Walsh, S.T.D.
Imprimatur   + Most Rev. William J. Levada, Archbishop of San Francisco
             January 23, 2001

The *nihil obstat* and *imprimatur* are official declarations that a book or pamphlet is free of doctrinal or moral error. No implication is contained therein that those who have granted the *nihil obstat* and *imprimatur* agree with the contents, opinions, or statements expressed.

The cover art is based on a fresco in the catacombs.
Symbolic elements include symbols of the Holy Eucharist
and the pillar, which represents the Church.
The lamb on the right represents the Faithful,
and the lamb on the left represents those who sadly turn away
from God's gifts in the Catholic Church.

Cover design by Riz Boncan Marsella

© 2001 Ignatius Press, San Francisco
Reprinted 2014
All rights reserved
ISBN 978-0-89870-798-4
Library of Congress control number 00-100231
Printed in the United States of America ∞

For Fr. Michael Scanlon, T.O.R.
President, Franciscan University of Steubenville,
my candidate for American Catholic of the century

If there are thank-you lines in heaven,
his will be one of the longest.

CONTENTS

PREFACE

I thought of calling this book *Mere Catholicism*, for it attempts to present simply the essential data, rather than any particular interpretation, of the Catholic faith, as C. S. Lewis did half a century ago in *Mere Christianity* for Christian faith in general.

Most converts from Protestantism say they have only added to, not subtracted from, their Protestant faith in becoming Catholics. A Catholic Christian is a "full gospel" Christian, a full or universal Christian ("Catholic" means universal). As Lewis pointed out in the preface to *Mere Christianity*, "mere" Christianity is not some abstract lowest common denominator arrived at by stripping away the differences between Protestant and Catholic or between one kind of Protestant and another. It is a real and concrete thing; and Catholicism is that thing to the fullest, not that plus something else.

Far from alienating Catholics from Protestants, this unifies them at the center. The part of the old *Baltimore Catechism* that a Protestant would affirm the most emphatically is its heart and essence, which comes right at the beginning: "Why did God make you? God made me to know him, love him, and serve him in this world and to enjoy him forever in the next." And the part of the Protestant *Heidelberg Catechism* that a Catholic would affirm the most emphatically is its heart, which also comes right at the beginning: "What is your only comfort in life and in death? That I belong—body and soul, in life and in death—not to myself but to my faithful Savior Jesus Christ, who at the cost of his own blood has fully paid for all my sins and . . . makes me wholeheartedly willing and ready from now on to live for him."

I also thought of calling the book *What Is a Catholic?* The emphasis should be on the word "is". But it seldom is. When I ask my students what a Catholic is, they tell me what a Catholic believes or (more rarely) how a Catholic behaves or (occasionally) how a Catholic worships. These are the three parts of this book, but the root of all three, and the unifying principle of all three, is the new *being*, the supernatural life, the "sanctifying grace", that is the very presence of God in us. The *Catechism of the Catholic Church* never loses sight of this essence and, therefore, of this same unity among its four parts. It is the very same thing, the same reality, that

9

(1) the Creed defines, (2) the Commandments command, and (3) the sacraments communicate. Therefore, at the beginning of its section on morality, the *Catechism* connects these three and says: "What faith confesses, the sacraments communicate: by the sacraments of rebirth, Christians have become 'children of God' [Jn 1:12; 1 Jn 3:1], 'partakers of the divine nature' [2 Pet 1:4]. Coming to see in the faith their new dignity, Christians are called to lead henceforth a life 'worthy of the gospel of Christ' [Phil 1:27]. They are made capable of doing so by the grace of Christ and the gifts of his Spirit, which they receive through the sacraments and through prayer" (*Catechism of the Catholic Church* [hereafter CCC] 1692). Every part of this organic body that is the Catholic faith is connected through its heart, which is Christ himself, "this mystery, which is Christ in you, the hope of glory" (Col 1:27). That is how St. Paul summarized the central mystery of the faith, and therefore that is how the Church has always taught it, and therefore that is how the *Catechism* teaches it, and therefore that is how this book teaches it. Its peculiar specialty is not to specialize; its peculiar angle is to have no angle but to stand up right at the center.

Half a century ago such a book would have been superfluous, for Catholics knew then twenty times more than they know now about everything in their faith: its essence, its theology, its morality, its liturgy, and its prayer; and there were twenty times more books like this one being written. The need was less, and the supply was more. Today the need is much more, and the supply is much less. Since "nature abhors a vacuum", spiritually as well as physically, I offer this unoriginal "basic data" book to those Catholics who have been robbed of the basic data of their heritage.

For the first time since the Council of Trent, in the sixteenth century, the Church has authorized an official universal catechism, the *Catechism of the Catholic Church*, because the current crisis is the greatest since the Reformation. All Catholics now have a simple, clear, one-volume reference work to answer all basic questions about what the Church officially teaches. There is no longer any excuse for the ignorance, ambiguity, or fashionable ideological slanting (at *any* angle) that has been common for over a generation. No one can be an educated Catholic today without having a copy of this *Catechism* and constantly referring to it. Let no one read this book instead of that one.

The expressed aim of the *Catechism* was defined as follows: "This catechism aims at presenting an organic synthesis of the essential and fundamental contents of Catholic doctrine, as regards both faith and morals, in the light of the Second Vatican Council and the whole of the Church's Tradition. Its principal sources are the Sacred Scriptures, the Fathers of the Church, the liturgy, and the Church's Magisterium" [living teaching authority]. "It is intended to serve 'as a point of reference for the catechisms or compendia that are composed in the various countries'[1]" (CCC 11).

This book is an attempt to be no more and no less than an extension of that.

---

[1] Extraordinary Synod of Bishops 1985, *Final Report* II B a, 4.

PART I

THEOLOGY

What Catholics Believe

Chapter 1

FAITH

1. Why we need faith

We need faith because our world is full of death.

And so are we. Each one of us will die. So will each nation. Many individuals and nations will also kill. Our world has always been a world at war with itself, because it has been at war with God. Thomas Merton wrote: "We are not at peace with others because we are not at peace with ourselves. And we are not at peace with ourselves because we are not at peace with God."

Human nature does not change. Today we live in what the Vicar of Christ has called "the culture of death", a culture that kills children before birth and kills childhood after birth, kills innocence and faithfulness and families. What is the answer to this culture of death?

Faith. The Catholic faith is the answer.

Faith in the God who has not left us in the dark but has revealed himself as our Creator; who, out of his love, designed us for a life of love, in this world and in the next.

Faith in the gospel, the good news of the man who said he was God come down from heaven to die on the Cross to save us from sin and to rise from the grave to save us from death.

Faith in the Church he left us as his visible body on earth, empowered by his Spirit, authorized to teach in his name, with his authority: to invite us to believe the truth of his gospel, to live the life of his love, and to celebrate the sacraments of his presence.

This Church is our only sure and certain light in this beautiful but broken world.

Faith is the answer to fear. Deep down we are all afraid: of suffering, or of dying, or of God's judgment, or of the unknown, or of weakness, or of our lives slipping out of our control, or of not being understood and loved. We sin because we fear. We bully because we are cowards.

Faith casts out fear as light casts out darkness. God has shone his light into our world, and it is stronger than darkness (Jn 1:5).

That light is Jesus Christ.

2. The role of faith in religion

The word "religion" comes from *religare* in Latin and means "relationship"—relationship with God.

All religions have three aspects: creed, code, and cult; words, works, and worship; theology, morality, and liturgy.

Thus there are three parts to this study of the Catholic religion: (1) what Catholics believe, (2) how Catholics live, and (3) how Catholics worship.

These are also the three parts of the *Catechism of the Catholic Church*. (The *Catechism* divides the third part into two: public worship and private prayer; thus it has four parts.)

The whole of religion stems from faith. The Creed is a summary of the faith. Morality is living the faith. Liturgy is the celebration of the faith. Prayer is what faith does.

The Catholic faith is summarized in the twelve articles of the Apostles' Creed. Catholic morality is summarized in the Ten Commandments. Catholic liturgy is summarized in the Mass. Catholic prayer is summarized in the seven petitions of the Lord's Prayer.

The Apostles' Creed is the teaching of *Christ* and his apostles. It specifies what we believe when we believe Christ's teachings. The Ten Commandments specify the way to obey *Christ's* two great commandments: to love

God and neighbor. The Mass makes *Christ* really present. The Lord's Prayer is *Christ's* answer to his disciples' plea: "Teach us to pray."

So the whole Catholic faith is summarized in Christ.

3. The act of faith and the object of faith

What do we mean by "faith"?

We must distinguish the human act of faith from the divine object of faith; *our* faith from *the* faith; the act of believing from the truth believed.

The act of faith is ours. It is our choice to believe or not to believe.

To believe *what*? What God has revealed, divine revelation. That is the object of faith.

The act of faith is relative to its object. We do not "just believe"; we believe *God*. And we do not just believe any god; we believe the true God, the Father of Jesus Christ, as revealed to us by the Church, her Bible, and her creeds.

The *Catechism* describes the act of faith this way: "Faith is a personal act—the free response of the human person to the initiative of God who reveals himself" (CCC 166). Faith is a response to data, to what has been divinely given ("data" means things given)—that is, faith is a response to divine revelation. Faith is not some feeling we work up within ourselves. Faith has data just as much as science does. But the data of faith are not the kind of thing the scientific method can discover or prove or comprehend. God does not fit into a test tube. He is not visible to the eye, only to the mind (when it is wise) and the heart (when it is holy).

4. Faith and creeds

The Church has always summarized the object of faith (what she believes) in her creeds, especially the first and most basic one, the Apostles' Creed, which we recite at the beginning of each Rosary, and the Nicene Creed, which we recite in every Sunday Mass. They are called "creeds" because they begin with "I believe", which in Latin is *credo*.

The ultimate object of faith is not creeds but God. Creeds define what we believe about God. (They do not define God himself. God cannot be defined. Only finite things can be defined.) The *Catechism* says: "We do not believe in formulas, but in those realities they express" (CCC 170). St. Thomas Aquinas says: "The believer's act [of faith] does not terminate in propositions, but in the realities [which they express]." [1] Creeds are like accurate road maps; they are necessary, but they are not sufficient. Looking at a road map is no substitute for taking the trip.

---

[1] St. Thomas Aquinas, *STh* II-II, 1, 2, ad 2.

So "[f]aith is first of all a personal adherence of man to God" (CCC 150). But "[a]t the same time, and inseparably, it is a *free assent to the whole truth that God has revealed*" (CCC 150). We believe all the truths God has revealed to us (which are summarized in the creeds) because we believe God, "who can neither deceive nor be deceived".

5. Sacred Tradition

What the Church teaches, and summarizes in her creeds, was not invented by the Church. It was handed down to her from Jesus Christ, God in the flesh. That is why it is called Sacred Tradition—"sacred" because it came from God, not mere man, and "tradition" because it was handed down (the word "tradition" means "handed down").

The Church gives us her Tradition like a mother giving a child hand-me-down clothing that has already been worn by many older sisters and brothers. But unlike any earthly clothing, this clothing is indestructible because it is not made of wool or cotton but truth. It was invented by God, not man. Sacred Tradition (capital "T") must be distinguished from all human traditions (small "t").

Sacred Tradition is part of "the deposit of faith", which also includes Sacred Scripture. It is comprised of the Church's *data*, given to her by her Lord.

It is authoritative because Christ authorized his apostles to teach it with his own authority (Lk 10:16). These apostles left bishops as their successors, and, *with the authority Christ had given them*, they ordained and authorized their successor bishops. This apostolic succession is the historical link between the Catholic Church today and Jesus Christ himself.

The Church has always been, is, and must always be faithful to her deposit of faith. It is the sum of her data; she is not its author or editor but only its mail carrier. It is God's mail. It is sacred. She does not have the authority to change or delete any part of it, no matter how unpopular it may become to any particular human society or individual. That is why she cannot approve things like fornication, divorce, contraception, or sodomy even today.

That does not mean that the faith cannot change. It constantly changes— but by growth from within, like a living plant, not by alteration or construction from without, like a machine or a factory—or a man-made ideology, philosophy, or political system. The Church can further explore and explain and interpret her original deposit of faith, drawing out more and more of its own inner meaning and applying it to changing times—and in *that* sense she "changes" it by enlarging it—but she cannot change it by shrinking it. She cannot conform it to demands from the secular world. She obeys a higher authority.

Important data of the deposit of faith are contained in the Sacred Scriptures (the Bible). The Bible does not contain all of the data but contains all that is needed for our salvation.

6. Faith and progress

The Catholic faith constantly progresses, in the way explained above (growing like a plant). It needs no "push" to make it go, like a stalled car. To try to make the faith more "progressive" is to assume it is a man-made artifact rather than a God-planted organism. Whenever the Church rejects a heresy, she rejects some external growth on this organism, like a parasite or a barnacle. When she defines her dogmas (articles of faith), she is only maturing and ripening her fruit.

This "development of doctrine" (Cardinal John Henry Newman's term) is both conservative and progressive at the same time and for the same reason (see Mt 13:52). For the Church's datum, divine revelation, is both complete (thus she conserves it) as well as ongoing (thus she helps it to progress).

The data are complete because the tradition was completely given by Christ two thousand years ago to his Church. She has all her data. She will never have new data, for Christ "is the Father's one, perfect, and unsurpassable Word. In him he has said everything; there will be no other word than this one . . . 'because what he spoke before to the prophets in parts, he has now spoken all at once by giving us . . . His Son' [2]" (CCC 65; cf. Heb 1:1-2).

The Church's Tradition is ongoing because it is alive and grows new fruits—not new in kind, like apple trees growing pears, but new in size and beauty, like bigger and better apples. "[E]ven if Revelation is already complete, it has not yet been made completely explicit; it remains for Christian faith gradually to grasp its full significance over the course of the centuries" (CCC 66). For instance, the Church's doctrine on the divine and human natures of Christ, on the Trinity, on the canon of Scripture (the list of books in the Bible), on the seven sacraments, on the nature of the Church, on the authority of the pope, on Mary, and on social ethics has developed in this way.

7. Faith and Scripture

In the Constitution on Divine Revelation, the Fathers of Vatican II write that "the Church does not derive her certainty about all revealed truths from

[2] St. John of the Cross, *The Ascent of Mount Carmel*, 2, 22, 3–5, in *The Collected Works*, trans. K. Kavanaugh, O.C.D., and O. Rodriguez, O.C.D. (Washington, D.C.: Institute of Carmelite Studies, 1979), 179–80: *Liturgy of the Hours*, Office of Readings, Advent, week 2, Monday.

the holy Scriptures alone. . . . [B]oth Scripture and Tradition must be accepted and honored" (DV 9).

Most Protestants reject all the Catholic doctrines they cannot find explicitly in Scripture—for example, Mary's Assumption into heaven—because they believe *sola scriptura*: that Scripture alone is the infallible authority. This is the fundamental reason behind all the differences between Protestant and Catholic theology.

There are at least six reasons for rejecting the idea of *sola scriptura*:

a. No Christian before Luther ever taught it, for the first sixteen Christian centuries.

b. The first generation of Christians did not even *have* the New Testament.

c. Without the Catholic Church to interpret Scripture authoritatively, Protestantism has divided into more than twenty thousand different "churches" or denominations.

d. If Scripture is infallible, as traditional Protestants believe, then the Church must be infallible too, for a fallible cause cannot produce an infallible effect, and the Church produced the Bible. The Church (apostles and saints) wrote the New Testament, and the Church (subsequent bishops) defined its canon.

e. Scripture itself calls the *Church* "the pillar and bulwark of the truth" (1 Tim 3:15).

f. And Scripture itself never teaches *sola scriptura*. Thus *sola scriptura* is self-contradictory. If we are to believe only Scripture, we should not believe *sola scriptura*.

Yet the Church is the servant of Scripture, as a teacher is faithful to her textbook. Her Book comes alive when the Holy Spirit teaches through her, as a sword comes alive in the hands of a great swordsman (see Heb 4:12).

Some of the most important principles of *interpreting* Scripture are:

a. All Scripture is a word-picture of Christ. The Word of God in words (Scripture) is about the Word of God in flesh (Christ).

b. Therefore the Old Testament is to be interpreted in light of the New (*and* vice versa), for Christ came not "to abolish the law and the prophets . . . but to fulfil them" (Mt 5:17).

c. Saints are the best interpreters of Scripture, because their hearts are closer to the heart of God, Scripture's primary Author. Christ said, "If any man's will is to do his [the Father's] will, he shall know whether the teaching is from God" (Jn 7:17).

d. The Gospels are the very heart of Scripture. The saints found no better material for meditation than these (see CCC 125–27).

e. Each passage should be interpreted in its context—both the immediate context of the passage and the overall context of the whole Bible in its unity, all the parts cohering together.

f. Scripture should be interpreted from within the living tradition of the Church. This is not narrow and limiting, but expansive and deep. It is also reasonable; for suppose a living author had written a book many years ago and had been teaching that book every day: Who could interpret that book better than he?

8. Faith and Church authority

"The Church's Magisterium" [teaching authority] "exercises the authority it holds from Christ to the fullest extent when it defines dogmas" (CCC 88). (Note that the Church *defines* dogmas; she does not *invent* them.)

These dogmas, or fundamental doctrines, are also called "mysteries" of the faith. "There are natural mysteries (for instance, time, life, love), just as there are supernatural mysteries (for instance, Trinity, Incarnation, Transubstantiation). Natural mysteries are like the sun, which enables us to see during the day, while the supernatural mysteries of faith are like the stars, which enable us to see at night. . . . Although we do not see as well at night, nevertheless we can see much farther—into the very depths of outer space" (Scott Hahn, *Catholic for a Reason*).

They are called "mysteries" because we could not have discovered them by our own reasoning (nor can we fully understand them), but God revealed them to us on a "need to know" basis, since they concern our ultimate destiny, our eternal salvation, and the way to it.

Because these dogmas are so necessary for us to know, God did not leave us only fallible and uncertain teachers. Sacred Scripture, Sacred Tradition, and the living Magisterium of the Church, when it defines dogma, are all infallible (preserved from error), certain (for God can neither deceive nor be deceived), and authoritative (binding in conscience).

The Church is our Mother and Teacher (*Mater et Magistra*). "Salvation comes from God alone" [our Heavenly Father]; "but because we receive the life of faith through the Church, she is our mother. . . . Because she is our mother, she is also our teacher in the faith" (CCC 169). "As a mother who teaches her children to speak . . . , the Church our Mother teaches us the language of faith" (CCC 171).

We now turn from the object of faith (*the* Faith) to the *act* of faith.

9. Faith and freedom

"The act of faith is of its very nature a free act" (*DH* 10, see CCC 160). Faith cannot be forced any more than love can be forced.

Therefore the attempt to threaten or coerce anyone into believing is not only morally wrong but also psychologically foolish. For what can be coerced is fear, not faith. The Church condemns coercion in religion: "Nobody may be 'forced to act against his convictions, nor is anyone to be restrained from acting in accordance with his conscience in religious matters in private or in public' " (CCC 2106 [quoting *DH* 2 § 1]). "Christ invited people to faith and conversion, but never coerced them. . . . '[H]e bore witness to the truth but refused to use force' [*DH* 11, cf. Jn 18:37]" (CCC 160).

Believing what God has revealed is submitting our mind to God's mind. This submission is not contrary to human freedom or human dignity. "Even in human relations it is not contrary to our dignity to believe what other persons tell us about themselves and their intentions or to trust their promises (for example, when a man and a woman marry)" (CCC 154).

Faith is our Yes to God's proposal of spiritual marriage. This Yes is doubly free: it comes from our free choice, and it leads us to our true freedom, for the God whose proposal we accept *is* truth ("I am the way, and the truth, and the life" [Jn 14:6], and "the truth will make you free" [Jn 8:32]).

Only if we believe will we see "the splendor of truth" (*Veritatis Splendor*). For only when we marry someone do we fully know that person, and only when we accept God's proposal of spiritual marriage, by faith, will we know the ultimate truth, who is a Person, personally.

But this Person is a gentleman. He will not compel us. He leaves us free to choose, Yes or No, for him or against him.

10. Faith and feeling

Faith is not some state of feeling we get ourselves into. It is much simpler than that. It is simply believing in God and therefore believing everything he has revealed—no matter how we feel. "God said it, so I believe it, and that settles it."

Feelings are influenced by external things, like fashions and fads, wind and weather, diet and digestion. But when God gives us the gift of faith, he gives it from within, from within our own free will.

The devil can influence our feelings, but he has no control over our faith.

We are not responsible for our (unfree) feelings, but we are responsible for our (free) faith.

Yet, though faith is not a feeling, it often produces feelings: of trust, peace, gratitude, and confidence, for instance. And faith can also be aided by feelings: for instance, when we feel trustful or grateful to someone, God or man, it is much easier for us to believe him than when we feel mistrustful or ungrateful.

But even when we do not feel trustful or peaceful, we can still believe. Faith is not dependent on feelings. It is dependent on facts: divinely revealed facts.

There is a Chinese parable about faith and feeling. Fact, Faith, and Feeling are three men walking along the top of a wall. As long as Faith keeps his eyes on Fact, ahead of him, all three keep walking. But when Faith takes his eyes off Fact and turns around to worry about how Feeling is doing, both Faith and Feeling fall off the wall. (But Fact never does.)

11. Faith and belief

Faith includes belief, but it is more than belief. Here are some of the differences:

Belief is an act of the mind; faith is also an act of the will.

Faith is an act by which one person says to another: "I choose to trust you and believe you."

The object of belief is an idea; the object of faith is a person.

Belief alone is not something to die for. But faith is. Faith is also something to live every moment.

Belief alone is not enough to save us from sin and bring us to heaven. "You believe that God is one; you do well. Even the demons believe—and shudder" (Jas 2:19). But faith does save us. We are "justified by faith" (Rom 5:1), if it is a faith that is alive and thus produces good works (cf. Jas 2:17).

Non-Catholics who, through no fault of their own, do not believe that the Catholic faith is true can still be saved by the faith in their hearts that leads them to love and seek God. For Christ promised that "he who seeks finds" (Mt 7:8). So while correct belief without faith cannot save anyone, faith without correct belief can.

12. Faith as a gift of God

"Salvation comes from God alone; but because we receive the life of faith through the Church, she is our mother . . ." [and] "teacher in the faith" (CCC 169). The faith, summarized in the creeds of the Church, comes to us, not from the Church, but through the Church from God—just as our bodily life comes from God through our mothers.

The human *act* of faith also comes to us from God, through the Holy Spirit, who inspires it. It is a gift of God.

So the faith comes to us from without, while the act of faith comes from within, but both are gifts from God.

God offers everyone the gift of faith, in both of these two senses. All have the free will to accept it or reject it, to the extent that they know it. No one can truly say, "I want to believe, but God just hasn't given me the gift of faith yet, so it's his fault, not mine, that I'm an unbeliever."

Perhaps such a person misunderstands what faith is, thinking of it as some irresistible mystical experience or sudden, undeniable light of certitude.

Instead, it is like pledging your loyalty to a king, or a friend, or a spouse: it is a choice.

13. The effect of faith

What does faith *do*? What is its power, its result, its effect?

The result of sexual intercourse is (often) a new physical life in the woman's body. The result of faith is (always) a new spiritual life in the believer's soul: the life of God himself. This is why Christ came to earth: "that they may have life [*zoē*, supernatural life], and have it abundantly" (Jn 10:10). "But to all who received him, who believed in his name, he gave power to become children of God" (Jn 1:12). Many different expressions are used for this result of faith: "salvation", "eternal life", "supernatural life", "regeneration", "sanctifying grace", "justification", "sanctification", or "being born again".

The principle is often repeated in the New Testament that if we believe, we will be saved; if not, not (see, for instance, John 3:36). Faith is necessary for salvation—not because God arbitrarily decreed this, but because of what faith is and what salvation is: If we let God into our souls (that is what faith is), then we will have God in our souls (that is what salvation is). If we do not, we will not. (For God respects our free will.) Faith is more like opening a faucet than passing a test. If you do not open the faucet of faith, you will not receive the water of salvation.

After death, those who have God's life in their souls will live in heaven in union with him forever, and those who have deliberately refused will be barren of his life forever. This is the essence of hell: to be without God, the source of all good and all joy. The biblical imagery of fire and torture is probably not meant to be taken literally, but it is certainly meant to be taken seriously. For what could ever be more serious than the loss of God forever?

Thus, there is simply nothing that makes a greater difference than faith.

14. Faith and love

This new life of God in our souls is like a plant. It has three parts. Faith is its root, its beginning. Hope is its stem, growing upward into the sky. Love is its fruit, or its flower, the best and most beautiful part of all. "So faith, hope, love abide, these three; but the greatest of these is love" (1 Cor 13:13).

Faith is invisible. Only God can see it. The works of love make our faith visible to others, as the fruits of a plant show what kind of plant it is. "Thus you will know them by their fruits" (Mt 7:20).

"So faith by itself, if it has no works, is dead" (Jas 2:17). If we have living faith, we will love, and if we love God, we will obey him. "If you love me, you will keep my commandments" (Jn 14:15). Faith's natural effect is obedience. "By faith Abraham obeyed" (Heb 11:8). "Abraham is the model of such obedience offered us by Sacred Scripture. The Virgin Mary is its most perfect embodiment" (CCC 144)—because she spoke her Yes to God with all her being (see Lk 1:38).

Good works—the works of love—are a requirement for salvation just as much as faith is, as roses are a requirement for a rose bush. Faith alone is not salvation, as roots alone are not a plant.

15. Faith and works

Most Protestants, following Luther, believe that faith alone is sufficient for salvation. The Catholic Church, following the New Testament (Mt 25; Jas 2), teaches that good works are also required. This was the single most important issue of the Protestant Reformation, the single most tragic division in the history of the Church.

But both Protestants and Catholics are beginning to see that their two apparently contradictory positions may have been saying the same essential thing in different words, words that seemed contradictory but perhaps were not. Returning to the common data—Scripture—reveals that both key words, "faith" and "salvation", are used in two senses: sometimes more narrowly and sometimes more broadly:

a. In Romans and Galatians, for example, St. Paul uses "faith" broadly, to mean acceptance of God and his offer of salvation in Christ. This is the free choice of the will that saves us. But in 1 Corinthians 13, St. Paul uses "faith" in a narrower sense in distinguishing faith from hope and love, and he says love is greater. And St. James uses faith in a narrower sense when he says that faith alone does not save us. That is, intellectual belief alone does not save us.

b. Scripture also uses "salvation" in two senses, broad and narrow. Salvation in the broad sense includes sanctification, being-made-saintly, being-made-holy; and this is a process that requires not faith alone but also good works. Salvation in the narrower sense means just being accepted by God, or justified, forgiven for sin, being in a state of grace. Catholics agree with Protestants that in this narrower sense of salvation we can be saved by faith alone—that is, by faith in the broader sense, faith as a choice of the will, not just a belief of the intellect. Faith is what lets the life of God into our soul. The thief on the cross (Lk 23:33–43) had no time for good works, but he was saved by his faith.

To summarize, then,

a. we are neither justified (forgiven) nor sanctified (made holy) by intellectual faith alone (belief);

b. we *are* justified by will-faith, or heart-faith alone;

c. but this faith will necessarily produce good works,

d. and we are not sanctified by faith alone, in either sense, but only by faith plus good works.

An analogy: a woman is made pregnant by her faith in a man, by letting him impregnate her. She is not made pregnant merely by right intellectual beliefs about him. This faith, or trust, is sufficient to *begin* her pregnancy, but she must choose to do the deeds that nourish and complete it (for example, eating the right foods).

The Protestant doctrine of justification by faith alone contradicts Scripture. St. Paul never says we are justified by faith alone, and St. James explicitly says we are *not* justified by faith alone (Jas 2:24).

But Protestants can remind us of an infinitely important truth that we often forget: that we are not saved by good works alone; that we cannot buy our way into heaven with "enough" good deeds; that none of us can deserve heaven; and therefore if we were to die tonight and meet God, and God were to ask us why he should let us into heaven, if we are Christians our answer should not begin with the word "I" but with the word "Christ".

16. Faith and reason

Faith can never contradict reason, when reason is properly used, though faith goes beyond reason. As a result of divine revelation, the Catholic faith tells us many things human reason could never have discovered by itself. But faith and reason are both roads to truth, and truth never contradicts truth.

There is one God who is the source of all truth, whether that truth is known by faith or reason; and God never contradicts himself. God is like a teacher who wrote two books and teaches from them: natural reason and supernatural revelation. There are no contradictions between the two books because they both come from the same author.

It follows that every argument against the true faith, every objection to the faith, makes some mistake in the use of reason. It either misunderstands the meaning of some terms or assumes some false premise or makes some mistake in reasoning, some logical error.

Faith cannot contradict science (see CCC 159). There are thousands of truths that make up the Catholic faith and billions of truths that the sciences have discovered; yet there is not a single real contradiction between any two of them.

When there seems to be such a contradiction—for instance, between creation and evolution—it always turns out to be no real contradiction at all. One or both have been misunderstood. For instance, the doctrine of creation does not say how or when God made man's body "of the dust from the ground" (Gen 2:7); and the theory of evolution (which is a theory, not a dogma!) does not say how souls were made, only bodies. (Souls leave no fossils!) Nor does evolution say where the very first matter that began to evolve came from.

Not only does faith not contradict reason, but reason leads to faith, discovers clues to faith, good reasons for faith. These include:

a. the power of the Gospels, and of the figure of Christ met there, to move readers' souls;

b. Christ's miracles, which continue today in various places throughout the world;

c. fulfilled prophecies (Christ in the Gospels fulfilled hundreds of specific Old Testament prophecies of the Messiah);

d. the history of the Church:

(1) her faithfulness to her doctrine, never abandoning or contradicting any point of it, despite many pressures to do so, both from without and from within, and despite the intellectual and moral weakness of her human teachers;

(2) her survival for two thousand years despite persecutions without and sins and follies within;

(3) her growth, her liveliness, her eternal youth, her production of new saints for every age; and

(4) the winsomeness and joy of her saints. If the Catholic faith is not supernatural truth, how could it have produced such supernatural goodness? Can truth and goodness contradict each other? How could humanity's two most perfect and absolute ideals lead in opposite directions? Could the human heart be so badly designed as that?

17. Faith as certainty yet mystery

Faith is not simply bright and clear, like the noonday sun. Nor is it simply dark, like an underground pit. It is like a sky full of stars on a clear night, or like a bright beam of light surrounded by darkness. Faith is certain but it is also mysterious.

The Catholic faith is certain. "It is more certain than all human knowledge because it is founded on the very word of God who cannot lie" (CCC 157). The objective (in itself) certainty of God's revelation does not depend on the subjective (in our minds) certitude of our feelings or reasons. The object of faith is not anything in ourselves; it is God. Our faith is not in our faith but in our Creator. We are certain not of our minds but of God's mind.

Faith is also mysterious, for the very same reason: because its object is God. God is infinite, and our understanding is finite. As St. Augustine said, we could sooner put all the ocean into a thimble than put all of God into our mind.

But faith naturally seeks understanding. ("Faith seeking understanding" was the definition of Christian wisdom for medieval philosophers.) If we love and trust a person—man or God—we want to know him better. A faith without curiosity is like a seed that does not grow. Indifference is farther from faith than doubt or rebellion.

Faith is like a bright light (certainty) surrounded by darkness (mystery), a light that keeps growing and illuminating new areas of the darkness.

18. Faith and beauty

Throughout history, the Catholic faith has produced great works of beauty, as naturally as the sun produces reflections on the water: in music, poetry, painting, sculpture, dance, plays, novels, and architecture. For instance, those medieval Gothic cathedrals that look like stone turned into angels ready to take flight from earth into heaven—they were built by faith: faith in the Real Presence of Christ in the Eucharist. They were built to house the Eucharist, to glorify Christ's presence there.

The Catholic faith naturally produces beauty because the God who is both the object of this faith and its author is the ultimate source and inventor of all beauty, both in nature and in the mind of the human artist.

The greatest beauty produced by faith is holiness. The most beautiful thing we will ever see in this life is the character and life of a saint, because nothing more closely resembles God. The most beautiful sight that ever appeared on this earth was Jesus Christ, divine beauty in human flesh, "full of grace and truth" (Jn 1:14)—like the "grace" of a great dancer or football player. His "moves" were perfect! The Gospels are the most beautiful of all works of art because they are portraits in man's words of the Word of God, the God-man, the Author who became a character in his own story.

Yet the divine Inventor of all earthly beauty, when he became a man, "had no form or comeliness that we should look at him, and no beauty that we should desire him" (Is 53:2). A man tortured and dying on a cross does not look beautiful. Yet this is the most beautiful thing that ever happened: God dying for us, for our sins, out of incomprehensible, infinite love. The Cross is supremely beautiful because it was the supreme work of love, and love is the supreme beauty.

19. Faith and trials

God tests our faith by allowing us to suffer. He does not make us suffer, but he allows it. He does not miraculously shield us from suffering, though he could. He does this so that we learn to trust him more; he does it to mature and strengthen our souls and thus to increase our ultimate happiness.

God also tests our faith by remaining invisible, so that we must believe him instead of seeing him. He could manifest himself in constant miraculous displays, but he does not do so, for our sake. For more "blessed are those who have not seen and yet believe" (Jn 20:29).

He tests our faith to make it stronger, as a gardener prunes a plant or a blacksmith forges iron in the fire or an athlete trains his muscles by exercise.

This is why he holds back and lets himself be forgotten, ignored, or even rejected. If we could not refuse him, our faith could not be a free choice. It is the Godfather who makes you "an offer you can't refuse", not God the Father.

We do not need to have faith in the moon: we can see it. We do not need to have faith in an equation: we can prove it. But we need to have faith in the goodness of our friends, our parents, our spouse. God is more like a friend, a father, or a husband than like the moon or an equation.

20. "Losing your faith"

No one "loses" his faith, as he loses his watch. Faith is never lost against our will, any more than it is chosen against our will. We choose to believe, and we choose not to believe.

Some of the main causes for the choice not to believe are the following (see CCC 29):

a. revolt against evil in the world and against the God who does not act as we think he should to defeat evil as quickly as we would wish;

b. ignorance or misunderstanding of the faith;

c. indifference or laziness;

d. the cares of the world, "having no time for religion" (that is, *making* no time for God);

e. greed for riches and the things money can buy, serving "the creature rather than the Creator" (Rom 1:25);

f. the scandal of bad example on the part of believers;

g. the unfashionableness of religion in a secular society;

h. the refusal to repent and give up some cherished sin;

i. fear of the unknown, fear of letting go and giving God a "blank check"; fear of trusting him;

j. fear of suffering rejection or reprisals from family, friends, or secular authorities;

k. pride, the demand to "play God", to be in control, to have our own way;

l. the difficulty in trusting God as Father if we have experienced broken families and absent or unloving human fathers.

But all these "reasons" not to believe can be answered.

21. Faith's answers

a. Faith's one-word answer to the problem of evil is: Wait. God will conquer all evil, in time, in the end. But we have to go through the middle of the story to get to the end.

b. A book like this one or the *Catechism* or a wise and good priest can usually clear up misunderstandings.

c. If we knew God as his closest friends, the saints, do, we could never be bored or indifferent to him. If we are bored with Catholic theology, morality, or liturgy, that is because we do not realize that they are the truth about this God, the good will of this God, and the celebration of the presence of this God.

d. If it is foolish to refuse to give up ten dollars to win a million, it is even more foolish to refuse to give up a little time to win eternity.

e. Everything we seek, desire, love, and enjoy in the things of this world, the things we hope money can buy—pleasure, beauty, freedom, power, peace, excitement, happiness—is to be found in God, multiplied to infinity. As St. Augustine says, "Seek what you seek, but it is not where you seek it."

f. Do we refuse to love because there are some bad lovers? Do we refuse to marry because there are some bad husbands and wives?

g. If you must choose between the two, which is better: to be accepted by God forever and be rejected by some men for a little time, or to be accepted by some men for a little time but rejected by God forever?

h. We are all sinners, sin addicts, sinaholics. We all find it hard to give up cherished sins, even after we believe (though it is much easier and happier then). But the question is not whether we can, but whether we will, whether we are willing to let God do it in us. We cannot, but he can and will, if we let him. And all who have done that say the same thing: that it is joyful liberation, like being freed from a drug habit.

i. Being born, falling in love, marrying, or travelling to a new place are all experiences of the unknown. All the greatest joys in life come from letting go.

j. Jesus promised us: "Every one who has left houses or brothers or sisters or father or mother or children or lands for my name's sake, will receive a hundredfold, and inherit eternal life" (Mt 19:29).

k. Pride was the first sin, the sin of Satan, who resented being Number Two to God. He would not obey God's will, only his own. ("Better to reign in Hell than serve in Heaven"—Milton.) This is also a selfish, spoiled baby's philosophy of life: "I want what I want when I want it." Two rather unwise models to live by, don't you think?

l. We know, from past bitter experience, that where there is no faith and trust there can be no joy. We know the past; but we do not know the future.

We do not know whether our trust will be disappointed again, by God, as it was by man. But we do know that our only hope, our only chance at joy, on earth and in heaven forever, is to trust and to love. If our trust is betrayed by men, that is all the more reason to trust God. It is not reasonable to refuse the only lifeboat that can save us when all the other boats have sunk.

22. Faith and Christ

The Catholic faith has one answer, ultimately, to all twelve of these problems; in fact, one answer to all problems: Jesus Christ, the one answer God provided. "God will supply every need of yours according to his riches in glory in Christ Jesus" (Phil 4:19).

Every Catholic home and every Catholic believer should have a crucifix. For the answer to all doubts, temptations, and trials is there. (In the reality it pictures, not just in the picture of it.) For instance, the problem of suffering and injustice. God's answer is not an explanation but a deed: he did not hover above it like a bird but came down and shared it as a man, as a victim. Instead of telling us why not to weep, he wept with us (Jn 11:12). Christ is God's tears. And Christ is the conqueror of tears—and of death.

Chapter 2

GOD

1. The priority of belief in God

"'I believe in God': this first affirmation of the Apostles' Creed is also the most fundamental. The whole Creed speaks of God, and when it also speaks of man and of the world it does so in relation to God. The other articles of the Creed all depend on the first, just as the remaining Commandments make the first" [You shall have no other gods before me] "explicit. The other articles help us to know God better as he revealed himself progressively to men" (CCC 199).

Scripture begins here too: "In the beginning God" (Gen 1:1)—because all reality begins here; and the Catholic faith, its Scriptures (its data), and its creeds (its summaries) all follow reality and teach us to live in reality. That is the essence of sanity: living in reality. It is also the basis of sanctity, which is the ultimate end of faith.

The first and most basic requirement for living in reality is to believe in God. Faith in God comes first because God comes first.

2. How can man know God?

We can know God in two ways: by reason and by faith; by our natural human minds and by God's supernatural divine revelation; by thinking and speaking about God and by listening to God speak to us.

32

3. The need for divine revelation

Human reason alone is radically insufficient when it comes to knowing God. For

a. We are finite, but God is infinite. We are closer to worms than to God. A worm can know us more adequately than we can know God.

b. We are fallible. We make mistakes—often very serious ones. Only God and his revelation are infallible.

c. We are selfish, prone to sin, and addicted to false gods. Addicts do not think clearly.

But the knowledge of God is the most important knowledge of all, because God is our ultimate end, our destiny, our happiness. We *must* know our true end and the true road to that end. Living without knowing God is like driving a car without seeing the road. Therefore we desperately need a better knowledge of God than our reason alone can provide.

4. The knowledge of God by human reason

Even without supernatural divine revelation, however, all men by nature know something about God. Scripture itself says so: "His invisible nature, namely, his eternal power and deity, has been clearly perceived in the things that have been made" (Rom 1:20).

We know God instinctively. Children and primitive peoples never begin as atheists. Even atheists like Freud admit that religion is a universal, innate instinct (though they think it is an innate illusion).

We also know God by reasoning, when we begin to think logically about the data we experience. We experience both outer data, about the universe, and inner data, about ourselves. Both lead us to God:

a. Data about the universe:

(1) We see order in nature. We could never design a machine as perfect as the universe. Its designer must be a very great intelligence.

(2) Its maker must also be a very great power. For when we ask why the universe as a whole exists, we see that no part of it can make the whole of it. What is its cause? The very existence of the universe points to a creator, a giver-of-existence.

(3) Everything in the universe changes, moves. All motion requires a mover, and ultimately a "first mover", a beginning. If there is no first, there is no second or third or any others.

(4) Time is finite. Time had a beginning: what modern physics calls the Big Bang, when all matter suddenly came into existence. Since nothing happens without an adequate cause, the Big Bang requires a "Big Banger".

b. Data about ourselves:

(1) Our minds can know unchangeable truths like "$2+2=4$" and "Injustice is evil" and "Nothing can be and not be at the same time." Where do we see these unchangeable truths? Everything in our world is changeable. Our minds themselves are changeable. Unchangeable truth is like a visitor from another world, another mind: an eternal Mind.

(2) Our conscience experiences an absolute moral obligation to do good, not evil. Not even moral sceptics and relativists think it is morally good to disobey your own conscience deliberately. But an absolute moral obligation can come only from an absolute moral authority, not from any fallible, human authority. Conscience appears as God's inner prophet.

(3) The experience of beauty often leads to God more directly and intuitively than does a process of argument. "There is the music of Mozart, therefore there must be God"—you either see this or you do not.

(4) Our desire for joy, for a joy we can never find in this world, even from other people, points to another world (heaven) and another Person (God); for every natural, innate, and universal desire corresponds to a reality that can satisfy it. The reality of hunger shows the reality of food; the same is true of the hunger for God and heaven.

(5) If there is no God, there is no ultimate meaning to life. If we came ultimately from nothing and die ultimately into nothing, we are ultimately nothing. If we are made in the image of God, we are the children of the King of Kings. But if we are made only in the image of King Kong, we are only clever apes.

(6) If we are only accidentally evolved matter, how could we have invented the idea of God? Compare this one idea—a Being infinitely perfect, good, wise, powerful, holy, loving, just, and eternal—with all other ideas we have ever invented, and it tips the scales infinitely. No effect can be greater than its cause; our minds could no more have created God than blind chance could have created our minds.

(7) Finally, "Pascal's wager" shows that faith in God is life's best bet, and atheism is life's most stupid one. For our only chance of winning eternal happiness is to believe, and our only chance of losing it is to disbelieve.

5. The knowledge of God by divine revelation

God has revealed much more of himself than human reason could ever discover, especially his love and his plan for the salvation of mankind. This revelation took place historically in three "trinitarian" steps:

First, he revealed himself to Israel, his "chosen people":

a. by establishing his covenant with them (a covenant is a relationship between two parties that is freely entered into and binds both parties. Marriage is the most intimate human covenant and a "horizontal" image of God's "vertical" covenant of salvation with us);

b. by giving them his law to live by as part of the covenant;

c. by giving them his promise of a Savior;

d. by sending them prophets, his "mouthpieces";

e. by performing miracles ("signs and wonders") for them;

f. by inspiring infallible Scriptures;

g. and by revealing to them the reason for his revelation: "God had only one reason to reveal himself to them, a single motive for choosing them from among all peoples as his special possession: his sheer gratuitous love"[1] (CCC 218).

Second, God revealed himself by the Incarnation. Christ is "the Word of God" in the flesh. He is the perfect and complete revelation of God (see Col 1:15–20).

Third, when Christ ascended to heaven, he left his Holy Spirit and his Body, the Church, to continue his work. The Church is the Mystical (invisible) Body of Christ, and the Holy Spirit is her soul (see CCC 813). That is why he said, "As you did it to one of the least of these my brethren, you did it to me" (Mt 25:40), and why he said to St. Paul, when Paul before his conversion was persecuting Christians, "Why do you persecute *me*?" (Acts 9:4, italics added). The Church is "the extension of the Incarnation"; that is why Christ said to his apostles, "He who hears you hears me" (Lk 10:16).

God gave his Church the authority and infallibility that is fitting for God's own instrument; anything less would have been unworthy of the honor of God and inadequate to the needs of fallen man.

6. How adequately can we know God?

"This alone is the true knowledge of God: to know that God is beyond knowing" (St. Thomas Aquinas).

Whatever can be known of God, even by the greatest theologian or the greatest mystic, is infinitely less than what God is.

God is "transcendent"; that is to say that God is *always more*—more than we can ever know or think or imagine. God transcends everything in our thoughts just as he transcends everything in our world. He is not some concept or feeling inside us, any more than he is some stone or star outside us.

Love grasps him better than knowledge; for love conforms itself to its object, while knowledge has to fit its object into itself, into the limitations

---

[1] Cf. Deut 4:37; 7:8; 10:15.

of the knower. A child can understand only a tiny part of a parent but can love the whole. Love can be more true to objective reality than knowledge can, in this sense: we can know others only as we can understand them, but we can love them as they are in themselves.

Thought cannot comprehend God, but love can apprehend him. Our minds cannot surround him and define him, but our wills can reach out to him and touch him. Even among ourselves, we can never fully understand each other, but we can fully love each other.

The ultimate goal of theology is to know God in this way, with the heart and will, not only with the mind: to "know" him as a person loved, not just a concept known. If we know God thus, we will fall on our knees and adore. Our deepest eyes are in our knees.

7. The nature of God

God is infinite; therefore he cannot be defined. But this does not mean he has no nature. He is not a "whatever", an "everything in general and nothing in particular". He has a character. He is one thing and not another: righteous, not wicked or indifferent; wise, not foolish; merciful, not cruel. But each of his attributes is infinite (unlimited): he is infinitely righteous, infinitely wise, infinitely merciful, and so on. He is infinite, but not indefinite. He is infinitely *himself*.

And we can get to know this character:

a. better by faith than by reason; better by trusting his own revelation of himself than by trusting our own cleverness;

b. better still by prayer, by real personal contact with him, both private and public, both spontaneous and liturgical;

c. and best of all by loving him, doing his will and obeying his commandments, especially that of loving each other; "for he who does not love his brother whom he has seen, cannot love God whom he has not seen" (1 Jn 4:20).

We can know something of God's nature, or character, from ourselves, from our deepest desires. God is our ultimate joy. God is the one whose presence will give us infinite and unimaginable ecstasy without boredom forever. What must God be, to do this? A sea of infinite beauty, a light of infinite understanding, a heart of infinite love. And more, always more, infinitely more, "what no eye has seen, nor ear heard, nor the heart of man conceived" (1 Cor 2:9).

8. The attributes of God

a. God is one (see Deut 6:4). This means (1) that God is unique, that there is only one God; and (2) that God is simple, not composed of parts. He is three Persons, not three parts. His Trinity does not lessen his unity. The unity of the Trinity, which is freely a love-unity of the three Divine Persons, is more of a unity, not less, than the mere arithmetical unity of any one Person.

b. God is good. This means (1) that he is perfect, that he is "whatever it is better to be than not to be" (St. Anselm). It also means (2) that he is right-eous: just, holy, right, moral. The moral law he gave us reflects his own nature: "Be holy, for I am holy" (Lev 11:44). This is why the essential prin-ciples of morality for mankind are absolute and unchangeable: because they "go all the way up" into the nature of God, and we are made in the image of this God (see Gen 1:27).

c. God is both just and merciful. With us it is usually either/or, but with God it is both/and. That is why the Father sent his Son to die in our place to save us from the just punishment for our sins: because God must be both just and merciful. On the Cross, Christ got the justice and we got the mercy.

d. "God is love" (1 Jn 4:8). Love (charity) is the highest meaning of "good-ness" for any person. Self-giving love is what God essentially is; therefore self-giving love is what motivates everything God does: his creation, his redemption, and his providential care over our lives, including his allowing us to suffer evil (pain) for our own eventual greater good, and even his allow-ing us to commit evil (sin), out of respect for our free will. Neither the evil we suffer nor the evil we do refutes God's goodness and love.

e. God is omniscient: all-knowing and all-wise. He numbers every hair (Mt 10:30).

f. God is omnipotent (all-powerful). He who created everything out of nothing can do anything. "With God all things are possible" (Mt 19:26).

If we consider these last three attributes together—all-loving, all-know-ing, and all-powerful—we can see that it is necessarily true that "all things work together for good for those who love God" (Rom 8:28 KJV). For there is no limit to his love and goodwill toward us, to his wisdom in knowing what is truly best for us, or to his power to arrange every detail in our lives—indeed, every atom in the universe—as a means to that end.

9. God's transcendence and immanence

God is transcendent. He is not part of our universe, like the pagan gods, who supposedly lived in the sky or in the earth. Nor is he part of our personal-ities, like the modern humanists' god, which is only all the good in man or all the ideals posited by the human spirit. God is always more—more than all his creation and more than all created minds can conceive.

"Transcendent" means "more", it does not mean "absent". God is imma-nent (present) as well as transcendent; in fact, he is omnipresent. He is both "higher than my highest and more inward than my innermost self". [2] When he created us, he did not then turn away from us like a parent abandoning his child; that is the God of eighteenth-century Enlightenment Deism, not the God of the Bible.

Therefore, a fundamental exercise in sanctity and sanity (that is, living in reality) is what Brother Lawrence called "the practice of the presence of God". For God is always present, right here, right now.

10. God's name

"God has a name; he is not an anonymous force" (CCC 203).

Man has given God many names, but once God spoke to man his own true name. Beyond all man-made names is the divinely revealed name given to Moses, and through Moses to Israel, and through Israel to the world. That name is "I AM" (YAHWEH in Hebrew)—a name so sacred no Jew will pronounce it. For "I" is the absolutely unique name, proper to the speaker alone. Jesus was attacked and eventually executed for speaking it (Jn 8:58), for claiming to bear this name; that is, claiming to be God.

The name signifies:

a. God's reality: "I AM."

b. God's oneness: "I" is the name of only one.

c. God's uniqueness: God is not just one being among others, but the Absolute Being. He is not a being, a finite being; he is infinite, unlimited Being itself.

d. God's personhood: "I" signifies the self-consciousness only a person can have. This is what essentially distinguishes man, whom God made in his image, from the animals.

e. God's eternity: he is present ("AM"), not past or future. God's being is not, like ours, limited by time. Nothing of him is dead, like the past, or unborn, like the future. He is not "what once was but is no more", nor is he "what will be but is not yet". He is present to all times; all times are present to him.

f. God's mystery: he does not tell us who he is, but says simply "I AM WHO I AM." The Hebrew verb can also be translated: "I WILL BE WHAT I WILL BE." The God of the Bible always surprises us, instead of fitting our little expectations. Like the Bible, the Church does not put God in a box for us, even a word-box or formula. She knows he does not sit still while we take his photograph. Like the Bible, the Church tells us only (1) what God is not, by rejecting heresies and idols, and (2) what God is like, by using parables and analogies.

---

[2] St. Augustine, Confessions, 3, 6, 11: PL 32, 688, see CCC 300.

(Actually, even these parables and analogies do not tell us that God is like the things we can understand, but that these things are a little like God. God is like nothing: "To whom can you compare me?" But everything is like God in some way, since he made it all.)

When the Church speaks of God, she does not claim to know or say what God is, to define his nature. Instead of defining him, she presents him, or rather introduces us to him as he presents himself, above all in Christ. For "he who has seen me has seen the Father" (Jn 14:9).

11. God as Father

Of all the names for God that are human analogies, the primary one is "Father". Jesus always used this name, and we cannot improve on his theology! To claim to have corrected Christ, for instance by a more fashionably gender-inclusive and less "patriarchal" term than "Father", is to claim far more than any prophet or saint ever claimed. As C. S. Lewis put it, "Christians believe that God himself has taught us how to speak of him."

"By calling God 'Father,' the language of faith indicates two main things: that God is the first origin of everything and transcendent authority" [for 'authority' means 'author's rights']; "and that he is at the same time goodness and loving care for all his children. God's parental tenderness can also be expressed by the image of motherhood,[3] which emphasizes God's immanence, the intimacy between Creator and creature. The language of faith thus draws on the human experience of parents, who are in a way the first representatives of God for man. But this experience also tells us that human parents are fallible and can disfigure the face of fatherhood and motherhood. We ought therefore to recall that God transcends the human distinction between the sexes. He is neither man nor woman: he is God" (CCC 239).

The name "God" can be used either for the Father, the first Person; or for the Divine Being or substance, which is fully expressed in all three Persons of the Trinity. Thus Jesus is both the Son of God and God. He both addressed his Father as "God" and accepted Thomas' worship of himself as "my Lord and my God" (Jn 20:28–29).

12. The reason for the doctrine of the Trinity

The doctrine of the Trinity is the primary doctrine of Christianity in that it reveals the ultimate truth, the nature of ultimate reality, the nature of God. (It does not define God, but it truly reveals God.) Other mysteries of our

---

[3] Cf. Isa 66:13; Ps 131:2.

faith tell us what God has done in time (the creation, the Incarnation, the Resurrection), but the Trinity tells us what God is in eternity.

Why do Christians believe the doctrine of the Trinity, that God is three Persons rather than only one? The doctrine sounds strange, even shocking, even after it is explained that this does not mean three Gods, or three parts to God.

We should not be surprised that the real God surprises us. Even created reality shocks our expectations—for instance, Einstein's theory of relativity. In fact, the reason for the doctrine of the Trinity is similar to the reason for Einstein's theory of relativity or any other good scientific theory: it alone explains all the data. The science of theology arises in a way similar to any other science: from data and the need to understand the data. The Church gradually defined the doctrine of the Trinity, in her first six ecumenical councils, to explain her data in Scripture. Theology has different data from other sciences, but it works by the same principle: that the data control the theory, not vice versa.

The datum for Christian theology is first of all Christ himself. On the one hand, he called God his Father, prayed to him, loved him, taught his teaching, and obeyed his will. On the other hand, he claimed to be one with, and equal to, the Father. And he also promised to send the Spirit. The scriptural data from which the Church derives the doctrine of the Trinity are essentially

a. that there is only one God (Deut 6:4);
b. that the Father is God (Jn 5:18);
c. that the Son is God (Jn 8:58); and
d. that the Holy Spirit is God (Mt 28:19).

The data are historical: God's progressive revelation of himself, first as the transcendent Creator "outside" us; then as the incarnate Savior "beside" us; then as the indwelling Spirit "inside" us. The reason for this progression, first Father (Old Testament), then Son (Gospels), then Spirit (Acts of the Apostles and the Church), is found in God's very being, which is love (1 Jn 4:18), and in the purpose and motive for God's self-revelation to man, which is love. For love's aim is always greater intimacy, deeper union with the beloved; so the stages of God's self-revelation are stages of increasing intimacy with man (from "outside" to "beside" to "inside").

As the *Catechism* explains it, "God's very being is love. By sending his only Son and the Spirit of Love in the fullness of time, God has revealed his innermost secret:[4] God himself is an eternal exchange of love, Father, Son, and Holy Spirit, and he has destined us to share in that exchange" (CCC 221).

---

[4] Cf. 1 Cor 2:7–16; Eph 3:9–12.

13. Trinity and love

The reason God is a Trinity is because God is love. Love requires twoness, in fact threeness: the lover, the beloved, and the act, or relationship, of love between them. God is Trinity because God is love itself in its completeness.

The doctrine of the Trinity makes the most concrete and practical difference to our lives that can possibly be imagined. Because God is a Trinity, God is love. Because God is love, love is the supreme value. Because love is the supreme value, it is the meaning of our lives, for we are created in God's image. The fact that God is a Trinity is the reason why love is the meaning of life and the reason why nothing makes us as happy as love: because that is inscribed in our design. We are happy only when we stop trying to be what we were not designed to be. Cats are not happy living like dogs, and saints are not happy living like sinners.

The doctrine of the Trinity also tells us the nature of love. Love is altruistic, not egotistic. God is other-love because he has otherness within himself; he is more than one Person.

Pope John Paul II says: "God in his deepest mystery is not a solitude but a family, since he has in himself fatherhood, sonship, and the essence of the family, which is love." The doctrine of the Trinity means that the family is not a mere sociological or biological human fact but "goes all the way up" into the nature of God.

The conventional division between the "liberal" emphasis on love and the "conservative" emphasis on dogma completely breaks down in the Trinity. For here it is the ultimate dogma that is the real foundation for love as the ultimate value. One might almost say that God himself is both a "stick-in-the-mud conservative" (the Trinity is his unchangeable nature) and a "bleeding-heart liberal" (the crucifixion revealed the deepest secret of his heart).

14. The Trinity and human reason

The doctrine of the Trinity surpasses human reason, but it does not contradict human reason.

Human reason could never have discovered this truth by itself without divine revelation. Nor can human reason ever fully comprehend it. Nor can human reason prove it.

But reason cannot disprove this doctrine either. It is not logically self-contradictory. It says that God is one in nature and three in Persons, but it does not say that God is both one Person and three Persons, or one nature and three natures. That would be a meaningless self-contradiction.

"The divine persons do not share the one divinity among themselves" [as triplets share humanity among themselves] "but each of them is God whole and entire. . . . 'Each of the persons is that supreme reality, viz., the divine substance, essence or nature' [5]" (CCC 253).

"[T]he Church confesses . . . 'one God and Father from whom all things are, and one Lord Jesus Christ, through whom all things are, and one Holy Spirit in whom all things are' [6]" (CCC 258).

15. The alternatives to God

God is the ultimate reality. What are the fundamental errors about ultimate reality? What are the alternatives to the true God?

(People who believe these errors, of course, may well be good and sincere people. But that fact cannot turn an error into a truth, any more than the faults of those who believe something true can turn that truth into a falsehood.)

First, one may be an agnostic and claim to know or believe nothing about God ("agnosticism" comes from Greek *a* + *gnosis*, meaning "no knowledge").

The essential problem with being an agnostic is death. Christianity is God's marriage proposal to the soul; atheists answer "No", Christians answer "Yes", and agnostics answer "I don't know." But at death, "I don't know" turns into "No".

Second, one may be an atheist and believe in no God at all ("theos" means "God" in Greek).

Fewer than 1 percent of all men who have ever lived have been atheists. To be an atheist you must be an elitist and believe that there was nothing but a fantasy and an illusion at the very center of the lives of over 99 percent of all men and women in history. (By the way, there have been extremely few women who were atheists until very recently.)

Third, one may be a polytheist and believe in many gods, like most ancient pagans ("poly" means "many" in Greek). Very few people today are polytheists.

Fourth, one may be a pantheist ("pan" means "all" in Greek) and believe that God is everything and everything is God or a part of God or an aspect of God.

Pantheism is the opposite error from atheism. While atheism denies any God separate from the universe, pantheism denies any universe separate from God. Atheism denies the Creator, and pantheism denies the creation. Most forms of Hinduism and "New Age" religions are pantheistic.

[5] Lateran Council IV (1215): DS 804.
[6] Council of Constantinople II: DS 421.

Fifth, one may be a deist. Deism is another error that is the opposite of pantheism. Deism denies God's immanence (presence), while pantheism denies God's transcendence. Deism arose in the eighteenth century as an attempt to keep a God to create the universe but to deny him any active role in it, especially through miracles, which deists mistakenly thought were disproved by modern science.

Sixth, one may be a theist. Jews, Christians, and Muslims are theists. Theists believe in one God who is both immanent (omnipresent) and transcendent, the Creator of the universe and man.

Jews and Muslims (and Unitarians) are unitarian theists: they believe this one God is only one Person.

Christians are trinitarian theists: they believe this one God is " 'three Persons indeed, but one essence, substance or nature entirely simple' "[7] (CCC 202). ("Simple" here means one.)

The two most distinctive doctrines of Christianity, the two things all orthodox Christians believe and no one else does, are the Trinity and the Incarnation. The Incarnation means that one of the three Divine Persons—the Son—became a man, while remaining God; that Jesus is both human and divine. Thus the Incarnation and the Trinity fit together.

Jews, Christians, and Muslims believe in the same God. God has the same attributes according to all three religions, because Christians and Muslims learned of this God from the same source: his revelation to the Jews, beginning with Abraham. The three theistic religions agree about (a) the oneness of God and about (b) the nature of God, but they disagree about (c) the Persons in God, because they disagree about Christ. Jews and Muslims do not believe in the Trinity because they do not believe in the Incarnation; Christians believe in the Trinity because they believe in the Incarnation.

---

[7] Lateran Council IV: DS 800.

Chapter 3

CREATION

1. The distinctiveness of the doctrine of creation

It is a simple and startling fact that no human mind on earth ever conceived the idea that the entire universe, visible and invisible, was created out of nothing, not just made or formed out of something, by a single all-powerful God—no one except the Jews and those who later learned this idea from the Jews, namely, Christians and then Muslims.

The Jewish idea of the universe as something *created* was as unique in history as the Jewish idea of God the Creator—the idea of a single all-perfect, all-powerful, all-wise, all-holy, all-just, and all-merciful God. The uniqueness of both ideas can be explained by the same fact: both came from God's revelation, not man's imagination (see Is 60:1–3).

The truth about our ultimate origin—the doctrine of creation—had the same supernatural source as the equally unique and startling doctrine about our ultimate destiny—to be spiritually married to the one perfect God. That too is something "no eye has seen, nor ear heard, nor the heart of man conceived, what God has prepared for those who love him" (1 Cor 2:9).

Different human cultures imagined different ultimate destinies: Nirvana, the Happy Hunting Grounds, the Elysian Fields, the Return to Paradise—

44

but all these pale in comparison with the divinely revealed truth about our destiny. Similarly, different cultures also invented many different so-called creation myths, but none ever got as far as a Creator of the universe out of nothing.

2. The meaning of the doctrine of creation

The Hebrew language had a unique word for this unique concept, found in no other ancient culture. "[T]he verb 'create'—Hebrew *bara*—always has God for its subject" (CCC 290). Man cannot literally create. Man can be "creative" in giving new form to matter, but God alone creates matter itself. Man can make something new out of something old, but God alone can make something out of nothing. For the gap between something new and something old is only finite, and man's finite power can often close that gap; but the gap between nothing and something is infinite, and only God's infinite power can close that gap.

To create a thing is to give it existence. To make a thing means to give new form to matter, to something that already exists. What is created is not just changed but made to exist in the first place.

The closest man ever comes to creating is "procreating". Procreating is cooperating with God's most important act of creation, which is not the creation of mindless galaxies, which are doomed to death in only a few trillion years, but the creation of human beings, with immortal souls, destined to exist eternally. When God creates a new human soul out of nothing, he does so only when a man and a woman make a new body out of their previously existing matter and genetic form by sexual intercourse. That is why sex is holy.

We will now explore some of the consequences of the doctrine of creation; that is, what difference does this idea of creation make?—to our idea of God, of the universe, and of ourselves and our lives? Hardly any other idea in human history has ever made a greater difference.

3. The consequences of the doctrine of creation for the nature of God

The God who creates is a radically different God from any other. No pagan, Gentile god-idea comes even close.

a. For one thing, he must have infinite power to bring things an infinite distance, from nothingness into being.

b. For another thing, the Creator and Designer of this whole universe must be infinitely wise, for any designer must know everything he designs.

c. Also, he must be infinitely loving, infinitely generous, for creation is the gift of existence itself, and none of us could possibly deserve any gift before we existed—including the gift of existence.

d. Finally, he must also be a great artist, with a great sense of beauty, to have invented, all by himself, the stars, the sea, the snow. "Poems are made by fools like me, / But only God can make a tree" (Joyce Kilmer).

God is the Creator; therefore God must be infinite in power, wisdom, love, and beauty.

What difference does knowing this truth about God make for our daily lives in this world? The difference is total. It is that *all* the power, wisdom, goodness, and beauty we ever see or desire or admire or love must come from this one God, for he has no rival. Because of the fact of creation, because God is the source of the very being of every good thing, he is not just one good among others, and we are fools to try to find any good apart from him. Thus the first and greatest commandment is to worship him alone and to love all that we love for him; for it is *from* him. All goodness is God's goodness. Only evil is not his.

4. The consequences of the doctrine of creation for the nature of the universe

If God created the universe, then the universe is really real, true, good, beautiful, and one.

a. It is real, not just an appearance or a dream, as taught in most Hindu, Buddhist, and New Age philosophies.

b. It is true—orderly and intelligible—for it came, not from mindless chance, but from divine wisdom. Thus the doctrine of creation is the strongest basis for natural science.

c. It is good and valuable and to be appreciated and cared for, for "God saw everything that he had made, and behold, it was very good" (Gen 1:31). When Scripture speaks disparagingly of "the world", the word used is not *gaia*, "the earth", the world of nature, which is full of God's glory, but *aiōn*, "this age", the man-made world of history, which is full of folly, sin, and sorrow.

d. It is beautiful. "The beauty of creation reflects the infinite beauty of the Creator" (CCC 341). The doctrine of creation explains why we find nature so beautiful and satisfying, why it moves us so and makes us happy.

e. It is one. "There is a *solidarity among all creatures* arising from the fact that all have the same Creator and are all ordered to his glory" (CCC 344). This is the ultimate basis for community: the fact that all things have the same origin (God's act of creation) and the same end (God's glory). It is one *uni*-verse because it has one Creator.

5. The consequences of the doctrine of creation
   for human life

a. Since God's act of creating the universe gave everything in it reality, order, goodness, beauty, and solidarity, and since we are a part of the universe (in fact, the highest, most recent, most complex, and most intelligent part, according to both Scripture and the theory of evolution), these five characteristics apply to us too, to us especially: reality, order, goodness, beauty, and solidarity.

   b. The doctrine of creation alters not only our origin but also our destiny (see CCC 282). The Church tells us that we are God's children, created in his image and destined to share his heavenly glory. The modern secular world tells us that we are only accidentally evolved dust—"dust in the wind"—destined only for the dust of death.

   c. If God is our Creator, we have no rights over against God, as we do over against each other. How could a character in a novel have rights over against his author? Since we are created out of nothing, we have nothing we can call our own over against God. No little corner of our lives, no little chunk of our time or money, or even our thoughts, can rightly be kept or grasped.

   d. Instead, all good is from the one Creator, everything is a free love-gift that has come down from him (Jas 1:17). And therefore everything is to be freely and lovingly offered up to him. Since every good thing is from him, every good deed can be for him. St. Thérèse of Lisieux said we can glorify God by picking up a pin for his sake.

   e. Since the Creator must be infinitely powerful, wise, and good, we can trust him totally. The God who can "do" the whole universe, the God who can do Everything, can do anything, and we can trust him with everything. The Creator and Lord of the universe and of every person in it lacks neither the love to will our good nor the wisdom to know it nor the power to effect it. That is why it is so reasonable that "Jesus asks for childlike abandonment to the providence of our heavenly Father who takes care of his children's smallest needs" (CCC 305; see Mt 6:31–33).

   f. Since the very existence of things is God's gift, God's deed; and since existence is not "outside" anything that exists, but "inside" it; therefore God is present in every existing thing, everything we touch. "[B]ecause he is the ... Creator, the first cause of all that exists, God is present to his creatures' inmost being: 'In him we live and move and have our being' [Acts 17:28]" (CCC 300).

6. Christ in creation

Scripture says about Jesus Christ that "all things were created through him and for him" (Col 1:16).

All things were made through him, for he is the Word of God (Jn 1:1), and when God created the universe, according to Genesis, he did so through his creative Word. He simply spoke ("Let there be light"), and it came to be ("And there was light"). This Word is the pre-incarnate Christ, the eternal Christ: "In the beginning was the Word, and the Word was with God, and the Word was God. . . . All things were made through him, and without him was not anything made that was made" (Jn 1:1, 3).

All things were made *for* him too, for he is the end and purpose for which the Father created the universe:

—"The world was made for the glory of God" [1] (CCC 293);

—And Christ *is* the glory of God, as a perfect son is the glory of his father and as sunlight is the glory of the sun. Christ is God's Sonlight.

—So the world was made for Christ. Christ is the reason for creation.

7. God's motive for creating

God had no need to create. He was not lonely or bored or incomplete. He has no imperfections. "God created all things 'not to increase his glory'" [for that is impossible] "'but to show it forth and to communicate it'" [2] (CCC 293).

Why did he do it? The motive for this sharing of his glory is pure unselfish love. "God has no other reason for creating than his love and goodness" (CCC 293). This love is natural to God. It is his nature, his character, his essence. It is the nature of goodness to be self-giving, or "diffusive of itself" (as St. Thomas Aquinas puts it).

This means willing the good of the other, or charity. God gained nothing by creating us, but we gained everything, first of all our very existence. God created us for the same reason good and generous parents have many children: to share their love.

But though it was natural for God to create, it was not necessary. The universe "is not the product of any necessity whatever, nor of blind fate or chance. We believe that it proceeds from God's free will" (CCC 295; see Rev 4:11). Nothing but God *has* to be; only God is necessary. Every creature is contingent, a "might-not-have-been".

8. Creation and evolution

The doctrine of creation and the theory of biological evolution do not necessarily contradict each other. We do not know how God arranged for

---

[1] *Dei Filius*, can. § 5: DS 3025.
[2] St. Bonaventure, *In II Sent.* I, 2, 2, 1.

the world he created to come to perfection. He could have used the evolution of species by natural selection ("the survival of the fittest") to produce the human body. Scripture says he "formed" it out "of dust from the ground" (Gen 2:7). However, the breath of life (the soul) was then "breathed" into man by God (Gen 2:7). Souls cannot evolve from matter but must be directly created by God.

Insofar as evolution explains bodies, it does not contradict the doctrine of creation. Insofar as it claims to explain souls, it does. But it is unscientific and illogical to try to explain immaterial souls by material biology.

Insofar as evolution explains natural processes, it does not contradict creation. Insofar as it denies supernatural divine design, it does; but then evolution goes beyond its scientific scope and becomes a theology instead of a natural science.

There can be no real contradiction, ever, between true science and true religion, because truth can never contradict truth.

9. The natural hierarchy

God created the universe as a hierarchy; some things are "higher", more valuable, and more important than others. Each human being may be equal in value in the sight of God, since all are made in his image; but irrational animals are not equal to human beings. They do not have rational souls, free choice, or the knowledge of God. If animals were equal to humans, eating meat would be cannibalism.

Democracy and equality are good ideas in politics, but nature is not a democracy. God is its absolute monarch, angels his ministers, men his children, animals his pets, plants his decorations, minerals his construction materials, and time his land. All are good, all are precious, and all are loved, but not *equally*. That would be chaos, not cosmos.

"The *hierarchy of creatures* is expressed by the order of the 'six days'" [of creation], "from the less perfect to the more perfect" (CCC 342). The theory of evolution agrees with this. Like the days of creation, evolution also proceeds in a progressive and hierarchical pattern.

10. Providence

God created the universe full of time. Everything in it changes. It was not complete all at once, like God, but it grows toward its proper perfection.

Divine providence is God's plan by which he guides his creation toward this perfection, toward its end (see CCC 302). The universe is a story, God is its Author, and providence is its plot. Man is its protagonist, or main character. (If there are creatures with rational souls on other planets, they are also protagonists in God's story. For God is the God of the whole universe, not only one little planet.)

11. First (supernatural) causes and second (natural) causes

When we thank God for the gifts of nature—for example, when we say grace at meals and thank him for our food—we acknowledge that things in nature have two causes: the Creator and other creatures; the ultimate cause and the proximate cause; first and second causes; supernatural and natural causes. This theological fact has two important practical consequences:

a. All good must be traced back to God, ultimately. We must give him all the gratitude and all the glory. "And so we see the Holy Spirit, the principal author of Sacred Scripture, often attributing actions to God without mentioning any secondary causes." [See Jonah 1:4, for instance.] "This is not a 'primitive mode of speech,' but a profound way of recalling God's primacy and absolute Lordship over history and the world,[3] and so of educating his people to trust in him" (CCC 304).

Our lives can be transformed by this simple truth: we can and should see God in everything and love God in everything. Creatures are like roads on which God comes to us and we come to God. We can become saints in the middle of the most active life in the world if we live in this light and "practice the presence of God".

b. But "[f]ar from diminishing the creature's dignity, this truth enhances it" (CCC 308). For God loves to use natural means to do his work, to exalt and glorify his creatures, especially man.

This is true of supernatural things like prayer as well as natural things like food. "God instituted prayer in order to give to his creatures the dignity of being causes" (Pascal).

"To human beings God even gives the power of freely sharing in his providence" [thus human free will and divine providence are not contradictory but complementary parts of the same divine plan] "by entrusting them with ... responsibility. ... Though often unconscious collaborators with God's will, they can also enter deliberately into the divine plan by their actions, their prayers, and their sufferings"[4] (CCC 307).

"God is the sovereign master of his plan. But to carry it out he also makes use of his creatures' cooperation. This use is not a sign of weakness, but rather a token of almighty God's greatness" (CCC 306). A great king exalts his subordinates; a weak and selfish king does not.

Catholics affirm the absolute sovereignty of God as strongly as Calvinists

---

[3] Cf. Isa 10:5–15; 45:5–7; Deut 32:39; Sir 11:14.
[4] Cf. Col 1:24.

or Muslims do, but they also emphasize second causes: for instance, the visible Church, physical sacraments, the saints, and Mary.

Non-Catholics often worry that the love and respect we give to these things will detract from God's glory. But the spirit of Catholicism refuses any rivalry between nature and grace. "Grace perfects nature", and nature points to grace. For instance, Mary always points us to her divine Son, not to herself. God exalts his saints, and his saints exalt God.

This unselfish exaltation of the other person begins in the Trinity itself, where the Father loves and glorifies the Son, and the Son loves and glorifies the Father, and the Spirit that eternally proceeds is that very love.

12. Man's place in creation

God created "the heavens and the earth" (Gen 1:1), that is, "all things visible and invisible" (CCC 325, referring to the Nicene Creed). Man lives in both dimensions. He lives in the visible world of matter by his body, and he lives in the invisible world of spirit by his soul. The acts of the soul are invisible and immaterial: thoughts, feelings, desires, and choices have no size, weight, shape, or color.

Man is the lowest of spirits and the highest of animals. He is the center and bridge of the created universe. He is creation's priest, for when he offers his whole self to God he offers all creation, since he is in himself all that creation is: spirit (mind and will), which he shares with angels; sensations and feelings, which he shares with animals; organic life, which he shares with plants; and physical matter, which he shares with chemicals.

13. Angels

Angels are not mythical but real. They are not an optional addition to the Catholic faith; their existence is a dogma of the faith (Lateran Council IV). Angels appear many, many times in Scripture. The life of Christ especially is surrounded by their work (see CCC 333).

"Angel" means "messenger". "St. Augustine says: '"Angel" is the name of their office, not of their nature. If you seek the name of their nature, it is "spirit"'[5]" (CCC 329). Angels are spirits who worship and serve God by ministering to men. (So do we!) They minister to men by announcing messages from God (their most important messages were at Christ's birth) and by guarding and guiding us.

Every human being has a guardian angel assigned to him from birth to death. Christ himself assured us of that: see Matthew 18:10 and Luke 16:22.

[5] St. Augustine, *En. in Ps.* 103, 1, 15: PL 37, 1348.

"Christ is the center of the angelic world. They are *his* angels" (CCC 331). When he returns at the end of the world, he will come with all his angels (Mt 24:31; 25:31).

14. Demons

Angels have intellect and free will, like man. Some angels chose, at their beginning, to rebel against God's will and became demons, or evil spirits.

Just as good spirits help us, evil spirits seek to harm us by tempting us to sin.

Any baptized and believing Christian has the power to resist temptation, whether it comes from "the world, the flesh, or the devil"—that is, (a) from the external world of fallen human society, (b) from the internal world of our own fallen, selfish instincts, of body or soul, or (c) from the supernatural world of evil spirits.

No faithful Christian can be demon-*possessed* against his will, though many will be severely *oppressed* and all will be *tempted*. The Church, like Christ, has the power to free those who are "possessed" by exorcising the evil spirits. Christ promised this gift to his Church (Mk 16:17). In most times and places, demon possession and exorcism are rare. But they are real.

If the devil is not real, the Bible lies (for example, 1 Pet 5:8), and Christ was a fool, for he certainly believed in demons and in Satan (see, for instance, Luke 10:18).

15. The mystery of evil

"If there is no God, why is there good? If there is a God, why is there evil?" That is how St. Augustine stated the famous "problem of evil" (or rather, the *mystery* of evil). If the all-powerful Creator is all-good (1 Jn 1:5), why is there evil in his creation? The doctrine of creation by a totally good God naturally gives rise to the problem of evil.

For other religions and philosophies, which do not have the doctrine of creation, evil is less of a scandal. For if God did not create matter, evil can be blamed on matter. Or if God is a little bit bad, or weak or foolish, evil can be blamed on God. But the God of the Judeo-Christian revelation is infinitely good and wise and powerful; and this wholly good God declared everything he made to be good (Gen 1:31); so where did evil come from? The question arises naturally from the story of creation in Genesis 1 and 2, so it is answered in the story of the Fall in Genesis 3.

Evil is not a thing, a being, an entity. If it were, it would have to be either the Creator or a creature created by him. But evil is not just an illusion either. If it were, it would be evil for us to fear a mere illusion! Evil is a real and tragic moral defect, as blindness is a real and tragic physical defect. It is real, like blindness, but it is not a *thing* created by God, like the eye.

The question of evil is really two different questions, for evil means two different things: moral evil and physical evil, sin and suffering, the evil we do and the evil done to us. "*Moral evil* [is] incommensurably more harmful than physical evil" (CCC 311) because it harms our eternal souls, while physical evil, however bad, harms only our temporal bodies.

Fortunately, the answer to the more important question (why moral evil) is clearer than the answer to the less important question (why physical evil). The answer is that moral evil comes neither from God nor from the material world he created but from our own choices. To find the origin of evil, look not up at the heavens nor out at the earth, but into a mirror. Man brought evil into the world by disobeying God's good will and law.

Even here, however, our religion is profoundly positive. Man is not evil by his nature, which God created, but by his own free choice. Human nature is the best of all God's creations, for it is made in his image. The worth of a single human being is more than that of all the galaxies. That worth can be gauged by the price God deemed it worth paying to redeem him: his own infinitely beloved Son's life.

Both the cause of evil (man's misuse of his free will) and the cure of evil (the death of Christ on the Cross) are deep mysteries, not simple problems. They are not wholly transparent to human reason. "[N]o quick answer will suffice. Only Christian faith as a whole constitutes the answer. . . . *There is not a single aspect of the Christian message that is not in part an answer to the question of evil*" (CCC 309), just as there is not a single aspect of a hospital that is not part of its answer to the problem of disease and pain.

So on the question of moral evil we may say that (1) its *origin* is man's free will, and (2) its providential purpose is (a) the good of preserving our free will and (b) the good of Christ's redemption from it. These are two reasons God allows it. But he does not cause it. "God is in no way . . . the cause of moral evil.[6] He permits it, however, because" [a] "he respects the freedom of his creatures and," [b] "mysteriously, knows how to derive good from it" (CCC 311), as he did on *Good* Friday, when "[f]rom the greatest moral evil ever committed—the . . . murder of God's only Son . . . —God . . . brought the greatest of goods: . . . our redemption" (CCC 312).

God's answer to evil is not a thought but a deed, not an explanation but a real cure—through the most amazing and unforeseeable means: his own death on the Cross. We cannot fully comprehend God's solution to evil, but we can contemplate it every time we look at a crucifix.

---

[6] Cf. St. Augustine, *De libero arbitrio* 1, 1, 2: PL 32, 1223; St. Thomas Aquinas, *STh* I-II, 79, 1.

Between the Cross and the Resurrection, between Good Friday and Easter Sunday, it looked very dark for Jesus' disciples. In a sense that is where we are now—Holy Saturday—for our resurrection is still in the future, and only faith, not sight, will bring us there. God's plan is not finished. Until it is, God struggles with us in time and history against evil, through his Incarnation in Christ and in Christ's Body the Church, which is the extension of the Incarnation.

This is God's solution to moral evil. But what of physical evil? That is different from moral evil and needs a different solution. Yet physical evil is closely connected with moral evil because our bodies are so closely connected with our souls. Thus Scripture traces suffering and death ultimately to sin. Our own individual sins ("actual sins") now cause most of the world's sufferings; and humanity's "original sin" (the state of alienation from God that was brought about in human nature by the Fall) caused suffering and death to be our lot in life.

Evil is the opposite of good; and God is the source of all kinds of good, spiritual and physical; so all evil, spiritual and physical, is some kind of separation from God. Evil takes the form of sin in the soul, and suffering and death in the body. Venial sin is to the soul what disease and suffering are to the body; mortal sin is to the soul what death is to the body.

We have only partial knowledge of precisely how this close body–soul connection works and of exactly what happened in the historical event poetically narrated in Genesis 3 that we call the Fall. God has told us more about the practical aspect, what to do about evil, than about the theory, how to explain it. At the heart of that practical answer are the two virtues of courage and charity. We are to bear our sufferings with active courage and work to relieve others' sufferings with active charity, especially to the weak, the poor, and the dying. We can do much more "solving" of the problem of evil by our actions than by our thoughts.

Pain and sin are tests of faith. The saints show us how to pass this test. If evil depresses you, read Romans 8:15–39, remembering that these are not subjective feelings from a fallible man but the objective truth from the infallible God.

Chapter 4

MAN

1. The dignity of man today

No century in history has spoken more about the dignity of man than the twentieth. Yet no century in history has threatened the dignity of man more, both in theory and in practice.

Note: "Man" does not mean "males", or "males more than females". Despite this fact, many publishers today strictly censor the traditionally inclusive use of "man" or "he"—a use we find until the 1960s in all English translations of the Bible, all the documents of the Church, and all the great secular books in the history of Western civilization.

This censorship is usually insisted on out of respect for the strong feelings of a small minority of influential feminists, and perhaps in guilt and reparation for the many real injustices done in the past by men to women.

Traditional language is maintained in this book, not out of any desire to exclude women or to deny the full equality between men and women (full equality is a biblical principle, by the way), but because of the conviction that past injustices against women are not atoned for by future injustices against language.

In the English language, the word "man" does double duty; it means two things, "humans" and "male humans". For English has only one word ("man") where many other languages

Threatened it in theory because the three thinkers who have had the most influence on the twentieth century—Darwin, Marx, and Freud—all reduced man to something soulless: either an accidentally evolved clever ape, a cog in the economic State machine, or a suppressed sex maniac.

Threatened it in practice because of the twentieth century's most dramatic invention, genocide: the deliberate murder of more than one hundred million innocent people, more than the entire population of the world for most of man's history. And not just by Hitler, Stalin, and Mao. In "free" America, well over a million human beings a year continue to be slaughtered in the womb.

The cause of this human carnage should be obvious to any Christian or Jew or Muslim. Once "God is dead" to any society or ideology, so is his image in man. "The abolition of man" (the title of a prophetic book by C. S. Lewis) follows from the abolition of God. For God is the source of all life, and when any culture says No to God, it says No to life and becomes what Pope John Paul II has dared to call a "culture of death".

The defense of man is thus bound up with the defense of God. They are inseparable. "If any one says 'I love God,' and hates his brother, he is a liar" (1 Jn 4:20).

For the same reason, if anyone says "I love man" and hates God, he is a liar. For a great building will not stand without a strong foundation. Everyone in our culture affirms "the dignity of man", but what is its foundation? What prevents its collapse?

2. The basis for the dignity of man

The Catholic answer is clear: "Of all visible creatures only man is 'able to know and love his creator.'[1] . . . [H]e alone is called to share, by knowledge and love, in God's own life. It was for this end that he was created, and this is the fundamental reason for his dignity" (CCC 356). This is one of the most crucial and challenging sentences in the *Catechism* for our time.

Man's dignity rests on his destiny. He is not simply from the dust and for the dust but from God and for God.

Even the theory of evolution agrees with the Genesis account in seeing man as the culmination of the natural process. We naturally wonder what is

---

have two. In Latin, for instance, *homo* means "human being" and *vir* means "male human being". In Greek, *anthropos* and *aner* make the same distinction. When English writers said "God and man" they did not mean "God and males".

Why not say "God and humanity" then? Because "God and man" not only sounds better than "God and humanity", but it means something different. "Man" is a concrete term, like "God"; but "humanity" is an abstract term, like "divinity".

[1] GS 12 § 3.

the point and purpose of the whole universe; the answer is not its gases and galaxies but the man who asks that question. The galaxies are only the stage, the setting for the play; we are the actors.

The universe is a great cathedral. The stars and seas are God's holy pictures on the walls to raise the mind of man to worship and adore his Creator. Without God, the cathedral loses its meaning, its dignity, and its destiny. So does man the worshipper.

Man has value and dignity because he is a holy thing, like the Eucharist. In man, too, Christ is truly hidden.

3. Christ as the meaning of man

"In reality it is only in the mystery of the Word made flesh that the mystery of man truly becomes clear" (GS 22). Man sees his own meaning and destiny much more clearly in Christ than in any of his own ideas or dreams, philosophies or psychologies, ethical or social ideals. Christ is the answer to the most important and challenging question we can ask: What am I supposed to be? What is the meaning of my life? To this question we have, not an abstract answer or a theory, but a concrete answer, a fact: the man Jesus Christ. He is the datum for man's knowledge of himself.

To understand this concrete datum, let us consult our written data, the Bible. (Both Christ and Scripture are called "the Word of God".) Christians read the Old Testament in light of the New, as a farmer interprets a seed in light of its fruit. So we should expect to find Christ at the center of the Old Testament, too. And we do, starting with God's creation of the universe and of man.

Genesis 1 says God created the universe by his Word, but it does not say what God's Word is. The New Testament does. Jesus Christ is the Word of God (Jn 1:1–14). Genesis 1:26–27 says God made man "in the image" of God, but it does not say what the image of God is. The New Testament does. Jesus Christ is the image of God (Rom 8:29; 1 Cor 15:49). Man's dignity is based on the fact that he is created to be like Christ.

In this fallen world, that means Christ's Cross: self-giving love culminating in death. And in the next world it means the full glory of Christ's Resurrection body.

4. Christ as the basis for human solidarity

Man finds his meaning in Christ not only as an example or ideal to imitate but as the "Head" of a "Body" that is organically one and one with its Head, just as the thing between your shoulders is organically one with the body it directs. We are Christ's "members" (1 Cor 12:14–27; Rom

12:4–5)—"members", not like stockholders in a corporation, but like the limbs of a body.

Human solidarity, like human dignity, is another idea modern man rightly praises but usually without knowing its true basis. *Why* are we one? Are all men one merely because of our material origin in Adam (or in apes)? Or is it rather because of our end, our destiny in Christ? The question is not merely theoretical. Our culture is now seriously asking why we should respect all human life, including the unborn, the severely handicapped, the retarded, the insane, the sick, the dying, even the wicked and the criminal. And our culture does not know the answer. Why should we treat these inconvenient and "unwanted" people as our brothers and sisters? The Church thunders the gentle answer: Because they *are* our brothers and sisters, "in Christ".

In the Incarnation, Christ assumed humanity—all humanity, not just one Jewish, male, white body. Christ became man, not just *a* man. All men are therefore carriers of the image of the Son as well as of the Father. Non-Christians cannot unmake the image of Christ in them by denying it, any more than atheists can unmake the image of the Father in them by denying it.

"The brotherhood of man" rests on "the Fatherhood of God" made incarnate in the Body of Christ. Why are we one? The Church not only *says* the answer, "the Body of Christ"; she *is* that answer.

5. The human body

Man was created "in the image" of God (Gen 1:26–27). What is the image of God? It is not only the soul. Although God's nature is spirit, not body (Jn 4:24), yet "[t]he human body shares in the dignity of 'the image of God': ... it is the whole human person that is intended to become, in the body of Christ, a temple of the Spirit [cf. 1 Cor 6:19–20; 15:44–45]" (CCC 364). That is why our bodies are holy, temples of the Holy Spirit (see 1 Cor 3:16–17; 6:19).

"For this reason man may not despise his bodily life. Rather, he is obliged to regard his body as good and to hold it in honor since God has created it and will raise it up on the last day" (GS 14).

We are neither animals nor angels. Our bodies are neither the whole of our nature, as with animals, nor outside our nature, as with angels. They are not external to us, not costumes for spirits to hide in, like Halloween masks, or instruments for minds to manipulate, like computers. We are essentially body as well as spirit.

Why did God design us this way?

God designed us to be the priests of the whole of creation. "God created

[2] Cf. GS 12 § 1; 24 § 3; 39 § 1.

everything for man,[2] but man in turn was created to serve and love God and to offer all creation back to him" (CCC 358). How then do we fulfill our destiny as the priests of the whole creation?

When we offer ourselves to God, we offer up the whole universe in our body, for our body is a "microcosm", a little cosmos, the universe in miniature. We are made of star-stuff and mineral-stuff and plant life and animal sensations, as well as mind and will and heart. "Through his very bodily condition [man] sums up in himself the elements of the material world. Through him they are thus brought to their highest perfection and can raise their voice in praise freely given to the creator" (GS 14; cf. Dan 3:57–90). In us, the floods clap their hands and the hills sing for joy (Ps 98:8).

So nature becomes humanized in us. And we become divinized in Christ. We are the bridge from matter to spirit, and Christ is the bridge from man to God. As Scripture says, "all are yours; and you are Christ's; and Christ is God's" (1 Cor 3:22–23).

6. The unity of soul and body

Man is not merely a body (that is materialism). Nor is he merely a soul (that is spiritualism). Nor is he two beings, like a ghost in a machine (that is dualism). He is one being in two dimensions, bodily and spiritual. "The unity of soul and body is so profound that one has to consider the soul to be the 'form' of the body"[3] ['form' here means not 'external shape' but 'intrinsic nature']; "i.e., it is because of its spiritual soul that the body made of matter becomes a living, human body; spirit and matter, in man, are not two natures united, but rather their union forms a single nature" (CCC 365).

The human soul is not imprisoned in the body, as Plato taught, but expressed in it, as the meaning of a play is expressed in its words. And the body is not enslaved by the soul but fulfilled by it, as a beautiful piece of marble is fulfilled and brought to perfection in a great work of sculpture.

7. The human soul

The human soul is not a pure spirit, like an angel. It is the "form" of the body; it is meant to inform a body. The body is not a house, and the soul is not a ghost. We are not haunted! The soul is not something strange, occult, or alien. Just the opposite. It is who we are; it is our personality. God gave it to us at conception (that magical moment that was the beginning of our body, too), and we shape it through all of life's choices.

The Church's most important teachings about the soul are (a) "that every

---

[3] Cf. Council of Vienne (1312): DS 902.

spiritual soul is created immediately by God—it is not 'produced' by the parents—and also" (b) "that it is immortal: it does not perish when it separates from the body at death, and" (c) "it will be reunited with the body at the final Resurrection"[4] (CCC 366).

On each of these three points there is good reason for our faith:

a. The soul must be created rather than evolved because matter cannot make spirit any more than space can make time or color can make sound. They are two different dimensions. "You can't get blood from a stone", and you cannot get self-consciousness and free will from atoms and molecules.

b. The soul must be immortal because it is not made of atoms spread out in space and capable of being cut into parts. It is not composed, so it cannot be decomposed.

c. The soul must be reunited with a new body because God made man as a soul-body unity, and God makes no mistakes. Therefore the resurrection of the body is needed to complete and perfect our human nature in heaven. (Between death and resurrection, we are incomplete.) We do not become angels any more than we become ants.

8. Human sexuality [5]

God invented sex. That is why it is not "bad" or "dirty". Nor is it merely neutral, to be used as we please. It is good and holy.

No aspect of the Church's teaching is more misunderstood and rejected today than her unchanging and unchangeable principles of sexual morality. For these cannot be understood except in the context of her vision of man.

Man has not evolved by accident or blind chance. Man has been loved into existence by God. Man is willed by God, deliberately designed, as male and female. That is the first reason why sex is holy.

The second reason is that God has designed and willed not only the existence of sex but also its purpose. It is holy not only because of its origin but also because of its end. That purpose is to be the means of procreating the greatest things in the universe: new persons, with immortal souls. "By transmitting human life to their descendants, man and woman as spouses and par-

---

[4] Cf. Pius XII, *Humani Generis*: DS 3896; Paul VI, *CPG* § 8; Lateran Council V (1513): DS 1440.

[5] A word about words. Throughout centuries of English usage, "sex" meant not merely something we do (copulation) but something we are (male and female). And "gender" meant something grammatical, not biological: *words* had gender (masculine and feminine nouns). Today, "gender" means what "sex" used to mean, and "sex" means simply copulation or even any erotic stimulation ("having sex"). In other words, we have taken the word "sex" away from our personal *being* and reduced it to our biological *doing* and taken the word "gender" away from grammar and exalted it to refer to human beings.

ents cooperate in a unique way in the Creator's work" (CCC 372; cf. *GS* 50 § 1).

Sexual intercourse is like the Consecration at Mass. It is a human work that God uses as the material means to do the most divine work done on earth. In the Mass, man offers bread and wine, the work of nature and human hands, for God to transform into the Body and Blood of Christ. In sex, man offers his work—the procreation of a new body—for God to do his work: the creation of a new soul. God grants priests the incredible dignity of being his instruments in working one of his two greatest miracles. God grants spouses the incredible dignity of being his instruments in working the other one.

Something that is so very good "ontologically", that is, in its being, essence, or nature, needs to be respected and rightly used. Misuse of something ontologically good is morally bad. The better and more important it is ontologically, the more seriously harmful its moral abuse is. We have rules for careful use of precious works of art, not for paper clips.

The principles of sexual morality are essentially unchanging because the meaning of sex is essentially unchanging. They stem from human nature itself, which God designed, not from the changing mores of society, which man designs. God's law is very clear: no adulterated sex, that is, sex outside of marriage. As Holy Mass is the place for Transubstantiation, holy marriage is the place for sex.

9. Complementarity of men and women

The biblical and Catholic vision of sexuality rejects both chauvinism, which sees one sex (either one) as superior, and unisexism, which sees the two sexes as different only by social convention, not by nature. God invented sex, and God created men and women *different in nature but equal in value*. Chauvinism and unisexism share the common false assumption that all differences must be differences in value.

Male and female were designed by God to complement, complete, and perfect each other, to love each other, and to find joy in each other, both biologically and spiritually. "Man and woman were made 'for each other'—not that God left them half-made and incomplete: he created them to be a community of persons, in which each can be 'helpmate' to the other, for they are equal as persons . . . and complementary as masculine and feminine" (CCC 372).

The first and foundational community was a man and a woman, Adam and Eve. The first foundation of all human community, no matter how wide, even worldwide, is the family. And the family, no matter how extended, is based on this first foundation: one man and one woman becoming "one flesh" (Mt 19:3–6).

10. Man and nature

On the one hand, man is part of nature. He is the culmination of creation, but he is a creature, not the Creator. Nor is he an angel, confronting nature from outside. Nature is not his machine but his "garden", to be loved, reverenced, and cared for (Gen 2:15).

On the other hand, man is superior to nature by his reason and free will; and God entrusted him with the "dominion" (lordship or mastery) of nature (Gen 1:28–29). Man is the artist. Nature is his material and his studio. An artist "masters" his material by knowing, loving, and respecting it.

To master his material, an artist must first master himself. "The 'mastery' over the world that God offered man from the beginning was realized above all within man himself: *mastery of self.* The first man was . . . free from the triple concupiscence"[6] [disordered desire] "that subjugates him" [like an addict] "to the pleasures of the senses" [lust], "covetousness for earthly goods" [greed], "and self-assertion" [pride], "contrary to the dictates of reason" (CCC 377).

Self-mastery comes through the three virtues of poverty, chastity, and obedience. (These three are formally taken as lifelong vows by Catholics in religious orders.) They are the three weapons that counter the three key vices of greed, lust, and pride, which come from the three sources of temptation, "the world, the flesh, and the devil" (competitive pride was the invention of the devil, who taught us to want to be "like gods": Gen 3:5).

11. The Fall of man

How did man succumb to temptation? Was the Fall a historical event?

"The account of the fall in *Genesis* 3 uses figurative language, but affirms a primeval event, a deed that took place *at the beginning of the history of man*"[7] (CCC 390). The Church does not require us to interpret the creation and Fall stories in Genesis literally, but she does insist that they must be interpreted historically, as something that really happened.

For if the creation was not a real historical event (however symbolically that event may have been expressed in Genesis) but a mere myth in the popular sense, like Santa Claus, then how did the universe get here?

And if the Fall was not a real historical event (also narrated in symbolical language) but only a myth, then how did sin get here? Sin is a historical fact, as real as the universe. Its cause must also be a historical fact.

---

[6] Cf. 1 Jn 2:16.
[7] Cf. GS 13: § 1.

12. The origin of evil

There are only two alternatives to the Fall, two other possible answers to the question of the origin of evil. If evil is not our fault, it must be the fault of either what is greater than us or of what is less than us: either God or nature. If a statue has defects, we must blame either its sculptor or its material—unless the statue has free will and altered the sculptor's design.

God is all-good, so he cannot be the origin of evil. And he is all-powerful and created the universe out of nothing, so matter is not the origin of evil; it is subject to his will and is good. The only remaining suspect is the one we see in the mirror.

In confronting the mystery of evil, we must at least be honest enough to begin by admitting the reality of our data: human evil, moral wickedness, sin. "Sin is present in human history; any attempt to ignore it or to give this dark reality other names would be futile" (CCC 386). G. K. Chesterton said sin was the only Christian dogma you could prove simply by reading the daily newspaper.

The only adequate explanation of "horizontal" evil, the evil we do to each other (like Cain's murder of Abel), is the prior story of "vertical" evil: the Fall, man declaring independence from God, the source of all good. "To try to understand what sin is, one must first recognize *the profound relation of man to God*, for only in this relationship is the evil of sin unmasked in its true identity" (CCC 386).

13. The need for divine revelation to understand man

This is why secular explanations of evil are not sufficient. "Without the knowledge Revelation gives of God we cannot recognize sin clearly and are tempted to explain it as merely a developmental flaw, a psychological weakness, a mistake, or the necessary consequence of an inadequate social structure" (CCC 387). Without God's revelation, without the knowledge that human nature in its present state is fallen from the true norm and thus not normal but abnormal, all our judgments of man are upside down. We then see sin as normal and human and see sanctity as abnormal and super-human, as drunks might see sober people as abnormal. This is precisely the fundamental error about man that is assumed by our secular society. "Ignorance of the fact that man has a wounded nature inclined to evil gives rise to serious errors in the areas of education, politics, social action,[8] and morals" (CCC 407).

Man is like a caged dog in a railroad station who has chewed off his tag,

[8] Cf. John Paul II, *CA* 25.

so that he does not know his true name or the name of his master. He does not know where he has come from or where he is supposed to be going. Divine revelation gives us back our name tag. It is crucial information. Our master is our Creator, our name is "beloved child of God", and our destiny is heaven. It is crucial to keep this tag, to cherish it, to read and remember it, and to live by it.

14. Sin

The Fall was a fall into sin. What is sin?

"The doctrine of original sin is, so to speak, the 'reverse side' of the Good News that Jesus is the Savior" (CCC 389). The Good News presupposes the Bad News, as the prognosis of a cure presupposes the diagnosis of the disease.

The idea of sin is very unpopular in the modern Western world. But it is an essential part of the Christian gospel, and "[t]he Church, which has the mind of Christ,[9] knows very well that we cannot tamper with the revelation of original sin without undermining the mystery of Christ" (CCC 389). For what does Christ the Savior save us from? "You shall call his name Jesus [which means 'Savior', or 'God saves'], for he will save his people from their sins" (Mt 1:21).

Sin does not mean that we are wholly evil or more evil than good (how could that be measured?) or that our very being is evil or that we are no longer infinitely valuable and infinitely loved by God. It means that we are seriously wounded, a defaced masterpiece. The greater the masterpiece, the more terrible its defacement is.

15. The consequences of the Fall

The Bible, in Genesis 3, "portrays the tragic consequences of this first disobedience. Adam and Eve . . . become afraid of the God of whom they have conceived a distorted image—that of a God jealous of his prerogatives . . ."[10] (CCC 399). "[T]he control of the soul's spiritual faculties over the body is shattered; the union of man and woman becomes subject to tensions, their relations henceforth marked by lust and domination.[11] Harmony with creation is broken: visible creation has become alien and hostile to man. . . .[12] Finally, the consequence explicitly foretold for this disobedience will come true. . . . *Death makes its entrance into human history*"[13] (CCC 400).

[9] Cf. 1 Cor 2:16.
[10] Cf. Gen 3:5–10.
[11] Cf. Gen 3:7–16.
[12] Cf. Gen 3:17, 19.
[13] Cf. Rom 5:12.

Once the harmony between our soul and God is broken, all harmonies dependent on that one are broken too: harmony with nature ("thorns and thistles", "the sweat of your brow", and pain in childbirth), harmony between body and soul (illness and death), harmony between man and woman (Adam blames Eve), and harmony between brothers (Cain murders Abel).

16. The three stages of history: Bad news and good news

Human history, like all the stories we tell, has three stages. A situation must always be first set up, then somehow upset, then somehow reset, whether successfully or not. The Bible's story follows these three stages: Creation, Fall, and Redemption. First, the good God creates a good world and man; then man defaces God's creation and himself; then God laboriously sets it right. The three stages are Paradise (Eden), Paradise Lost (the Fall), and Paradise Regained (the Redemption).

(The Rosary goes through these three stages too: first five joyful mysteries, then five sorrowful mysteries, then five glorious mysteries. "One for sorrow, two for joy" [Fulton Sheen].)

Already in Genesis 3 we see the beginning of the third stage, Redemption, when God promises Christ's eventual victory over all evil. Genesis 3:15 is the first prophecy of the gospel, the "protoevangelium".

17. Why did God allow sin?

"But *why did God not prevent the first man from sinning?* St. Leo the Great responds, 'Christ's inexpressible grace gave us blessings better than those the demon's envy had taken away.' [14] And St. Thomas Aquinas wrote, 'There is nothing to prevent human nature's being raised up to something greater, even after sin; God permits evil in order to draw forth some greater good. Thus St. Paul says, "Where sin increased, grace abounded all the more"; and the [Easter liturgy's] Exultet sings, "O happy fault, that earned so great, so glorious a Redeemer!"' [15]" (CCC 412).

18. Is man good or evil?

He is both.

Two extremes are perennially possible and popular: pessimism, which denies the goodness of man, and optimism, which denies the evil. The Church rejects both errors.

[14] St. Leo the Great, *Sermo* 73, 4: PL 54, 396.
[15] St. Thomas Aquinas, *STh* III, 1, 3, ad 3; cf. Rom 5:20.

Thus she rejected Pelagianism, the fifth-century heresy that taught that man is so good that he can save himself without God's grace. Pelagius underestimated original sin and "reduced the influence of Adam's fault to bad example" (CCC 406). But the Church also rejected the teaching of Luther and Calvin in the sixteenth century that man is so bad ("totally depraved") that he cannot freely choose to cooperate with God's grace.

Chapter 5

JESUS CHRIST

"I believe in God, the Father Almighty, creator of heaven and earth. I believe in Jesus Christ, his only Son, our Lord. He was conceived by the power of the Holy Spirit and born of the Virgin Mary. He suffered under Pontius Pilate, was crucified, died, and was buried. He descended into hell. On the third day he rose again. He ascended into heaven, and is seated at the right hand of the Father. He will come again to judge the living and the dead."

1. The centrality of Christ

In the Apostles' Creed, 65 percent of the words (seventy-three of 113) are about Christ. Why then is only 10 percent of this part on the Creed (one chapter out of ten) about him? Not because Christ is only 10 percent of Christianity. He is 100 percent. Christ is the essence of Christianity. Pascal says: "Not only do we only know God through Jesus Christ, but we only know ourselves through Jesus Christ; we only know life and death through Jesus Christ. Apart from Jesus Christ we cannot know the meaning of our life or our death, of God or of ourselves" (*Pensées* 417).

Why then is the gospel, or "good news", about Jesus Christ covered in only one chapter? Because we have four perfect supplements to it: the four Gospels in the New Testament.

Do you want to be a Christian? Then read the Gospels, for there you meet Christ.

Do you want to be a saint? Then read the Gospels, for they were the main spiritual food of all the saints. No human words ever written have come even close to equaling their power to change lives.

2. The distinctive doctrine of Christianity

What distinguishes Christianity from all other religions? The answer is simple: Christ himself. The essence of the Christian faith is in its first and shortest creed: "Jesus Christ is Lord [*Kyrios*, God]" (Phil 2:11). All Christians believe that Jesus Christ is God incarnate, God in human flesh. If they did not believe that, they would not be Christians. No non-Christians believe that; if they did, they would be Christians. "Belief in the true Incarnation of the Son of God is the distinctive sign of Christian faith" (CCC 463).

3. The message and the person

All other great religious teachers subordinated themselves to their message. They pointed away from themselves to their teachings. For instance, Buddha said, "Look not to me, look to my *dharma* [doctrine, teaching]." But Christ said, "Come to me" (Mt 11:28). Buddha said, "Be lamps unto yourselves." But Christ said, "I am the light of the world" (Jn 9:5). Moses and Muhammad claimed only to be prophets of God; Jesus claimed to be God (Jn 8:58).

Any other religion could survive the loss of its founder. If Muhammad or Buddha or Confucius were proved to be mythical and not historical figures, the religions that stem from them might still survive. But Christianity could never survive without Christ. For other religious founders only claimed to teach the truth; Christ claimed to *be* the Truth (Jn 14:6).

4. The essence of catechesis

"The transmission of the Christian faith consists primarily in proclaiming Jesus Christ in order to lead others to faith in him. From the beginning, the first disciples burned with the desire to proclaim Christ: 'We cannot but speak of what we have seen and heard' [Acts 4:20]" (CCC 425). " 'At the heart of catechesis' " [instruction in Christianity] " 'we find, in essence, a Person' [*CT* 5]" (CCC 426). "In catechesis 'Christ . . . is taught—everything else is taught with reference to him' [*CT* 6]" (CCC 427).

5. The essential qualification for all Christian teachers

You cannot teach what you do not know. You cannot give what you do not have. The primary requirement for any Christian teacher, preacher, evangelist, or catechist is not just to know *about* Christ but *to know Christ*. "Whoever is called 'to teach Christ' must first seek 'the surpassing worth of knowing Christ Jesus' [Phil 3:8]" (CCC 428).

6. Christ the supreme surprise

Throughout the biblical narrative, God takes the initiative, and reveals himself. It is a story not of man's search for God but of God's search for man. (C. S. Lewis says, "To speak of man's search for God is like speaking of the mouse's search for the cat" [*Surprised by Joy*].) And his acts always astonish us. They go "far beyond all expectation" (CCC 422). "God is the great iconoclast; the Incarnation leaves all previous ideas of the Messiah in ruins" (C. S. Lewis, *A Grief Observed*). The Incarnation was the most astonishing of all God's acts, the most surprising, unforeseeable, unimaginable thing that ever happened. The immortal God, who has no beginning or end, became a mortal man, with a beginning (he had a mother!) and an end (he died!). The Author of all of history stepped into the drama he created and became one of his own characters, without ceasing to be the Author. The Creator became a creature. "He whom the world could not contain was contained in a mother's womb" (St. Augustine). No man ever dreamed this could happen. (See Is 48:6–8.)

If it really happened, it is the greatest fact that ever entered the universe. If it did not really happen, then it is the greatest fantasy that ever entered the universe of human thought. Why do Christians believe it is a fact rather than a fantasy or myth?

The world was convinced and converted by the Incarnation. Not by arguments for it, but by it—or, rather, by him, by the concrete Person Jesus Christ. Even after he ascended, the world kept meeting him in the Gospels and in his saints and simply could not help falling in love with him. The gospel is a love story—the story of God's love for man. And the story of the world's conversion is also a love story—the story of man's love for this God.

They were not converted by the reasonableness of the story. The story is *not* reasonable. It is a story of crazy, passionate love that led the eternal

Creator, infinitely perfect and lacking nothing, to become a mortal man and suffer torture, death, and hell ("My God, my God, why hast thou forsaken me?") to save us rebels from our sins. Our sin was irrational, and his redemption was irrational too. We sinned for no reason but lack of love, and he redeemed us for no reason but excess of love. Our sin was sub-rational, his salvation was super-rational.

It is the heart that makes us accept the gospel, not just the head. The head understands what the heart must desire and believe. Tolkien says of the Gospels, "There is no tale that [good] men would rather believe is true." The unbeliever's only defensible defense against the gospel is that it is "too good to be true". Only the hard or despairing heart can look on that face on the Cross, know who that is, what he is doing, what love made him do it, and whose sin made it necessary, without melting.

7. The meaning of the Incarnation

But what does this astonishing thing—the "Incarnation"—mean?

It means that the second Person of the eternal Trinity, who is called the "Logos" or "Word" of God (Jn 1:1–3), became "flesh" (Jn 1:14), that is, added our human nature (body and soul) to his divine nature some two thousand years ago and was called "Jesus". That is the Incarnation looked at "from the top down", so to speak. Looked at from the bottom up, it means that this man Jesus is, in the words of the Nicene Creed recited at every Sunday Mass, "the only Son of God eternally begotten of the Father, God from God, Light from Light, true God from true God, begotten, not made, one in Being with the Father. Through him all things were made."

8. The two natures of Christ

The Creed confesses that Christ is both conceived "by the power of the Holy Spirit" and "born of the Virgin Mary". This one Person has two natures: he is both fully divine and fully human.

This is a mystery and a paradox, but not a logical contradiction, not impossible. It is not one person and two persons, or one nature and two natures, but one person with two natures. Human nature itself contains a similar though not identical paradox. Each of us, though only one person, is both visible and invisible, tangible and intangible, material and spiritual at once, by having both body and soul.

"The unique and altogether singular event of the Incarnation of the Son of God does not mean that Jesus Christ is part God and part man, nor does it imply that he is the result of a confused mixture of the divine and the human. He became truly man while remaining truly God" (CCC 464). He is not half human and half divine, as a centaur is half human and half horse, or as Mr. Spock in *Star Trek* is half human and half Vulcan. The Church rejected all heresies that denied his full humanity (such as ancient Gnosticism or modern New Age versions of it) and all heresies that denied his full divinity (such as ancient Arianism or contemporary Modernism).

9. God as one in nature and three in Persons

God is one: "Hear, O Israel: The LORD our God is one LORD; and [therefore] you shall love the LORD your God with all your heart, and with all your soul, and with all your might" (Deut 6:4–5). We are to give our all to him and no other precisely because he *is* all; there is no other God.

The doctrines of the Incarnation and the Trinity do not compromise God's oneness at all. Christianity is as monotheistic as Judaism or Islam. There is but one God.

But this one God is three Persons: Father, Son, and Holy Spirit. All three are called God in the Bible. Scripture is our datum for the doctrine of the Trinity.

10. Christ as both God and the Son of God

Christ claimed to be God ("I AM", Jn 8:58) and accepted St. Thomas' worship of him as "My Lord and my God!" (Jn 20:28).

But he also claimed to be the Son of God, whom he called his "Father". He received his teaching from his Father: "My teaching is not mine, but his who sent me" (Jn 7:16). He prayed to his Father, obeyed his Father, and subordinated his will to his Father's: "I have come down from heaven, not to do my own will, but the will of him who sent me" (Jn 6:38).

How can he be both God and God's Son?

Because the word "God" is used in two ways in Scripture: (a) "God" means the one Divine Being, who exists equally and totally in each Divine Person. (b) "God" also means the personal name for the Father, as distinct from Christ, who is the Son of God the Father.

11. The meaning of the names "Jesus" and "Christ"

"Jesus" (*Yeshua* or *Joshua*) means "Savior" or "God saves". This name was given at the command of God's angel: "You shall call his name Jesus, for he will save his people from their sins" (Mt 1:21).

"Christ" (*Christos* in Greek), or "Messiah" (*Ha-mashia* in Hebrew) means "the anointed one", that is, "the promised one", the one God promised through the prophets of his chosen people.

The promised Messiah was to have three offices, or functions: prophet, priest, and king (see Is 11:2; 61:1; Zech 4:14; 6:13; Lk 4:16–21).

But what kind of kingdom did Jesus establish to fulfill the prophecies and show that he was the Messiah? The prophets had promised that the Messiah would save God's people from their enemies. Many of the Jews in Jesus' day rejected Jesus as the Messiah because they looked for a worldly king who would save them from their worldly masters, the Romans, not realizing that their worst enemies, the ones he came to save them from, were their own sins and not realizing that his kingdom would be, not a political kingdom, but a kingdom "not of this world" (Jn 18:36).

Jesus' miracles were not meant to be the tools of a this-worldly salvation but signs of an otherworldly salvation. "By freeing some individuals from the earthly evils of hunger, injustice, illness, and death,[1] Jesus performed messianic signs. Nevertheless he did not come to abolish all evils here below,[2] but to free men from the greatest slavery, sin" (CCC 549). (The sharpest distinction between traditional, orthodox Catholicism and Modernist, "liberal", revisionist Catholicism is probably right here.) The Messianic promises in the prophets were deliberately ambiguous, to test people: those whose hearts were set on righteousness and salvation from sin recognized and accepted him as their Savior; those whose hearts worshipped other gods did not. The same is true today.

12. The meaning of the name "Son of God"

The Old Testament sometimes uses the term "sons of God" loosely to include angels and righteous men. But Jesus called himself the "only Son" of God (Jn 3:16). The Nicene Creed says he is "eternally begotten . . . , not made [created]."

A son has the same nature as his father. As the son of a man is a man, and the son of an ape is an ape, and the son of a Martian would be a Martian, so the Son of God is God.

He is both Son of God (thus divine) and Son of Man (thus human), for he has a divine Father from eternity and a human mother in time. The Virgin Birth shows both his divinity and humanity, conceived "by the power of the Holy Spirit" and "born of the Virgin Mary", " 'Son of the Father as to his divinity and naturally son of his mother as to his humanity'[3] " (CCC 503).

---

[1] Cf. Jn 6:5–15; Lk 19:8; Mt 11:5.
[2] Cf. Lk 12:13–14; Jn 18:36.
[3] Council of Friuli (796): DS 619; cf. Lk 2:48–49.

13. The meaning of the name "Lord"

"Jesus Christ is Lord" (Phil 2:11) is probably the earliest and shortest Christian creed. The name "Lord" is given to Jesus hundreds of times in the New Testament. It is clearly a divine title. "In the Greek translation of the Old Testament, the ineffable Hebrew name YHWH" [I AM], "by which God revealed himself to Moses [cf. Ex 3:14], is rendered as *Kyrios*, 'Lord.' . . . The New Testament uses this full sense of the title 'Lord' both for the Father and—what is new—for Jesus, who is thereby recognized as God Himself [cf. 1 Cor 2:8]" (CCC 446).

"Throughout his public life, he demonstrated his divine sovereignty by works of power over nature, illnesses, demons, death, and sin" (CCC 447)—five miraculous signs of his divinity.

14. Only one Lord

A consequence of Christ's lordship is liberation from the idolatry of worshipping any earthly lord. "From the beginning of Christian history, the assertion of Christ's lordship over the world and over history has implicitly recognized that man should not submit his personal freedom in an absolute manner to any earthly power, but only to God the Father and the Lord Jesus Christ: Caesar is not 'the Lord' "[4] (CCC 450). There is a higher law than human law and a higher Lord than human lords. There is only one absolute Lord: Christ, not Caesar or "society" or "public opinion" or "the spirit of the times" or all the authorities on earth. If Christ's Church is contradicted by all the powers of this world—as she was nineteen centuries ago and increasingly is again today—we must say, with St. Paul, "Let God be true though every man be false" (Rom 3:4).

Life is full of choices between lords. We will not be happy, and Christ will not rest, until he is the lord of all: our time, our money, our bodies, our souls, our lives, our deaths.

15. Reasons for faith in Christ's divinity

The titles "Lord" (God) and "Savior" (from sin) come together in Jesus' claim to forgive sins—all sins, any sins, for every person, at every time in history. The Jewish religious authorities, hearing him do this, rightly asked, "Who can forgive sins but God alone?" (Mk 2:7). All sin is against God; that is why God alone can forgive all sins.

If Christ is not God, he is a blasphemous pretender. For he claimed to be

[4] Cf. Rev 11:15; Mk 12:17; Acts 5:29.

God. He said such things as "I and the Father are one" (Jn 10:30) and "Truly, truly, I say to you, before Abraham was, I am" (Jn 8:58). This claim forced men either to worship him as God (if they believed he spoke the truth) or to crucify him as the worst blasphemer in history (if they believed he did not speak the truth). Thus the earliest Christian apologists (defenders of the faith) argued that Christ must be "either God or a bad man". What nearly all non-Christians believe him to be—just a very good man—is the one thing he could not possibly be. For a mere man who says he is God is not a good man; he is either a liar or a lunatic. And if the Gospel records make it impossible to call this man either a liar or a lunatic, either a wicked blasphemer or a deranged egomaniac, then he is Lord. Not only faith but also logic forces us to our knees.

16. Why God became man

There are at least four reasons:

a. "The Word became flesh for us *in order to save us*" [from sin and its consequence, eternal separation from God] "*by reconciling us with God*, who 'loved us and sent his Son to be the expiation" [atonement] "for our sins" [1 Jn 4:10; 4:14]; (CCC 457). It is as if the governor voluntarily became a prisoner and went to the electric chair in place of the condemned murderer, to set the murderer free. He came most fundamentally to die, to give his life for ours.

b. "The Word became flesh *so that we might know God's love*" (CCC 458; cf. Jn 3:16). Once you have heard this word—the word of divine love—in the most supernatural thing that ever happened, the Incarnation, you can then hear this same word in the most natural things as well, in the whisper of every breeze and the trickle of every brook. Every ray of sunlight becomes a ray of Sonlight; every creature becomes a little love letter when you recognize the Creator's big love letter that is Christ. We now know why he banged out the Big Bang billions of years ago: for the same reason he died on the Cross two thousand years ago: so that we might know him and his love for us.

c. "The Word became flesh *to be our model of holiness*" (CCC 459)—to show us, not just tell us (as he had done in the Mosaic law), what is the design and purpose of our life, what kind of person he made us to be. He came to show us our own ultimate identity; to reveal man to man as well as to reveal God to man.

d. Most incredibly of all, "The Word became flesh to make us '*partakers of the divine nature*' [2 Pet 1:4]. . . .' " " '[T]he Son of God became man so that we might become' " [sons of] " 'God.' [5] " " 'The only-begotten Son of God,

---

[5] St. Athanasius, *De inc.* 54, 3: PG 25, 192B.

wanting to make us sharers in his divinity, assumed our nature, so that he, made man, might make men gods.'[6]" He transforms our *bios* (natural life) into *zoē* (supernatural life).

"We are brethren" [of the God-man, of God] "not by nature, but by the gift of grace, because that adoptive filiation" [adopting us as his brothers] "gains us a real share in the life of the only Son" (CCC 654).

By nature we are created in God's image, or resemblance, as a statue is sculpted in the image of its sculptor, but we do not have God's life any more than a statue has the human life of its sculptor. What Christ called being "born anew" (Jn 3:3) is like the statue coming to life, to share not only the image and likeness of the sculptor, but his very life—like Pinocchio, transformed from mere wooden puppet to real boy, miraculously sharing the life of a boy: thinking, choosing, talking, playing. In St. Paul's terms, our destiny is to be not merely "flesh" (human nature) but "spirit", living off the life of the Holy Spirit. In St. Augustine's formula, the Holy Spirit becomes the life of our soul as the soul is the life of our body.

17. When God became man: "The fullness of time"

"The coming of God's Son to earth is an event of such immensity that God willed to prepare for it over centuries. He makes everything converge on Christ [Col 1:15-20]: all the rituals and sacrifices, figures and symbols of the 'First Covenant' [Heb 9:15]. He announces him through the mouths of the prophets who succeeded one another in Israel. Moreover, he awakens in the hearts of the pagans a dim expectation of this coming" (CCC 522) through their philosophers and poets and myth-makers (see Acts 17:16–28). He also providentially prepares the world for the spread of the gospel by unifying it as never before or since under a single Roman law, language, communications, transportation, and peace: the *pax Romana* was God's providential preparation for the *pax Christi*.

18. The universality of Christ and the salvation of non-Christians

Christ is the Savior of all men, without exception. "*Everyone* is called to enter the kingdom" (CCC 543). "The Church, following the apostles, teaches that Christ died for all men without exception: 'There is not, never has been, and never will be a single human being for whom Christ did not suffer'[7]" (CCC 605).

---

[6] St. Thomas Aquinas, *Opusc.* 57: 1–4.
[7] Council of Quiercy (853): DS 624; cf. 2 Cor 5:15; 1 Jn 2:2.

Jesus claims to be not only Savior but *the* Savior, the *only* Savior from sin and the only way to heaven (Jn 10:7; 14:6; Acts 4:12). This "exclusivism" invariably offends non-Christians. But the Church cannot water down his claim. She cannot revise Scripture. Her data are non-negotiable, because they are not man-made but God-given. She has no authority to correct her Lord's words.

However, she does have authority to interpret them. There are three interpretations of Christ's "narrow way" sayings, such as John 14:6 ("I am the way . . . no one comes to the Father, but by me"):

a. The Church's traditional interpretation is Christocentric: one must have faith in Christ to be saved, but that faith may possibly be implicit or unclear or unaware of itself, as with the good, God-seeking pagan.

b. The very narrow or fundamentalist interpretation is ecclesiocentric: one must have *explicit* faith in Christ and be in his *visible* Church to be saved.

c. The very broad or liberal interpretation is theocentric without being Christocentric. It maintains that all who seek God in any way are saved, whether through Christ or not.

The Church does not teach the fundamentalist interpretation. The Church does teach that "outside the Church is no salvation". But she also teaches that this can refer to the invisible, or "mystical", Body of Christ, not just the visible Church, and that a just and loving God does not condemn those who through no fault of their own do not know that Christ and his Church are the means of salvation.

The Church bases her Christocentric interpretation on her data. The scriptural data tell us that Christ is the only Savior, but they do not tell us that those who call themselves Christians are the only ones saved.

If any are saved, they are saved by Christ. But Christ is divine as well as human. Many of the saved may not have known him on earth in his human incarnation, but only as the "Logos", the Truth, "the true light that enlightens every man" (Jn 1:9). Every man knows God innately, by reason and conscience and nature (Rom 1:19–20). And the only way to know God is through the light of truth that he gives us. And that light is the "Logos", the Word or Mind or Revelation of the Father. And that Logos is the Son of God. Therefore, everyone who knows God does so through the Son. Just as all who see the creation see it through the light of the sun, all who know the Creator know him through the light of the Son.

Who then are saved? We do not know who or how many. When his apostles asked him, "Lord, will those who are saved be few?" (Lk 13:23), he replied, "Strive to enter." He did not satisfy our curiosity about comparative population statistics of heaven and hell. What he did tell us is that he is the only Savior. If he is not what he claimed to be, then he is no Savior at all, but a liar, an egomaniac, a blasphemer, or a madman.

It remains to be seen what is wrong with the "liberal" interpretation. People often ask: If one can be saved without being a member of Christ's visible Church by being baptized, or even without explicitly believing in Christ, then why be a Catholic?

The answer is, first of all, because the Catholic faith is true! Surely this is the first and last reason to believe anything if you are honest. The very asking of the question is its own answer and refutation. For if anyone asks the question, he knows about the claims of Christ to be God and of the Catholic Church to be the one Church he founded, and he is now seeking an excuse to evade an honest confrontation with these claims.

A second, equally absolute reason is: because God gave us Christ, and you do not want to refuse God. And Christ gave us the Church, and you do not want to refuse Christ.

Third, because the Church gives us far more knowledge of Christ, and far more of God's sacramental graces that come from Christ, than anything else can. So it is more likely that you can be saved as a Catholic. The more complete the road map, the more likely it is that you will reach your destination.

19. Christ and the Jews

"In the magi" [the wise men from the East who followed the star to find Christ], "representatives of the neighboring pagan religions, the Gospel sees the first-fruits of the nations, who welcome the good news of salvation through the Incarnation: The magi's coming to Jerusalem . . . means that pagans can discover Jesus and worship him as Son of God and Savior of the world only by turning toward the Jews and receiving from them the messianic promise as contained in the Old Testament"[8] (CCC 528).

Through Christ the Jews fulfill their destiny as the people chosen to show the true God to the world. In fact, half the world today worships the God of the Jews mainly because Christian missionaries made him known.

Vatican II's *Nostra Aetate* made clear that although "Jerusalem did not recognize God's holy moment when it came (cf. Lk 19:42)," the Jews remain very dear to God, and " 'neither all Jews indiscriminately at that time, nor Jews today, can be charged with the crimes committed during [Jesus'] passion. It is true that the Church is the new people of God, yet the Jews should not be spoken of as rejected or accursed' " (NA 4). Rather, " 'sinners were the authors and the ministers of all the sufferings that the divine Redeemer endured'[9] " (CCC 598). The charge against him, the sign on his Cross, was

---

[8] Cf. Jn 4:22; Mt 2:4–6.
[9] Roman Catechism I, 5, 11; cf. Heb 12:3.

written in Hebrew, Greek, and Latin (Jn 19:20), signifying that the whole world was implicated in the crucifixion. The whole world crucified him because the whole world's sins necessitated his death and were atoned for by it. The *Roman Catechism* of the Council of Trent said that " '[s]ince our sins made the Lord Christ suffer the torment of the cross, those who plunge themselves into disorders and crimes crucify the Son of God anew in their hearts (for he is in them) and hold him up to contempt. And it can be seen that our crime in this case is greater in us than in the Jews. As for them, according to the witness of the Apostle, "None of the rulers of this age understood this; for if they had, they would not have crucified the Lord of glory." We, however, profess to know him' [10] " (CCC 598).

The Jews are our fathers in the faith; they taught us who the true God is. To hate the Jews is to hate our fathers. And since Christ was a Jew, to hate Jews is to hate Christ.

20. Of whom is Christ not the Savior?

In God's eyes there is none, but in some men's eyes there are: themselves. They think they do not need forgiveness and salvation.

God gives forgiveness to all in Christ, but not all receive it. Forgiveness, being a spiritual gift, is free: it must be freely given *and* freely received. A bullet does not have to be freely received for it to do its work of killing, but forgiveness has to be freely received for it to do its work of healing.

Thus Christ says to the self-righteous Pharisees, who would not repent, that he is not their Savior: "Those who are well have no need of a physician, but those who are sick; I came not to call the righteous, but sinners" (Mk 2:17). Confession of sin and repentance are the preconditions for faith and salvation.

21. Christ's death and descent to the dead

Christ really died and really rose. It was not merely a show. If he did not really die, he could not have really risen from death. And if he did not really die, he did not really pay for our sins.

The Apostles' Creed says he "descended to the dead". This means *Hades* (Greek) or *Sheol* (Hebrew): the realm of the physically dead, the grave. It does not mean *Gehenna*, the realm of the spiritually dead, the eternally damned. "Jesus, like all men, experienced death and in his soul joined the others in the realm of the dead. But he descended there as Savior, proclaiming the Good News to the spirits imprisoned there [cf. 1 Pet 3:18–19]" (CCC 632).

---

[10] Roman Catechism I, 5, 11; cf. Heb 6:6; 1 Cor 2:8.

22. Christ's Resurrection

"Christ's resurrection is a real event, with manifestations that were historically verified" (CCC 639). "The faith of the first community of believers is based on the witness of concrete men. . . . Peter and the Twelve are the primary 'witnesses to his Resurrection,' but they are not the only ones—Paul speaks clearly of more than five hundred persons to whom Jesus appeared [I Cor 15:4–8; cf. Acts 1:22]" (CCC 642).

This is concrete evidence, not abstract myth (see 2 Pet 1:16). The Resurrection did not come from the apostles' faith; their faith came from the Resurrection. It was not some inner mystical experience. "Far from showing us a community seized by a mystical exaltation, the Gospels present us with disciples demoralized ('looking sad' [Lk 24:17; cf. Jn 20:19]) and frightened" (CCC 643). "Even when faced with the reality of the risen Jesus the disciples are still doubtful, so impossible did the thing seem" (CCC 644).

If Christ did not really rise, then those who say he did—his apostles and the five hundred other witnesses—were not telling the truth. They either knew their story was untrue, or they did not. If they knew, they were deliberate liars, deceivers; if not, they were deceived. But liars do not suffer and die for a lie as they did; nothing proves sincerity like martyrdom. And if they were deceived rather than deceivers, they must have been hallucinating or projecting their subjective faith into objective reality. But they had touched the risen Christ (Jn 20:24, 29). He had eaten food (Lk 24:36–43). He had had long conversations with many men at the same time (Lk 24:13–35; Acts 1:34). He had been seen by all who were present, not just some (Mk 16:14; Jn 24:36, 50). No hallucination in history ever behaved like that.

And no hallucination ever had such power to transform lives and to give love, joy, peace, hope, and meaning to millions of men for thousands of years. For the sake of this "hallucination" saints joyfully endured tortures, persecutions, crucifixions, and martyrdoms. This "hallucination" changed soft, cowardly hearts into hard, courageous ones and converted the hard, cruel Roman Empire to a religion of unselfish love. "By their fruits you shall know them"—how could such true fruit have come from such a false tree? Pascal asks the simple question: "If Christ was not risen and present, who made the apostles act as they did?"

If the Resurrection did not really happen, then an even more incredible miracle happened, as St. Thomas Aquinas argues in his *Summa contra Gentiles*, "In this faith there are truths preached which surpass every human intellect; the pleasures of the flesh are curbed; it is taught that the things of the world should be spurned. Now for the minds of mortal men to assent to these things is the greatest of miracles. . . . For it would be truly more wonderful than all miracles if the world had been led by simple and lowly men to believe such lofty truths, to accomplish such difficult actions, and to have such high hopes" on the basis of a hallucination or a lie.

23. The importance of the Resurrection

What difference does the Resurrection make? Here are two different answers.

Answer no. 1: "If the bones of the dead Jesus were discovered in some Palestinian tomb tomorrow, all the essentials of Christianity would remain unchanged." So wrote Rudolf Bultmann, the founder of Modernist "demythologizing", a century ago.

Answer no. 2: "If Christ has not been raised, then [1] our preaching is in vain [2] and your faith is in vain. [3] We are even found to be misrepresenting God. . . . [4] If Christ has not been raised, . . . you are still in your sins. [5] Then those also who have fallen asleep [died] in Christ have perished. [6] If for this life only we have hoped in Christ, we are of all men most to be pitied" (1 Cor 15:14-19). Six rather important consequences! So wrote St. Paul, who was far closer to Christ in time, in space, in culture, and in spirit than Bultmann.

Nothing more concretely and conclusively proves Christ's divinity than his Resurrection. No one but God can conquer death. And no one but the One who can conquer death can conquer sin. We cannot be saved by a dead Savior. The difference the Resurrection makes is nothing less than this: our hope of salvation.

Even more, the personal and practical importance of the Resurrection is not a past event but a present one: Christ *is* risen. The tomb of every other man who lived says: Such and such a man is here. But at Christ's tomb his disciples heard these words from the angel: "He is not here" (Lk 24:5).

Where is he, then? He is *here*! He is not absent but present: "Behold, I am with you always" (Mt 28:20). He is not in the dead past but in the living present, as really present as we are. The angel's question continually reminds us: "Why do you seek the living among the dead?" (Lk 24:5).

24. The meaning of the Resurrection for our future

Christ's Resurrection was not just a resuscitation, like the raising of Lazarus. For Christ rose with a new kind of body, "not limited by space and time but able to be present how and when he wills" (CCC 645). And this resurrection body can no longer die.

This is the kind of body he promises us. That is one very practical consequence of the Resurrection (see 1 Cor 15). As Christ's death conquered sin for us, his Resurrection conquered death for us. We will have immortal bodies like his.

25. The Ascension

Christ's Ascension, like his Resurrection, is not only about him, it is also about us.

Christ's Ascension to heaven was not the undoing of the Incarnation. The Incarnation was not a temporary visit. It was more like a hunting expedition, in which he captured a trophy and brought it home (Eph 4:8). The trophy was humanity.

And Christ brought humanity home to heaven in the Ascension not only in the sense that his death and Resurrection allowed us to enter heaven, and he ascended to prepare a place for us to live with him forever (Jn 14:1–3), but also in the sense that humanity was united with divinity in the Person of Christ forever. Not only were we changed forever, so was he! "The Father's power 'raised up' Christ his Son and by so doing perfectly introduced his Son's humanity, including his body, into the Trinity" (CCC 648). Christ's Ascension brought his human body and soul to heaven into the Godhead forever. The second Person of the Trinity, God himself, is forever human as well as divine, and bodily as well as spiritual! The incorporation of humanity into divinity was completed in the Ascension.

26. The Second Coming

"He will come again in glory to judge the living and the dead", says the Creed. He promised he would return (Lk 21:27–28), and he keeps his promises.

One of the reasons the early Christians lived in such great hope and expectation was their faith in this promise. Where we see only darkness when we peer into the future, they saw light; where we see clouds of fog, they saw a golden glory.

The quantity of years between his first and second comings is irrelevant; the quality of this time is the point. We are now living in "the last hour" (1 Jn 2:18). The final age of the world is with us now, whether it lasts ten years or ten million. The most important event in history has already happened, the Incarnation, the First Coming, the event that divides all time into two, into B.C. ("before Christ") and A.D. (*anno Domini*, "in the year of our Lord"). Only one more Great Event will happen: his Second Coming. There will be no more Lords, no more revelations, no more Bibles, no more Churches, no more Saviors until the end of time.

Scripture promises that this last age will not be one of sheer progress and goodness but will also be one of great evil and "tribulation" (Jn 16:33), of spiritual warfare between the Spirit of Christ and the spirit of Antichrist (2 Thess 2:3–12; 1 Jn 2:18). All Christians now live in two worlds, two kingdoms: the world and the Church, the flesh and the spirit, "the old man" and "the new man" (Rom 6:6; Eph 4:22; Col 3:9), what St. Augustine called "the City of the World" and "the City of God".

27. Christ the conqueror of the world

Christ promised, "In the world you have tribulation; but be of good cheer, I have overcome the world" (Jn 16:33).

Only three men in history ever made good on that claim: Buddha, Alexander the Great, and Christ. Buddha overcame the world by "waking up" from it as a dream, an illusion. (It is not an illusion; it is a creation of God!) Alexander the Great overcame the world by arms, then wept because he thought there were "no more worlds to conquer". (He forgot the world of his own soul! As Buddha ignored the world without, Alexander ignored the world within.)

Christ overcame the world, not by spilling its blood for himself, like Alexander, but by spilling his blood for it. The Cross is God's sword, held at the hilt by the hand of heaven and plunged down into the earth, not to take blood but to give it.

Chapter 6

THE HOLY SPIRIT

Introduction

This chapter, on the Holy Spirit, is in two parts: first the data, then the theology that explains the data.

Christian theology, like science, is based on data; its principles are not up-in-the-clouds abstractions but divinely revealed explanations of human experiences, both past experience in history (especially as recorded in Scripture) and present experience in our own lives. This is true of the Holy Spirit and the doctrine of the Trinity, just as it is true of Christ and the doctrine of the Incarnation.

Therefore we begin with the experienced data: What difference did the Holy Spirit make in the lives of Jesus' disciples and in the life of the Church in the New Testament? What difference does he make in our lives today?

1. The Holy Spirit: The "Missing Person"

Acts 19 tells a story that could be repeated in most parishes today. Paul the Apostle "came to Ephesus. There he found some disciples [Christians]. And he said to them, 'Did you receive the Holy Spirit when you believed?'" (Acts 19:1-2). They had not.

How did Paul know that? Why did he ask that question? What did he sense was missing at Ephesus? Might he ask the same question today if he came to one of our parishes? Did he perhaps find them sincere but vague, good but boring, nice but wishy-washy? You certainly could not use those words to describe the Church of the martyrs, which changed the world.

2. The difference the Spirit makes: Solving our "power shortage"

St. Paul must have noticed a spiritual power shortage. The Ephesians knew Christ, but they did not know his spiritual power in their lives. It was as if they had maps of the road up God's mountain and the vehicle to travel up the road, but not the fuel for it. They had the ideal but not the power to live it. (Does this sound familiar?)

After his Resurrection and just before his Ascension, Christ told his disciples not to go out and preach his gospel but to wait in Jerusalem for the Holy Spirit, because only then would they have the power for this world-changing work (see Acts 1:4–5, 8). They could not do divine deeds with only human power. (Neither can we.)

The Kingdom of God could not be built with the tools of men. The Church (visible and invisible) is the Kingdom of God, and God gave her the three power tools we summarize in the three parts of this book: theology, morality, and liturgy; creed, code, and cult; words, works, and worship; dogmas, laws, and prayers; and he supplies the Holy Spirit as the energy for all three power tools. All three are composed of words, and it takes the Holy Spirit to give them power. "For the Kingdom of God does not consist in talk but in power" (1 Cor 4:20), the power to transform words into works, ideals into realities, the abstract into the concrete, "life-styles" into lives, nice people into new people (see 2 Cor 5:17).

For the Spirit is not something vague and ethereal and abstract, like "the spirit of the times" or "the spirit of democracy" or "school spirit". He is a Person. He is Almighty God!

3. The difference the Spirit makes: Sharing God's very life

The Eastern churches use the Greek word *theosis* ("divinization") for the Spirit's essential work in us: that "you may . . . become partakers of the divine nature" (2 Pet 1:4). He enables us to share in the very life of God himself—not just the ideals or principles of that life, not just God's "life-style", but God's life itself, something as real as blood (though not made of molecules but of love). This transformation, from merely human life to a participation in divine life, is as great a transformation as the ones in the fairy tales, from a frog to a prince, or from a wooden puppet to a boy.

This state of our spirit, in which we share God's own life, is called by various names, such as "sanctifying grace" or "the state of grace" in Catholic theology, "deification" in Eastern theology, "salvation" in Evangelical Protestantism, and many other names in Scripture, such as "eternal life" (*zoē*, supernatural life), being "born anew" as God's child, being adopted into God's family, or entering God's Kingdom. This is the work of the Holy Spirit.

4. The difference the Spirit makes: Intimacy

The word for "spirit" in both Hebrew and Greek also means "breath". The Spirit is God's "breath". What does this image mean?

When we breathe, the air actually enters into our lungs and becomes one with us. When the Spirit comes, he enters into us and becomes one with us. For this reason, he is not visible as an external object. He is also invisible because he is spirit, not matter, of course. He is within; he is hard to objectify as if he were without. He is too intimate, too close to see. When he is within us, our soul breathes God as our lungs breathe air: he is that intimate. He is like the wind. In fact, that is the image Christ used in John 3. He becomes the very life of our souls. In St. Augustine's formula, the Spirit is to our souls what our souls are to our bodies.

5. The difference the Spirit makes: The world's amazement

What did the world call the first Christians? Acts 17:6 tells us: "these men who have turned the world upside down". Are we doing that today? Why not? Because the world needs it any less today? Or because we have forgotten how?

The word used for the world's reaction to Christians was the same word used for the world's reaction to Christ: *thaumadzein* (to be amazed, astonished, wondering). Everyone, friend and foe alike, wondered at Christ. The friends went on from wonder to worshipping him, and the foes from wonder to crucifying him; but both began in wonder. The world sat up and took notice of Christians just as they did of Christ, and the world was polarized by Christians just as it was by Christ (Mt 10:34–39).

6. The difference the Spirit makes: A radically new kind of love

What the world noticed above all was a new kind of love. The New Testament calls it *agapē*. It is almost a new word. Greek before the New Testament rarely used the word *agapē*, for it meant then only "some kind of love", not any specific kind. It now received a new, specific meaning: the love Christ showed and lived, to the Cross—and poured out on the world through his Spirit.

This was the kind of love that often led to martyrdom. Christians went to their death with hymns on their lips, forgiving their killers, as Christ had done (Lk 23:34). When the world saw these Christians, they said: "See how they love one another!" Christ had promised exactly that: "By this all men will know that you are my disciples, if you have love for one another" (Jn 13:35). Notice that this presumes that Christian love is not the same as any other kind of love, but so distinctive that the whole world will be able to see the difference. It was radical. It was supernatural. It was a miracle—the miracle that converted the world.

The image Scripture uses for this love that "turned the world upside down" is fire. The early Christians were on fire with love: the fire Jesus said he came to earth to kindle: "I am come to cast fire upon the earth, and would that it were already kindled!" (Lk 12:49).

7. The source of this love

What kindles this fire? The Holy Spirit. All four Gospels distinguish Jesus from John the Baptist, the last Old Covenant prophet, by this: John said, "I baptize you with water; but he who is mightier than I is coming, the thong of whose sandals I am not worthy to untie; he will baptize you with the Holy Spirit and with fire" (Lk 3:16).

Everyone wants "true love". True love is *agapē*, the honest, self-forgetful love of the other for the sake of the other. Everyone responds to this love; everyone admires true love; everyone deeply longs for a relationship of mutual love. Everyone knows that love is the meaning of life, life's highest value, the *summum bonum*, or greatest good.

But not everyone knows how to get it, where to go to get it. Where does this love come from? (Could there be a more practical question than that?)

The answer is the Holy Spirit. "God's love has been poured into our hearts through the Holy Spirit who has been given to us" (Rom 5:5). Love is the first fruit of the Spirit (Gal 5:22). To get the fruit, you need the plant.

For the Spirit is the very love of God, the love that eternally circulates, like divine electricity, between the Father and the Son. "God is love" (1 Jn 4:8). God is made of love as the sun is made of sunlight. As the Son is the Father's Word, or truth (*logos*), the Spirit is their love. The Son is God's light, and the Spirit is God's fire. This is the fire Christ came to earth to kindle among us even now as "the 'pledge' or 'first fruits' of our inheritance: the very life of the Holy Trinity" (CCC 735).

8. The difference the Spirit makes: Wisdom

Another difference the Spirit makes, both to the early Church and today, is wisdom, or understanding. He gives light as well as fire.

This is why the saints understand Scripture so much more profoundly than the theologians. This is why simple-minded saints like Mother Teresa seem so smart and sophisticated scholars so silly when it comes to understanding the mind of God. For the mind of God can be understood only through the heart of God. The truth of God is understood through the love of God. (The Son of God, the "Word of God", is understood through the Spirit of God, who is the love of God.)

Thus Jesus says that the way to understand his teaching is to will (love) his Father's will (Jn 7:17). The heart leads the head here.

The kind of wisdom the Spirit gives is the kind Christ had (for it is *his* Spirit!): "They were astonished at his teaching, for he taught them as one who had authority, and not as the scribes" (Mk 1:22).

9. The Spirit and Scripture

When a Spirit-filled Christian reads the Word of God—the Word this very Spirit inspired—the book seems to "come alive" and "light up" from within itself. This is because its primary Author is really present in the reader, alive, interpreting his own words.

The human writers of Scripture, after all, were only the secondary authors, the instruments. That is why Scripture has such a wonderful unity, though it was written by many different authors, with different personalities, issues, problems, presuppositions, limitations, times, places, and situations.

Scripture is "the sword of the Spirit" (Eph 6:17), and the difference the Spirit makes to understanding Scripture is the difference between a sword in a museum case and a sword in the hands of a great swordsman, when it comes alive and cuts to the heart. "For the Word of God is living and active, sharper than any two-edged sword, piercing to the division of soul and spirit, of joints and marrow, and discerning the thoughts and intentions of the heart" (Heb 4:12).

When Christ appeared to his disciples on the road to Emmaus after his Resurrection, he explained the Old Testament Scriptures to them, and they said later, "Did not our hearts burn within us while he talked to us on the road, while he opened to us the scriptures?" (Lk 24:32). That fire was the Spirit, and that heart-light still burns, for his Spirit still teaches the saints. Read St. Augustine or St. Bernard of Clairvaux or St. Catherine of Siena or St. John of the Cross (or a clear and faithful summary of them, like *The Fire Within*, by Fr. Thomas Dubay), and see whether Scripture does not suddenly light up and ignite under their teaching. Where did they get this wisdom? The same place all the saints did: the Spirit.

10. How to "get" the Holy Spirit

Do you want this wisdom? Do you want the wisdom of the saints? Do you want to be a saint? The source is the Spirit. Do you want the love that turned the world upside down? The source is the Spirit. But how do you get the Spirit?

We cannot "get" him; we can only let him get us. He is God. Only God can give him. Christ gives him. He comes from the Father through the Son.

To whom does God give the Spirit? And what must we do to receive him? Scripture's answer is scandalously simple—so simple it is hard for us:

"I tell you, Ask, and it will be given you; seek, and you will find; knock, and it will be opened to you. For every one who asks receives, and he who seeks finds, and to him who knocks it will be opened. What father among you, if his son asks for a fish, will instead of a fish give him a serpent; or if he asks for an egg, will give him a scorpion? If you then, who are evil, know how to give good gifts to your children, how much more will the heavenly Father give the Holy Spirit to those who ask him!" (Lk 11:9–13).

The Spirit is free. He is God's gift. There is nothing we can do to "get" him; we must simply ask, in faith, like a child trusting his father's love. The same is true of the Spirit's gifts, such as wisdom: we get them simply by asking and believing: "If any of you lacks wisdom, let him ask God, who gives to all men generously and without reproaching, and it will be given him. But let him ask in faith" (Jas 1:5–6).

But be careful what you ask for, because God will take you at your word. The Spirit's work is to sanctify, to make saints, and saints are not safe! They are like the One who makes them. God is not safe. Rabbi Abraham Heschel says: "God is not nice. God is not an uncle. God is an earthquake."

11. The Spirit and saints

Saints are wild. Saints risk everything on God. Saints are lovers: in love with God (and therefore with God's children), on fire with God's fire. That fire is the Holy Spirit.

The meaning of life is to be a saint. "There is only one tragedy, in the end: not to have been a saint" (Léon Bloy). If we are not saints when we die, God will not rest until we are; that is why most of us will probably need purgatory before heaven. All heaven's citizens are saints.

Sainthood is the culmination of God's work in us, the final end of our lives. And this end—sanctification, saint-making—is especially the work of the Holy Spirit. The Father made this end possible by creating us, and the Son made it possible by redeeming us, and now the Spirit makes actual what the other two Persons made possible.

12. The Spirit and intimacy with God

The essence of sanctity is intimacy with God, "knowing" God. This is also the essence of eternal life (Jn 17:3), what we will be doing in heaven forever. But how? We can know some facts *about* God by our own human reason, but we cannot know *God*, personally, intimately, without the Holy Spirit. (Most languages, unlike English, have two different words for knowing facts and knowing persons: for instance, *savoir* and *connaître* in French, *wissen* and *kennen* in German.)

Intimacy is the ultimate aim of love. What love seeks is always union with the loved object or person, whether it is ice cream, sports, music, friendship, romance, marriage, or God. And intimacy with us is the ultimate aim of God's love throughout history and throughout our lives.

The Spirit gives us this intimacy. The Spirit moves us to call God our "Father": "When we cry, 'Abba! Father!' it is the Spirit himself bearing witness with our spirit that we are children of God" (Rom 8:15–16). "Abba" is the intimate Aramaic word for "Father". Our equivalent would be "Daddy". Jesus called God "Abba" (Mk 14:36), and so can we. We can have something of the same intimacy with God the Father that God the Son had! How? Through God the Holy Spirit.

And God wants all his children to have this intimacy through his Spirit. This is not an optional extra for super-saints; this is part of the basic "package deal" of being a Christian: "Any one who does not have the Spirit of Christ does not belong to him" (Rom 8:9). And God wants more for us than just having the Spirit; he wants us to experience the fullness of the Spirit, the release of the Spirit, "baptism" in the Spirit. (The Greek word *baptism* means "immersion", like a sunken ship in the sea.)

13. The Spirit and prayer

Because of this intimacy with God, prayer (talking with God) becomes as natural as breathing. The Spirit moves us to talk with the infinitely perfect Creator as we talk with our own closest friend. We want to pray, because we want to be in the presence of the One we love. Love replaces fear or duty as the motive for prayer (and for obedience, too). Of course we will still have problems and temptations and distractions, but they will be the problems of life, not of death. They will be growing pains.

This is true of public, liturgical prayer just as it is true of private, personal prayer. Like Scripture, liturgy too lights up, comes alive, and springs into flame when the same Spirit who inspired the Church to compose it inspires us to enact it.

14. The Spirit's work in relation to the Father and the Son

(We now turn from experience to theology, from data to explanation.)
We have seen Christocentrism in every part of our faith so far, and we will continue to see it. But this in no way lessens the centrality of the Father and of the Spirit. There is no rivalry in the Trinity, no "either/or", only "both/and", as in a good marriage. For Christ has no teaching or will or glory of his own, but refers all to the Father (Jn 6:57; 7:16; 8:50). And the only way we can know Christ is through the Spirit (1 Cor 12:3). All three must be present, or none is. All three must be active, or none is.

This altruism, or other-directedness, is true both "going down" and "going up", so to speak: both for God revealing himself to us and for our knowing God.

First, "on the way down". Christ did not teach on his own authority but on the Father's (Jn 5:30–32; 6:38; 7:16). And the Spirit does not teach on his own authority but on Christ's (Jn 16:13–14). The Spirit does not glorify himself, he glorifies the Son. The Son does not glorify himself, he glorifies the Father, and the Spirit glorifies him. The Father does not glorify himself, the Son glorifies him.

Second, "on the way up", the *Catechism* tells us that " '[i]t is impossible to see God's Son without the Spirit, and no one can approach the Father without the Son' [1] " (CCC 683). Scripture tells us this too: "No one can say 'Jesus is Lord' except by the Holy Spirit" (1 Cor 12:3), and "No one has ever seen God; the only Son, who is in the bosom of the Father, he has made him known" (Jn 1:18).

---

[1] St. Irenaeus, *Dem. ap.* 7: SCh 62, 41–42.

This is why we must forget ourselves and love others, if we are to be happy: because we are made in the image of the God whose whole life is self-forgetful love. Love "goes all the way up".

15. Why the Holy Spirit was revealed last

"[T]he Holy Spirit is the first to awaken faith in us. . . . But the Spirit is the last of the persons of the Holy Trinity to be revealed. St. Gregory of Nazianzus . . . explains this progression in terms of the pedagogy of divine 'condescension': 'The Old Testament proclaimed the Father clearly, but the Son more obscurely. The New Testament revealed the Son and gave us a glimpse of the divinity of the Spirit. Now the Spirit dwells among us and grants us a clearer vision of himself. It was not prudent, when the divinity of the Father had not yet been confessed, to proclaim the Son openly and, when the divinity of the Son was not yet admitted, to add the Holy Spirit' [2] " (CCC 684).

16. Why it is better for us to have the Holy Spirit than Christ visibly present

Christ told his apostles before his Ascension, "It is to your advantage that I go away, for if I do not go away, the Counselor [the Holy Spirit] will not come to you; but if I go, I will send him to you" (Jn 16:7).

If Jesus Christ would appear visibly in person anywhere on earth, a billion people would probably come. Yet we have something better than that, according to Christ's own teaching. We have the Holy Spirit.

But why is this better?

Because the Spirit's presence to us can be even more intimate than Christ's. Or, rather, Christ himself can be more intimately present through his Spirit than he was bodily to his apostles. They knew him better—more intimately and more accurately—after he left them and sent his Spirit. This is clear by comparing the apostles, especially Peter, in the Gospels, with the same apostles in Acts.

The same is true for us. The visible Christ is separated from us by two thousand years of time and four thousand miles of space. We are not first-century Jews; we did not see him. The Father is separated even more: he is infinitely transcendent and "dwells in inaccessible light". But the Spirit makes Christ known to the eyes of our spirit, as Christ made the Father known to our bodily eyes. The Father is God outside us; the Son is God beside us; the

[2] St. Gregory of Nazianzus, *Oratio theol.*, 5, 26 (= *Oratio* 31, 26): PG 36, 161–63.

Spirit is God inside us, God haunting us, God "possessing" us. He is maximal intimacy. That is why it is "better".

17. The Holy Spirit as the culmination of God's love and plan for us

This "indwelling of the Holy Spirit" is the culmination of the plan God had for us before the foundation of the world.

"God is love", therefore all he does comes from his love, his essence.

What love seeks above all is intimacy.

Therefore God seeks intimacy with us.

He reveals himself in three stages of intimacy:

a. Throughout Old Testament history, the Father "gets his hands dirty" with his chosen people. He makes noise, like a good parent to his children. He does not keep to himself but comes out of himself to us. (For love is *ekstatic*, "beside itself", out of itself.)

b. In the Gospels, the Son becomes even more intimate; he comes down from heaven to earth and becomes one of us—in fact, the lowest. This is as if a parent became a child to become more intimate with his children.

c. Yet even that is not enough. He has to get "under our skin". After Pentecost, the Spirit dwells within us. This is the ultimate goal of love: to get into your beloved's heart.

This is the ultimate reason for God's creation of the universe, the reason for each detail of his providence (see Rom 8:28), the reason for the Incarnation, and the reason for the Church. That is what they are *for!* The universe and the Church are divinely designed saint-making machines. They are bridal chambers.

18. How the three Persons of the Trinity cooperate to bring us to perfection

All three Persons act together in all three stages of our destiny.

First, the Father creates us—not alone, but by his Word (the Son) (Gen 1:3) and his Spirit (Gen 1:2).

Then, the Son redeems us—not alone, but by obeying his Father's will unto death and by being baptized with the Spirit (Jn 1:33).

Finally, the Holy Spirit sanctifies us—not alone, but by showing us Christ (Jn 16:14–15) and, through Christ, the Father.

The work of creation is especially "appropriated" to the Father, redemption to the Son, and sanctification to the Spirit. But each Person of the Trinity works for another:

The Father created us for the Son and for redemption. Colossians 1:16

says that "all things were created [by the Father] through him [the Son] and for him."

The Son redeemed us for the Spirit's work of sanctifying us. Justification (redemption) was *for* sanctification. He was called Jesus ("Savior") not only because he would save us from the *punishment* due for our sins, but "because he will save his people from their sins" (Mt 1:21).

And the Spirit sanctifies us in order to bring us back to the Father, so that God can be all in all, Alpha and Omega.

19. The Holy Spirit in history

"When the Father sends his Word, he always sends his Breath" (CCC 689). His Breath, here, means his Spirit.

"The Holy Spirit is at work with the Father and the Son from the beginning. . . . But in these 'end times,' ushered in by the Son's redeeming Incarnation, the Spirit is revealed and given, recognized and welcomed as a person. Now can this divine plan, accomplished in Christ, the firstborn and head of the new creation, be embodied in mankind by the outpouring of the Spirit: as the Church, the communion of saints, the forgiveness of sins, the resurrection of the body, and the life everlasting" (CCC 686). These last five articles of the Creed are the Spirit's work, too. All the rest of the Creed belongs to the Holy Spirit. The Creed is totally trinitarian. It is not trinitarian plus anything else. The Trinity has no postscripts.

20. Why is the Holy Spirit so obscure?

The *Catechism* explains why.

"[T]he Spirit does not speak of himself. The Spirit who 'has spoken through the prophets' makes us hear the Father's Word, but we do not hear the Spirit himself. We know him only in the movement by which he reveals the Word to us. . . . The Spirit . . . 'will not speak on his own' [Jn 16:13]. Such properly divine self-effacement" (CCC 687) is remarkable. *God* is self-effacing! *God* is humble! How dare we be proud?

Humility, subordination, submission, obedience to authority—this is very unpopular in our secular world, but it is the very life of the Trinity, the nature of God himself. It "goes all the way up". It is not merely a human virtue; it is certainly not an old-fashioned superstition; it is the nature of ultimate reality.

No man was ever more obedient than Jesus Christ, God incarnate. Since it was not demeaning for God the Son to obey God the Father (they are equals!), it is not demeaning for human equals to obey each other: for children to obey their parents, wives their husbands, or citizens their rulers, as

Scripture clearly commands (see Eph 5:21—6:9; Col 3:18; 4:1, and Jesus' radical words in Mt 20:20–28). Obedience means something totally different in the Christian life from what it means in the world. It does not signify inferiority in any way. Christ was obedient to the Father, but he was equal to the Father in all things. The Spirit is equally divine, yet he is self-effacing. Therefore Scripture's command that some of us obey others "in Christ" in no way signifies inferiority, as it does in the world.

21. Symbols of the Holy Spirit: Water, fire, dove

We cannot speak of the invisible God directly but only through visible symbols. Three of the most prominent symbols for the Holy Spirit in Scripture are fire, water, and the dove.

Water. "The symbolism of water signifies the Holy Spirit's action in Baptism. . . . [J]ust as the gestation of our first birth took place in water, so the water of Baptism truly signifies that our birth into the divine life is given to us in the Holy Spirit" (CCC 694).

Water is the most important element in nature, and it is necessary for all life. It was the second thing God created, after light. It is the element most of us naturally love the most. Our favorite vacation spot is the sea. We have a mysterious love of moving water. And some of the great saints, like St. Teresa of Avila, say it has taught them more than books.

Jesus spoke of the Spirit as "living [moving] water"; "Jesus stood up and proclaimed, 'If anyone thirst, let him come to me and drink. He who believes in me, as the scripture has said, "Out of his heart shall flow rivers of living water."' Now this he said about the Spirit, which those who believed in him were to receive" (Jn 7:37–39).

Fire. God revealed himself to Moses in a burning bush. Scripture describes him as "a consuming fire" (Heb 12:29). Mystical experiences of him, such as Pascal's, often take that fiery form.

"[F]ire symbolizes the transforming energy of the Holy Spirit's actions. The prayer of the prophet Elijah, who 'arose like fire' and whose 'word burned like a torch,' brought down fire from heaven on the sacrifice on Mount Carmel [Sir 48:1; cf. 1 Kings 18:38–39]. This event was a 'figure' of the fire of the Holy Spirit, who transforms what he touches. . . . In the form of tongues 'as of fire,' the Holy Spirit rests on the disciples on the morning of Pentecost" [Acts 2:3–4] (CCC 696).

Dove. The dove symbolizes peace, one of the most precious fruits of the Spirit (Gal 5:22). "When Christ comes up from the water of his baptism, the Holy Spirit, in the form of a dove, comes down upon him and remains with him [cf. Mt 3:16 and parallels]" (CCC 701). The Spirit is both fire and peace, and both fire and water; paradoxically opposite symbols from nature must be used to express adequately the One who transcends everything in nature.

22. The Spirit and the Scriptures

The Nicene Creed confesses that the Holy Spirit spoke "through the Prophets". "By 'prophets' the faith of the Church here understands all whom the Holy Spirit inspired in living proclamation and in the composition of the sacred books, both of the Old and the New Testaments" (CCC 702).

On the one hand, this inspiration was not necessarily audible or even verbal (word for word), but, on the other hand, it was more than "inspiration" in the common sense of the word, more than a vague help or inclination. On the one hand, the Spirit did not reduce his human instruments to puppets but spoke through the different personalities, backgrounds, and styles of his human authors; for "grace does not destroy nature but perfects it." But, on the other hand, he insured that their writings (Scripture) would have infallibility and divine authority, so that we can be certain of its truth; for "God can neither deceive nor be deceived." A sinful and fallible mankind needed no less; and a wise and merciful God provided no less.

23. The Spirit and the Law

"God gave the Law as a 'pedagogue'" [a tutor] "to lead his people towards Christ [Gal 3:24]. But the Law's powerlessness to save man ... along with the growing awareness of sin that it imparts [cf. Rom 3:20], enkindles a desire for the Holy Spirit" (CCC 708). For without the Spirit within us, we cannot obey God's Law. Thus St. Augustine prays, "Give what you command [that is, give the power, through the Spirit, to obey your command], and then command what you will."

Augustine also says "Love God and then do what you will", for, as Christ says, "If you love me, you will keep my commandments" (Jn 14:15). It is the Spirit who gives us that greatest gift, the gift of loving God.

24. The Spirit and Mary

Only one merely human being in history was so "full of grace" and of the Holy Spirit in this world that she was sinless and perfectly obeyed the "first and greatest commandment", to love God with her whole heart and soul and mind and strength. Mary is the Spirit's masterpiece, "our tainted nature's solitary boast".

"The Holy Spirit *prepared* Mary by his grace. It was fitting that the mother of him in whom 'the whole fullness of deity dwells bodily' [Col 2:9] should herself be 'full of grace.' She was, by sheer grace, conceived without sin as the most humble of creatures, the most capable of welcoming the inexpressible gift of the Almighty" (CCC 722).

25. The Spirit and the Church

The Holy Spirit is to the Church what the soul is to the body. He is the Church's soul, the Church' life. The Church is "the Temple of the Holy Spirit" (CCC 737). Our bodies, too, are temples of the Holy Spirit (see 1 Cor 6:19), because we are cells in the Body of Christ.

The Holy Spirit infallibly guided the Church's earliest ecumenical councils to formulate the doctrine of the Trinity—including the doctrine of the Holy Spirit. Why do Catholics believe in the Holy Spirit? On the authority of the Holy Catholic Church, which teaches it. And why do Catholics believe this Church has infallible authority? Because the Holy Spirit, and not any human spirit, is her soul.

"[T]he Church's mission is not an addition to that of Christ and the Holy Spirit, but is its sacrament" (CCC 738).

26. The Spirit and morality

The Holy Spirit is also the power of our moral life, "life in Christ, according to the Spirit" (CCC 740).

The Spirit gives us both the (long-developing) "fruits of the Spirit" (Gal 5:22–23) and the (more immediately given) "gifts of the Spirit" (1 Cor 12:4–11).

27. The Spirit and sacraments

And "[t]hrough the Church's sacraments, Christ communicates his Holy and sanctifying Spirit to the members of his Body" (CCC 739).

28. The Spirit and prayer

The Spirit also teaches us—both through the Church, which he ensouls, and individually—to pray and worship. "The Holy Spirit . . . is the master of prayer" (CCC 741).

Chapter 7

THE HOLY CATHOLIC CHURCH

1. The Church was founded by Christ

The fundamental reason for being a Catholic is the historical fact that the Catholic Church was founded by Christ, was God's invention, not man's—unless Christ, her founder, is not God, in which case not just Catholicism but Christianity itself is false. To be a Christian is to believe that "Jesus Christ is Lord." To acknowledge him as Lord is to obey his will. And he willed the Catholic ("universal") Church for all his disciples, for all Christians. We are Catholics because we are Christians.

Many Protestants become Catholics for this reason: they read the Church Fathers (earliest Christian writers) and discover that Christ did establish, not a Protestant Church that later became Catholic, but the Catholic Church, parts of which later broke away and became Protestant ("protesting").

2. Why did Christ establish the Church?

Suppose he had not established a single, visible church with authority to teach in his name. Suppose he had left it up to us. Suppose the Church was our invention instead of his, only human and not divine. Suppose *we* had to figure out the right doctrine of the Trinity, the two natures of Christ, the sacraments, Mary, and controversial moral issues like contraception and homosexuality and euthanasia. Who then could ever know with certainty the mind and will of God? How could there then be one Church? There would be twenty thousand different churches, each teaching its own opinion.

Instead, we do have one Church, with divine authority. As the Father gave authority to Christ (Jn 5:22; Mt 28:18–20), Christ passed it on to his apostles (Lk 10:16), and they passed it on to the successors they appointed as bishops. After two thousand years of unbroken apostolic succession, we Catholics have the immense privilege of knowing the mind and will of God through the teaching authority (Magisterium) of the Church visibly incarnated in the bishops. (A very early formula was: "Where the bishop is, there is the Church.")

3. The Church's authority

The Church is not a democracy. She is the Body of the Christ who "taught them as one who had authority, and not as their scribes" (Mt 7:29).

"Authority" does not mean "power" but "right"—"author's rights". The Church has authority only because she is *under* authority, the authority of her Author and Lord. "No one can give himself the mandate and the mission to proclaim the Gospel. The one sent by the Lord does not speak and act on his own authority, but by virtue of Christ's authority" (CCC 875).

This authority of the Church, then, is not arrogant but humble, both (a) in its origin, as received from Christ, under Christ; and (b) in its end, which is to serve, as Christ served (see Jn 16)—if necessary, to the point of martyrdom.

Mother Teresa's most oft-quoted saying describes these two things: the origin of the Church's authority and her essential end as well as every Christian's: "God did not put me on earth to be successful, he put me here to be faithful."

4. Sacred Tradition

"Tradition" means "what is handed over" or "handed down". Sacred Tradition, with a capital "T", is a technical theological term. It does not mean human tradition, but, with Scripture, it comprises the deposit of faith that the Church has received from Christ. We learned of Christ through the apostles he authorized and their successors (the bishops of the one, visible, universal Church) whom *they* authorized to teach in his name and with his authority. The Church reveres Sacred Tradition only because she reveres Christ.

5. Church authority: The basis for the doctrine of the Trinity

The authority of the Church was necessary for us to know the truth of the Trinity. This most distinctively Christian doctrine of all, the one that reveals the nature of God himself, the nature of ultimate reality, was revealed by God clearly only to the Church. It was not clearly revealed to his chosen people, the Jews. It is not clearly defined in the New Testament. God waited to reveal it to the Church.

Scripture contains the data for the doctrine of the Trinity; but that is not enough, for every heretic, too, throughout history has appealed to Scripture. As a matter of historical fact, it has proved impossible for men to know the nature of the true God without the true Church. The dogmas of the Trinity and the Incarnation (and the two natures of Christ) were in fact derived from the Catholic Church.

6. Church authority: The basis for our knowledge of Christ

No Christian has ever learned of Christ except through some ministry of the Church. This is not a controversial opinion but a simple historical fact. We know Christ only because the Church has witnessed to us about him: by passing down through the centuries the gospel ("good news") of the historical events of Christ's life, death, and Resurrection witnessed by the apostles; by teaching true doctrine about him; by living his supernatural life, his love, and his Spirit; and by celebrating his sacred rites, making him really present in the sacraments. Christ lived on earth two thousand years ago. Who brings him across the millennia to us? Who makes us contemporaries with Christ? The Church.

7. Church authority: The basis for Biblical authority

St. Augustine wrote, "I would not believe the authority of the Scriptures except for the authority of the Catholic Church."

It is unreasonable to believe, as most Protestants do, that the Bible is infallible but the Church is not. For

a. Why would God leave us an infallible book in the hands of fallible teachers and interpreters? That would destroy the whole purpose of an infallible book: to give us certainty about the things God knew we needed to know.

b. It is a matter of historical fact that the Church (the apostles) wrote the New Testament. But a fallible cause cannot produce an infallible effect.

c. It is also a historical fact that the Church "canonized" the Bible (defined which books belong to it). If the Church is merely fallible, how can we be sure what this infallible book *is*?

d. The Bible itself calls the Church, not the Bible, "the pillar and bulwark of the truth" (1 Tim 3:15).

e. Scripture never teaches the Protestant principle of *sola scriptura* (Scripture alone). Thus *sola scriptura* contradicts itself.

8. The College of Bishops and its head, the Pope

One visible Church needs one visible head. Christ appointed Peter the head of the apostles. Peter's successors, the popes, are the heads of the apostles' successors, the bishops. Pope and bishops are mutually dependent in pastoring the whole Church.

" 'The sole Church of Christ [is that] which our Savior, after his Resurrection, entrusted to Peter's pastoral care' [Jn 21:15–19; Mt 16:13–19]".... " 'This Church ... subsists in ... the Catholic Church, which is governed by the successor of Peter and by the bishops in communion with him'[1]" (CCC 816).

"The *Pope*, Bishop of Rome and Peter's successor" [in an unbroken chain of historical continuity] " 'is the perpetual and visible source and foundation of the unity both of the bishops and of the whole company of the faithful' [LG 23]" (CCC 882). This Vatican II document continues, "For the Roman Pontiff, by reason of his office as Vicar [servant-representative] of Christ, and

[1] LG 8 § 2.

as pastor [shepherd] of the entire Church, has full, supreme and universal power over the whole Church. . . . The college or body of bishops has no authority unless united with the Roman Pontiff, Peter's successor, as its head" (*LG* 22).

9. Infallibility

Vatican Council I defined what Catholics had always believed: that the pope, like the ecumenical (worldwide) councils, is infallible (preserved by God from error) when defining doctrine or morality for the whole Church. He is not *personally* infallible, but his *office* is.

God did not let us wonder and wander in darkness about the most important truths we had to know in order to fulfill our most important task in life, union with him. No human lover would allow that if he could help it. Neither did God. Papal infallibility, like every other Catholic dogma, is properly understood only by the primacy of love.

Infallibility is God's loving gift in response to our need to persevere in the unity of love and truth—which is what God wants above all because that is what he is: love (1 Jn 4:18) and truth (Jn 6:14). Without infallibility, uncertainties and schisms are inevitable among us fallen and foolish humans for whom Christ designed his Church.

The gift of infallibility flows from God's character. He is so generous that he does not hold back anything that we need. He is not a stingy God! The creation of the world, the Incarnation and death of Christ, the gift of the Holy Spirit, the Eucharist, and heaven are six spectacular examples of God's unpredictable and amazing generosity. The gift of infallibility to the Church fits this same pattern.

10. When the Church is infallible

a. "The Roman Pontiff, head of the college of bishops, enjoys this infallibility in virtue of his office, when, as supreme pastor and teacher of all the faithful . . . , he proclaims in an absolute decision a doctrine pertaining to faith or morals" (*LG* 25).

b. "The infallibility promised to the Church is also present in the body of bishops when, together with Peter's successor, they exercise the supreme teaching office" (*LG* 25).

c. Even doctrines not explicitly labeled infallible can be binding on Catholic belief because "[d]ivine assistance is also given to the successors of the apostles, teaching in communion with the successor of Peter, . . . when, without arriving at an infallible definition and without pronouncing in a 'definitive manner,' they propose in the exercise of the ordinary Magisterium a teaching . . . of faith and morals. To this ordinary teaching the faithful 'are to adhere . . . with religious assent' [LG 25]" (CCC 892). Wise and good parents do not explicitly label everything they say to their children as "infallible", yet wise and good children trust them. Similarly, we should trust Holy Mother Church, the Church of the apostles, saints, and martyrs, the Church with a two-thousand-year-long memory, much more than we trust our own opinions.

d. The sign the Church attaches to an infallible teaching is Christocentric: "When the Church through its supreme Magisterium proposes a doctrine 'for belief as being divinely revealed,' [2] and as the teaching of Christ, the definitions 'must be adhered to with the obedience of faith' [3]" (CCC 891).

11. Why the Church is infallible

The Church is infallible because she is faithful. Our faith in the Church is grounded in the Church's faithfulness to Christ. Infallibility is Christocentric.

The Church does not have authority over Sacred Tradition because she is not its author. Its author is Christ. She can interpret it and draw out its inner meanings, but she can never correct it. She can add to it but never subtract from it; and when she adds, she adds from within, organically, as a tree adds fruit, not mechanically, as a construction crew adds another story to a house.

Because she does not claim to have the authority other churches claim to have, to change "the deposit of faith" entrusted to her by Christ, she cannot allow such things as divorce or priestesses or homosexual sex (or the hating of homosexuals), however fashionable these things may become in society. Her Lord is not society or the world, but Christ.

12. The Church is necessary for salvation

> Since we have no salvation without Christ,
> And we do not know Christ without the Church,
> It follows that there is no salvation without the Church.

This traditional formula of the Church Fathers (see CCC 846), "Outside the Church there is no salvation", does not mean that Protestants and others are not saved, because this formula is not an answer to the mind's curiosity about the populations of heaven and hell, but an answer to the sincerely seeking heart's question "Where is salvation? Where is the road? What has God done

[2] DV 10 § 2.
[3] LG 25 § 2.

to show me how to be saved?" Similarly, Christ's words to his disciples about "many" choosing the "wide" road to destruction and only "few" finding the "narrow" road to life (Mt 7:14) are not the words of a statistician spoken to a census taker, but the words of a loving heavenly Father to his beloved children, warning them of danger. To the Good Shepherd even one out of a hundred sheep is too many to lose and ninety-nine too few to save (Mt 18:12).

In fact the Church explicitly teaches that many who call themselves non-Catholics are saved. Vatican Council II said that "they could not be saved who, knowing that the Catholic Church was founded as necessary by God through Christ, would refuse either to enter it, or to remain in it" (LG 14), but also that "[t]hose who, through no fault of their own, do not know the Gospel of Christ or his Church, but who nevertheless seek God with a sincere heart, and, moved by grace, try in their actions to do his will as they know it through the dictates of their conscience—those too may achieve eternal salvation" (LG 16)—not because conscience is an adequate substitute for the Church, but because conscience, too, is contact with God.

13. Why the Church sends out missionaries if non-Catholics can be saved

We do not know exactly how God saves non-Catholics or how many are saved; but we do know by whom they are saved: the One who said "No man comes to the Father, but by me" (Jn 14:6). Therefore "the Church, nevertheless, still has the obligation and also the sacred right to evangelize" (AG 7)—not because of consequences but commandments: not because she knows how many would be lost if they did not hear the gospel, but because Christ has commanded her to preach it (Mt 28:19).

Fundamentalists send out missionaries because they claim to know that all are damned except those who consciously know and accept Christ. Modernists send out missionaries, if they do, just to do good human works. They also claim to know the number of the damned: none. Catholics make neither claim. They just preach the truth.

"God wills the salvation of everyone through the knowledge of the truth. Salvation is found in the truth. Those who obey the prompting of the Spirit of truth are already on the way of salvation. But the Church, to whom this truth has been entrusted, must go out to meet their desire, so as to bring them the truth" (CCC 851).

Two things are needed, not just one: seeking the truth and finding it. Each individual must supply the first by himself, but the Church is needed to supply the second, because divine revelation is needed for us to know God's plan of salvation.

14. The Church and Mary

The Church is like Mary in pointing beyond herself to Christ. Her last words recorded in Scripture are: "Do whatever he tells you" (Jn 2:5).

The Church is also like Mary in being a womb in which Christ's body grows. "Mother Church" brings forth the mature Christ as Mary did, having first received him as a seed. She brings forth words (creeds), having first received the Word by her faith, her *fiat* (Yes), just as Mary did (Lk 1:38).

And the Church is holy in the same way Mary is holy: by receiving Christ, divine Love incarnate. "In the Church this communion of men with God, in the 'love [that] never ends,' is the purpose which governs everything in her. . . .[4] '[The Church's] structure is totally ordered to the holiness of Christ's members.'[5] . . . Mary goes before us all in the holiness that is the Church's mystery. . . . This is why the 'Marian' dimension of the Church" [holiness] "precedes the 'Petrine'" [authority] (CCC 773).

15. The Church and the Holy Spirit

"The article" [of the Creed] "concerning the Church also depends entirely on the article about the Holy Spirit, which immediately precedes it. . . . The Church is, in a phrase used by the Fathers, the place 'where the Spirit flourishes'[6]" (CCC 749). It is the fireplace for the fire of the Spirit.

The Holy Spirit is the Church's spirit. "'What the soul is to the human body, the Holy Spirit is to the Body of Christ, which is the Church'[7]" (CCC 797).

Though the Spirit is not limited to the Magisterium of the Church, the Spirit never works contrary to it. Those who claim the inspiration of the Spirit when they denounce official Church teachings that they do not like— for instance, those who in the name of the so-called "spirit of Vatican II" reject the actual teachings of Vatican II—are judging and "correcting" the teachings of the Church by their own desires and opinions, instead of letting their desires and opinions be instructed and corrected by the Church. That is not the work of the Holy Spirit. That is the work of an unholy spirit.

16. Why be a Catholic?

If you want to invent your own religion, do not be a Catholic. If you want to teach the Church rather than let the Church teach you, there are plenty

[4] 1 Cor 13:8; cf. *LG* 48.
[5] John Paul II, *MD* 27.
[6] St. Hippolytus, *Trad. Ap.* 35: SCh 11, 118.
[7] St. Augustine, *Sermo* 267, 4: PL 38, 1231D.

of other churches for you, churches that welcome theologies without miracles, moralities without absolutes, and liturgies without adoration. Please do not be a Catholic unless you believe the Church's claim to speak in these areas in the name of Jesus Christ.

There is no such thing as a "cafeteria Catholic". Catholics do not pick and choose among the Church's doctrines and laws; we receive them gratefully from God, we "eat all the food Mother puts on our plate".

A "cafeteria Catholic" or a half Catholic or a 95 percent Catholic is a contradiction in terms. If the Catholic Church does not have the divine authority and infallibility she claims, then she is not half right or 95 percent right, but the most arrogant and blasphemous of all churches, a false prophet claiming "thus says the Lord" for mere human opinions. It must be either/or, as with Christ himself: if Christ is not God, as he claims, then he is not 95 percent right or half right or merely one of many good human prophets or teachers, but the most arrogant and blasphemous false prophet who ever lived. Just as a mere man who claims to be God is not a fairly good man but a very bad man, a merely human church that claims divine authority and infallibility is not a fairly good church but a very bad church.

The only honest reason to be a Christian is because you believe Christ's claim to be God incarnate. The only honest reason to be a Catholic is because you believe the Church's claim to be the divinely authorized Body of this Christ.

17. What is the Church?

The Church is not something man makes after he is saved, but something God makes to save man. We are not first saved as individuals and then form a Church; we are saved by getting aboard the one Ark of salvation. (Noah's Ark was a favorite image of the Church for the Fathers.)

"The word 'Church' (Latin, *ecclesia*, from the Greek *ek-ka-lein*, to 'call out of') means a convocation or an assembly" (CCC 751) that Christ himself calls out of the world to be holy ("set apart"), to be Christ's own Body on earth, "the extension of the Incarnation".

The Church was founded by Christ; the Church is the Body of Christ; and the Church's purpose is to make us into little Christs, to spread Christ's life. Christ is the whole key to the Church's origin, nature, and end—and to ours.

18. Is the Church visible or invisible?

The Church is much more than what we can see. The Church is "the mystical [invisible] Body of Christ." But she is also "the (visible) People of God."

As man is both invisible (soul) and visible (body), so is Christ, and so is his Church. "The Church is at the same time:

"— a 'society structured with hierarchical organs *and* the mystical body of Christ;

"— the visible society *and* the spiritual community;

"— the earthly Church *and* the Church endowed with heavenly riches' [*LG* 8]" (CCC 771; italics added by author).

Two common opposite errors are to reduce the Church to what is visible in human history and to reduce the Church to an invisible community of souls.

19. The Church as the ultimate reason for creation

"Christians of the first centuries said, 'The world was created for the sake of the Church.'[8] God created the world for the sake of" [our] "communion with his divine life, a communion brought about by . . . the Church. . . .

"'Just as God's will is creation and is called "the world," so his intention is the salvation of men, and it is called "the Church"'[9]" (CCC 760).

The Church is the reason for creation, the reason for the Big Bang. The universe is a Church-making machine, and the Church is a saint-making machine.

20. The Church as the "spiritual marriage"

The consummation of all human history, according to Scripture (Rev 21), is a marriage: between Christ and the Church, his Bride. St. Paul sees, as a symbol of Christ, a husband and wife becoming "one flesh" and the Church becoming one Body: "'The two shall become one.' This is a great mystery, and I mean in reference to Christ and the church" (Eph 5:31–32). What the Church is ultimately for, what all the Bibles and creeds and priests and sacraments and music and fund-raising and social service and commandments and buildings are for—the one ultimate purpose of everything the Church is and does, right down to each sweep of the janitor's broom, is lovemaking: the love relationship, the life of love, between Christ and his Bride (us!). The Catholic Church is the Church of Love.

This parallel between the Church and a marriage shows why there can be only one true Church: because Christ is no polygamist. The parallel also shows why this Church is not merely invisible, any more than a bride is— or any more than the Bridegroom (Christ) is!

---

[8] *Pastor Hermæ*, Vision 2, 4, 1: PG 2, 899; cf. Aristides, *Apol.* 16, 6; St. Justin, *Apol.* 2, 7: PG 6, 456; Tertullian, *Apol.* 31, 3; 32, 1: PL 1, 508–9.

[9] Clement of Alexandria, *Pæd.* 1, 6, 27: PG 8, 281.

21. The Church as the total Christ

"Christ and his Church . . . together make up the 'whole Christ'" (CCC 795) as head and body are one person. Christ is not the "head" of the Church the way Henry Ford was the "head" of Ford Motor Company, but the way that round hairy thing between your shoulders is the head of your body. He is the head of a corpus, not a corpse; something living, not something dead; a real organic body, not a legal fiction.

St. Augustine writes, "'Let us rejoice then and give thanks that we have become not only Christians, but Christ himself. Do you understand and grasp, brethren, God's grace toward us? Marvel and rejoice: we have become Christ. For if he is the head, we are the members; he and we together are the whole man. . . . But what does "head and members" mean? Christ and the Church'[10]" (CCC 795).

St. Thomas Aquinas writes: "'Head and members form as it were one and the same mystical person'[11]" (CCC 795).

That is why Christ says: "[A]s you did it to one of the least of these my brethren, you did it to me" (Mt 25:40)—because "I am the vine, you are the branches" (Jn 15:5) of one organism, with one life, one blood. This vine has its roots in heaven and its foliage on earth. The Church is an upside-down tree.

"'A reply of St. Joan of Arc to her judges sums up the faith of the holy doctors and the good sense of the believer: "About Jesus Christ and the Church, I simply know they're just one thing, and we shouldn't complicate the matter"'[12]" (CCC 795).

22. The Church and the Eucharist

The Church is the People of God, "who themselves, nourished with the Body of Christ, become the Body of Christ" (CCC 777). "The Body of Christ" means both the Church and the Eucharist. The Church "makes" the Eucharist, and the Eucharist makes the Church. The Church is where we "eat" Christ and Christ "eats" us, assimilates us to his life. The Eucharist is not just one of the many things the Church does but the one thing she essentially *is*: Christ's Body.

23. How does one enter the Church?

"One becomes a *member* of this people not by a physical birth, but by being 'born anew,' a birth 'of water and the Spirit' [Jn 3:3–5], that is, by faith in

[10] St. Augustine, *In Jo. ev.* 21, 8: PL 35, 1568.
[11] St. Thomas Aquinas, *STh* III, 48, 2.
[12] Acts of the Trial of Joan of Arc.

Christ, and Baptism" (CCC 782). Since the Church is both invisible and visible, one enters her by both an invisible, inner act of sincere faith and a visible, public rite of Baptism.

24. The three offices in the Church

In ancient Israel God established prophets, priests, and kings.

Christ fulfills all three "job descriptions": the perfect prophet (the Word of God himself), the perfect priest (offering the perfect sacrifice on the Cross), and "Christ the King" of the whole universe.

Christ then established these three offices in his Church: (prophetic) teaching, (priestly) sacraments, and (kingly) apostolic authority. These offices are hierarchical, but they are not limited to the clergy only. In a sense every Christian is a prophet, a priest, and a king, for "[t]he whole People of God participates in these three offices of Christ" (CCC 783).

25. The meaning of Christ's kingship— and the Church's

Christ the King ruled by serving (Mt 20:28). Therefore his Church, too, rules by serving, as does each Christian. "For the Christian, 'to reign is to serve him,' particularly when serving 'the poor and the suffering, in whom the Church recognizes the image of her poor and suffering founder' [LG 8; cf. 36]" (CCC 786).

Most of God's chosen people, the Jews, did not recognize and accept Christ as the promised Messiah when he came because they misunderstood this kingly office. The prophets had promised that the Messiah would deliver God's people from their "enemies". God was testing his people's hearts by the very ambiguity of these prophecies; for those whose hearts were set on worldly success interpreted these enemies as the Romans and did not recognize Christ as Messiah because he was apolitical, but those whose hearts were set on God and holiness knew their enemies were really their own sins and recognized Christ as their Savior. All who sought him (that is, sought what he was: holiness, not power) found him, just as he promised (see Mt 7:7-8).

26. The "four marks of the Church"

The Nicene Creed mentions four "marks of the Church": "We believe in one holy catholic and apostolic Church." If anyone wonders which of the twenty thousand different churches that claim to be Christ's true church is really the one Christ established, this is how to recognize it. Only one church has all four marks in their fullness: the Catholic Church.

This is discovered by both faith and reason. "Only faith can recognize that the Church possesses these properties from her divine source" [as opposed to a merely human source]. "But their historical manifestations are signs that also speak clearly to human reason" (CCC 812).

27. The first mark of the Church: Oneness

How is the Church one?

a. Essentially, the Church is one because Christ her Head is one. A head with many bodies is a monstrosity, like a body with many heads. For the Church is an organic unity (though spiritual rather than biological), not only a legal one. A CEO can head many companies, but your head cannot have two bodies.

b. Scripture tells us that the Church is one because she has "one Lord, one faith, one baptism" (Eph 4:5). Because it is Christ her Lord that makes her one, the Church insists on right faith—creedal orthodoxy—not for its own sake but so that we know who Christ is. The "one faith" identifies the "one Lord". So does the "one baptism", which begins that Lord's divine life in the soul of the baptized. The creeds define, and the sacraments communicate, this "one Lord".

c. The Church is also one in love. Her Lord's essential command is love (Jn 15:9–12), for "God is love" (1 Jn 4:16). Therefore "put on love, which binds everything together" (1 Cor 3:14).

d. "But the unity of the . . . Church is also assured by visible bonds of communion:

"— profession of one faith received from the Apostles;

"— common celebration of divine worship, especially of the sacraments;

"— apostolic succession through the sacrament of Holy Orders [cf. UR 2; LG 14; CIC, can. 205]" (CCC 815). For it is a matter of historical fact that "the apostles were careful to appoint successors" (LG 20).

28. Unity and diversity in the Church

"From the beginning, this one Church has been marked by a great *diversity*. . . . 'Holding a rightful place in the communion of the Church there are also particular Churches that retain their own traditions' [LG 13 § 2]" (CCC 814).

A body is both one and many. "For just as the body is one and has many members [organs, limbs], and all the members of the body, though many, are one body, so it is with Christ" (1 Cor 12:12).

Pennies in a pile are neither profoundly one (they are not dependent on each other) nor profoundly different (they are identical and replaceable). Organs in a body are both profoundly one (for they are dependent on each other for life, and all work together for the health of the whole body) and profoundly different (for example, the lung and the kidney).

29. Solidarity

The unity in a body is so great that "if one member suffers, all suffer together; if one member is honored, all rejoice together" (1 Cor 12:26)—for instance, in a family or a nation. The assassinations of Lincoln and Kennedy harmed all of America and, thus, all Americans.

There is a Russian word for this kind of unity: *sobornost* (usually translated as "universality" or catholicity). A similar Polish word is *solidarność*: solidarity. It is the basis in objective reality for the life of charity. Charity is realistic. It is how bodies stay alive.

All prayers help all members of Christ's Body, not just the ones consciously prayed for. Every good deed makes the whole Body stronger. And every evil deed makes it weaker. All sins harm all members of the Body, not only the ones visibly and immediately harmed. There are no private sins, no victimless crimes. Every failure of love harms everyone. As Dostoyevsky says, "We are each responsible for all."

30. Ecumenism and "other churches"

Though there are particular Churches and rites within the one Church, there are no "other churches"; there is but one Church. Christ has only one Body, one Bride. He is not a bigamist.

However, his one Body is torn and wounded. Though her essential unity is indestructible, her visible signs of unity are not. Already in New Testament times there were divisions: schisms, heresies, and apostasies. The Apostle Paul found this not merely unfortunate but intolerable. No one can read 1 Corinthians 1–3 and be in doubt what Paul would say about our far worse and wider divisions today.

These wounds must be healed. Working and praying for ecumenical reunification is not an option but a requirement. (So said Pope John Paul II in *Ut unum sint*.)

We can find the right road, back to unity, only by retracing our path back to where the wrong road, the road to divisions, began. They began with sin. We are not one with each other because we are not one with God. "The ruptures that wound the unity of Christ's Body . . . do not occur without human sin" (CCC 817); "'often enough, men of both sides were to blame'

[*UR* 3 § 1]" (CCC 817). Therefore our divisions will be undone only if sin is conquered. And only Christ can conquer sin. Reunion will come when all Christians put Christ's will above their own. Only when all the musicians follow the conductor's baton does the orchestra play in harmony. The key to ecumenism is the same as the key to all Catholic ideas: the lordship of Christ.

31. How to work for reunion

"The desire to recover the unity of all Christians is a gift of Christ and a call of the Holy Spirit" [cf. *UR* 1] (CCC 820). "Certain things are required in order to respond adequately to this call:

"— a permanent *renewal* of the Church in greater fidelity to her vocation ... [cf. *UR* 6]." [Note the paradox here: the re-*new*-al comes by fidelity, that is, faithfulness to the old, the origin, the marriage vows between Christ and the Church. All significant ecumenical progress so far has come about through a return to common sources, as called for by Vatican II: the Church Fathers, the Bible, and ultimately Christ himself.]

"— [C]*onversion of heart* as the faithful 'try to live holier lives according to the Gospel' [*UR* 7 § 3]; for it is the unfaithfulness of the members to Christ's gift which causes divisions." [If it took sin to cause the divisions, it will take sanctity to heal them.]

"— [P]*rayer in common* ... 'should be regarded as the soul of the whole ecumenical movement, and merits the name "spiritual ecumenism"' [*UR* 8 § 1]." [When Catholics and Protestants put their knees together in common prayer, God will put their heads together to understand common truths.]

"— [F]*raternal knowledge of each other* [cf. *UR* 9]" [for many divisions originated and are maintained by mutual ignorance and misunderstanding]. ...

" [C]*ollaboration* among Christians in various areas of service to mankind [cf. *UR* 12] (CCC 821). Protestants and Catholics who share a jail cell for trying to save lives by protesting abortion or who run inner city homeless shelters or drug rehabilitation programs have often found that their common orthopraxy (right action) has opened their eyes to a common orthodoxy (right belief). The heart and the hands can sometimes lead and educate the head.

"But we must realize 'that this holy objective—the reconciliation of all Christians in the unity of the one and only Church of Christ—transcends human powers and gifts' [*UR* 24 § 2]" (CCC 822). We can no more save the Church from the divisions our sins caused than we can save ourselves. Only Christ can save us from sin, and only Christ can save his Church from division.

32. Are Protestants to blame for church divisions?

Yes. And so are Catholics.

"'However, one cannot charge with the sin of the separation those who at present are born into these communities [that resulted from such separation] and in them are brought up in the faith of Christ, and the Catholic Church accepts them with respect and affection as brothers. . . . All who have been justified by faith in Baptism are incorporated into Christ' [UR 3 § 1]" (CCC 818); they are our "separated brethren".

"Christ's Spirit uses these Churches and ecclesial communities as means of salvation, whose power derives from the fullness of grace and truth that Christ has entrusted to the Catholic Church" (CCC 819). The Protestant limbs that broke off from the Catholic tree can still have enough life-giving sap (God's truth and grace) from the root (Christ) through the trunk (the Catholic Church) to be the means of salvation for their members. The Church of Christ "subsists in" (CCC 816; LG 8 § 2) the Roman Catholic Church most completely but not exclusively.

33. The second mark of the Church: Holiness

The Church is "holy" in a way her members are not. Her doctrine, her moral principles, and her sacraments are pure because they are from Christ. But her human members, clergy as well as laity, are far from pure in their understanding of those doctrines, in their living according to those principles, and in their participation in those sacraments. For Christ established his Church, not as a museum for saints, but as a hospital for sinners. "I came not to call the righteous, but sinners" (Mk 2:17).

The Church's perfect Head (Christ) is perfectly holy. "'The Church, however, clasping sinners to her bosom, at once holy and always in need of purification, follows constantly the path of penance and renewal.'[13] All members of the Church, including her ministers, must acknowledge that they are sinners [cf. 1 Jn 1:8–10]" (CCC 827).

34. Saints

In the most important sense—the sense used in the New Testament—all members of Christ's Body are "saints": that is, they are "holy" (not perfect but "set-apart"), taken out of the "world" (not the earth) and the "flesh" (not the body), and made to share in the very life of Christ; and constantly being "sanctified", or made more saintly, by "sanctifying grace". Who are

[13] LG 8 § 3; cf. UR 3; 6; Heb 2:17; 7:26; 2 Cor 5:21.

the saints? All the faithful—that is, all who have faith in Christ and remain faithful to him.

In a more specific sense, "[b]y *canonizing* some of the faithful, i.e., by solemnly proclaiming that they practiced heroic virtue" (CCC 828), the Church singles out a few thousand men and women as ideals for the rest of us as heroes for our reverence and models for our lives.

The Church also canonizes saints to assure us publicly that they will intercede for us from heaven and to encourage us to pray to them.

35. Society's need for saints

Society needs saints. A society is unified only by sharing a common end, a common value, a common love; and this is concretized in its heroes and in shared stories about them. Without true heroes there is no true society. And the saints are the truest heroes.

The early Church won the world mainly through her saints. She can win it back only in the same way. This means you and I must do it, we must become saints—not only for our own sakes, but also for the sake of our society, that is, all those we love.

36. Praying to saints

Protestants usually criticize the Catholic practice of praying to saints because they think it is idolatry to pray to anyone but God.

Catholics do not worship saints; we worship God alone. The Church distinguishes between *latria* (adoration, due to God alone), *hyperdulia* (the greatest human respect, which is due to Mary as the only sinless saint), and *dulia* (great human respect, which is due to all the saints).

However, Catholics "pray" to saints as they "pray" to holy friends on earth: that is, they ask these friends to pray to God for them. It is no more idolatrous to ask another human being to pray for you after he dies than before. The issue that divides Protestants and Catholics here is not idolatry but the "communion of saints", the interaction between the Church on earth and the Church in heaven (see the next section).

37. The communion of saints

The Catholic vision differs from the Protestant, not about whether there is a real communion of saints on earth, who pray for each other, but about whether this communion extends to heaven.

The Catholic Church exists in three places: "the Church Militant" on earth, "the Church Suffering" in purgatory, and "the Church Triumphant" in heaven.

We on earth and those in heaven can pray for the souls in purgatory, that their purification in preparation for heaven be hastened. This is biblical: "It was a holy and pious thought. Therefore he made atonement for the dead, that they might be delivered from their sin" (2 Mac 12:45). And those in purgatory and heaven can pray for us, and we can ask them to. Death itself cannot sever the unity of the Church.

The communion of saints is far more powerful than we imagine. Our prayers to God for the souls in purgatory help them much more than we know. And the saints in heaven and also those in purgatory help us by their prayers much more than we know. St. Dominic said, when dying, " 'Do not weep, for I shall be more useful to you after my death and I shall help you then more effectively than during my life' [14] " (CCC 956). St. Thérèse of Lisieux wrote, "I want to spend my heaven in doing good on earth" [15] (CCC 956).

38. The third mark of the Church: Catholic

"Catholic" means "universal", one-in-many, like the "uni-verse" itself. The Church is one Church though spread over many places on earth as well as over purgatory and heaven.

Just as the Church is one because Christ her Head is one, so the Church is universal because Christ is universal. "[T]he Church is catholic because Christ is present in her. 'Where there is Christ Jesus, there is the Catholic Church' [16] " (CCC 830).

"Secondly, the Church is catholic because she has been sent out by Christ on a mission to the whole of the human race [cf. Mt 28:19] (CCC 831)".

Where Christ is, there is the Catholic Church, his Body; therefore *insofar* as Christ is present in churches Orthodox, Anglican, Evangelical, Reformed, Pentecostal, and so on, they are parts of the Catholic Church, partially "catholic", for they share the Church's Scripture, the Church's Baptism, and above all the Church's Lord.

39. Who belongs to the Catholic Church?

The Church answers this question in degrees:

First, baptized, believing, and practicing Roman Catholics are "[f]ully incorporated into the society of the Church" [LG 14] (see also CCC 837).

[14] St. Dominic, dying, to his brothers.
[15] St. Thérèse of Lisieux, *The Final Conversations*, trans. John Clarke (Washington, D.C.: ICS, 1977), 102.
[16] St. Ignatius of Antioch, *Ad Smyrn.* 8, 2: *Apostolic Fathers*, II/2, 311. [St. Ignatius of Antioch was the disciple of St. John the Evangelist.]

However, "[e]ven though incorporated into the Church, one who does not . . . persevere in charity is not saved. He remains indeed in the bosom of the Church, but 'in body' not 'in heart' [LG 14]" (CCC 837).

Second, "[t]hose 'who believe in Christ and have been properly baptized are put in a certain, although imperfect, communion with the Catholic Church' [UR 3]. *With the Orthodox Churches*, this communion is so profound 'that it lacks little to attain the fullness that would permit a common celebration of the Lord's Eucharist' " [17] (CCC 838). The most troublesome difference concerns papal jurisdiction.

Third, members of Protestant churches, "separated brethren", are parts of Christ's Mystical Body if they are Christians, though they are separated from his visible Body on earth in various degrees. "The Church knows that she is joined in many ways to the baptized who are honored by the name of Christian, but who do not however profess the Catholic faith in its entirety or have not preserved unity or communion under the successor of Peter" (LG 15).

Fourth, "[t]hose who have not yet received [believed] the Gospel are related to the People of God [the Church] in various ways [LG 16]"—most of all, the Jews, " 'to whom the Lord our God spoke first.' [18] The Jewish faith, unlike other non-Christian religions, is already a response to God's revelation in the Old Covenant" (CCC 839). Biblical Judaism is divinely revealed and the foundation for Christianity; the Jews are our "fathers in the faith", for they taught us who the true God is. But Judaism is incomplete without its capstone, Christ. Jews who accept Christ as the Messiah and become Christians today usually see themselves as completed Jews, just as the first Christian converts did.

Fifth, " '[t]he plan of salvation also includes those who acknowledge the Creator, in the first place amongst whom are the Muslims; these profess to hold the faith of Abraham, and together with us they adore the one, merciful God, mankind's judge on the last day' [19] " (CCC 841). Christians, Jews, and Muslims worship the same God.

Sixth, "[t]*he Church's bond with non-Christian religions*" [especially Hinduism and Buddhism] "is in the first place the common origin and end of the human race" [in God as the Alpha and Omega] (CCC 842). "The Catholic Church recognizes in other religions that search, among shadows and images, for the God who is unknown yet near" [this is true even of pagan polytheism; see Acts 17:22–23]. . . . "Thus, the Church considers all goodness and truth found in these religions as 'a preparation for the Gospel' [20] " (CCC 843)—prophets outside Israel, so to speak, though not infallible ones.

---

[17] Paul VI, Discourse, December 14, 1975; cf. UR 13–18.
[18] Roman Missal, Good Friday 13: General Intercessions, VI.
[19] LG 16; cf. NA 3.
[20] LG 16; cf. NA 2; EN 53.

But though there may be profound truth and goodness in other religions, they are incomplete because they lack the fullness of Christ. The Church's claim of superiority is not for herself but for her Lord. And therefore, as Christ commanded her, she "still has the obligation and also the sacred right to evangelize. And so, today as always, missionary activity retains its full force and necessity" (*AG* 7).

40. The fourth mark of the Church: Apostolic

The Church is apostolic because of her mission, her "apostolate" to evangelize (preach the gospel), and because she is "built upon the foundation of the apostles" (Eph 2:20), who ordained their successors (bishops) as Christ had ordained *them*. "[T]he bishops have by divine institution taken the place of the apostles as pastors of the Church, in such wise that whoever listens to them is listening to Christ and whoever despises them despises Christ" (*LG* 20 § 3); see also Lk 10:16.

Not only the bishops, the successors of the apostles, but "[t]he whole Church is apostolic. . . . All members of the Church share in this mission, though in various ways" (CCC 863).

Chapter 8

THE FORGIVENESS OF SINS

1. The importance of forgiveness

It is very foolish to fear or resent the authority of the Church, for that authority is the basis on which she forgives our sins.

When he was asked why he became a Catholic, G. K. Chesterton, the great English writer, replied: "To get my sins forgiven." Jesus came to earth for that purpose. "You shall call his name Jesus ["Savior"], for he will save his people from their sins" (Mt 1:21). And the Church, since she is his Body, continues his work. Therefore the Church's purpose on earth is to extend through time and space this kingdom of forgiveness.

Not merely forgiveness, but *Christ's* forgiveness. Forgiveness, like the Church herself, is wholly Christocentric.

How important is forgiveness? Eternally important! " 'Were there no for-giveness of sins in the Church, there would be no hope of life to come or eternal liberation. Let us thank God who has given his Church such a gift' [1] " (CCC 983).

2. The need for forgiveness: The reality of sin

Why do we need forgiveness? Because we are sinners.

Sin is life's greatest problem, for sin is separation from life's greatest solu-tion, God, the source of all goodness and life and joy.

Sin is real. So is justice. Sin deserves punishment. The fear of divine jus-tice is wise because that justice is true. If it is not, every book of the Bible lies.

The work of Christ and his Church is "the forgiveness of sins". Not imper-fections or mistakes or immaturities, but sins. Brain damage is an imperfec-tion, $2 + 2 = 5$ is a mistake, and "puppy love" is an immaturity, but acts of greed and lust and pride are sins.

But the sense of sin, the conviction of sin, is increasingly absent from mod-ern minds. This is a radically new development in the history of Western civilization. Ancient pagans took sin for granted and doubted salvation; mod-ern pagans take salvation for granted and deny sin. Our society's most pop-ular prophets, the pop psychologists, see sin as a superstition, guilt as a mental illness, and "the fear of the Lord"—which Scripture calls "the beginning of wisdom"—as emotional immaturity.

Why is it "the beginning of wisdom" (Prov 9:10)? Because the wisdom of gospel love presupposes the wisdom of religious fear; the "good news" of the forgiveness of sins presupposes the "bad news" of sins to be forgiven.

In fact, Christ said he did not come for those who do not believe they are sinners: "Those who are well have no need of a physician, but those who are sick. . . . I came not to call the righteous, but sinners" (Mt 9:12–13). If there is no confession of sin, there is no forgiveness and no salvation. "If we say we have no sin, we deceive ourselves, and the truth is not in us" (1 Jn 1:8). This is Scripture's constant assumption. Deny that assumption, and everything else in Scripture loses its meaning. The prophets become quaint exaggerations, and Christ's Incarnation and crucifixion become unnecessary overreactions.

3. Seven ways to deny the reality of sin

The very concept of sin presupposes seven other ideas that are historically derived from God's revelation to Abraham and the three religions (Judaism,

---

[1] St. Augustine, *Sermo* 213, 8: PL 38, 1064.

Christianity, and Islam) that stem from that; seven ideas that are denied by alternative religions and philosophies:

a. Atheism ("no-God") denies that there is a God to sin against.

b. Polytheism ("many-gods") denies that there is only one God, who is all-good and deserves to be obeyed.

c. Pantheism ("everything is God") denies that God has a will that discriminates between good and evil.

d. Deism (a God, but an absent God) denies that God has intervened in history to make his will known by establishing a covenant and giving commandments.

e. Scepticism denies that we can know God's law, God's will, or God's character.

f. Determinism denies that we have a free will and are therefore personally responsible for our choices of good or evil.

g. And naïve optimism denies that evil exists in humanity.

4. The meaning of sin

"Sin" means more than merely bad behavior or bad habits. It means a No to God, his will, his law, and his love. It means breaking the love-covenant relationship with God. It is like marital infidelity (an analogy often used by the prophets). It concerns a relationship, not an isolated individual; and a personal relationship, not a relationship to an abstract principle; and a relationship with God, not only with man.

Forgiveness is the beginning of the restoration of the relationship. It is reconciliation.

But the "good news" of forgiveness presupposes the "bad news" of sin, as a cure presupposes a disease. Christianity does not appear as good news at all to the self-righteous, any more than a free heart transplant operation appears as good news to the patient who does not know he is dying.

5. Two kinds of sin: Original sin and actual sin

"Actual sin" is something we do; "original sin" is something we have, like a disease. (The analogy is not too insulting; it is not insulting enough: sin is far worse than any physical disease.)

Actual sin means *sins*, particular acts, choices to obey our own will when it conflicts with God's will as revealed in God's law, the moral law that is written both in the Ten Commandments and in our own hearts and consciences.

"Original sin" means, not the first actual sin committed by Adam and Eve (that is a popular confusion), but the *state or condition* of being deprived of supernatural life; the state of separation from God that we are born with, the fallen human nature that we inherit from our first parents' first actual sin—much as the state of divorce results from the choice to divorce, or the state of death results from an act of killing, or the state of drug addiction results from the choice to take the first drug.

The analogy to drugs also sounds insulting, but it, too, is not insulting enough. For sin is worse than drugs. Drugs can ruin only our life; sin can ruin our eternity.

6. The meaning of original sin

Original sin could be called "original selfishness". Our instincts are selfish. We are born with the selfishness principle in us by nature. This is observable even in infants. We do not, of course, personally blame them for being selfish, but, as St. Augustine argued, "As we grow older we root out such ways and cast them from us: which means that we hold them to be bad—for no man engaged in removing evil would knowingly cast out what is good" (*Confessions* 1, 7).

Original sin is a very unpopular idea in the modern world. But it is an essential part of the Christian gospel, and "The Church, which has the mind of Christ [cf. 1 Cor 2:16], knows very well that we cannot tamper with the revelation of original sin without undermining the mystery of Christ" (CCC 389). For sin is precisely what this "Savior" saves us from.

Original sin does not mean that we are "totally depraved" (Calvin's term) or wholly evil or more evil than good (how could that be measured?) or that our very *being* is evil or that we are no longer infinitely valuable and infinitely loved by God. It means that we are mortally wounded, a defaced masterpiece. The greater the masterpiece, the more terrible its defacement is.

Original sin is a difficult concept for us because we cannot appreciate the great difference between our present state and mankind's first state of unfallen innocence, which we have never experienced. Our instincts spontaneously take our present state of selfishness as the norm rather than the abnormality. But our faith and our reason tell us that the good God could not have created us selfish by nature; that we are all now "abnormal".

Original sin, the inborn state of all humanity, explains why all of us commit actual sins. If we were all born sin-free and innocent like Adam, surely *some* of us would have chosen to remain so. Yet none does. (And the better and more saintly we are, the more readily and clearly we admit it.) Why?

Because we are not born innocent of original sin, only innocent of actual sins. And our original sin leads us to commit actual sins. Our being conditions our actions. We sin because we are sinners, just as we sing because we are singers. Our nature conditions our acts, as an alcoholic's brain chemistry and chemical dependency condition his act of drinking.

This does not mean we are not responsible for actual sins, for the will's choice is also involved in the act—sometimes a lot, sometimes a little. We are not *determined*, but we are conditioned—led, pulled, influenced—by our sinful nature and instincts. But we also are free to choose to obey our instincts or to resist them. We can and often do choose contrary to our instincts— for instance, when we fast or sacrifice.

How original sin is transmitted from our first parents to all their descendants is a mystery about which we have very inadequate knowledge. The same is true of the mystery of our very selves, about the union of body and soul. The transmission is by heredity, not only environment—a kind of spiritual heredity. Our selfishness comes from our nature, not from society, not merely by imitation.

The origin of sin may be mysterious, but its existence, its reality and presence now, in our individual and social experience, is very clear. The dogma is confirmed by the data. "What Revelation makes known to us is confirmed by our own experience. For when man looks into his own heart he finds that he is drawn towards what is wrong and sunk in many evils which cannot come from his good creator" (GS 13), or from the wholly good world he created; so it must come from man's own free "fall".

7. The historical background of the Christian concept of sin

All mankind has a religious instinct, a tendency to worship something. We also have a moral instinct, a tendency to judge between right and wrong. Only one people in history joined these two instincts definitively: the Jews (and Christians and Muslims, who learned from them). For the God they worshipped, the God who revealed himself to them, unlike all other gods, was wholly good, and his will was the origin of the moral law. The worship-object and the moral-ideal were the same for the Jews, unlike any other ancient people. This was not their doing but God's. They knew the true God only because God chose to reveal himself to them, chose them to be his collective prophet to the world.

The Jews knew two relationships with this God that no other ancient people had with any of their gods, two possibilities of personal intimacy unknown to pagans: faith and sin. Faith to them meant more than belief; it meant personal trust and fidelity, as in marriage. (Indeed, the marriage covenant is the closest human parallel to this covenant relationship with God.) Sin meant the breaking of this intimate relationship: spiritual infidelity or divorce. Since no pagan knew such wonderful intimacy with God, no pagan knew such awful alienation from God either. The height of the mountain measures the depth of the valley; the greater the treasure, the greater the tragedy when it is lost.

Christians inherited these two categories, faith and sin, as the two fundamental options in relationship to God. Thus St. Paul can write: "Whatever does not proceed from faith is sin" (Rom 14:23). Christians knew an even greater intimacy with God because of the Incarnation and a greater horror of sin because of the crucifixion. When you see the murder of God, no other evil can come close.

So real and so terrible is sin that the price God had to pay for its forgiveness was his own Son's precious blood and that terrible cry from the Cross, from the depths of hell: "My God, my God, why hast thou forsaken me?" (Mt 27:46).

No greater price was ever paid for anything than God paid for our forgiveness. For nothing in the world is more valuable than forgiveness.

8. Why could God not forgive our sins without Christ's death?

Because that would mean *ignoring* them. And God is Truth.

Suppose you have done something real and terrible to a good friend. You know the harm you have done, and your guilt haunts you with its truth. Now suppose, when you plead for forgiveness, your victim says, "Forget it. There's nothing to forgive." That does not free you. The truth must be faced and dealt with. "Forget it" is not the same as "forgive it."

Sin is a reality, as death or disease or divorce is a reality. It must be dealt with by a reality, not a blinking of the eye. A real debt is owed, and it must be really paid.

And that must cost something. If I forgive you your debt of $1,000 to me, that costs me $1,000, and I must pay my creditors $1,000 out of my own pocket. If I assume another's debt, I must really pay it.

And the human debt God assumed was death.

"Without the shedding of blood there is no forgiveness of sins" (Heb 9:22). God taught this to his chosen people for almost two thousand years by displaying before their eyes every day in the Temple the ritual slaughter of animals, especially the sacrificial lamb. It was the central act of their liturgy.

For sin involves the shedding of blood, or at least the harming of human life in some way. Nothing less than human lifeblood can redeem (buy back) human lifeblood. So God, through Mary, took our blood, took human nature and human blood, so that he could give his lifeblood as the price of our forgiveness.

9. Only Christ can forgive sins

There can be no forgiveness without Christ. The Pharisees recognized his claim to forgive sins as a claim to divinity and objected, "Who can forgive sins but God alone?" (Mk 2:7).

No sinful man, who himself needed to be redeemed, could pay the price for mankind's redemption. But God's divine nature, perfect and immortal, could not die or suffer. So God assumed human nature to effect the forgiveness of sins. Forgiveness is the reason for the crucifixion, and the crucifixion is the reason for the Incarnation.

10. The power of the Church to forgive sins

Only God can forgive sins. But God became man in Christ, and Christ gave the Church the power to transmit Christ's forgiveness. She forgives in Christ's name, not her own. She has the authority to forgive sins because Christ gave it to her: "As the Father has sent me, even so I send you. . . . If you forgive the sins of any, they are forgiven; if you retain the sins of any, they are retained" (Jn 20:21–22).

" 'When . . . Baptism . . . cleansed us, the forgiveness we received then was so full and complete that there remained in us absolutely nothing left to efface, neither original sin nor offenses committed by our own will. . . . Yet the grace of Baptism delivers no one from all the weakness of nature. On the contrary, we must still combat the movements of concupiscence" [sinful desire, desire to sin] "that never cease leading us into evil' [2]" (CCC 978).

And when we do sin, "[i]t is through the sacrament of Penance that the baptized can be reconciled with God and with the Church" (CCC 980). Penance forgives all actual sins if they are confessed and sincerely repented of. This sacrament gives us liberation, pardon, and peace. The devil hates and fears the confessional more than any place on earth outside the Eucharist itself.

St. John Chrysostom wrote, " 'Priests have received from God a power that he has given neither to angels nor to archangels' [3]" (CCC 983). This is the power to forgive sins.

11. Is there an "unforgivable sin"?

No sin is too great for God and his Church to forgive, if repentance is honest. "There is no offense, however serious, that the Church cannot forgive" (CCC 982). Only impenitence, only refusal to believe in and accept God's gift of forgiveness, is unforgivable. God never withholds his forgiveness, but we sometimes withhold our repentance.

How could any finite human sin exhaust the infinite mercy of God? How could evil be stronger than good? No sin is too great for God's forgiveness to save us from, but no sin is too small to damn us if we refuse to repent of it.

---

[2] *Roman Catechism*, I, 11, 3.
[3] St. John Chrysostom, *De sac.* 3, 5: PG 48, 643.

12. Nothing worse than sin

There is nothing better than God. And sin separates us from God. Therefore there is nothing worse than sin.

Nothing but sin can separate us from God, in time or in eternity. For sin is departure from God's will, and God's will for us is nothing but our own happiness. In fact, it is to share his own divine life in unimaginable joy. Once you realize how great God's love is and how great the joy he wills for us, there is nothing—no pain, no failure, no horror—that can be worse than the one and only thing that can separate us from that end: our unrepented sin.

13. The reality of eternal punishment

It is difficult for modern minds to believe that the alternative to forgiveness is eternal punishment; that to die in unrepented, unforgiven sin is to deserve eternal separation from God.

But we have free will, therefore we *can* choose to die in this state. And since there is no reincarnation, no second chance ("It is appointed for men to die once, and after that comes judgment"—Heb 9:27), it follows that eternal separation from God—hell—is really possible.

No one talked more, or more seriously, about hell than sweet and gentle Jesus. Why did he do that? For the same reason loving parents talk more seriously than anyone else to their children about not running into a busy street or playing with matches.

The popular images of hell—brimstone, pitchforks, and torture—and even the biblical imagery of fire, are not to be taken literally (that is part of what is meant by calling them "images"), but they are to be taken seriously. The reality of hell—eternal separation from God—is much more terrible, not less, than the imagery.

God does not force heaven on those who refuse it. If he did, it would not be heaven to them anyway, any more than an opera is heavenly to a captive audience who would rather be at a rock concert—or vice versa. Hell is real because free will is real. No one wants hell to be real, and everyone wants free will to be real, but the two imply each other: if we are free, we are free to refuse heaven.

Thus, the forgiveness of sins is infinitely and eternally important. "Salvation" *means* salvation from sin and its eternal consequence, hell. If sin and hell were myths, what would Christ's salvation be salvation from? How could Jesus be Jesus ("Savior")?

14. Does Christ save us from sin or punishment?

The Savior saves us from two things: the punishment for sin and sin itself.

The punishment for sin is death. "The wages of sin is death" (Rom 6:23).

There are two kinds of death: temporal and eternal, death of the body and death of the soul. Christ warns us, "Do not fear those who kill the body but cannot kill the soul; rather fear him who can destroy both soul and body in hell" (Mt 10:28).

Death (of both body and soul) is the inevitable punishment for sin as a stomach ache is the inevitable punishment for an infant eating twenty cookies, or as ignorance is the inevitable punishment for not studying. It is not an external, optional punishment added on by God's choice, like a spanking to the infant or a grade of F to the student.

But Christ does not just save us from sin's punishment; he was called "Savior" because "he will save his people from their sins" (Mt 1:21). He is not merely an eternal fire insurance policy. We are to be perfectly sanctified as well as perfectly justified. He does not only forgive our sins, he also destroys our sins. He does not rest until he has made us perfectly holy, in this life or in purgatory. ("You, therefore, must be perfect, as your heavenly Father is perfect"—Mt 5:48.)

15. Is forgiveness a legal change or a real change?

When God forgives us, that changes not only our legal relation to God, but it changes us too. Luther taught that the result of repentance and faith was only freedom from the penalty and punishment of God's law, or legal justification, not real sanctification. He said that God saw us *as if* we were righteous because Christ had paid our debt.

But this is a very inadequate image for God. God is not a lawyer! More seriously, God cannot deceive himself; what he sees is true. We are made really righteous; we are sanctified as well as justified by God's grace. Baptism really wipes away original sin and gives us supernatural life.

Therefore sanctification, being-made-holy by doing good works, is a necessary part of the forgiveness of sins and salvation. We are forgiven in order to forgive others; we are given God's love in order to pass it on. We are justified (forgiven) by pure grace, without our deserving it; but we are justified (forgiven) for good works. St. Paul teaches both points at once when he writes: "For by grace you have been saved through faith; and this is not your own doing, it is the gift of God—not because of works, lest any man should boast. For we are his workmanship, created in Christ Jesus for good works, which God prepared beforehand, that we should walk in them" (Eph 2:8–10).

16. Catholic vs. Protestant theologies of forgiveness;
    faith and works

The controversy that primarily provoked the Protestant Reformation was the controversy about faith and works. Luther taught that we are justified and forgiven by faith alone, while the Church held that good works were also necessary for salvation.

Protestants and Catholics agree that faith is necessary for salvation. The Bible clearly teaches that it is. Good works alone do not merit salvation. No one can "buy" heaven with enough good works, or good enough motives. The ticket to heaven is not being nice or sincere or good enough; the ticket to heaven is the Blood of Christ, and faith is the acceptance of that free gift.

But the Church insists that good works are necessary too. This means the works of love. Good works are not mere external deeds, but the works of love. And love is not mere feelings, but the *works* of love (charity, *agapē*). That is why Christ can command them; feelings cannot be commanded.

St. James clearly teaches that "faith by itself, if it has no works, is dead" (Jas 2:17). And some of Christ's parables teach that our salvation depends on our charity (Mt 25:40: "as you did it to one of the least of these my brethren, you did it to me"). St. John of the Cross wrote: " 'At the evening of life, we shall be judged on our love'[4]" (CCC 1022).

It is not that we purchase heaven with our good works; Christ has already purchased heaven for us with his work of love on the Cross. We do not do good works to get to heaven, but we do good works because heaven has gotten to us. If we do not do good works, that shows that heaven has not gotten to us. For "you will know them by their fruits" (Mt 7:20).

The differences between the Catholic and the Protestant (especially Lutheran) theologies of forgiveness are as follows:

a. Luther thought forgiveness was only external and legal ("forensic"). Catholic theology teaches that it actually changes our souls. In fact, it gives us a share in the divine nature (what Eastern theologians call *theosis*, divinization): " '[God] gave himself to us through his Spirit. By the participation of the Spirit, we become communicants in the divine nature'[5]" (CCC 1988).

b. Catholic theology teaches that justification and sanctification, faith and works, are not separated, as Luther thought. Rather, " '[j]ustification is not only the remission of sins, but also the sanctification and renewal of the interior man'[6]" (CCC 1989).

---

[4] St. John of the Cross, *Dichos* 64.
[5] St. Athanasius, *Ep. Serap.* 1, 24: PG 26, 585 and 588.
[6] Council of Trent (1547): DS 1528.

c. Catholic theology teaches that human free will cooperates with divine grace. (Luther denied free will.) "Justification establishes *cooperation between God's grace and man's freedom*. . . . '[M]an himself is not inactive while receiving that inspiration, since he could reject it' [7]" (CCC 1993).

d. Catholics agree with Protestants that man, "'without God's grace, . . . cannot by his own free will move himself toward justice in God's sight' [8]" (CCC 1993). Yet since grace perfects nature, with grace man can do precisely that.

e. Catholics believe, therefore, that there is real merit. "The merit of man before God in the Christian life arises from the fact that *God has freely chosen to associate man with the work of his grace*. The fatherly action of God is first on his own initiative, and then follows man's free acting through his collaboration, so that the merit of good works is to be attributed in the first place to the grace of God, then to the faithful" (CCC 2008). To deny merit, as the Protestant Reformers did, is to demean not only man's work but God's work in man. For as St. Augustine wrote, "'Our merits are God's gifts' [9]" (CCC 2009).

f. But Catholics agree with the Protestant, biblical emphasis on our total dependence on God. St. Thérèse of Lisieux wrote, "'After earth's exile, I hope to go and enjoy you in the fatherland, but . . . I want to work for your *love alone*. . . . In the evening of this life, I shall appear before you with empty hands, for I do not ask you, Lord, to count my works.' [10]" "The saints have always had a lively awareness that their merits were pure grace" (CCC 2011).

"Since the initiative belongs to God in the order of grace, *no one can merit the initial grace* of forgiveness and justification. . . . Moved by the Holy Spirit and by charity, *we can then merit* for ourselves and for others the graces needed for our sanctification" (CCC 2010). For grace always perfects nature rather than setting it aside.

17. Forgiveness must be passed on

Christ makes our being forgiven by him contingent on our forgiving others: "For if you forgive men their trespasses, your heavenly Father also will forgive you; but if you do not forgive men their trespasses, neither will your Father forgive your trespasses" (Mt 6:14–15).

He even commands us, in the Lord's Prayer, to pray for our own damnation if we hold back our forgiveness: "Forgive us our debts, *as we also have*

---

[7] Council of Trent (1547): DS 1525.
[8] Council of Trent (1547): DS 1525.
[9] St. Augustine, *Sermo* 298, 4–5: PL 38, 1367.
[10] St. Thérèse of Lisieux, "Act of Offering" in *Story of a Soul*, trans. John Clarke (Washington, D.C.: ICS, 1981), 277.

forgiven our debtors" (Mt 6:12, emphasis added). Our refusal to forgive—to do this first deed of charty—will, quite simply, send us to hell if not repented of. Gentle Jesus says so! Why is this? It is not that God refuses to give forgiveness to us until we forgive but that we cannot receive forgiveness from God if we have unforgiving hearts. If our heart is closed, like a clenched fist, to giving forgiveness to others, it will also be closed to receiving it from God.

The difference between the forgiving and the unforgiving heart is like the difference between the Sea of Galilee and the Dead Sea. The same water— the water of the Jordan River—flows into both bodies of water. But the Dead Sea lives up to its name—nothing can live there—because it does not pass on the living water it receives. It has no outlet. But the Sea of Galilee is so alive that it is still fished today as it was in Jesus' time. For the water it receives, it also gives. Forgiveness is like that.

God forgave us a far greater debt than any debt we owe to each other. We owe God far more than anyone owes us. We owe him not only our very existence, since he created us, and our hearts' total love, since he is completely good, but also our salvation, our hope of heaven, which he won for us on the Cross, at a cost no mortal can comprehend.

18. Who are forgiven? How many?

We do not know.

When Jesus' disciples asked him, "Lord, will those who are saved be few?" He replied, "Strive to enter" (Lk 13:23–24). He did not give us statistics about others, only directions for ourselves.

Whatever their number, the forgiven and saved are always far too few for divine love. To the Good Shepherd, ninety-nine of one hundred sheep saved were too few, and he spent all day searching for the one that was lost (Lk 15). God revealed to us his infinitely merciful character, which we need to know, but not the comparative population statistics of heaven and hell, which we do not need to know.

We do know that "every one who asks receives, and he who seeks finds, and to him who knocks it will be opened" (Mt 7:8). Clearly Christ is speaking of forgiveness and salvation here, not of worldly goods. Not all who seek wealth or health or fame find it, but all who seek God with a sincere and honest heart find him, whether in this life or in the next. We do not know what proportion of mankind truly seek God in the depths of their hearts, because we do not know the hearts of men; but we do know what proportion of those who do seek God find him and his forgiveness (100 percent!), because we know the heart of God (Eph 3:14–19).

19. How are our sins forgiven?

Objectively, by Christ's death. That paid sin's price. Subjectively, by our repentance and faith. That appropriates Christ's payment. This is applied to us as individuals publicly in Baptism, which forgives original sin, and the Sacrament of Penance, which forgives all actual sins that are confessed and repented of.

Sincere repentance is a condition of receiving forgiveness. We cannot be forgiven while we are planning to sin again. But our repentance does not cause forgiveness. All of the sacraments, including Penance, work *ex opere operato*, that is, objectively, from the power and presence of Christ in them, not from the power of our souls' right subjective dispositions. We are like faucets; we need to turn the handle, turn our wills around, to turn the faucet of forgiveness on; but the living water of forgiveness and salvation comes to us not from within ourselves but from the sacraments themselves, from the power of Christ in them.

God has given this power to his Church: "If you forgive the sins of any, they are forgiven; if you retain the sins of any, they are retained" (Jn 20:23). "Whatever you bind on earth shall be bound in heaven, and whatever you loose on earth shall be loosed in heaven" (Mt 16:19).

20. How does God's forgiveness work?

Theologians have different explanations. The Church does not dogmati- . cally assert any one of them to the exclusion of others. As with electricity or gravity, we do not need to know how it works, we just need to know *that* it works.

Some explanations, or human analogies, given by Scripture are:
— the legal: Christ satisfied the demands of the law
— the financial: Christ paid the price
— the military: Christ defeated the devil
— the mathematical: Christ restored the balance sheet ·
— emancipation: Christ released us from the slavery into which we had sold ourselves
— laundry: Christ washed us clean in his blood
— scapegoat: Christ became our substitute
— shield: Christ endured God's just wrath and shielded us from it

If any of these analogies is helpful to us, we are invited to use it in our thinking; if not, not. What we know is not the spiritual technology, so to speak—the theory of how it works. What we know is something much more practical: what God did and what we must do (points 21 and 22, below).

21. What did God do to forgive our sins?

He died. Christ's death caused our sins to be forgiven. That is our divinely revealed data. How it worked is theological theory.

What God did was to become a man and suffer the hell we deserved ("My God, my God, why hast thou forsaken me?"), in our place, for us. God got us off the hook by putting himself on the hook, on the Cross. The price of our soul was his body.

22. What must we do to receive the forgiveness of sins?

To the world's most practical question, "What must I do to be saved?", God has given us a clear answer: Repent, believe, and live in charity.

a. We must repent of sin, reject sin, turn around, turn to God, seek God, say (and mean) "Your will, not mine, be done."

b. We must believe in Christ and accept God's forgiveness and salvation as a free gift.

This faith has an intellectual component, for we must know what Christ we believe. The creeds define who this Christ is who saves us. However, merely intellectual belief is not enough to save us. For "even the demons believe—and shudder" (Jas 2:19).

Saving faith also has a personal component: we must really open up our souls to Christ, choose him, commit ourselves to him, accept him with an act of will, "just say yes." This is so simple that it is hard to define. It is what Mary did when God asked permission to come into her womb; she said, "Let it be to me according to your word" (Lk 1:38). And when we do this, we really receive him, receive his supernatural life, into our souls. "Believing" equals "receiving" (Jn 1:12).

When do we receive Christ? In Baptism. Faith includes Baptism. They are not separated. "For as many of you as were baptized into Christ have put on Christ" (Gal 3:27). Baptism is more than a symbol or ceremony. "Baptism . . . now saves you" (1 Pet 3:21). "Baptism is the first and chief sacrament of forgiveness of sins because it unites us with Christ, who died for our sins" (CCC 977).

c. We must then live this new life of charity we have received in Baptism. "Faith apart from works is dead" (Jas 2:26). "If you do not forgive men their trespasses, neither will your Father forgive your trespasses" (Mt 6:15).

These three requirements for salvation correspond to the three "theological virtues", faith, hope, and charity (1 Cor 13:13). Repentance involves hope in Christ, seeking God's forgiveness. Baptism involves faith in Christ, accepting God's forgiveness. Charity involves love of Christ and the members of his Body, loving the forgiven ones.

23. Why forgive?

Because we should, we must, and we can.

We should forgive others because God forgave us.

We must forgive others because God will not forgive us if we do not.

We can forgive because we know Christ—not just as a figure in history, but as a present and permanent resident of our souls. We can forgive because we have his Spirit and his divine life in our souls, which *is* the life of charity and forgiveness. We have the power.

24. The power of forgiveness to save the world

It worked once. It can work again. What Christ did, his Church can and must do, both institutionally and personally, both sacramentally and individually. She has always done it sacramentally; Baptism and Penance have always been available. If her people do it more resolutely, like the saints—if we become saints—we can win the world again.

It is costly to forgive. When we forego justice and forgive, it means giving up something. But it can never cost us a fraction of what it cost Christ.

The Christian does more than work for "peace and justice", necessary as those two things are. The Christian works for peace through *forgiveness*.

Pope John Paul II has given us an example of forgiveness: by forgiving the man who tried to assassinate him and by asking for forgiveness from all who have been harmed by members of the Church in the past when Catholics failed to live up to Catholic principles: for example, heretics, Protestants, Jews, women, Galileo. Forgiveness is a two-way street; we must both ask for and give forgiveness.

If we follow the Pope's Christlike lead, the world can be won again for Christ. If not, not. There is no other way. It is God's way.

Chapter 9

THE RESURRECTION OF THE BODY

1. The importance of death

Nothing brings home to us the importance and value of human life more sharply than death. We seldom appreciate life until we realize how fragile it is, when friends and family are taken away from us by death.

"[D]eath lends urgency to our lives: remembering our mortality helps us realize that we have only a limited time in which to bring our lives to fulfillment" (CCC 1007). The Psalmist prays: "Teach us to number our days that we may get a heart of wisdom" (Ps 90:12). If you knew that you had only one year to live—or only one day—wouldn't you live differently? Then why not live like that right now? Live as if this day were your last—because it may be and, one day, certainly will be!

Samuel Johnson said, "I know of no thought that so wonderfully clarifies a man's mind as the thought that he will be hanged tomorrow morning." When we think of our (certain!) forthcoming death, trivia no longer seem important, and truly important things no longer seem trivial. Death clarifies our perspective, sharpens our sight, and brings our whole life to a point, like the single summit of a many-sided mountain. Death teaches us all the truth of Jesus' words: "Martha, Martha, you are anxious and troubled about many things; one thing is needful" (Lk 10:41).

That "one thing" is God, and—for us—our relationship to God. Only God is eternal, and only our relationship to God is eternal. Only God is necessary in his own being, and only our relationship to God is absolutely necessary for our being. Of everything else it is true to say "This too shall pass." God alone remains.

2. What does the Church know about death?

I do not know any specific facts about you, the individual who is reading these words right now. I do not know your present life, whether you are believer or unbeliever, saint or sinner, old or young. I do not know your past, whether your life has been full of pains or full of joys. I do not know your future, what the rest of your life in this world will be like or whether you will spend eternity in heaven or in hell. Only one concrete fact do I know with certainty about you: you will die.

The Church knows that about you too, but the Church also knows the meaning of death. The Church comes to you as a newspaper reporter with a startling piece of good news about death and life after death from the Man who claimed to be God and proved it by rising from death. The sceptic asks, "What do you know about life after death anyway? Have you ever been there?" And the Catholic answer is: "No, but I know Someone who has, and I believe him." We Catholics know *him*—that is the essential thing we know and the essential reason to be a Catholic—and therefore we know the meaning of death, through his witnesses, his apostles and their successors, the Church.

3. Why do we die?

The first part of the Church's wisdom about death concerns its origin. Why do we die? How did death come into the world?

This is the "bad news" from the past that comes before the gospel, which is the "good news" about the future, about our conquest of death through Christ.

The good news is that Christ is the Savior from both sin and death, the Savior of both soul and body. But just as the good news of salvation from sin presupposes the bad news of sin, so the good news of salvation from death presupposes the bad news of death.

Why do we die? The Church tells us three reasons. The first is natural, the second unnatural, and the third supernatural.

a. "In a sense bodily death is natural" (CCC 1006), for we have animal bodies. We are not angels or pure spirits. We are "rational animals".

b. "[B]ut for faith it" [death] "is in fact 'the wages of sin' [Rom 6:23; cf. Gen 2:17]" (CCC 1006), and thus unnatural. "God did not make death, and he does not delight in the death of the living" (Wis 1:13). God originally made man free from death, but when he tested man and man failed the test, man fell into death (Gen 3:3–4, 19). The cause of death is sin (Rom 6:23).

This is not as unbelievable as it appears to be to many people today. It is confirmed by reason, by ancient myths, and by modern psychology. By reason, for sin is separation from God, and God is the source of all life. By the ancient myths, for they teach the same point: that man was once innocent and immortal but fell from this paradise. By modern psychology, for the "psychosomatic unity" means that body and soul are not two independent beings but two interdependent dimensions of one being. Thus spiritual death in the soul (that is, sin) is naturally connected to physical death in the body.

c. Finally, death is now a supernatural event, a highway to heaven. For Christ has given death this new meaning. "For those who die in Christ's grace it is a participation in the death of the Lord, so that they can also share his Resurrection"[1] (CCC 1006). A Christian can even sing: "Thou hast made death glorious and triumphant, for through its portals we enter into the presence of the living God."

4. Is death good or evil?

It is both. Just as God made the worst spiritual evil—the sin of man murdering God—into the best thing that ever happened to us in this world, the event that saved man from sin, so that we celebrate this event as *Good* Friday, so God also made the worst physical evil—the loss of all physical goods in death—into the best thing that ever happens to us in this life, the door to eternal life, through Christ's bodily Resurrection, which is also ours if we are incorporated into that Body by faith and Baptism.

Death is thus both very bad and very good (if we are in Christ). It is very bad because what is lost is very precious: life, the body, the whole world to the individual who dies. Christ wept at his friend Lazarus' grave, and so should we if we love life as he did. But death is also very good if we die in Christ, because what is gained is infinitely more than what is lost. "For to me to live is Christ, and to die is gain", said St. Paul (Phil 1:21). For if we live in Christ, death means only more of Christ and more of life. This body dies, like a precious little seed, but a greater body rises, like a greater and glorious plant (see Jn 12:24 and 1 Cor 15:35–53).

5. How does Christ transform death?

"*Death is transformed by Christ.* . . . The obedience of Jesus has transformed the curse of death into a blessing [cf. Rom 5:19–21]" (CCC 1009).

---

[1] Cf. Rom 6:3–9; Phil 3:10–11.

Death, too, is Christocentric. Death's deepest meaning is revealed only in Christ's death and Resurrection. As Pascal says, "Apart from Jesus Christ we cannot know the meaning of our life or of our death, of God or of ourselves"—the four greatest questions we can ask (*Pensées* 417).

"Jesus links faith in the resurrection to his own person: 'I am the Resurrection and the life' [Jn 11:25]" (CCC 994). He is not just the giver of the Resurrection, he *is* the Resurrection. Our resurrection is not just caused by him, it is found in him. We rise because we are incorporated into Christ's Body.

"God revealed the resurrection of the dead to his people progressively" (CCC 992). The Old Testament is full of hope that God will do some great, mysterious deed of resurrection after death; but only the later prophets clearly announce it. God trained his chosen people to love him not for his gifts but for himself ("I am the LORD your God; . . . be holy, for I am holy"—Lev 11:44). Only after that lesson was learned did he reveal his great gift of the resurrection.

This is now much more than a "hope" in the weak, worldly sense of a *wish*. It is part of our hope in the strong, biblical sense of a *guarantee* from God, who always keeps his promises. The Church's funeral service calls it "the sure and certain hope of the resurrection". For it is God's promise that "just as Christ is truly risen from the dead and lives for ever, so after death the righteous will live for ever with the risen Christ [cf. Jn 6:39-40]" (CCC 989).

6. The Christian attitude toward death

Since death is both natural, unnatural, and supernatural (see section 3 of this chapter), we should have three corresponding attitudes toward it:

Since it is natural, we honestly confront it and accept it as a fact of our being, instead of avoiding it by endless diversions of our attention or, by living in denial, pretending it is not there.

Since it is also unnatural, the inescapable punishment for sin, we hate it and fight it as our enemy, "the last enemy" (1 Cor 15:26).

Finally, since it is also supernatural, transformed by Christ's Resurrection, we welcome it. For if we are in Christ, death comes to us as God's golden chariot sent to fetch his Cinderella bride from the cinders of this dying world to his golden castle to live with him in eternal ecstasy.

The element that pervades all three of these attitudes is readiness. "The Church encourages us to prepare ourselves for the hour of our death. In the ancient litany of the saints, for instance, she has us pray: 'From a sudden and unforeseen death, deliver us, O Lord';[2] to ask the Mother of God to

---

[2] *Roman Missal*, Litany of the Saints.

intercede for us 'at the hour of our death' in the *Hail Mary*; and to entrust ourselves to St. Joseph, the patron of a happy death" (CCC 1014).

" 'Every action of yours, every thought, should be those of one who expects to die before the day is out. Death would have no great terrors for you if you had a quiet conscience. . . . Then why not keep clear of sin instead of running away from death? If you aren't fit to face death today, it's very unlikely you will be tomorrow' [3] " (CCC 1014).

7. What happens at death?

We naturally fear death because we fear the unknown, and death appears to us as the great unknown, an immense darkness. The Church gives us a light from Christ in this darkness, so that we can truly pray, with David in the Twenty-third Psalm, "Though I walk through the valley of the shadow of death, I fear no evil; for thou art with me."

What happens at death is not extinction. Souls cannot be destroyed as bodies can.

What happens at death is not reincarnation into another earthly body and another earthly life. "It is appointed for men to die once, and after that comes judgment" (Heb 9:27).

What happens at death is not a change into an angel. God created angels, men, and animals to be different, not to be confused. Angels have no mortal bodies, animals have no immortal spirit, man has both.

What happens at death is not a change into a ghost, a pale copy of what we were in life. God has something more substantial, not less, in store for us. (By the way, though the Church explicitly denies reincarnation, she does not deny the existence of ghosts.)

What happens at death is the particular judgment. God infallibly knows and judges each soul as either (a) able to enter heaven immediately, or (b) needing to be purified in purgatory first and then able to enter heaven, or (c) set forever (since our lifetime is over) in unrepented sin and capable only of hell.

Then, at the general judgment at the end of time, there is the general resurrection of the body, which will share in the soul's eternal destiny.

The answer to "What happens at death?" depends on three things:

a. It depends on us: on our free choice for or against God and on our degree of holiness. There are two roads: one to life, and one to death (Ps 1; Wis 3:1–8), and God gave us the incredible and fearful dignity of deciding our own eternal destiny.

b. But it does not depend wholly on us, because it depends on eternal

---

[3] *The Imitation of Christ*, I, 23, I.

justice and truth, which we cannot change. Even God cannot change this, because it is his own nature. Truth is eternal and unavoidable. We can hide from it only temporarily, and even then we can only hide God from our sight, not ourselves from him—like a baby playing peek-a-boo.

c. It also depends on God's grace and mercy. No one can buy heaven or force God's hand. All who are saved are saved by God's free choice to be merciful. We are saved by mercy, not by justice. Hell's citizens stand on justice and get it; heaven's citizens stand under The Mercy.

8. The meaning of resurrection

We can discover the fact that our souls are immortal by the proper use of our natural reason, for souls are immortal by their own nature: they are not material or biological. But only divine revelation can inform us of the resurrection of the body, for it takes a supernatural act of God to resurrect bodies.

"The term 'flesh' refers to man in his state of weakness and mortality.[4] The 'resurrection of the flesh' . . . means not only that the immortal soul will live on after death, but that even our 'mortal body' will come to life again [Rom 8:11]" (CCC 990).

What does this mean? "*What is 'rising'?* In death, the separation of the soul from the body, the human body decays and the soul goes to meet God" [in the particular judgment], "while awaiting its reunion with its glorified body" [in the general judgment]. "God, in his almighty power, will definitively grant incorruptible life to our bodies by reuniting them with our souls, through the power of Jesus' Resurrection" (CCC 997).

Our resurrection is dependent on Christ; we are resurrected only in him. His Body is resurrected, and we are put into his Body. This is done by faith and Baptism. For the Church *is* his Body.

9. Resurrection is more than immortality

The significance of Christ's Resurrection was not merely that it was visible proof of life after death. The soul was always immortal, a fact always knowable by human reason. But Christ's Resurrection brought a new reality into the universe: a new kind of body, a human body that was as immortal as the soul.

The immortality of the soul is not an idea that is unique to Christianity. Most religions teach it. But the resurrection of the body, foretold by the Jewish prophets, came true only in Christ.

Resurrection with Christ is a far greater hope than mere immortality. Immortality is not even necessarily a good thing. If science should ever

---

[4] Cf. Gen 6:3, Ps 56:5, Isa 40:6.

discover how to make our present bodies immortal by genetic engineering, this would not give us heaven on earth but hell on earth. We would be like eggs that never hatched. We know that smell.

A person who commits suicide does not want immortality. He wants to die but cannot. He wants to kill his soul but cannot. He is eternally frustrated. Immortality can be hell.

("*Can* be"—those who commit suicide do not necessarily all go to hell, for many have mixed motives, confused minds and hearts, and not the full knowledge and full consent necessary for a mortal sin. The partly sane are only partly responsible for their sins.)

10. Is the resurrection irrational?

The Christians at Corinth to whom St. Paul wrote two epistles in the New Testament apparently thought Christ's Resurrection (and their own) could not be literally real, but (as many Modernist theologians today teach) a "resurrection of faith" in the disciples' hearts and lives rather than a real Resurrection of Christ's body; a "resurrection of Easter faith" without a real Easter! The Corinthians thought the idea of a literal resurrection crude, naïve, and irrational. For St. Paul's reply, read 1 Corinthians 15, especially verses 12 to 19.

"From the beginning, Christian faith in the resurrection has met with incomprehension and opposition.[5] . . . It is very commonly accepted that the life of the human person continues in a spiritual fashion after death. But how can we believe that this body, so clearly mortal, could rise to everlasting life?" (CCC 996).

The answer is: Because "with God all things are possible" (Mt 19:26). The God who created the whole universe out of nothing can surely perform the lesser miracle of making an immortal body out of a mortal one.

The question should rather be: How could we *not* believe it, since it is Christ who tells us (and his apostles, and their successors in the great chain of witnesses to the Resurrection that is the Church). Resurrection is not a philosophical idea accepted on the very fallible authority of human reason; it is a historical fact accepted on the infallible authority of divine revelation.

11. Who will rise?

"*Who will rise?* All the dead will rise, 'those who have done good, to the resurrection of life, and those who have done evil, to the resurrection of judgment' [Jn 5:29; cf. Dan 12:2]" (CCC 998).

---

[5] Cf. Acts 17:32; 1 Cor 15:12–13.

12. When will they rise?

" '[A]t the last day,' 'at the end of the world.' [6] . . .

" 'For the Lord himself will descend from heaven, with a cry of command, with the archangel's call, and with the sound of the trumpet of God. And the dead in Christ will rise first' [1 Thess 4:10]" (CCC 1001).

13. How will they rise?

"Christ is raised with his own body . . . but he did not return to an earthly life. So, in him, 'all of them will rise again with their own bodies which they now bear,' but Christ 'will change our lowly body to be like his glorious body' [7] " (CCC 999).

We do not know how God will do this—whether he will use the matter of our old, dead bodies or whether he will make new matter, a new *kind* of matter, for our new bodies. But we know that "we shall be like him" (1 Jn 3:2).

"This 'how' exceeds our imagination and understanding" (CCC 1000). It should not, however, exceed our understanding that God's deeds should exceed our understanding. Wonder and amazement (*thaumadzein*) is the typical mark of his presence throughout the scriptural narrative.

14. What do we know about our resurrection bodies?

Our only real data for what we know about our own future resurrection bodies come from the Gospel accounts of Christ's Resurrection body. This body was recognizable as Christ; it had a continuity with his former body; it was he and not another. And yet it was different—so different that at first his own disciples did not recognize him—and then they did (Lk 24:13–32; Jn 20:11–16; 21:1–13). It could walk through walls (Jn 20:19) and ascend to heaven (Acts 1:9–11). Yet it was a body, not a ghost; it could eat and be touched (Lk 24:36–43; Jn 20:19–29; Mt 28:9).

15. Why will we rise?

Because God loves us and loves life. He who has commanded us, through his prophet Moses, to "choose life" (Deut 30:19) practices what he preaches. He who is life itself, eternal life, chose to create many forms of temporal life, culminating in man; and when man chose death, God chose to restore

---

[6] Jn 6:39–40, 44, 54; 11:24; *LG* 48 § 3.
[7] Lateran Council IV (1215): DS 801; Phil 3:21; 1 Cor 15:44.

man to full life, body and soul. "The wages of sin is death, but the free gift of God is eternal life in Christ Jesus our Lord" (Rom 6:23).

16. The importance of the body in Christianity

Christ's Resurrection bestows new dignity on our bodies by revealing to us a new, unexpected, and glorious eternal destiny for them. C. S. Lewis says, "These small and perishable bodies we now have were given to us as ponies are given to schoolboys. We must learn to manage: not that we may some day be free of horses altogether, but that some day we may ride bare-back, confident and rejoicing, those greater mounts, those winged, shining and world-shaking horses which perhaps even now expect us with impatience, pawing and snorting in the King's stables" (*Miracles*). "In expectation of that day, the believer's body and soul already participate in the dignity of belonging to Christ" (CCC 1004).

In most religions (such as Hinduism), only spirit is immortal. In some (such as Gnosticism), only spirit is good. In some (such as Buddhism), only spirit is real. But for Christians, the body is real, good, and immortal. No religion exalts matter and the body as Christianity does:

a. God created it and declared it "good" (Gen 1).

b. God united man's body with his immortal soul to make one substance, one being.

c. And therefore he made the body immortal like the soul, through resurrection.

d. In sexual intercourse, he uses a material act to make new immortal souls.

e. He incarnated himself into matter and a human body.

f. And he kept his human body forever. Ever since Christ took his human nature, body and soul, to heaven in the Ascension, God has a body forever. Christ did not "un-incarnate" when he ascended.

g. He now uses matter to save souls in Baptism and the Eucharist.

" 'The flesh is the hinge of salvation.'. . .[8] We believe in God who is creator of the flesh; we believe in the Word made flesh in order to redeem the flesh; we believe in the resurrection of the flesh, the fulfillment of both the creation and the redemption of the flesh" (CCC 1015).

Almost all other religions are religions of spirit only. They identify goodness only with good intentions and good will. But Christianity does not separate spirit as holy from matter as unholy; matter is holy too. God did not confine religion to spirituality or inwardness only. He created bodies as well as spirits; he commanded and forbade certain external actions as well as certain inner intentions; and he redeemed us from sin and death

[8] Tertullian, *De res.* 8, 2: PL 2, 852.

by assuming a human body, shedding his blood, and rising bodily from death.

Other religions seek "spirituality". But Christianity seeks holiness. To be a spirit is not necessarily to be good; the most evil being that exists is a pure spirit, a fallen angel. Sin cannot be blamed on matter or the body, which God made and will remake, but on our own bad will and choices. Our sins will be destroyed eternally, but not our bodies.

The practical moral consequences of this doctrine of the resurrection as the body's destiny are radical, especially to contemporary culture. "This dignity entails the demand that he should treat with respect his own body, but also the body of every other person" (CCC 1004). "Do you know that your bodies are the members of Christ? . . . Your body is a temple of the Holy Spirit. . . . You are not your own; you were bought with a price. So glorify God in your body" (1 Cor 6:15, 19–20).

The origin of modern hedonism and materialism (especially "the sexual revolution") is not the discovery of the goodness or greatness of the body, but the *denial* of it, by the Gnostic separation of body from spirit, by the confinement of religion and morality to subjective intention (the idea that if it is motivated by love, anything is moral). The "materialism" of the play-boy really stems from the denial of the sacredness of matter and the body, which is then used as a mere tool, a means to the end of pleasure and excitement. His end is subjectively good feelings in the soul, not the objective good of the body.

Chapter 10

LIFE EVERLASTING

1. Our destiny is "life everlasting"

The life story of any individual or community gets its meaning, point, and purpose from its end. So to know what kind of story we are in, to know what is the "meaning of life", we must know our end.

The Church tells us our end. It is one with our origin. In the words of the old *Baltimore Catechism*, "God made me to know him, love him, and serve him in this world and to be happy with him forever in the next."

2. Reason confirms faith in life after death

Life after death cannot be proved scientifically, for it cannot be observed publicly. But even apart from religious faith, the human mind can find good reasons for believing it, by using the basic rule of scientific reasoning: to accept a theory because it alone adequately accounts for the data. The data here include at least three pieces of evidence for immortality:

There is, first of all, our universal longing for "something more" than this world can ever give us. A real "life everlasting" is the only thing that makes sense of humanity's deep, innate desire for "life everlasting", a desire that is present in nearly all times and places and cultures. "Thou hast made us for thyself, and [that is why] our hearts are restless until they rest in thee", says St. Augustine at the beginning of the *Confessions*.

All natural and innate desires of the human heart, all desires that are found in all times and places because they come from within rather than from without, correspond to realities that can satisfy these desires: food, drink, sex, sleep, friendship, knowledge, health, freedom, beauty. The same must be true of the desire for everlasting life.

A second reason for believing in everlasting life is the data perceived by love. The eye of love perceives persons as intrinsically valuable, indispensable, irreplaceable. If death ends all, if life treats these indispensable persons as if they were dispensable and disposable things, "then life is an outrageous horror. No one can live in the face of death knowing that all is utter emptiness." So says even the agnostic Ingmar Bergman in *The Seventh Seal*.

A third good reason for belief in everlasting life is the fact that we have spiritual, rational souls that are able to know eternal truths (2 + 2 is *eternally* 4) and to know the eternal value of love. This at least strongly suggests that we have a kinship with eternity, that we are more than merely temporal creatures.

Our destiny depends on our nature and our origin. If our origin is mere matter without mind or purpose, and if our nature is thus comprised of only material organisms, atoms and molecules, then our destiny can only be material: to return to the dust from which we came. For whatever is made of material parts can come apart and die. But if we are also persons, selves, souls, subjects, I's, then we are immortal, for those are not composed of parts, like atoms. We cannot have half an *I*. Souls cannot be divided by swords.

3. Mankind's instinctive knowledge of the "Four Last Things"

What does the Church tell us about life after death? Her teaching is summarized in the "Four Last Things": death, judgment, heaven, and hell. But even humanity outside the Church instinctively knows something about these four things.

Life's one certainty is death. Everyone knows this, though not everyone knows what comes next.

Nearly all religions, cultures, and individuals in history have believed in some form of life after death. For man's innate sense of justice tells him that there must be an ultimate reckoning, that in the final analysis no one can cheat the moral law and get away with it or suffer undeserved injustices throughout life and not be justly compensated. And since this ultimate justice does not seem to be accomplished in this life, there must be "the rest of the story". This instinctive conviction that there must be a higher, more-than-human justice is nearly universal. Thus the second of the Four Last Things, judgment, is also widely known. As Scripture says, "Whoever would draw near to God must believe that he exists and that he rewards those who seek him" (Heb 11:6). And most men do "draw near to God"; most men have a religion; most men believe that God justly "rewards those who seek him".

Most men also know that justice distinguishes the good from the evil and, therefore, that after death there must be separate destinies for us, rewards for good and punishments for evil. Thus mankind also usually believes in some form of heaven and hell.

4. Judgment as encounter with Christ

What the Church adds to this universal human wisdom—what man could not discover without divine revelation—centers in Christ. The Church gives a radically sharper focus to mankind's instinctive but vague sense of justice by telling us about God, and then gives an even sharper focus to our knowledge of God by showing us Christ.

This applies to the final judgment too. It is an encounter with Christ. For

a. " 'At the evening of life, we shall be judged on our love' [1] " (CCC 1022).

b. And our love is a response to God's love, which was given to us in Christ (1 Jn 4:16).

c. Therefore the standard at the final judgment is Christ. Like life, judgment is Christocentric. "In the presence of Christ, who is Truth itself" [Jn 14:6], "the truth of each man's relationship with God will be laid bare [cf. Jn 12:49]" (CCC 1039).

"Death puts an end to human life as the time open to either accepting or rejecting the divine grace manifested in Christ [cf. 2 Tim 1:9–10]. The New Testament speaks of judgment primarily in its aspect of the final encounter with Christ" (CCC 1021).

5. The final options

In this judgment, "[e]ach man receives his eternal retribution in his immortal soul at the very moment of his death, in a particular judgment that refers his life to Christ: either entrance into the blessedness of heaven—whether through a purification" [2] [purgatory] "or immediately [3]—or immediate and everlasting damnation [4] " (CCC 1022), hell.

---

[1] St. John of the Cross, *Dichos* 64.

[2] Cf. Council of Lyons II (1274): DS 857–58; Council of Florence (1439): DS 1304–6; Council of Trent (1563): DS 1820.

[3] Cf. Benedict XII, *Benedictus Deus* (1336): DS 1000–1001; John XXII, *Ne super his* (1334): DS 990.

[4] CF. Benedict XII, *Benedictus Deus* (1336): DS 1002.

There are only two eternal destinies: heaven or hell, union or disunion with God, the one and only ultimate source of all goodness and joy. Each one of us will be either with God or without him forever.

There is no reincarnation, no "second chance" after time is over. There is no annihilation, no end of the soul's existence. There is no change of species from human being to angel or to anything else.

The particular judgment occurs immediately after each individual's death. The general judgment takes place at the end of all time and history.

So the scenario of final events is: (a) first, death; (b) then, immediately, the particular judgment; (c) then, either hell, or purgatory as preparation for heaven, or heaven; (d) and, at the end of time, the general judgment; (e) and the "new heavens and new earth" for those who are saved.

6. "New heavens and a new earth"

God created the earth, loved it into existence, and declared it good (Gen 1). He made us its custodians, and we failed. But despite our sin, God will restore the earth in the end. "The universe itself will be renewed ... 'in the glory of heaven.... [T]ogether with the human race, the universe itself, which is so closely related to man and which attains its destiny through him, will be perfectly re-established in Christ' [5]" (CCC 1042). "Sacred Scripture calls this mysterious renewal, which will transform humanity and the world, 'new heavens and a new earth' [2 Pet 3:13; cf. Rev 21:1]" (CCC 1043).

"We know neither the moment ... nor the way the universe will be transformed" (GS 39). But we know its consequences. The consequences of a pregnant woman's hope for childbirth are a much greater care and love for her body. Analogously, the consequences of our hope for "new heavens and a new earth" are a greater love and care and appreciation and proper use of this earth. This universe is like a pregnant woman; she is more precious, not less, because another is to be born from her. "'Far from diminishing our concern to develop this earth, the expectancy of a new earth should spur us on, for it is here that the body of a new human family grows.... That is why, although we must be careful to distinguish earthly progress clearly from the increase of the kingdom of Christ, such progress is of vital concern to the kingdom'" [GS 39 § 2] (CCC 1049). For "'[w]hen we have spread on earth the fruits of our nature and our enterprise ... , we will find them once again, cleansed this time from the stain of sin, illuminated and transfigured' [GS 39 § 3]" (CCC 1050).

This vision frees us at once from two opposite errors: the disdain for this world that tempts the "spiritualist" and the worship of this world that tempts

[5] LG 48; cf. Acts 3:21; Eph 1:10; Col 1:20; 2 Pet 3:10–13.

the secularist. The Christian gospel cannot be identified with or reduced to either some internal, spiritual "transformation of consciousness" (Gnosticism, Buddhism, New Age Movement, "spirituality") or some external, secular social program of this-worldly peace and justice (Modernism, Marxism, "the social gospel"). It centers neither in our souls nor in our world, but in God, who created both our souls and our world and who recreates both our souls and our world in Christ.

7. The reality of hell

C. S. Lewis says about the doctrine of hell: "There is no doctrine which I would more willingly remove from Christianity than this, if it lay in my power. But it has the full support of Scripture, and, especially, of Our Lord's own words; it has always been held by Christendom; and it has the support of reason. If a game is played, it must be possible to lose it. If the happiness of a creature lies in self-surrender, no one can make that surrender but himself (though many can help him to make it), and he may refuse" (*The Problem of Pain*).

If hell is not real, then Jesus Christ is either a fool or a liar. For he warned us repeatedly and with utmost seriousness about it. If hell is not real, the Church and the Bible are also liars, for they do the same.

But these three authorities are also our only sure foundation for believing in heaven and in God's love and forgiveness. This forgiveness is something human reason alone cannot know, since it depends on God's free choice, and our knowing it depends on his revealing this amazing surprise to us. So our basis for believing in the reality of hell is exactly the same authority as our basis for believing in the reality of heaven: Christ, his Church, and her Scriptures.

8. The cause of hell: Human free choice

Hell is a real possibility because our will is free. If we look into the implications of the doctrine of free will, we will see the doctrine of hell there as a necessary part of the package.

Our salvation consists essentially in union with God, spiritual marriage to God, a love-relationship with God. And love by its essence is free, a free choice of the will. God has freely done his part in loving us into existence by creating us and then redeeming us from our sin at infinite cost to himself, on the Cross. But if we do not freely do our part, we cannot attain this end of a love-union with God. God cannot force us to love; if freedom is forced, it is no longer freedom; and if it is free, it is no longer forced.

"We cannot be united with God unless we freely choose to love him. . . . 'He who does not love remains in death . . .' [1 Jn 3:14–15]. . . . To die in mortal sin without repenting and accepting God's merciful love means remaining separated from him for ever by our own free choice. This state of definitive self-exclusion from communion with God and the blessed is called 'hell' " (CCC 1033).

"God predestines no one to go to hell"[6] (CCC 1037). The cause of hell is not God but man.

9. No "second chance" after death

God forgives every sin—if only we repent while there is still time (life-time).

God has already forgiven us. But forgiveness is a gift—a gift of love—and a gift must be freely received as well as freely given. If we do not freely receive it while there is still time, we do not have it ever, we are not forgiven, we have justice instead of mercy. "The [just] wages of sin is death, but the free gift of God is eternal life in Christ Jesus our Lord" (Rom 6:23).

There is no "second chance" after death because there is no more time. Our life-time comes to an end. The time for repentance and salvation is *now*: "Behold, now is the acceptable time; behold, now is the day of salvation" (2 Cor 6:2). After death our soul is no longer in this material body and this material universe, which is the place where time resides. Death is a final, definitive "point of no return". "It is appointed for men to die once, and after that comes judgment" (Heb 9:27).

10. What is hell really like?

It was typical of medieval writers to use vivid imagery for hell: for instance, hell was described as a prison surrounded by thousand-mile-thick iron walls against which a pin makes one scratch every century. The damned have less hope of eventual escape than prisoners would have from there.

The point of such images is not literal, but it is infinitely serious. Christ used equally serious imagery. For instance, "If your hand causes you to sin, cut it off; it is better for you to enter life maimed than with two hands to go to hell, to the unquenchable fire" (Mk 9:44).

The Church does not ask us to take literally the popular imagery for hell: demons with horns, pointed tails, and pitchforks, a torture chamber, and physical fire. However, she does ask us to take seriously the imagery that comes from Christ. Images can be true even when they are not literal. And Christ's images must be true because they come to us from Truth himself.

The most prominent image is *fire*. Fire is an agent of destruction. "Jesus often speaks of 'Gehenna,' of 'the unquenchable fire' reserved for those who

[6] Cf. Council of Orange II (529): DS 397; Council of Trent (1547): 1567.

to the end of their lives refuse to believe and be converted, where both soul and body can be lost"[7] (CCC 1034). Gehenna was a valley (Ge Hinom) outside the holy city of Jerusalem. When the Jews first entered the Promised Land, under Joshua about fifteen centuries before Christ, they found the pagan Caananite tribes who lived there using this valley as the place where they sacrificed their own children to their evil demon-gods by burning them alive. The Jews recognized this as so supernaturally evil that they refused to live in this accursed place and used it only to burn garbage day and night with unending fire.

Fire is a natural image for hell because fire destroys. Christ tells us, "Do not fear those who kill the body but cannot kill the soul; rather fear him [Satan] who can destroy both soul and body in hell" (Mt 10:28). The fire of hell may not be a physical, external fire, but it is certainly the spiritual, self-destructive fire of pride, egotism, selfishness, or rebellion: the self-destructive state of a self shut up in itself, destroying itself by refusing to give itself in faith or hope or love. Any soul that will not die to its own self-will, and will God's will, cannot live with God in heaven. For dying to self-will and living in unselfish love is the very essence of God's own life and the essence of heaven. The identification of eternal salvation with unselfish love is not an "option" for "religious people" only; it is a necessity for every person, for it is dependent, not on man's changeable choice, but on God's unchangeable nature. Since self-giving love is the essential nature of the life of the Creator and Designer of all human souls, it is the only source of life for any such soul, in time or in eternity. It is what we are designed for. The alternative is not another form of life, but death. In time, this is the state of mortal sin; in eternity, it is hell.

Whatever else is in hell, "[t]he chief punishment of hell is eternal separation from God, in whom alone man can possess the life and happiness for which he was created and for which he longs" (CCC 1035). "All your life an unattainable ecstasy has hovered just beyond the grasp of your consciousness. The day is coming when you will wake to find, beyond all hope, that you have attained it, or else, that it was within your reach and you have lost it forever" (C. S. Lewis, *The Problem of Pain*).

There are many different terms for the essential state of soul that leads to heaven: the state of grace, being "born again" of the Spirit, penitence (repentance), faith, hope, and love (*agapē*), willing God's will, dying to self, humility, and submission (*islam*). There are also many different terms for the opposite essential state of soul that leads to hell: the state of mortal sin, impenitence, unbelief, despair, lovelessness, selfishness, pride, egotism. The simplest way to say it is this: "There are only two kinds of people in the end:

---

[7] Cf. Mt 5:22, 29; 10:28, 13:42, 50; Mk 9:43–48.

those who say to God: 'Thy will be done;' and those to whom God says, in the end, '*Thy* will be done'" (C. S. Lewis, *The Great Divorce*). Everyone who arrives in hell can sing: "I did it my way."

11. Purgatory

Purgatory exists because God is both just and merciful.

Purgatory is "like a refiner's fire" (Mal 3:2). It refines and purifies those who at the moment of death are neither good enough for an immediate heaven nor bad enough for hell. "All who die in God's grace and friendship, but still imperfectly purified, are indeed assured of their eternal salvation; but after death they undergo purification, so as to achieve the holiness necessary to enter the joy of heaven" (CCC 1030). "The Church gives the name *Purgatory* to this final purification of the elect, which is entirely different from the punishment of the damned" [8] (CCC 1031).

St. Catherine of Genoa says that although purgatory is incomparably painful because we see all the horror of our own sins, yet it is incomparably joyful because God is with us there, and we are learning to endure his truth, his light. It is also joyful because all those in purgatory have already passed the particular judgment and are assured of their eventual entrance into heaven.

The existence of purgatory logically follows from two facts: our imperfection on earth and our perfection in heaven:

a. At the moment of death, most of us are not completely sanctified (purified, made holy), even though we are justified, or saved by having been baptized into Christ's Body and having thereby received God's supernatural life into our souls, having accepted him by faith and not having rejected him by unrepented mortal sin.

b. But in heaven, we will be perfectly sanctified, with no lingering bad habits or imperfections in our souls.

c. Therefore, for most of us, there must be some additional change, some purification, between death and heaven. This is purgatory.

Purgatory is like heaven's porch, or heaven's incubator, or heaven's wash room. Unlike heaven or hell, purgatory is only temporary. Purgatory takes away the *temporal* punishment still due for our sins after our Baptism, faith, and repentance have already saved us from the *eternal* punishment due to our sins, that is, hell. There are only two eternal destinies, not three: heaven or hell, being with God or without him.

The reason for purgatory is not the past, not an external, legal punishment for past sins, as if our relationship with God were still under the old

---

[8] Cf. Council of Florence (1439): DS 1304; Council of Trent (1563): DS 1820; (1547): 1580; see also Benedict XII, *Benedictus Deus* (1336): DS 1000.

law. Rather, its reason is the future; it is our rehabilitation, it is training for heaven. For our relationship with God has been radically changed by Christ; we are adopted as his children, and our relationship is now fundamentally filial and familial, not legal. Purgatory is God's loving parental discipline (see Heb 12:5–14).

12. Is purgatory found in Scripture?

a. The reality of purgatory is found in Scripture, though not the word—just like the Trinity. For instance, Scripture speaks of a cleansing spiritual fire (1 Cor 3:15; 1 Pet 1:7).

b. The two principles mentioned above (in section 11 of this chapter) are found in Scripture: that at death many of us are still imperfect (1 Jn 1:8) and that in heaven we will all be perfect (Mt 5:48; Rev 21:27). Put these two principles together, and purgatory necessarily follows.

c. Scripture also teaches us to pray for the dead, "that they might be delivered from their sin" (2 Mac 12:46)—which is impossible for those in hell and already finished for those in heaven.

d. Scripture also distinguishes sins that cannot be forgiven either before or after death from sins that can be forgiven after death (see Mt 12:31–32).

e. Finally, the Church, which Scripture calls "the pillar and bulwark of the truth" (1 Tim 3:15), has always taught and has solemnly and officially defined purgatory as a divinely revealed dogma (Councils of Florence and Trent).

13. What is heaven?

a. The essence of heaven is the truth or light of God's presence. Thus Christ describes it: "This is eternal life, that they know thee the only true God" (Jn 17:3). The Church calls this the Beatific Vision: to "'see the divine essence with an intuitive vision, and even face to face'[9]" (CCC 1023).

b. Heaven is our home, our destiny, our fulfillment, our completion. Whatever else it will be, whatever else it will feel like, it will feel like home, for it is the place we were made for, designed for.

c. Heaven is joy. "Heaven is the . . . fulfillment of the deepest human longings, the state of supreme, definitive happiness" (CCC 1024).

d. Heaven is the ecstasy (the word means "standing outside one's self") of self-forgetful, self-giving love (*agapē*)—the love of God and of all the other blessed creatures of God. This is what God is—"God is love [*agapē*]" (1 Jn 4:8)—and this is the reason why God is eternal joy. Nothing but love can

---

[9] Benedict XII, *Benedictus Deus* (1336): DS 1000; cf. LG 49.

give us complete joy, because we are made in God's image, Love's image. Love (*agapē*) on earth is our best appetizer for heaven; it is the only thing we can do forever without being bored.

e. St. Paul describes the life of heaven in one word: "For to me to live is Christ, and [therefore] to die is gain" (Phil 1:21). "To live in heaven is 'to be with Christ.' The elect live 'in Christ' [10]" (CCC 1025).

f. To be in heaven is also to be your true self. All men are born into a lifelong identity crisis, and in heaven they find "their true identity, their own name" [cf. Rev 2:17] (CCC 1025). God promised that "to him who conquers I will give ... a white stone, with a new name written on the stone which no one knows except him who receives it" (Rev 2:17). "What can be more a man's own than this new name which even in eternity remains a secret between God and him? And what shall we take this secrecy to mean? Surely, that each of the redeemed shall forever know and praise some one aspect of the Divine beauty better than any other creature can. Why else were individuals created?" (C. S. Lewis).

g. But perhaps the best definition of heaven is that it is indefinable. "This mystery of blessed communion with God and all who are in Christ is beyond all understanding and description. Scripture speaks of it in images: life, light, peace, wedding feast, wine of the kingdom, the Father's house, the heavenly Jerusalem, paradise: 'no eye has seen, nor ear heard, nor the heart of man conceived, what God has prepared for those who love him' [1 Cor 2:9]" (CCC 1027).

14. The price of heaven

Christ speaks of heaven as "one pearl of great value" (Mt 13:46) and as the "one thing ... needful" (Lk 10:42) that makes life infinitely simple in the long run. For there is only one infinite good: God, and our union with God in heaven. "What shall it profit a man, if he shall gain the whole world, and lose his own soul?" (Mk 8:36 KJV). Who ever uttered words more practical than those?

God thought each human soul so infinitely precious that the price he paid for its salvation was far more than the whole creation; it was the lifeblood of the Creator, on the Cross.

The whole creation would be far too small a price for us to pay for heaven. "Were the whole realm of nature mine / That were a present far too small. / Love so amazing, so divine, / Demands my soul, my life, my all" (Isaac Watts). All God wants from us is our all: our heart, our free love. That is the one thing he cannot give to himself.

---

[10] Phil 1:23; cf. Jn 14:3, 1 Thess 4:17.

T. S. Eliot speaks of Christianity as "a condition of complete simplicity/ Costing not less than/ Everything".

15. The way to heaven

The way to heaven is a "way down" from God, not a "way up" from man. It is divine grace.

That is why there is one way, not many. If getting to heaven were a matter of man-made roads up the mountain, then all the roads—all the religions of the world—might be basically equal. But the way is the one way God made, not the many ways man made. No man, not even a man who found his way to God, can be equal to the God who found his way to man. Even the world's greatest mystic, saint, or prophet cannot found a religion equal to the one founded by the incarnate God himself. No religion is comparable to Christianity because no man is comparable to the God-man.

Other religions teach that the way to heaven (or ultimate happiness and fulfillment) is some human way: for instance, practicing yoga, or experiencing a transformation of consciousness in "enlightenment", or obeying a law well enough, or being sincere and kind enough. But Christianity's answer is a *Person*: the One who claimed, "I am the way, and the truth, and the life; no one comes to the Father but by me" (Jn 14:6). Christ does not merely teach the way to heaven; he is the way to heaven.

And the only one. He himself says that; the idea was not invented by any man or by the Church. The Church must be faithful to her Master's words and not change them into something more politically correct.

Men have made many roads up the religious mountain, seeking God; and there is much truth, goodness, and beauty to be found on these roads. But God made one road down—God *became* the road down—the One who "descended from heaven" (Jn 3:13), seeking man. If this man is not who he claims to be—God incarnate and the only way to heaven—then he is the world's most arrogant liar or lunatic. And if he is who he claims to be, then "there is no other name under heaven given among men by which we must be saved" (Acts 4:12). All who are saved, whether Christian, Jew, Muslim, Hindu, Buddhist, pagan, or atheist, are in fact saved by Christ, however imperfectly they may know him.

Catholics can know him in greater detail and depth than any others through the teachings of the Church he founded to teach in his name and with his authority. Therefore Catholics have a much greater responsibility to practice the truth they know so much more fully and to share it with the world in both word and deed. In the words of St. Francis of Assisi, "Our task is to preach the gospel. Use words if necessary."

PART II

MORALITY

How Catholics Live

Chapter 1

THE ESSENCE OF CATHOLIC MORALITY

1. The place of morality in the Catholic faith

Like the faith itself, this book has three parts:
1. How Catholics think (Catholic theology)
2. How Catholics live (Catholic morality)
3. How Catholics pray (Catholic worship)

These are the three essential parts of every religion: faith, morality, and spiritual life; "creed, code, and cult (liturgy)", or "words, works, and worship".

They correspond to the three powers of every human soul: mind, will, and heart.

All three are equally central to being a Catholic.

The three parts do not come separately but simultaneously. Catholics do not first decide what to believe, then begin to live morally after that, and then move on to prayer and worship after that. In fact, the order is sometimes the reverse; for the most usual source of a loss of faith is an immoral life, and the most powerful source of a moral life is prayer and the sacraments. The more prayer, the more virtue; the more virtue, the more faith.

The three parts are like the three legs of a tripod. The legs may be weak or strong, long or short, but if all three are not there, it is not a tripod. A person is not a Catholic without belief in the essence of what the Church teaches as God's revealed truth or without a sincere effort to obey what the Church teaches as God's commandments or without facing God in prayer as the Church does. To refuse to believe, to obey, and to pray is to be a non-Catholic; to believe, obey, and pray weakly is to be a weak Catholic; to believe, obey and pray well is to be a strong Catholic. God alone can know whether anyone is a weak Catholic or a strong Catholic; but you can and should know whether you are a Catholic or not.

2. The three parts are parts of one single thing

These three parts of the Catholic religion—faith, works, and worship—are three aspects or dimensions of the same single reality, like the three dimensions of space. The reality we confess in the Creed is the same reality we obey in the commandments and participate in in the sacraments. That one reality is the life of Christ. Not *imitating* the life of Christ, but that life itself; not trying to copy its imagined essence, but continuing its real existence; not merely "What would Jesus do?" but "What is Jesus doing?"

The *Catechism* says this: "What faith confesses, the sacraments communicate: by the sacraments of rebirth" [Baptism, first of all], "Christians have become 'children of God' [Jn 1:12; 1 Jn 3:1], 'partakers in the divine nature' [2 Pet 1:4]. . . . Christians are called to lead henceforth a life 'worthy of the gospel of Christ' [Phil 1:27]" (CCC 1692) because this means living morally the very life of Christ that we receive sacramentally and confess creedally. It is one thing, one life.

3. The centrality of Christ in Catholic morality

In our busy, complex world Christ surely says to us what he said to Martha in Luke 10:41–42: "Martha, Martha, you are anxious and troubled about many things; one thing is needful." That "one thing" is Christ himself.

As the Eucharist is not simply a rite or symbol but Christ himself, so the moral life of the Christian is Christ himself living his life in his people. We are his own Body! Christ is present in our moral life in a different way from that in which he is present in the Eucharist, of course: mixed with human imperfections, so that we do not worship good men or good deeds as we worship the Eucharist. But the moral life of the Christian is not merely a human effort to imitate Christ; it is what St. Paul called "this mystery, which is Christ in you, the hope of glory" (Col 1:27).

Christ is not merely a teacher of a moral code but God himself, the One who is the sole source of all good things. Two very good things are the moral law and our obedience to it. It follows that both originate in him: he is the God who gave the moral law to Moses (compare John 8:58 with Exodus 3:14) and the God who gives us the grace to live it. Whenever we obey the commandments, we obey Christ, for they are *his* commandments.

Christian morality is not merely a means to the end of a better world, peace and justice, the welfare of the family, or social harmony (though all of these are very, very good things). These things are relative to Christ, not Christ relative to them. They are ways of obeying his will. They are good because they are from him; he is not good because he is for them.

The *Catechism* clearly states its Christocentrism at the beginning of each of its major sections, including the one on morality: "The first and last point of reference of this catechesis will always be Jesus Christ himself, who is 'the way, and the truth, and the life' [Jn 14:6]" (CCC 1698)—and then the same paragraph quotes St. Paul's one-word summary of Christian morality, the best one ever given: "For to me, to live is Christ" (Phil 1:21).

4. The practical consequences of Christocentrism

Consciousness of the Christocentric nature of Catholic morality not only is the most accurate way to clear up our mental perspective and understanding of it, but is also the most powerful and effective way to practice it and overcome our sins and weaknesses. The very first words of the section on morality in the *Catechism* are:

" 'Christian, recognize your dignity and, now that you share in God's own nature, do not return to your former base condition by sinning. Remember who is your head and of whose body you are a member' [1] " (CCC 1691)

Nothing comparable exists in secular morality. No other basis for human dignity can rival this: that God has given us a share in his own divine nature by incorporating us into Christ's Body. At the beginning of this section on Catholic morality, at the beginning of each day, and before each moral choice, we should take time to let this essential point sink in, to listen to the heartbeat of this heart of Catholic morality.

5. The personalism of Catholic morality

What is the image of "Catholic morality" propagated by today's secular world, especially the media establishment, which forms modern minds through TV, movies, journalism, and public education? It is that of a joyless, repressive,

---

[1] St. Leo the Great, *Sermo 21 in nat. Dom.*, 3: PL 54, 192C.

dehumanizing, impersonal, and irrational system, something alien and inhuman and often simply stupid.

How totally different Catholic morality looks from the inside, from the viewpoint of those who live it, especially the saints! When the media meet a saint, like Mother Teresa, their stereotypes dissolve and die. Nothing looks more different from inside than from outside than Catholic morality—except perhaps being in love. Nothing appears more foolish to non-lovers, or more wise and wonderful to lovers.

For Catholic morality *is* a love affair with Christ and his people, though not "romantic" love. It has its laws and rules, as a city has its streets. Streets are essential to a city, but they are not the very essence of a city. And they are not to live in (though unfortunate "street people" do). Streets are a means to the end of getting home. Home is where the real living takes place. Similarly, moral rules are the street map to the good life, but they are not the thing itself. The thing itself is a relationship of love, like a marriage. The marriage covenant has laws, like God's covenant with us. But husband and wife are faithful to each other first of all, not to the laws. The laws define and command their fidelity to each other. Principles are for persons, not persons for principles. Catholic morality is personalistic—it is person-centric because it is Christocentric, and Christ is a person, not a principle.

But though they are only means to the greater end of the good of persons, laws are essential means. As you cannot be an engineer without knowing and following the laws of physics, of matter, you cannot be a Christian without knowing and following the laws of morality, of spirit.

Christianity is essentially a love relationship with persons: God and neighbor. What is it to love God? Here is how God himself defines it: "If you love me, you will keep my commandments" (Jn 14:15). Christ does not contrast love and law, but joins them, like soul and body. Love without law is like a soul without a body—like a ghost. Law without love is like a body without a soul—like a corpse. Ghosts and corpses speak of death; Christ says: "I came that they may have life, and have it abundantly" (Jn 10:10).

6. "Seeing the big picture"

Nothing is more necessary in re-evangelizing modern man than this vision of human life, this "big picture" in Catholic morality: seeing what the Church sees. One of the main reasons we fail to practice our morality well is that we fail to understand it well. We fail to understand that it is not just a way of behaving but a way of being; not simply "living a good life" but becoming "a new creation" (2 Cor 5:17), becoming "a little Christ". When we read what the saints say about the perfection of charity, or what Christ himself says in the Beatitudes, we are startled to see how different this vision is from the common conception of morality, how high and holy and beautiful and full of joy. If we forget this "big picture", this ultimate reason for being moral (to enter into Christ's own life and love), then even if we remember all the rest of Catholic morality—its realism, its reasonableness, its justice—we will miss its beauty, and we will miss the joy of its adventure.

For Catholic morality means, not following laws but following Christ; and that is more like following a speeding car than following a set of directions: it is alive! Annie Dillard says that when we go to Mass we are "like children playing on the floor with their chemistry sets, mixing up a batch of TNT to kill a Sunday morning. It is madness to wear . . . velvet hats to church; we should all be wearing crash helmets. Ushers should issue life preservers and signal flares; they should lash us to our pews. For the sleeping God may wake someday and . . . draw us out to where we can never return."

Pagans, ancient or modern, love goodness in man, where they can see it; Jews and Muslims as well as Christians love goodness also in God, where they cannot see it, but Christians love goodness most of all where we saw it perfectly on earth: in Christ, the God-man. What did goodness look like then? It looked like a cross: God loving us to death, to the end, no matter what it cost him and no matter how undeserving we are. It is not a love-until, or a love-unless, but a love-unqualified. That is the source of Catholic morality: a source as real and as fiery as the burning bush where Moses saw God.

7. The relation between religion and morality: Can we be good without God?

"If God does not exist, everything is permissible", wrote Dostoyevsky. For if it is only man's will and not God's that makes moral laws, then they are as changeable and contingent as the rules of a game. If we make the rules, we can change them or unmake them. Destroy religion, and you destroy morality.

Yet many great pre-Christian pagan thinkers, such as Socrates, Plato, Aristotle, Cicero, Confucius, and Lao Tzu, knew much of the content of the moral law and recognized its binding force without knowing much of God. And St. Paul wrote that all men, pagan as well as Christian, know God's moral law through natural reason and conscience (Rom 1:17-21), and he used this principle in preaching to the pagan philosophers in Athens (Acts 16). So there can be true morality without true religion.

Both Dostoyevsky and Paul are right. Dostoyevsky is right because if God, the first cause and ultimate origin of the moral law, did not exist, then an objectively real and universally binding moral law would not exist either. But Paul is also right because man can know God's effects, in morality as in natural science, without explicitly knowing God as their cause. All men know the creation; not all know the Creator. All men know the moral law; not all know the Lawgiver.

But we cannot know the moral law as well without knowing the Lawgiver and his character. God's supernatural revelation clarifies the knowledge of morality we have by natural reason and corrects our errors. For fallen man's moral knowledge by natural reason is not infallible, but God's revelation is.

A practical consequence of Paul's point that all men have knowledge of morality by natural reason (conscience) is that we can argue against such errors as abortion and euthanasia by universal rational principles, just as we can argue against slavery or racism. These are not "religious issues" or attempts to impose a specific religious morality on unbelievers. "Thou shalt not kill" is not for Catholics only.

A practical consequence of Dostoyevsky's point that without God everything is permissible is that one cannot really be good without God. Even if he does not know God, whenever anyone is good, that is God's grace working, whether the person knows it or not. God deserves the credit and the thanks because he is the source of "every good endowment and every perfect gift" (Jas 1:17), especially our natural moral knowledge and our good moral choices. They are ours, and they are free, but they are also God's grace, for God's grace turns our freedom on, not off.

8. If you can live a good moral life without being a Catholic, why be one?

You can be moral without being a Catholic, without being a Christian, without being religious at all. You can also live a long and healthy life without knowing or practicing anything about diet or exercise or medicine. But it is not easy! Your chances of succeeding in doing anything are always increased when you know more truth. So you are much more likely to live a good life if you have better knowledge of what "a good life" really means, from divine revelation.

You also have a far greater power to be good if you use the sacraments of the Church, channels of divine grace established by Christ for that very purpose.

But you can honestly be a Catholic only if you believe the Catholic faith is *true*. You cannot believe a falsehood even if it makes you good. You do not believe in Santa Claus, even though that belief probably made you quite good each Christmas when you were a child. Why not? Because you know there really is no Santa Claus.

"Why be a Catholic if you can live a good life without it?" If you are asking this question as a reason to avoid becoming a Catholic, or as a reason to cease being a Catholic, you are really saying that you do not care about truth, only about being good. Goodness is absolutely important. But so is truth. Both make absolute demands on us. It is never right to compromise either one.

9. The absolute importance of morality in Scripture

Catholic morality (deeds) is based on Catholic theology (beliefs). That theology teaches what God has revealed, and the primary data of this revelation is Scripture. And Scripture tells us that right morality, not just right theology, is the main source of God's blessings. This simple point is repeated constantly in Scripture—by Moses (Deut 30), by David (Ps 1), by Christ (Mt 25). Right faith ("orthodoxy") is crucial, but right practice ("orthopraxy") is even more crucial. Orthodoxy is indispensable, but it does not exist for itself alone but for a further end, as a plant's roots exist for its fruits. The Pharisees had correct theology, but they rejected Christ and were rejected by Christ, because they were not honest or humble but hypocritical and proud.

The two-thousand-year-long historical narrative of the Old Testament proves one unmistakably clear principle: whenever God's people obey his laws, they are blessed; whenever they disobey, they are punished, to bring them to repentance and obedience and then blessing again. The same principle is clear in the history of the Church, the New Israel: in the first few centuries she was a Church of saints and martyrs, and she conquered the world. She converted the pagan Roman Empire to Christ. When Catholics were distinctive, when it cost something to be a Catholic (often your blood!), the Church flourished. Increasingly, in the last few centuries in the West, Catholics have been behaving no differently from the secularized world— and have been steadily losing that world. Statistics show that in the United States, the West's most religious nation, Catholics murder, rape, commit adultery, abort, fornicate, euthanize, and commit suicide at the same rate as everyone else. Can anyone who knows Scripture wonder why God is not blessing the Church in the United States? Muslims, Mormons, Protestant Evangelicals, and Orthodox Jews, on the other hand, who *are* living and behaving differently, distinctively, "counter-culturally", are growing in numbers and vitality, even though they have defective theologies, because they are obeying God's moral laws.

10. The role of morality in the decision to believe

How do people decide whether or not to believe in any religion?

Consciously or unconsciously, it is on the basis of three qualities: truth, goodness, and beauty.

In Scripture, "faith" can mean all three things: (a) intellectual belief and (b) moral action (see the roll call of the Old Testament heroes of faith in Hebrews 11), and (c) the indefinable sense of grace and spiritual beauty that is the hallmark of truth (see Jn 1:18). These are three attributes of God: God is infinite truth, infinite goodness, and infinite beauty. And God created man in his image (Gen 1:27). That is why man naturally seeks truth, goodness, and beauty.

All the religions of the world, all man's searchings for God, seek these three ideals. Christianity fulfills them because it is not man's search for God but God's search for man, not man's way up but God's way down, divine revelation. Thus we find supreme truth, goodness, and beauty in Christ. And the Catholic Church is essentially Christ's continuing presence on earth. Catholic Christianity, when it is true to its essence, attracts man's spirit, when man is true to his nature, by all three qualities.

It is goodness that is the most powerful attraction. If the Church did not produce saints, then even her most brilliant theologians and her most gifted artists would not convince man to entrust his soul to her care. From the Virgin Mary to Mother Teresa, saints have always been the Church's most effective evangelists. The most common path to God is through goodness; the most common argument for God is the argument from goodness to truth, from the trustworthiness of saints to the trustworthiness of their faith, from the good fruit to the good tree (Mt 7:16). For truth and goodness could not fundamentally contradict each other.

11. The importance of morality historically:
    Our Jewish moral heritage

Both man's moral instinct (conscience) and man's religious instinct (to worship) are innate and natural to man and, therefore, present in all times and places in human history. But these two eyes of the soul have not always worked in united vision. Their perfect union was accomplished by only one people in ancient times: the people God chose to be his collective prophet to the world, to reveal his true character as moral and good and holy and demanding holiness from us. Today, nearly half of humanity knows this God, for the world's two largest religions, Christianity and Islam, learned of him from the Jews. But before Christ only Abraham and the people God formed from him knew the true God. Morality was not central to pagan religions as it was to Judaism. The gods of the pagans were as immoral as the men who made them in their own image.

While the common error in ancient times was to separate religion from morality, the common error in modern times is to confine religion to morality and to reject or ignore religion's supernatural elements. The two main motives behind this "modernism" were an unjustified embarrassment at the supernatural as supposedly unscientific and a justified embarrassment at the history of religious warfare, persecution, and hatred, which modernists thought came not from sin but from the contradictions between different theologies and the belief that theological orthodoxy was important and truth was objective. If we ignore theological dogma and reduce religion to morality, the modernists argued, we will find unity and peace among the different religions of the world.

But this good end does not justify the less-than-honest means. We cannot ignore truth. We cannot negotiate away any part of the gift of divine revelation, for it is God's unchanging truth. This does not mean that our knowledge of the truth is unchanging. The Church is a living thing. Like a tree growing new branches from within, her teaching grows in both theology and morality. Her theology grows in the depth with which she understands her original and unchangeable deposit of faith; and her morality grows by applying the unchanging principles to changing situations.

12. The importance of morality today:
The moral crisis of our time

The development from the Middle Ages to modern times is both progress and regress, judged by Christian moral standards.

On the one hand, there has been substantial progress not only in science and technology but also in morality: for instance, sensitivity to human rights, the humane treatment of the handicapped, and the nearly universal consensus against torture, cruelty, slavery, and racism.

On the other hand, especially since the so-called "Enlightenment", Western civilization has been increasingly secularized and de-Christianized, morally as well as theologically and ecclesiastically. The attempt to preserve Christian morality without Catholic doctrine, Catholic authority, or Catholic sacraments has not worked. Today the secular media, the mind-molders of our civilization, are increasingly sceptical of traditional morality, especially sexual morality; of the very idea of any certainty or any absolutes in morality; and of the idea of morality as God's commandments rather than man's ideals.

Perhaps man's behavior is not less moral today than in the past (though the twentieth century's record is far bloodier than any other), but his thinking certainly is. For the first time in human history a civilization has ceased to believe in an objectively real, universally binding moral law—and that civilization used to be called "Christendom".

The crisis exists within the Church as well. In most European countries and in America, Catholics, too, say they believe morality is subjective and relative. There have always been crises in the Church, but those of the past were usually theological rather than moral. The Church in the first six centuries confronted many heresies and hammered out the doctrines of the Trinity and the Incarnation; medieval Christendom did the same with the sacraments, and the Counter-Reformation with the doctrines of salvation and Church authority. But today the controversies are almost always about morality. So the critical teachings of the Church today are her moral teachings, her response to the moral crisis both in the Church and in the world.

13. The supernatural character of Catholic morality

The crisis of faith today is rooted in a loss of the sense of the supernatural: in theology (for example, "demythologizing" miracles and Christ's Resurrection), in liturgy (for example, substituting the "horizontal" human community for the "vertical" divine worship), and in morality (for example, changing God's absolute commandments into man's relative values). But Christian morality is supernatural in its essence, in its origin (see the following section 14), and in its end (section 15).

The essence of Christian morality is a relationship with God and his will, not just human self-fulfillment or society or abstract ideals or values, however important these aspects of morality are. The quest for personal happiness, for social justice and peace, and for higher and deeper human values is still quite popular in modern secular civilization, fortunately. But the idea of submission to God's authority and obedience to his laws certainly is not. (What immediate reaction is produced by the words "submission", "authority", "obedience", and "laws"?)

14. The supernatural origin of Catholic morality

Morality has a supernatural origin: God's will and God's character. This is made known to us in two ways: naturally, through human nature and our natural knowledge of morality by reason and conscience; and supernaturally, through God's special revelation to Abraham, Moses, and the Jewish prophets; and, most completely, in Christ and the Church he established, beginning with the apostles, to teach in his name and with his authority (Lk 10:16).

15. The supernatural end of Catholic morality

Morality's supernatural end is eternal heavenly happiness. This is why we exist in the first place, why God created us, the ultimate meaning and purpose of human life: "God put us in the world to know, to love, and to serve him, and so to come to paradise" (CCC 1721).

"[T]he natural desire for happiness [is] . . . of divine origin: God has placed it in the human heart in order to draw man to the One who alone can fulfill it" (CCC 1718).

Catholic morality is a road map on our path through this world to heaven. Its single most important teaching is its answer to life's single most important question: What is the *summum bonum*, the greatest good, the final end, the meaning of life? Of course the answer is "happiness", for " '[w]e all want to live happily; in the whole human race there is no one who does not assent to this proposition' [2] " (CCC 1718). But where is happiness to be found? That is the crucial question. The Church teaches us the true home of happiness: "[T]rue happiness is not found in riches or well-being, in human fame or power, or in any human achievement—however beneficial it may be—such as science, technology, and art, or indeed in any creature, but in God alone, the source of every good and of all love" (CCC 1723). Or, in just three words, " 'God alone satisfies' [3] " (CCC 1718).

16. The two ways

There are many ways to live, many paths through this world. But ultimately there are only two. "The way of Christ 'leads to life'; a contrary way 'leads to destruction' [Mt 7:13; cf. Deut 30:15–20]. The Gospel parable of the *two ways* . . . shows the importance of moral decisions for our salvation: 'There are two ways, the one of life, the other of death; but between the two, there is a great difference' [4] " (CCC 1696).

This antithesis, this dualism, this either-or, life-or-death vision is not familiar to the modern secular mind. But it is familiar to all other cultures. The most common image for life in all the world's literature is the "road" of life. Roads fork, and at each fork the traveler must make a choice. Thus the need for morality.

Christ, Church, and Scripture teach this; so do natural reason, conscience and experience. It is moral realism. In the real world, choices have real consequences: you cannot get from Chicago to the Pacific by walking east, however sincerely you try. Subjective sincerity is not enough. We must not only choose in the right spirit, but we must also choose the right thing.

Moses summarizes all God's moral demands in the two words "choose life" (Deut 30:19); for moral choice is ultimately a matter of life or death, for each

---

[2] St. Augustine, *De moribus eccl.* 1, 3, 4: PL 32, 1312, quoted in CCC 1718.
[3] St. Thomas Aquinas, *Expos. in symb. apost.* I.
[4] *Didache* 1, 1: SCh 248, 140.

individual and each civilization. If our civilization is becoming a "culture of death", as Pope John Paul II has dared to call it, we must call it back to the path to life, both human and divine. But we must first find and walk that path ourselves.

17. Beatitude

On this road to life, the Ten Commandments (Ex 20:1–17) summarize a kind of minimum, or what is necessary, and the Beatitudes (Mt 5:1–11) summarize a kind of maximum, or what is sufficient. The Beatitudes describe beatitude (the perfection of charity and supreme happiness). Beatitude is supernatural in three ways: it is beyond human nature, beyond human reason, and beyond human power.

"Beatitude makes us 'partakers of the divine nature' and of eternal life [2 Pet 1:4; cf. Jn 17:3]. With beatitude, man enters into the glory of Christ [cf. Rom 8:18] and into the joy of the Trinitarian life" (CCC 1721). "Such beatitude surpasses the understanding and powers of man. It comes from an entirely free gift of God: whence it is called supernatural" (CCC 1722).

This supernatural end gives Catholic morality a greater hope and a greater joy than any other. True morality is a prescription for joy—in heaven and also on the way (for "all the way to heaven is heaven", says St. Thérèse). The Church will not canonize a saint without evidence of heroic, supernatural joy in his life as well as heroic virtue. It is secular, godless morality that is joyless and dull; Catholic morality is something more full of joy than *The Joy of Sex*. It could rightly be titled *The Joy of Love*.

Chapter 2

HUMAN NATURE AS THE BASIS

FOR MORALITY

1. Human nature is the basis for morality
2. The meaning of the natural law
3. The characteristics of the natural law
4. How is a "natural law" morality Christian?
5. Four kinds of law
6. Morality is a science
7. The relation between morality as a science of natural reason and divinely revealed Catholic morality
8. Morality and man's place in the universe
9. The basis for Catholic morality in the origin of man
10. The basis for morality in the destiny of man
11. Is man good or evil?
12. Man as spiritual
13. The human body as part of man's dignity and God's image
14. An outline of the basis of Catholic morality in reality
15. The moral importance of the mind
16. Conscience
17. The will
18. Love
19. Free will
20. Law and freedom
21. Emotions

1. Human nature is the basis for morality

There are two very different ideas in the world today about the basis for morality. The typically modern idea is that moral laws are man-made rules like the rules of a game such as tennis, created by human will and therefore changeable by human will. The traditional idea, on the other hand, which is taught not only by the Catholic Church but by all the world's major religions and nearly all pre-modern philosophies, is that the laws of morality are not rules that we make but principles that we discover, like the laws of a science such as anatomy. They are based on human nature, and human nature is essentially unchanging; and therefore the laws of morality are also

167

essentially unchanging, like the laws of anatomy. Just as our anatomical nature makes it necessary for us to eat certain foods and to breathe oxygen for our bodies to be healthy, our moral nature makes certain virtues necessary for our souls to be healthy. There are universal principles, based on human nature, for bodily health and for mental health—and also for moral health.

Because our human nature is composed of body and soul, with powers of intellect, will, and feelings, and because it is our nature to love the good but also to be tempted by evil, it is necessary for us to cultivate such virtues as self-control, wisdom, courage, and honesty. Catholic morality follows the classical Greek philosophers Socrates, Plato, and Aristotle in deriving the essential principles of morality from unchanging human nature and its real, objective needs rather than from the changing subjective feelings and desires of individuals or societies. Thus its essential principles are universal (the same for everyone), objective (discovered, not invented), and unchangeable.

2. The meaning of the natural law

Such a morality is often called a morality of "natural law". This means two things: (a) that moral laws are based on human nature, derived from human nature; and (b) that they are naturally and instinctively known by human reason. ("Reason" means more than just "reasoning"; it includes an intuitive awareness of our obligation to "Do good and avoid evil" and of the meaning of "good" and "evil".)

a. Moral laws are based on human nature. That is, what we ought to do is based on what we are. "Thou shalt not kill", for instance, is based on the real value of human life and the need to preserve it. "Thou shalt not commit adultery" is based on the real value of marriage and family, the value of mutual self-giving love, and children's need for trust and stability.

b. The natural law is also naturally known, by natural human reason and experience. We do not need religious faith or supernatural divine revelation to know that we are morally obligated to choose good and avoid evil or to know what "good" and "evil" mean. Every culture in history has had some version of the Ten Commandments. No culture in history has thought that love, kindness, justice, honesty, courage, wisdom, or self-control was evil, or that hate, cruelty, injustice, dishonesty, cowardice, folly, or uncontrolled addiction was good. Speaking of pagans, St. Paul says that "they show that what the law requires is written on their hearts, while their conscience also bears witness" (Rom 2:15).

The term "natural law" is sometimes misunderstood. "This law is called 'natural,' not in reference to the nature of irrational beings" [that is, animals—it is not a law of *biology*], "but because reason which decrees it properly belongs to human nature" (CCC 1955). For example, the Church teaches that artificial contraception is against the natural law, not because it is a rational human intervention rather than an irrational biological process, but because it is contrary to right reason. It violates the integrity of human nature by divorcing the two naturally united aspects of the essence of the sexual act, "the unitive and the procreative", that is, personal intimacy and reproduction. "Test-tube babies" do the same thing. (See below, part 2, chapter 8.)

3. The characteristics of the natural law

a. "The natural law, present in the heart of each man and established by reason, is universal in its precepts and its authority extends to all men" (CCC 1956). It is not universally obeyed, or even universally admitted, but it is universally binding and authoritative. ("Authority" means "right", not "might"; see part 2, chapter 6, sections 2–4.)

b. "Even when it is rejected in its very principles, it cannot be destroyed or removed from the heart of man. It always rises again in the life of individuals and societies" (CCC 1958).

c. "The natural law is *immutable* and permanent throughout the variations of history" [cf. GS 10] (CCC 1958), because it is based on God-made essential human nature, which does not change with time or place, rather than man-made cultural developments, which do.

d. Because man's essence does not change but his accidental features do (that is, his circumstances and situations), "[a]pplication of the natural law varies greatly" (CCC 1957). For instance, capital punishment may be morally necessary in a primitive society but needlessly barbaric in a society with secure laws and prisons; and the moral restrictions on warfare today, with its weapons of mass destruction, must be far stricter than those in the past.

e. "[I]t provides the necessary basis for the civil law" (CCC 1959), for civil law forbids many acts, such as rape and torture and slavery, because they are morally wrong and harmful to human nature's health and flourishing. Without a natural law basis for civil law, civil law becomes based on power, whether collective or individual. The French Revolutionary slogan "The voice of the people is the voice of God" is just as idolatrous, and proved to be just as totalitarian, as "the divine right of kings", which it replaced.

4. How is a "natural law" morality Christian?

Since human nature finds its perfection and ultimate meaning in Christ, the one perfect man, and since morality is based on human nature, therefore morality finds its perfection and ultimate meaning in Christ. "The moral law finds its fullness . . . in Christ. Jesus Christ is in person the way of perfection" (CCC 1953). The ultimate end of all morality is to become Christlike, to be able to say, with St. Paul, "For to me to live is Christ" (Phil 1:21).

This chapter, like the rest of the book, is all about Christ. It is about his perfect human nature, not his divine nature. That is just as much a part of Christ as his divine nature. To be fully human is an essential part of being fully Christian.

5. Four kinds of law

Catholic tradition, following St. Thomas Aquinas, distinguishes four kinds of law:

a. *Human laws* are laws made by communities of men and are therefore changeable or revocable by men. Many of these are conventions with no intrinsic moral rightness or wrongness, such as traffic rules. But many of them are based on the moral law, if they are good laws (for example, laws requiring the just payment of debts), or in violation of the moral law if they are bad laws (for example, laws that deny essential human rights to Jews [Nazi Germany], black slaves [United States, *Dred Scott*], or unborn children [United States, *Roe v. Wade*]).

b. The *natural law*, as we have seen, is the moral basis of human (civil) laws. It is the law of human nature.

c. The natural law, in turn is "man's participation in the *eternal law*" of God. This "law" refers to the moral character of God, the ultimate reason why we must be moral: "Be holy, for I [the LORD your God] am holy." This formula is repeated many times in Scripture (for example, Lev 11:44).

The natural law points to the eternal law; it is strong evidence for the existence of God. " '[T]his command of human reason" [natural law] "would not have the force of law if it were not the voice and interpreter of a higher reason" [eternal law] "to which our spirit and our freedom must be submitted" [1] (CCC 1954).

d. *Divine law* means laws supernaturally revealed by God, whether for all (the Ten Commandments) or for one people (ancient Israel's liturgical laws) or to one individual (a command to one of his prophets). The "eternal law" is the eternal nature or character of God himself; a "divine law" is God's choice to intervene at a certain time to reveal a command or establish a covenant.

The *Catechism* sums up the four kinds of law as follows: "There are dif-

---

[1] St. Leo XIII, *Libertas præstantissimum*, 597.

ferent expressions of the moral law, all of them interrelated: eternal law—the source, in God, of all law" [c, above]; "natural law" [b]; "revealed law, comprising the Old Law and the New Law, or Law of the Gospel" [d]; "finally, civil and ecclesiastical laws" [a] (CCC 1952).

The summary above adds the important distinction within divine, revealed law between the Old Law (Old Testament) and New Law (New Testament). The purpose of the two is different. Speaking of the Old Law, the *Catechism* says, "The Law is holy, spiritual, and good, [cf. Rom 7:12, 14, 16] yet still imperfect. Like a tutor [cf. Gal 3:24] it shows what must be done, but does not of itself give the strength, the grace of the Spirit, to fulfill it. Because of sin, which it cannot remove" [only Christ can], "it remains a law of bondage. According to St. Paul, its special function is to denounce and *disclose sin* [cf. Rom 7]" (CCC 1963)—like an X ray, to move us to go to Christ the surgeon.

6. Morality is a science

Morality is obviously not an empirical science (good and evil have no shape or color) or a mathematical science. But it is a science in the broader, earlier meaning of the word:

a. It is a rationally organized body of knowledge.

b. Like all sciences, it consists of universal laws. In morality, these are not laws of how things really do in fact behave, as in physics, but laws of how people really ought to behave.

c. It is about objective truths, not subjective opinions or feelings. (Note the word "really" in (b) above: it characterizes both physical and moral sciences.)

d. It has data: human nature.

e. And it is discoverable by natural human reason.

7. The relation between morality as a science of natural reason and divinely revealed Catholic morality

a. Divine revelation, in the Catholic religion, includes this naturally knowable morality, reminds us of it, formulates it, clarifies it, defends it, and gives it a divine sanction.

b. It also builds on it. We know more about morality by faith in divine revelation than we know by reason alone.

c. But this supernatural knowledge never contradicts the morality of natural reason, since it comes from the same source, the same Teacher: God, who is Truth. Truth never contradicts truth. And God never contradicts himself—though he increases his demands and expectations as his children mature, just as good human parents do.

8. Morality and man's place in the universe

Human nature is not isolated. Man is defined by his place in the created order of things, the cosmic hierarchy. He is on the highest level of the visible, material world, which includes minerals, vegetables, and animals below him, and he is also on the lowest level of the invisible, spiritual world, which includes angels (created pure spirits) above him.

Since man is neither angel nor animal, moral law for man is not the same as moral law for angels or animals. Angels have no bodies and therefore no temptations to things like lust, greed, or gluttony. And there is no moral law for animals, who do not have self-conscious reason, free will, or conscience. Catholic morality takes account of this two-sidedness of man and is neither "angelistic" (ignoring our animality) nor "animalistic" (ignoring our spirituality and rationality).

9. The basis for Catholic morality in the origin of man

Morality is about human persons in their relationships with other human persons, with themselves, and with God. Therefore the nature and dignity of man is a fundamental basis for morality.

So what is the basis for the dignity of man? Is that basis something uncertain, changeable, and fallible, such as the state or popular consensus or one's own opinions and feelings and desires?

No, "[t]he dignity of the human person is rooted in his creation in the image and likeness of God" (CCC 1700). This is one of the most important sentences in the *Catechism*. The real basis for natural morality is this supernatural fact. It is also the ultimate basis for social and political order; for "human law" (social and political law) rests on "natural law" (moral law), and natural law rests on eternal law. We outlaw things because they are wrong, and they are wrong by their own nature ultimately because that nature is opposed to the nature and character of God (see part 2, chapter 3, section 5).

However, this ultimate basis need not be explicitly known or believed by people before they can be moral; even atheists can respect persons as ends and obey their own conscience.

10. The basis for morality in the destiny of man

A second basis for the dignity of man, and thus for morality, is man's ultimate end. "The dignity of the human person is . . . fulfilled in his vocation to divine beatitude" (CCC 1700).

Since man's end is to share God's own beatitude, man is a high and holy mystery, not a thing to be used. "[T]he human person is 'the only creature on earth that God has willed for its own sake' [GS 24 § 3]" (CCC 1703). And we must do the same: love persons for their own sake, not use them for the sake of anything else—in other words, love persons as ends and use things as means rather than using persons as means and loving things as ends. This rule is rooted in the fact that God created man to be an end, like himself, and all other things to be means for man (1 Cor 3:22–23).

This "religious" fact makes great "secular" differences. For instance:

a. We have a responsibility to take good care of the earth, the environment, and the ecology—not for its own sake, but for the sake of mankind and a better human life on earth. Material things are means, not ends; persons are ends, not means. The material world is precious, not as an end in itself, but as a means to the good of persons. The good of persons must never be sacrificed for the good of the natural environment.

b. Humans must not be harmed by being used as guinea pigs for scientific experiments, however important the purpose of those experiments.

c. Politicians and businesses must recognize that the ruling purpose of the economy is not power or profit but human welfare.

11. Is man good or evil?

Morality for man also depends on the fact that man is created by God in his image and is therefore very good, yet at the same time is also a fallen and imperfect creature, capable of reason but often irrational. Catholic morality does not ignore this two-sidedness of man, either, and is neither pessimistic, denying our intrinsic goodness, nor naïvely optimistic, denying our intrinsic capacity for evil.

If man were simply good, there would be no sin, guilt, repentance, or punishment. (This is the view of extreme optimists like Rousseau.) If man were simply evil, morality could be only external compulsion, forcing us to act contrary to our nature and evil instincts. (This is the view of extreme pessimists like Machiavelli and Hobbes.) But if man is by nature both good and evil, then morality is an aid to his good instincts and a threat to his evil ones, and appeals to both the love of good and the fear of evil are appropriate. (When there are real dangers around, it is better to feel afraid than secure.) This is the morality of common sense and of the Catholic faith.

Man is very good in his being, his essential nature. Man is the most valuable thing in the universe. For man is God's creature and God's child.

But man is fallen from moral innocence (though not from ontological goodness, goodness in his very being) and into original sin, instinctive selfishness. Life is now a spiritual warfare between good and evil, both of which lie in all of us. ("There's a little good in the worst of us and a little bad in the best of us.") The best of us, the saints, are the most honest and clear-eyed about their own evils. "There are two kinds of people: sinners, who think they are saints, and saints, who know they are sinners" (Pascal)— just as there are two kinds of people: fools, who think they are wise, and the wise, who know they are fools (Socrates).

"Man . . . is divided in himself. As a result, the whole life of men, both individual and social, shows itself to be a struggle, and a dramatic one, between good and evil, between light and darkness" (GS 13).

12. Man as spiritual

Here is the most obvious and radical difference between Catholic morality and the morality of the modern secularized society the Church confronts today. For Catholic morality, as for all the world's religions, man is a spiritual being, with a soul. He is not a mere clever ape, a mere biological organism. He is "[e]ndowed with 'a spiritual and immortal' soul" [GS 14 § 2] (CCC 1703).

The consequences for morality are obvious: in a word, we act like what we think we are. If we believe we are apes, we will act like apes. We ape the apes we think we are. And if we believe we are beloved children of a pure and holy God, we will act like the King's kids.

The broader social consequences are also radical. The secular view of man contains no guarantee against totalitarianism. For if we are not immortal spirits but only mortal animals, what is the eighty-year life of one animal compared with the centuries-long life of a nation of millions? The state seems greater than the individual person. But if we are spirits, it is the opposite, for each individual is immortal. Long after all nations, races, and galaxies have died, each of us will still exist. The refutation of totalitarianism is the soul.

13. The human body as part of man's dignity and God's image

Many philosophers, ancient and modern, sharply divide our souls from our bodies and see glory and greatness and the divine image only in the soul (for example, Platonism in ancient philosophy, Gnosticism in the early Christian era, Cartesianism in early modern philosophy, and the New Age Movement today).

a. But God deliberately designed and made our bodies. They are no accident or mistake. God meant our souls to be the life of our bodies. Bodies are not prisons. We are not meant to be pure spirits, like the angels.

b. No temple in the world is holier than the human body, for God incarnated himself into a human body (and soul) in Christ.

c. And God has this human body forever. The Ascension was not the undoing of the Incarnation.

d. Our bodies are ours as much as our souls are ours. We cannot take our bodies off as we can our clothes. They are part of our essential being, not our external containers, like hotel rooms.

e. Our bodies shared the fall of our souls into sin by receiving death as their penalty. And they will share our souls' redemption by resurrection. God will resurrect our bodies, as he resurrected Christ's. We will have bodies forever.

The *Catechism* sees the "image of God" not only in the spiritual, rational, and immortal soul but also in the body: "The human body shares in the dignity of 'the image of God': it is a human body precisely because it is animated by a spiritual soul, and it is the whole human person" [N.B. 'human person' includes 'body'!] "that is intended to become, in the body of Christ, a temple of the Spirit" [cf. 1 Cor 6:19–20; 15:44–45] (CCC 364).

The consequences for morality are shocking to many people today: a good spiritual intention—love and sincerity—is not enough. For instance, the difference between morally right sex and morally wrong sex is not merely a spiritual attitude but a physical fact: not merely what motives or feelings occur but which bodies are copulating: sex with anyone but your spouse is wrong. So is "mercy-killing"; even though the spiritual motive is mercy, the physical deed is killing.

Whenever we deal with objective reality, subjectively good intentions are not enough. (Are they enough for your dentist? Or for your financial advisor?) So if you say they are enough for morality, you say morality is not about objective reality.

The modern world has difficulty understanding this objective morality because it misses "the big picture" behind the rules. The "big picture" about our bodies is that they are neither gods to be worshipped nor devils to be resented nor mere animals to be fed nor mere tools to be used, but the matter of a great artist's masterpiece, the oils of a painting or the notes of a symphony or the words of a poem. The soul supplies the form, the meaning. But in any art work the matter is as essential as the form. In all good art the two are inseparably one.

14. An outline of the basis of Catholic morality in reality

Catholic morality is based on reality. The basic outline of reality is the reason behind the basic principles of morality, the reason for labeling some things right and some things wrong:

a. Because the Creator is not a creature and no creature is the Creator, we should not worship any creature as our end or try to use the Creator as a means.

b. Because spirit is greater than matter, we should not value things like money above things like wisdom and virtue. Yet matter is God-created and good. Our goal is self-control, not "liberation" from matter.

c. Because man is not an animal, he should not be treated as one (for example, through slavery or euthanasia).

Because animals are not persons, they should not be loved as persons but as animals—that is, they may be used as pets or clothing or even food. But persons may not.

d. Because the soul is more than the body, the body should serve the soul. The body should not be served as a lord, but it should be respected as a good.

e. Reason ought to guide, since it alone has understanding of truth. Will ought to obey reason and guide the emotions, since it is free and, therefore, responsible. The emotions ought to be neither served nor avoided, but formed, since they are the raw material for the work of the will guided by the reason.

Each *ought* is based on what *is*.

15. The moral importance of the mind

"By his reason, man recognizes the voice of God which urges him 'to do what is good and avoid what is evil' [GS 16]. Everyone is obliged to follow this law, which makes itself heard in conscience" (CCC 1706).

In Catholic morality, moral goodness cannot be divorced from truth and from that power of the soul by which we know truth, namely, the mind or reason. ("Reason" in the traditional sense means more than the ability to do logical reasoning or calculating. It means also the ability to understand the true natures of things. It has very little to do with I.Q.)

Typically, modern morality does not speak of the "intellectual virtues" because it usually underestimates the moral importance of the mind or intellect or reason. But in Catholic morality there are intellectual virtues (virtues of the mind) that are necessarily connected with moral virtues (virtues of the will). The most important of these is prudence, or practical wisdom.

The virtues of the mind and the will help each other to grow: wisdom makes us more charitable, and charity makes us more wise. The vices of the mind and will also reinforce each other: foolishness makes us selfish, and selfishness makes us foolish.

A prerequisite for all moral virtues is the fundamental virtue of honesty, or sincerity, or the will to truth, the refusal to deceive or be deceived, the absolute demand for light and not darkness. Truth, like love, is an absolute, for it is what God is (Jn 14:6); it is an eternal and infinite attribute of God (see part 2, chapter 10).

The sins of the intellect can be as serious as those of the will. Christ denounced dishonesty more vigorously than any other sin when he found it in the Pharisees. For God is Truth. To refuse Truth is to refuse God.

16. Conscience

Conscience is to good and evil what sight is to color. It is the power of the soul that gives us awareness of the moral dimension, the goodness or evil of human acts.

The moral importance of the mind becomes obvious once it is understood that conscience is an intellectual power. It is essentially a power of knowing, not feeling (though feeling is usually associated with it). To know that an act is morally obligatory, morally forbidden, or neither is not the same as to feel it. Sometimes our moral knowledge, or moral awareness, is accompanied by feeling and sometimes not. For instance, sometimes we know we are guilty of a certain wrong but we do not feel guilty, just as sometimes we know that a certain thing or person or deed is really beautiful without feeling subjectively attracted, or know it is ugly without feeling repulsed.

Conscience is powerfully aided by right feelings. It is much easier for us to become saints if we feel attracted to the life of sanctity than if we feel afraid of it. But conscience itself is essentially a power of knowing. It is an intuitive or immediate awareness of good and evil. At the heart of true morality there is knowledge; true morality involves living in the truth, in reality; true sanctity is true sanity.

17. The will

If the intellect is the soul's navigator, the will is its captain. A wise captain listens to his navigator, but it is the captain who is in charge and ultimately responsible for the ship.

The human will is free and, therefore, responsible. We have free will, or free choice. "By virtue of his soul and his spiritual powers of intellect and will, man is endowed with freedom, an 'outstanding manifestation of the divine image'[GS 17]" (CCC 1705). This does not mean we are not influenced or "conditioned" by many factors that come to us. But our choices come *from* us. We are not passive links in a chain of causes.

The will is close to the heart of the self, the "I". When we say "I promise you", or "I choose (or refuse) to do that", we stake our very selves to what we do or promise. It is by the will, the power of free personal choice, that we do this. Our free will makes us morally responsible.

Just as with the intellect and its conscience, the will and its choice is not essentially a feeling or emotion. It may be *accompanied* by emotion, and rightly ordered emotions make it much easier for the will to choose the right thing; but the will is distinct from the emotions. "I feel like doing this" is not the same as "I choose to do this."

18. Love

This point is especially important when it comes to love. The essence of love in the biblical sense (*agapē*) is not an emotion or feeling; the essence of love is a choice of will, good will, the willing of the other's good, the choosing of what is really best for the other. This is the unspectacular, unemotional essence of love. The exciting feelings are additions to the essence.

We can love someone even when we do not feel loving toward them. We can will someone's good even when we feel aversion or embarrassment toward them. For we often do this to ourselves: we do not always "feel good about ourselves", but we always will good to ourselves, we always seek our own welfare and happiness. When we feel sick, we seek healing; when we feel stupid, we seek to be wise; when we feel evil and guilty, we seek to become better persons.

Christ commands us to love our neighbor "as ourselves", that is, as we already do love ourselves. This love cannot be a feeling because feelings cannot be commanded; only free choices of the will can. Therefore love—the love Christ commands—is essentially a free choice of the will rather than a feeling.

This point becomes extremely practical when applied to questions like homosexuality. Homosexual feelings are not sins, since they are not freely chosen. Homosexual acts are sinful (as are heterosexual acts outside marriage) insofar as they are freely chosen acts of disobedience to God's known will and law. Homosexual desires, feelings, and emotions are *disordered*; they are troubles, but not sins, unless freely chosen by the will.

19. Free will

a. *The meaning of free will.* "God created man . . . a person who can initiate and control his own actions. . . . '[H]e is created with free will and is master over his acts' [2] " (CCC 1730)

"Freedom is the power, rooted in reason and will, to act or not to act, to do this or that, and so to perform deliberate actions on one's own responsibility. By free will one shapes one's own life" (CCC 1731).

---

[2] St. Irenaeus, *Adv. haeres.* 4, 4, 3: PG 7/1, 983.

b. *Free will is necessary for morality.* Free will "is the basis of praise or blame" (CCC 1732). If our wills are not really free, morality is really meaningless. All moral language—language about good and evil, right and wrong, ought and ought not, sin and virtue, praise and blame, all counseling and commanding—makes sense only when addressed to free persons, not necessitated and "determined" animals or machines. We do not praise or blame, reward or punish a machine. When the Coke machine fails to deliver a Coke, we do not reason with it or call it a sinner; we kick it.

c. *Freedom can be increased or decreased.* "The more one does what is good, the freer one becomes . . ." (CCC 1733). "Progress in virtue . . . enhance[s] the mastery of the will over its acts" (CCC 1734). And the more one does evil, the less free he becomes. He who sins is a slave to sin (see Rom 6:16). Sin is using our freedom to sell ourselves into slavery and addiction to sin. We forge the chains of our bondage with the power of our freedom. Freedom is not a constant: we are free to increase our freedom or decrease it. There is total freedom in heaven, no freedom in hell.

20. Law and freedom

The modern mind perceives the value of human freedom more deeply than previous ages did. But it often makes a key error about freedom: opposing it to the authority of law and obedience to law. Pope John Paul II's encyclical *The Splendor of Truth* addresses that problem very profoundly.

The very idea of law is in a state of crisis because our culture views law negatively, as a set of prohibitions and, therefore, as something that seems to lessen freedom. But good laws ensure freedom even when they are negative, like guard rails along mountain roads or labels on bottles of poison.

Submission to God, his will, and his law cannot lessen freedom, for God is the author of man and his freedom—both his free will to choose and his freedom from evil and sin. The author of freedom cannot be the enemy of freedom! The same is true of good human laws, laws that express the natural law, which in turn expresses God's eternal law (see part 2, chapter 5). It is the secular concept of freedom as self-will, or license—freedom as the opposite of law—that has proved terribly destructive to freedom, especially in the twentieth century, in many nations, families, and individual lives.

21. Emotions

One of the real benefits of modern psychology has been more attention to and understanding of the emotions, including their role in making moral choices. Though they are not free, like the will, they are important for morality because emotions are closely connected with the will and powerfully help or harm it. Well-ordered emotions make moral goodness more attractive and easier; unnatural, unrealistic, or uncontrolled emotions make it unattractive and difficult. Thus, good psychological counseling can be a powerful aid to good morality (as can good bodily health habits). Just as a good instrument helps a musician make good music, good emotions help us to live good moral lives.

"Strong feelings are not decisive for the morality or the holiness of persons; they are simply the inexhaustible reservoir of images and affections in which the moral life is expressed" (CCC 1768). But this expression is a part of human perfection: "The perfection of the moral good consists in man's being moved to the good not only by his will but also by his 'heart' " (CCC 1775). (Here *heart* means emotions.)

Emotions are part of God's design for human nature. Even emotions we find hard to control, like sexual desire, anger, and fear, are not evil but good in themselves and play a necessary role; without them we are not completely human. Christ did not ignore or suppress his emotions but accepted and used them rightly, including "negative" ones like sadness (see Mk 14:34, Jn 11:33–36) and anger (Jn 2:13–17).

"It belongs to the perfection of . . . human good that the passions be governed by reason"[3] (CCC 1767). Emotions are like horses. Some are tame, some are wild, all need to be cared for and ruled by prudence (practical wisdom), fortitude (courage), temperance (self-control), and justice (fairness), the four cardinal virtues (see part 2, chapter 3), as a horse needs to be ruled by a rider. The horse should not lead the rider, nor should the rider lock the horse up in the stable all the time. Wise governance is good for the horse as well as for the rider, and wise governance of the emotions is good for the emotions as well as for the mind and will that govern them.

[3] Cf. St. Thomas Aquinas, *STh* I-II, 24, 3.

Chapter 3

SOME FUNDAMENTAL PRINCIPLES

OF CATHOLIC MORALITY

(What follows, in chapters 3 and 4, are some basic principles of "natural law" morality, as defined in chapter 2. Chapters 5 through 10 will focus on the "divine law", the Ten Commandments.)

1. The point of principles
2. Moral principles are necessary for salvation
3. The three kinds of goods
4. The three moral determinants: What makes any act good or evil?
5. The three relationships
6. The three levels of love
7. Three universal moral rules
8. Three kinds of acts
9. The meaning of conscience
10. The three functions of conscience
11. Corrections to some common errors about conscience

1. The point of principles

a. Principles are *certain*.

If there is one thing the modern secular mind claims to be certain of about morality, it is that no one can really be certain about morality. If there is any one thing about religious believers that is utterly incomprehensible to most of media, public education, and journalism today, it is the fact that believers claim they can know what is really, truly good and evil—in other words, moral principles. Typically, modern people say that morality is always a "complex issue". G. K. Chesterton explained why: "Morality is always terribly complicated—to a man who has lost all his principles."

b. Principles are *universal*.

They are like scientific laws of formulas, like "$F = MA$" or "$E = MC^2$": statements that are true for all times and places and situations. Just as all matter obeys the laws of physics, all men are obligated to obey the laws of morality. In any field, universal principles bring order into chaos.

c. Principles are *objective*.

Moral principles such as the Golden Rule ("Do unto others what you would have them do unto you") are based on objective facts (in this case the fact that all persons are equal in moral value and rights).

Moral principles are not arbitrary or subjective but realistic and objective, just as scientific principles are. (The method of discovering and proving them, of course, is not the "scientific method", for good and evil have no qualities that appear to the senses, such as color or shape, and cannot be measured mathematically.)

2. Moral principles are necessary for salvation

If you do not believe in any moral principles as objectively true and binding, you will probably not believe in sin either, for sin means disobeying real moral laws. ("Sin" means more than that—divorce from God—but not less.) And if you believe there is no sin, you cannot repent for sin. And if there is no repentance for sin, there is no salvation.

This is not merely the teaching of some individual writer, or even of the *Catechism* or of the Church; it is the serious and repeated teaching of all the prophets and especially of Christ himself.

That does not mean that people whose minds are so confused that they do not clearly understand sin and repentance cannot be saved. If you are lost in a forest, it is possible to get out with only a faded road map, or even none at all. But it is far better and safer to have a map that is clear and accurate.

Having moral principles—believing them—is very important, but following them is even more important. "For it is not the hearers of the law who are righteous before God, but the doers of the law who will be justified" (Rom 2:13).

Again, this does not mean that only saints, not sinners, are saved. There are no other kinds of people besides sinners, and the saints are the first to tell us that. The difference between the saved and the damned is not the difference between saints and sinners but between repentant sinners and unrepentant sinners.

3. The three kinds of goods

Goods are traditionally classified into three different kinds. *Moral* goods are only one of three kinds of goods. The other two are *useful* goods (tools, instruments, anything sought as means to further ends) and *pleasant* goods (things sought as ends in themselves, as ingredients in happiness: joy, peace, beauty, delight, contentment, pleasure). These are the three things human nature seeks: righteousness, efficiency, and delight.

There are therefore only three good reasons why anyone should ever do anything: because it is moral, practical, or delightful. Our lives are very complicated today; here is a way to simplify them radically. If you find that many of the things you do are not necessary for morality, practicality, or delight, then there is no good reason to do them.

Of the three kinds of goods, moral goods clearly take precedence: it is not justifiable to sacrifice a moral duty for efficiency or pleasure. Thus "it would save the taxpayers money" is not a good argument for suddenly cutting off all welfare programs, and "it feels good" is not a good argument for drugs, adultery, or revenge.

4. The three moral determinants: What makes any act good or evil?

"The morality of human acts depends on
  "—the object chosen;
  "—the end in view or the intention;
  "—the circumstances of the action" (CCC 1750).
  That is, (a) the act itself, (b) the motive, and (c) the situation.

a. "The *object* chosen is a good toward which the will deliberately directs itself. It is the matter of a human act" (CCC 1751).

"Matter" here does not mean merely physical matter, like "giving a man money" or "fighting a war", but the moral "raw material" or content of the act, what the act objectively is in itself. For instance: Is this money bribery or repayment of a debt? Is this war aggression or defense?

b. "In contrast to the object, the *intention*" [the motive] "resides in the acting subject" [person] (CCC 1752).

But although personal intentions are subjective, they can be good or evil just as objective acts can be good or evil. An objectively good act can have a good or a bad subjective intention. (For instance, giving alms is a good act; relieving another's suffering is a good intention for it, but showing off is not.) An objectively bad act can also have a good or a bad intention. (For instance, robbing a rich man is an evil act; the intention of harming the rich man is a bad intention, and the motive of helping the poor with the money is a good intention.)

But a good intention does not excuse an evil act, any more than a good act excuses an evil intention. This is why "mercy killing" is wrong: though its intention is mercy (to relieve pain), it is an act of killing. "A good intention ... does not make behavior that is intrinsically" [by its own nature] "disordered, such as lying or calumny, good or just. The end" [the intention] "does not justify the means" [the act] (CCC 1753). If Hitler had instigated the Holocaust "to improve the human race" and not to vent his hate and prove his power, it would still have been a terribly evil deed.

c. The third element is the situation, or the circumstances. "The *circum-stances*, including the consequences, are secondary elements of a moral act. They contribute to increasing or diminishing the moral goodness or evil of human acts (for example, the amount of a theft). They can also diminish or increase the agent's responsibility (such as acting out of a fear of death). Circumstances of themselves . . . can make neither good nor right an action that is in itself evil" (CCC 1754). They can, however, do the reverse: they can make an act that is good in itself evil: for example, making love to your spouse when it is medically dangerous, or giving sugar candy to a diabetic.

Any one of the three elements alone is enough to make an act evil, but one alone is not enough to make it good, because for any human work to be good, *each* of its essential elements must be good. For instance, a good building can be spoiled by a bad foundation, bad walls, or bad electrical wiring. In a story, one good feature (for example, a good plot) is not enough to make a good story if the story lacks good characterization or a good theme. So with a human act. The act itself and the motive and the circumstances must all be right. You must (a) do the right thing (b) for the right reason (c) in the right way.

Each of three common oversimplified moralities focuses on only one of the three factors and ignores the other two. Legalism focuses only on the objective act itself, as specified by the moral law. Subjectivism focuses only on the subjective intention. And "situation ethics", or moral relativism, focuses only on changing situations or circumstances. Catholic morality is more complete, realistic, and balanced.

5. The three relationships

Life is largely a series of relationships. Every person in the world is related, in right or wrong ways, to others, to self, and to God. Thus morality has three parts: social ethics (your relationships with others), individual ethics (your relationship to yourself: virtues and vices, character), and the ultimate meaning and purpose of human life: your relationship with God.

As C. S. Lewis says, humanity is like a fleet of ships, and morality is like their sailing orders. It tells them three things: (1) how the ships should cooperate with each other and not impede each other; (2) how each ship should stay shipshape and afloat; and (3) most important of all, the fleet's mission, why they are at sea in the first place.

The three parts are related in a hierarchy of dependence: social morality depends on individual morality, and both depend on the purpose of human life. The ships cannot cooperate socially if each one is sinking individually, and it does no good for them to be afloat, individually or collectively, if they have no reason to be there, no destination. Modern secular morality usually shies away from this last question, for "the ultimate purpose of human life" is really what religion is all about. But it is clearly the most important of all.

As Thomas Merton said, "We are not at peace with others because we are not at peace with ourselves, and we are not at peace with ourselves because we are not at peace with God." All the problems of human life fit into that one sentence.

6. The three levels of love

Love is the most basic human drive, the strongest human energy, and the most important human relationship. "Love makes the world go round." And therefore it is the most basic moral value. St. Augustine defines morality as *ordo amoris*, the right ordering of love, and immorality as disordered love.

We find ourselves able to love on three different levels: we can love what is greater than ourselves (God), we can love ourselves and what is equal to ourselves (other human persons), and we can love what is less than ourselves (things in the world).

The essential moral rule for right loving is to love according to reality. This means *adoring* God, *loving* persons, and *using* things.

a. How are we to love God? "With all your heart, and with all your soul, and with all your mind, and with all your strength" (Mk 12:30). God deserves total love, the love of worship and adoration, because of what he *is*: infinitely good and the Creator of our very existence. Adoring things, or even human persons, is idolatry and foolishness. Only God is God. To treat non-God as God is to live in unreality. Even other persons, though their value cannot be measured in things, money, or quantity, are not God, not infinite, not perfect, and not to be worshipped. Great harm will come if we place divine burdens on human shoulders.

b. We are to love our neighbor "as ourselves", that is, with the same kind of love with which we love ourselves. However we may feel about ourselves at the moment, we always will our own good, our own best interest, our own true happiness; and we should do the same for others.

This love is in our power, for it is a free choice, not a feeling. We are not commanded to *like* all men, for liking is a form of love that is not under our power. It is a feeling, not a voluntary choice. If Christ had commanded us to like everyone, he would have been a very foolish psychologist.

The reason we are commanded to love our neighbor is the same as the reason we are commanded to adore God: to conform to reality, to face the facts—in this case the fact that others are in fact the same kind of beings we are: neither God to be adored, nor things to be used, but created persons made in God's image, to be loved as equals, as children of the same divine Father.

Neighbor-love is violated by loving our neighbors either too much (idol-atrously, as God) or too little (using them as things).

c. The things of this world are to be loved proportionately to what they are—for example, we should respect higher animals, which have feelings, more than lower animals such as insects, which do not; we should respect animals more than plants (we kill plants to feel animals but do not kill animals to feed plants); and we should respect living things more than non-living things.

God created things to be used for people. When things such as money are treated as ends, people are usually treated as means. This reverses the order of reality.

Things can be loved too little (not appreciated) or too much (treated as ends); persons can be loved too little (used as means) or too much (wor-shipped as gods), but God cannot be loved too much, only too little.

7. Three universal moral rules

If there are three moral rules that are obvious to every morally sane indi-vidual and culture, they are probably the following three mentioned in the *Catechism:* "Some rules apply in every case:

"—One may never do evil so that good may result from it" [that is, a good end does not justify an evil means];

"—the Golden Rule: 'Whatever you wish that men would do to you, do so to them.' [1]

"—charity always proceeds by way of respect for one's neighbor and his conscience" (CCC 1789).

These three rules are not sufficient for morality, but they are a necessary minimum, a foundation.

8. Three kinds of acts

Human acts are divided into (a) the morally *indifferent* (which are permit-ted), (b) the morally *evil* (which are forbidden), and (c) the morally *good* (which are commanded).

Within the third category, some morally good acts are strictly commanded or required as our moral duties. Other moral acts are not commanded but commended (or recommended), as going "beyond the call of duty", such as martyrdom, heroic sacrifice, and "turning the other cheek". These are "the evangelical [gospel] counsels", summarized in Christ's Beatitudes (Mt 5). They go beyond the Ten Commandments. One does not sin against the

---

[1] Mt. 7:12; cf. Lk 6:31; Tob 4:15.

Commandments if one is less than heroically saintly in following these higher counsels, or ideals. We should not feel guilty about not being heroes all the time. But if we never aim higher than the minimum, it is very unlikely that we will attain even the minimum. And, above all, we will miss the joy and drama and beauty of morality—the "beatitude".

9. The meaning of conscience

Conscience is our morality-detector.

"Deep within his conscience man discovers a law which he has not laid upon himself but which he must obey . . . , calling him to love and to do what is good and to avoid evil" (GS 16). Deep down, we all know we are really (objectively) obligated to do good and avoid evil, whether we (subjectively) want to or not.

Since this obligation binds us even when we do not want it to, it could not have come from our human will and wants. It comes to us, not from us, and is powerful evidence for the existence of God. Even the atheist treats conscience as an absolute moral authority; for like everyone else he admits that it is always right to obey your conscience and wrong to disobey it. But what could give conscience such absolute authority except God? The only explanation of this fact is that "man has in his heart a law inscribed by God. His dignity lies in observing this law, and by it he will judged. His conscience is man's most secret core. . . . There he is alone with God whose voice echoes in his depths" (GS 16). "When he listens to his conscience, . . . man can hear God speaking" (CCC 1777). " 'Conscience is the aboriginal Vicar of Christ' [2] " (CCC 1778).

10. The three functions of conscience

Conscience gives us three things:
  a. an awareness of good and evil;
  b. a desire for good and aversion to evil;
  c. a feeling of joy and peace and rightness at having done good and of unease and guilt at having done evil.

These three functions of conscience correspond to the three parts of the soul, (a) the mind, or intellect, or reason, (b) the will, and (c) the emotions, or feelings.

  a. "Conscience is a judgment of reason" [understanding] "whereby the human person recognizes the moral quality of a concrete act that he is going

[2] John Henry Cardinal Newman, "Letter to the Duke of Norfolk," V, in *Certain Difficulties Felt by Anglicans in Catholic Teaching* II (London: Longmans Green, 1885), 248.

to perform, is in the process of performing, or has already completed" (CCC 1778).

b. "Moral conscience" [3] ... [also] "enjoins him at the appropriate moment to do good and to avoid evil" (CCC 1777).

c. Conscience is also an intuitive feeling "approving those that are good and denouncing those that are evil" [cf. Rom 1:32] (CCC 1777).

11. Corrections to some common errors about conscience

a. Conscience is not just a feeling. It is first of all a knowing, an awareness of the truth about good and evil.

b. Conscience is not infallible. It can err, like anything in us. It can mistake what is evil for good, or good for evil. Therefore one of the first things conscience obligates us to do is to educate and inform our conscience. This "education of the conscience is a lifelong task" (CCC 1784), like the education of the mind or the training of the body.

c. "A human being must always obey the certain judgment of his conscience. If he were deliberately to act against it, he would condemn himself" (CCC 1790). We are always obliged to obey our conscience, even though it is not infallible. If your conscience leads you honestly to believe that a certain act is morally obligatory, it is morally wrong for you to avoid the act your conscience commands. If your conscience tells you something is morally forbidden, it is wrong for you to do the thing your conscience forbids, even if your conscience is wrong, because (assuming you are honest) you do not know that your conscience is wrong, and you believe it is right, and it has the authority of God's prophet in your soul (see CCC 1777–78). When you hear "Thus says the Lord", you must obey, even though your ears are fallible.

d. Ignorance of good and evil—that is, errors of conscience—may be either vincible ignorance or invincible ignorance.

Vincible ignorance is ignorance that can and should be overcome and conquered. We are responsible for this very ignorance in our conscience: for example, getting drunk and then murdering someone in thoughtless, blind rage. The excuse "I didn't know what I was doing" may be true but it does not excuse the act, because you *should* have known.

Invincible ignorance is ignorance you could not conquer and are not responsible for: for example, giving money to a rich "con man" cleverly disguised as a beggar.

e. Conscience is not merely negative but positive. Like the prophets in Scripture, it always offers a message of hope. Even when it condemns us for

[3] Cf. Rom 2:14–16.

having done evil, it offers hope of repentance and forgiveness, like a map that tells you of the right road as well as the wrong ones. "If man commits evil, the just judgment of conscience can remain within him as the witness to the universal truth of the good, at the same time as the evil of his particular choice. The verdict of the judgment of conscience remains a pledge of hope and mercy" (CCC 1781). Conscience, like God, hates sins but loves sinners.

f. Conscience is not a passive "given" but can be trained, like a muscle. It can also atrophy, like a muscle unused. Its first and most important exercise is honest listening. "It is important for every person to be sufficiently present to himself in order to hear and follow the voice of his conscience" (CCC 1779).

For the voice of conscience speaks softly. It respects our freedom and requires an effort of free will on our part to hear it. The voice of God usually speaks this way: in a "still, small voice" (see 1 Kings 19:12). We must train ourselves to hear it.

The two most important keys to hearing it are these:

a. We must honestly and passionately will to hear it, to know the truth.

b. We must be alone with ourselves and God to hear this gentle voice. It can easily be drowned out by external noise. "This requirement of interiority" [an inner life] "is all the more necessary as life often distracts us from any reflection, self-examination or introspection" (CCC 1779), especially in our complex, fast-paced, materialistic modern society. Kierkegaard's "prescription for all the ills of the modern world" was: "First, create silence."

Chapter 4

Virtues and Vices

1. The meaning of virtue

"Virtue" is a very simple concept to define. As vice is a bad habit, so virtue is a good habit. "A virtue is an habitual and firm disposition to do the good" (CCC 1803). Virtues and vices form a person's "character".

2. The importance of virtue

a. Without personal virtue, we will do good only sporadically. The main source of a good and happy life—for the human race, for each nation and community, and for each family—is the personal virtue of each individual. No system or set of laws, however perfect, can work for good without virtuous individuals. A Chinese parable says: "When the wrong man uses the right means, the right means work in the wrong way." Bad bricks, however well arranged, do not make a good building. Nothing can improve the world more than saints.

b. Virtues are forever. They are "marks on the soul", deeper and more permanent than any external deeds, for souls are immortal.

c. Virtues improve not just what you *do* but what you are. And every lover knows that the object of love is not just deeds but persons. Your boss may care more about what you do (your work) than about what you are (your character), but the opposite is true for those who love you. And God is not our boss but our loving Father.

3. The goal of virtue

"Why should I be good?" The question is simple and profound and requires a simple and profound answer.

Personal virtue is the key to improving the world, finding happiness, and helping other people to be good and happy, too; yet the ultimate end of virtue is even greater than these great goals: " 'The goal of a virtuous life is to become like God' [1] " (CCC 1803).

No secular answer to the question of the goal of virtue can rival this one.

4. The four cardinal virtues

From ancient times (Plato, Aristotle) and in various cultures (Hindu, Confucian, Jewish, Islamic) four virtues have traditionally been recognized as the indispensable foundation of all the others, as the "hinges" (*cardines*, in Latin, thus "cardinal") on which all others turn. "Four virtues play a pivotal role and accordingly are called 'cardinal'; all the others are grouped around them. They are: prudence" [or wisdom], "justice" [or fairness], "fortitude" [or courage], "and temperance" [or self-control] (CCC 1805). They are mentioned in Scripture by name (Wis 8:7) and "are praised under other names in many passages of Scripture" (CCC 1805).

5. Prudence

Prudence "is not to be confused with timidity or fear" (CCC 1806). Perhaps "practical moral wisdom" is a clearer term for this virtue today. Prudence is "the virtue that disposes practical reason" [the mind thinking about what should be done] "to discern our true good in every circumstance and

[1] St. Gregory of Nyssa, *De beatitudinibus*, 1: PG 44, 1200D.

to choose the right means of achieving it. . . . With the help of this virtue we apply moral principles to particular cases" (CCC 1806).

6. Justice

"*Justice* is the moral virtue that consists in the constant and firm will to give their due to God and neighbor. Justice toward God is called the 'virtue of religion' " [or 'piety']. "Justice toward men disposes one to respect the rights of each and to establish in human relationships . . . harmony" (CCC 1807).

Justice gives to each "what is due", or "what is right", or "just desserts". This logical and almost mathematical aspect of justice, focusing on equality and rights for individuals, is balanced and complemented by a more intuitive and holistic aspect that aims at harmony and right relationships. Typically, men are especially sensitive to the first aspect, and women to the second. Complete justice requires both.

Justice transforms power and is transformed by love.

Power is meant to serve justice—might should serve right—and justice is meant to serve love.

We are born first knowing power and weakness, like the animals. As children, we learn a sense of justice, from our innate conscience and from parents and teachers. As adults, we realize that justice, though necessary, is not sufficient; that our only hope is love and mercy and forgiveness—from God and from each other.

Wars will not cease and peace will not come, to nations or to families or to individuals, without justice. But neither will lasting peace come through justice alone.

7. Fortitude

"*Fortitude* is the moral virtue that ensures firmness in difficulties and constancy in the pursuit of the good. It strengthens the resolve to resist temptations and to overcome obstacles in the moral life. The virtue of fortitude enables one to conquer fear, even fear of death, and to face trials and persecutions. It disposes one even to renounce and sacrifice his life in defense of a just cause" (CCC 1808).

Of all the virtues this is perhaps the one most conspicuously lacking in the lives of most people today in technologically developed and relatively pain-free modern societies. Alexander Solzhenitsyn gave a very challenging Harvard Commencement Address in 1978 on this subject.

Fortitude is a necessary ingredient in all virtues, for no virtue "happens", but must be fought for.

8. Temperance

"*Temperance* is the moral virtue that moderates the attraction of pleasures" (CCC 1809), as fortitude moderates the fear of pains. (Thus it is also called "moderation".) Without it we do not rise above the level of animals, who live by their instincts, desires, and fears, especially the instinct to seek pleasure and flee pain. Temperance "provides balance" [that is, moderation: not too little and not too much] "in the use of created goods. It ensures the will's mastery over instincts" [thus it is also called "self-control"] "and keeps desires within the limits of what is honorable" (CCC 1809).

Our instinctive desire for pleasure and fear of pain is the matter, or raw material, to be formed and controlled by all four cardinal virtues. Prudence provides the map, fortitude tames the fears, temperance tames the appetites, and justice regulates the resulting activities.

All four cardinal virtues have deeper and wider meanings than their names suggest in current usage. Prudence is not "playing it safe", justice is not simply punishment, fortitude is not bull-headedness, and temperance is not simply sobriety.

9. The three theological virtues

The four cardinal virtues are natural. That is, (a) they are known by natural human reason; (b) their origin is human nature; and (c) their goal is the perfecting of human character and life. They are also (a) known more perfectly by divine revelation, (b) aided and increased by divine grace, and (c) incorporated into the higher goal of union with God (see section 3 in this chapter).

The three theological virtues, on the other hand, are supernatural, for they are (a) revealed by God and known by faith, (b) "infused by God into the souls of the faithful" (CCC 1813), and (c) their good is our participation in the divine nature.

They are called "theological" because they have God as their object. "Faith, hope, and love" mean faith in God, hope in God, and love of God (and of neighbor for God's sake).

10. The relation between the natural and the supernatural virtues

The three theological virtues are not an "extra", a second story added onto the natural virtues. "The theological virtues are the foundation of Christian moral activity; they animate it and give it its special character" (CCC 1813) as the soul animates the body. The Christian is prudent, just, courageous, and temperate out of faith in God, hope in God, and love of God.

11. Faith

"Faith is the theological virtue by which we believe in God and believe all that he has said and revealed to us, and that Holy Church proposes for our belief, because he is truth itself" (CCC 1814).

The proximate, or immediate, object of faith is all the truths God has revealed. The ultimate object of faith is the person of God himself (see part 1, chapter 2).

Faith is living and not dead only when it " 'work[s] through charity' [Rom 1:17; Gal 5:6]" (CCC 1814). "Faith apart from works is dead" (Jas 2:26). Faith, hope, and charity are three parts of the same living organism; the root, stem, and flower of the same living plant.

12. Hope

"Hope is the theological virtue by which we desire the kingdom of heaven and eternal life as our happiness, placing our trust in Christ's promises and relying not on our own strength, but on the help of the grace of the Holy Spirit" (CCC 1817). "The virtue of hope responds to the aspiration to happiness which God has placed in the heart of every man" (CCC 1818).

Hope is not merely our natural desire for happiness; everyone has that. Like faith, hope is our freely chosen affirmative response to a divine revelation: in the case of hope, our response to divinely revealed *promises*. Hope is faith directed to the future.

Hope is the strongest source of fortitude. If you trust God's promises of the incomparable happiness of heaven, you can give up any earthly good or endure any earthly deprivation for that. "Man can endure almost any how if only he has a why", wrote Viktor Frankl from the Auschwitz death camp (*Man's Search for Meaning*). A "why" is a hope, a goal, a meaning and purpose to your life.

13. Love

What word shall we use to translate *agapē* in the New Testament? It is a crucial point, for this is the most indispensable of all virtues (1 Cor 1:1–3), the greatest of all the virtues (1 Cor 13:13), the greatest of the commandments (Mt 22:36–37), and the very nature of God (1 Jn 4:16), of ultimate reality.

"Love" is too broad a word, for it usually connotes the natural loves—of sex, food, beauty, comfort, friends, and so on. "Charity", the old word for *agapē*, is now too narrow, for it usually connotes only giving money to good causes. We shall use both words, to correct the defects in each.

"Charity is the theological virtue by which we love God above all things for his own sake" [because he is worthy of such love], "and our neighbor as ourselves for the love of God" (CCC 1822).

Charity is not a feeling or emotion, but a choosing by the will and an obeying. Here is how it was defined by Christ, the perfect incarnation of charity and the supreme authority on the subject: "He who has my commandments and keeps them, he it is who loves me" (Jn 14:21).

Christ commands charity to everyone, even our enemies: "You have heard that it was said, 'You shall love your neighbor and hate your enemy.' But I say to you, Love your enemies and pray for those who persecute you, so that you may be sons of your Father who is in heaven; for he makes his sun rise on the evil and on the good, and sends rain on the just and on the unjust" (Mt 5:43–45). "Christ died out of love for us while we were still 'enemies' [Rom 5:10]. The Lord asks us to love as he does" (CCC 1825).

Charity is freeing. "The practice of the moral life animated by charity gives to the Christian the spiritual freedom of the children of God. He no longer stands before God as a slave, in servile fear, or as a mercenary looking for wages, but as a son responding to the love of him who 'first loved us' [cf. 1 Jn 4:19]" (CCC 1828). "Perfect love casts out fear" (1 Jn 4:18). Indeed, "the fear of the LORD is the beginning of wisdom" (Prov 9:10). But it is not the end. Love is.

14. The seven gifts of the Holy Spirit

Seven virtues are traditionally listed as the "gifts of the Holy Spirit". "The seven *gifts* of the Holy Spirit are wisdom, understanding, counsel, fortitude, knowledge, piety, and fear of the Lord [cf. Isa 11:1–2]" (CCC 1831).

15. The twelve fruits of the Holy Spirit

"The *fruits* of the Spirit are perfections that the Holy Spirit forms in us as the first fruits of eternal glory. The tradition of the Church lists twelve of them: 'charity, joy, peace, patience, kindness, goodness, generosity, gentleness, faithfulness, modesty, self-control, chastity' [Gal 5:22–23 (Vulg.)]" (CCC 1832).

16. The Beatitudes

"The Beatitudes are at the heart of Jesus' preaching" (CCC 1716). "The Beatitudes depict the countenance" [face, character] "of Jesus Christ and portray his charity. They express the vocation of the faithful" (CCC 1717) to be like Christ. They all appeal to the theological virtue of hope by including promises of rewards to be fully given in the next life.

They are:

"Blessed are the poor in spirit, for theirs is the kingdom of heaven.

"Blessed are those who mourn, for they shall be comforted.

"Blessed are the meek, for they shall inherit the earth.

"Blessed are those who hunger and thirst for righteousness, for they shall be satisfied.

"Blessed are the merciful, for they shall obtain mercy.

"Blessed are the pure in heart, for they shall see God.

"Blessed are the peacemakers, for they shall be called sons of God.

"Blessed are those who are persecuted for righteousness' sake, for theirs is the kingdom of heaven.

"Blessed are you when men revile you and persecute you and utter all kinds of evil against you falsely on my account. Rejoice and be glad, for your reward is great in heaven" (Mt 5:3-12).

17. Vices

The four cardinal virtues (prudence, justice, fortitude, and temperance) have opposite vices: folly, injustice, cowardice, and intemperance.

The three theological virtues have even more serious opposite vices—more serious because they directly imperil our eternal salvation.

a. The knowing and deliberate repudiation of faith is *apostasy*.

b. The deliberate refusal of hope is *despair*. This is not to be confused with feelings like pessimism or depression, for two reasons. First, no mere feeling in itself is virtuous or vicious; only the will's free consent to a feeling makes it morally good or evil. Second, despair is not psychological but theological. That is, just as the theological virtues have God as their object—they are three ways of saying Yes to God—so their opposites are three ways of saying No to God.

Presumption is the opposite extreme from despair, and an equally serious sin against hope. "There are two kinds of *presumption*. Either man presumes upon his own capacities (hoping to save himself without help from on high), or he presumes upon God's almighty power or his mercy (hoping to obtain his forgiveness without conversion)" (CCC 2092).

c. The deliberate refusal of charity includes indifference, ingratitude, lukewarmness, spiritual sloth, and hate. Hate wills evil and harm to another and refuses to forgive. Christ clearly tells us that if we do not forgive, we cannot be forgiven (Mt 6:14–15).

18. Sin

Sin is any deliberate thought, word, or deed contrary to God's law. Sin is disobedience to God's law, thus God's will, thus God himself. It is "a revolt against God" (CCC 1850). Sin is the very worst thing there is, since it is the contrary of God, the very best thing there is.

"Sin" means more than "evil" or "vice". It is a specifically religious term. It means evil *in its relation to God*. It means damaging or breaking the relationship with God, the spiritual marriage covenant.

19. Kinds of sin

"Sins can be distinguished" [a] "according to their objects, as can every human act;" [b] "or according to the virtues they oppose, by excess or defect;" [c] "or according to the commandments they violate." [d] "They can also be classed according to whether they concern God, neighbor, or oneself;" [e] "they can be divided into spiritual and carnal sins;" [f] "or again as sins in thought, word, deed, or omission" (CCC 1853).

The most important distinction is between mortal and venial sins (section 20 below).

20. Mortal and venial sin

"The distinction between mortal and venial sin, already evident in Scripture [cf. 1 Jn 5:16–17], became part of the tradition of the Church. It is corroborated by human experience" (CCC 1854).

Venial sin damages the relationship with God; mortal sin destroys it. Venial sin is like a fight between spouses; mortal sin is like a divorce. To die in a state of mortal sin is to lose heaven forever. For there is no more time for repentance and conversion after death. To die with venial sins on the soul is to need purgatory to purify the soul before heaven. To die with neither kind of sin or their consequences in the soul is to merit heaven without the need for purgatory.

21. The three conditions for mortal sin

There are three conditions necessary for mortal sin. All must be present for the sin to be mortal; if any one is missing, the sin is venial.

They are: "grave matter", "full knowledge", and "full consent".

First, the sin must be a grave matter, an act in itself seriously sinful, like adultery, grand larceny, blasphemy, or murder (including the murder of unborn children or old people). The objective act itself must be seriously (gravely) sinful.

Second, there must be full knowledge that the act is a serious sin.

Third, there must be full consent of the will. Sins of weakness, committed reluctantly, in spite of a sincere effort to avoid them, are not mortal sins.

Fear, addiction, and compulsion diminish personal freedom and therefore responsibility for evil acts, but they do not wholly remove it. "The promptings of feelings and passions can also diminish the voluntary and free character of the offense, as can external pressures or pathological disorders" (CCC 1860)—as is probably the case in many suicides.

The first of the three conditions for mortal sin is public, objective, and the same for everyone; it is easy to tell whether a sin is a serious sin, or grave matter, since "*grave matter* is specified by the Ten Commandments" (CCC 1858). But the other two conditions are subjective, psychological, personal conditions. They are much harder to discern, even in oneself, much less in others. Therefore although we can define and judge what mortal sin is in itself, we cannot judge who is in the state of mortal sin and should not try to (see Mt 7:7). "[A]lthough we can judge that an act is in itself a grave offense, we must entrust judgment of persons to the justice and mercy of God" (CCC 1861), for we do not know others' deepest minds, hearts, and motives.

22. Why venial sins are serious

Venial sins are not light. All sins are serious.

The *Catechism* (CCC 1863) gives three specific reasons why venial sins are serious:

a. "Venial sin weakens charity . . .", that is, weakens the life and grace of God in us.

b. "[I]t merits temporal punishment . . ." (in purgatory).

c. Worst of all, "[d]eliberate and unrepented venial sin disposes us little by little to commit mortal sin."

" 'While he is in the flesh, man cannot help but have at least some light sins. But do not despise these sins which we call "light". . . . A number of light objects makes a great mass; a number of drops fills a river; a number of grains makes a heap. What then is our hope? Above all, confession' [2] " (CCC 1863). For sacramental confession is not just an X ray; it is an operation: it really removes the cancer of sin (see part 1, chapter 8, and part 3, chapter 5).

23. The seven deadly sins

Tradition highlights seven sins as especially dangerous, or "deadly". They are the soul-deadening opposites to the soul-enlivening virtues commended in the Beatitudes:

[2] St. Augustine, *In ep. Jo.* 1, 6: PL 35, 1982.

Pride is self-assertion and selfishness (the opposite of poverty of spirit, which is humility and selflessness).

Avarice is greed, the selfish reach to grab and keep for oneself (the opposite of mercy, which is the reach to give, to share with others, even the undeserving).

Envy resents another's happiness (the opposite of mourning, which shares another's unhappiness).

Wrath wills harm and destruction (the opposite of meekness, which refuses to harm, and peacemaking, which prevents destruction).

Sloth refuses to exert the will toward the good even when it is present (the opposite of hunger and thirst for righteousness, which is the passionate desire for good even when it is absent).

Lust dissipates and divides the soul, desiring every attractive body (the opposite of purity of heart, which centers and unifies the soul, desiring the one God alone).

Gluttony wants to consume an inordinate amount of worldly goods (the opposite of being persecuted, which is to be deprived of even ordinate necessities).

24. Sin and grace

The saints understand both sin and grace most clearly. For sanctity clarifies our vision, while sin clouds it. The saints are always clearer than anyone else about four facts about human sin and divine grace:

a. they themselves are sinners;

b. great harm is done by all sins to human souls, to their true happiness, both in time and in eternity (thus the saints often pity the murderer more than the murdered);

c. divine mercy and forgiveness are inexhuastible ("where sin increased, grace abounded all the more"—Rom 5:20);

d. we need to repent and confess in order to receive this forgiveness.

"To receive his mercy, we must admit our faults" [repent and confess] (CCC 1847). Thus the denial of the very existence of sin ("I'm OK, you're OK") imperils our very salvation, as living in denial of a life-threatening disease imperils our life. God offers free grace and mercy, like a doctor offering a free operation. "But to do its work grace must uncover sin" (CCC 1848).

This is a very unpopular and misunderstood message to our modern "therapeutic" culture of self-esteem. But it is far better to experience undeserved rejection from a million ignorant men than deserved rejection from the one all-knowing God.

Chapter 5

THE FIRST THREE COMMANDMENTS:
DUTIES TO GOD

1. What are the Ten Commandments?

Talking about them is pointless if we do not know them. And few people can list all ten. For many generations, most Christians knew them from memory. Today, it is illegal in America even to display them in public schools. So we had better begin by simply listing them, word for word, as the Bible records them in Exodus 20:1–17:

God spoke all these words, saying:

"I am the LORD your God, who brought you out of the land of Egypt, out of the house of bondage.

"You shall have no other gods before me.

"You shall not make for yourself a graven image, or any likeness of anything that is in heaven above, or that is in the earth beneath, or that is in the water under the earth; you shall not bow down to them or serve them; for I the LORD your God am a jealous God, visiting the iniquity of the fathers upon the children to the third and the fourth generation of those who hate me, but showing steadfast love to thousands of those who love me and keep my commandments.

"You shall not take the name of the LORD your God in vain; for the LORD will not hold him guiltless who takes his name in vain.

"Remember the sabbath day, to keep it holy. Six days you shall labor, and do all your work; but the seventh day is a sabbath to the LORD your God; in it you shall not do any work, you, or your son, or your daughter, your manservant, or your maidservant, or your cattle, or the sojourner who is within your gates; for in six days the LORD made heaven and earth, the sea, and all that is in them, and rested the seventh day; therefore the LORD blessed the sabbath day and hallowed it.

"Honor your father and your mother, that your days may be long in the land which the LORD your God gives you.

"You shall not kill.

"You shall not commit adultery.

"You shall not steal.

"You shall not bear false witness against your neighbor.

"You shall not covet your neighbor's house; you shall not covet your neighbor's wife, or his manservant, or his maidservant, or his ox, or his ass, or anything that is your neighbor's."

2. The numbering of the Commandments

"The division and numbering of the Commandments have varied in the course of history. The present catechism follows the division of the Commandments established by St. Augustine, which has become traditional in the Catholic Church. It is also that of the Lutheran confessions. The Greek Fathers worked out a slightly different division, which is found in the Orthodox Churches and Reformed communities" (CCC 2066).

Catholics distinguish "You shall not covet your neighbor's wife", as the ninth commandment, which forbids lust, from "You shall not covet your neighbor's goods", as the tenth, which forbids greed. Reformed Protestants distinguish "You shall have no other gods before me", as the first commandment, from "You shall not make any graven images", as the second. The numbering makes no difference to the substance; all Christians accept all the words in Exodus 20:1–17.

3. The Ten Commandments and Christ

What did Christ do with the Commandments?

a. Christ acknowledged the Commandments (Mt 5:17; 19:16–21).

b. "He unfolded all the demands of the Commandments. 'You have heard that it was said to the men of old, "You shall not kill." . . . But I say to you that every one who is angry with his brother shall be liable to judgment' [Mt 5:21–22]" (CCC 2054).

c. He exceeded the Commandments. He demanded more, not less: a "righteousness [which] exceeds that of the scribes and Pharisees" (Mt 5:20; see also CCC 2054).

d. He summarized the Commandments and showed their unity as the Law of Love: "You shall love the Lord your God with all your heart, and with all your soul, and with all your mind. This is the greatest and first commandment. And a second is like it: You shall love your neighbor as yourself. On these two commandments hang all the Law and the prophets" [1] (see also CCC 2055).

Love does not worship idols; love keeps God's sabbath; love honors parents; love does not kill, steal, adulterate, lie, or covet. "The Ten Commandments state what is required in the love of God and love of neighbor. The first three concern love of God, and the other seven love of neighbor" (CCC 2067).

e. He fulfilled the Commandments by obeying them perfectly.

f. He freed us from "the curse of the law" (Gal 3:13) and its punishment by taking that curse on himself on the Cross.

g. He freed us from the obligation of keeping the burdensome Jewish law (Torah) with its 613 distinct regulations. But not from the obligation to keep the Ten Commandments. "The Council of Trent teaches that the Ten Commandments are obligatory for Christians and that the justified man is still bound to keep them" [2] (CCC 2068). "They are fundamentally immutable, and they oblige always and everywhere. No one can dispense from them" (CCC 2072).

---

[1] Mt 22:37–40; cf. Deut 6:5; Lev 19:18.
[2] Cf. DS 1569–70.

h. However, these Commandments are no longer an impossible burden now, since Christ, by giving us the Holy Spirit, gave us the power to keep them, as well as the motive and the desire to keep them: out of free love, not servile fear. By his Spirit, the Law of God becomes a law of our own hearts.

4. The origin of the Commandments

The Commandments are to the moral order what the creation story in Genesis 1 is to the natural order. They are God's order conquering chaos. They are not man's ideas about God, but God's ideas about man. "They were written 'with the finger of God' [Ex 31:18; Deut 5:22], unlike the other commandments written by Moses" [cf. Deut 31:9, 24] (CCC 2056).

5. The end of the Commandments: Life and freedom

"The Decalogue is a path of life" (CCC 2057; see also Deut 30 and Ps 1).

It is also the path to freedom. The Commandments do not limit freedom; they protect freedom, as the fence around the city schoolyard does not imprison the children playing there but protects them from life-threatening dangers (cars, muggers) and frees them to play and enjoy their games within that fence.

"This liberating power of the Decalogue appears, for example, in the commandment about the sabbath rest. . . . '[Y]ou were a servant in the land of Egypt, and the LORD your God brought you out' [Deut 5:15]" (CCC 2057). Resting one day each week frees us from perpetual labor. It is slaves who have no "free time".

6. The Commandments, like the Creeds, summarize our response to God's initiative

Just as faith, whose content is summarized by the Creeds, is essentially a response to a given revelation of God, not a state or feeling we work up in ourselves, the same is true of morality, whose content is summarized in the Commandments. "Moral existence is a *response* to the Lord's loving initiative" (CCC 2062), not a lifestyle we invent.

7. The Ten Commandments and the natural law

"The Ten Commandments belong to God's revelation" (CCC 2070). Thus they are "divine law". "At the same time they teach us the true humanity of man. They bring to light the essential duties, and therefore, indirectly, the fundamental rights inherent in the nature of the human person. . . ." [They are] "a privileged expression of the natural law: 'From the beginning, God had implanted in the heart of man the precepts of the natural law. Then he was content to remind him of them. This was the Decalogue' [3] " (CCC 2070). (The word decalogue comes from *Deca-logos*, meaning "ten laws" or Ten Commandments.) Although they are knowable by natural reason, and all societies have some knowledge of them, that knowledge is clouded and imperfect. " 'A full explanation of the commandments of the Decalogue became necessary in the state of sin because the light of reason was obscured and the will had gone astray' [4] " (CCC 2071).

8. The unity of the Ten Commandments

The Ten Commandments are one law, not ten laws. They are one thing: the will of the one God. Therefore "whoever keeps the whole law but fails in one point has become guilty of all of it. For he who said, 'Do not commit adultery,' said also, 'Do not kill.' If you do not commit adultery but do kill, you have become a transgressor of the law." "To transgress one command-ment is to infringe all the others [cf. Jas 2:10–11]. One cannot honor another person without blessing God his Creator. One cannot adore God without loving all men, his creatures. The Decalogue brings man's religious and social life into unity" (CCC 2069).

9. Negative and positive sides to the Commandments

There is a negative and a positive side to all the Commandments. The fact that their original formulation is usually negative ("You shall *not* . . .") does not mean they are "negative" in the sense of being repressive, joyless, or pes-simistic. This is so for three reasons:

a. Each negation is "the other side of the coin" of a positive command; for example, "no idolatry" means "worship God"; "do not kill" means "respect life"; and No to adultery means Yes to unadulterated love.

b. Having just a limited number of negative commandments frees us to do an infinite number of positive things within these "foul lines".

c. The negative commandments free us from negative things, protect us from threats to our positive happiness.

---

[3] St. Irenaeus, *Adv. haeres.* 4, 15, 1: PG 7/1, 1012.
[4] St. Bonaventure, *Comm. sent.* 4, 37, 1, 3.

10. The priority of the first commandment

All sins are sins against the first commandment; the first commandment contains the whole of the Decalogue. For all sin serves some other god, obeys another commander: the world or the flesh or the devil. So if we obeyed only this one commandment perfectly, we would need nothing more. St. Augustine says, "Love God and then do what you will." For if you give your whole heart and will and love to God, then what you will will be all that God wills.

How liberatingly simple is the moral life of the Christian (or the Jew or the Muslim): only one God, therefore one ultimate object of love and obedience.

11. The positive side of the first commandment

The negative side of the first commandment is: "You shall have no other gods before me" (Ex 20:3). The positive side is: "You shall worship the Lord your God" (Mt 4:10).

What is here commanded is what Scripture calls the "fear" of the Lord (Deut 6:13). This is not the craven, servile fear of something evil, but the awe and adoration of something infinitely good.

This is positive, for "[t]he worship of the one God sets man free from turning in on himself, from the slavery of sin and the idolatry of the world" (CCC 2097).

12. Worship includes faith, hope, and charity

" 'The first commandment embraces faith, hope, and charity' [5] " (CCC 2086). The reasons for all three are the character of God himself.

a. Faith: " 'When we say "God" we confess a constant, unchangeable being, always the same, faithful and just, without any evil. It follows that we must necessarily accept his words and have complete faith in him and acknowledge his authority' [6] " (CCC 2086).

b. Hope: " 'He is almighty, merciful, and infinitely beneficent. . . . Who could not place all hope in him?' [7] " (CCC 2086).

c. Charity: " 'Who could not love him when contemplating the treasures of goodness and love he has poured out on us? Hence the formula God employs in the Scripture at the beginning and end of his commandments: "I am the LORD" ' [8] " (CCC 2086).

[5] Roman Catechism 3, 2, 4
[6] Roman Catechism 3, 2, 4
[7] Roman Catechism 3, 2, 4
[8] Roman Catechism 3, 2, 4

13. Sins against faith

There are various sins against faith.

" '*Heresy* is the obstinate post-baptismal denial of some truth which must be believed with divine and catholic faith' " [as supernaturally revealed for all]. . . . " '[A]*postasy* is the total repudiation of the Christian faith. . . . [S]*chism* is the refusal of submission to the Roman Pontiff' " [9] (CCC 2089).

14. Sins against hope

There are two opposite sins against hope: despair and presumption.

"By *despair*, man ceases to hope for his personal salvation from God . . . or for the forgiveness of his sins" (CCC 2091).

As indicated in Chapter 4, *presumption* can take two forms. One might presume upon his own abilities, or he might presume upon God's power or mercy (see CCC 2092).

15. Sins against charity

"One can sin against God's love in various ways:
 "—*indifference* . . .
 "—*ingratitude* . . .
 "—*lukewarmness* . . .
 "—*acedia* or spiritual sloth goes so far as to refuse the joy that comes from God . . .
 "—*hatred of God* . . . from pride" (CCC 2094).

16. The social aspect of the first commandment

"The duty of offering God genuine worship concerns man both individually and socially" (CCC 2105). Freedom of religion, or religious liberty, is a fundamental social right. This freedom "means that . . . nobody is forced to act against his convictions, nor is anyone to be restrained from acting in accordance with his conscience in religious matters in private or public, alone or in associations with others" (*DH* 1).

As the *Catechism* points out, this applies "within due limits" (CCC 2106; *DH* 2 § 1). These "due limits" may vary from one society to another. But even "[i]f because of the circumstances of a particular people special civil recognition is given to one religious community in the constitutional organ-

---

[9] CIC, can. 751: emphasis added.

ization of a State, the right of all citizens and religious communities to religious freedom must be recognized and respected as well" (*DH* 6).

17. The negative side of the first commandment

"You shall have no other gods before me" means that we must worship and adore God alone because God *is* alone. Idolatry—worship of anything except God—is forbidden by the nature of reality. "Idolatry consists in divinizing what is not God. Man commits idolatry whenever he honors and reveres a creature in place of God, ... whether this be gods" [pagan polytheism, worshipping imaginary gods] "or demons (for example, satanism), power, pleasure, race, ancestors, the state, money, etc." (CCC 2113).

Treating God as a creature is utterly contrary to reality. So is treating any creature as God.

18. How the prohibition against idolatry is positive and freeing

Idolatry enslaves us. That is why avoiding it frees us.

This can be explained in a number of ways.

a. A first way comes from the Psalms, which point out that you become like whatever you worship; therefore, just as you become more godly by worshipping God, you become more like a subhuman thing by worshipping it. The idols of wood and stone that ancient pagans worshipped, or the idols of money, power, or pleasure that modern idolaters worship, all work the same "black magic" on the soul: these idols are "the work of men's hands. They have mouths, but do not speak; eyes, but do not see. They have ears, but do not hear. . . . Those who make them are like them; so are all who trust in them" (Ps 115:4–8). "These empty idols make their worshippers empty" (CCC 2112).

To worship the God of life is to become more alive; to worship a dead idol is to become more dead.

b. A second way to explain how avoiding idolatry frees us is this: since we become more like whatever we worship, we attain our oneness, our integration of personality, by adoring the one Creator rather than the many creatures. We become one great person by having one great goal, one great love. As the *Catechism* explains it, "[h]uman life finds its unity in the adoration of the one God. The commandment to worship the Lord alone integrates man and saves him from an endless disintegration" (CCC 2114). The extreme form of this disintegration can be seen in the demon-possessed man who, when Christ asked his name (the word-symbol for one's individual self), replied, "My name is Legion; for we are many" (Mk 5:9).

c. If we are absolute about God the Absolute, we are free from absolutizing anything else. Reality offers only one absolute good: God. Everything is good if it leads to God or comes from God as his will and evil if it leads away from God or his will. Obeying "the first and greatest commandment" gives us a meaning, point, goal, and direction in life and a liberating simplicity. It is like a single lighthouse in a confusing storm.

19. Specific sins against the first commandment

a. "*Superstition* is the deviation of religious feeling and of the practices this feeling imposes . . . e.g., when one attributes an importance in some way magical to certain practices otherwise lawful or necessary. To attribute the efficacy of prayers or of sacramental signs to their mere external performance, apart from the interior dispositions that they demand, is to fall into superstition" [cf. Mt 23:16–22] (CCC 2111, italics added).

b. "The first commandment condemns *polytheism*" [worship of many gods] (CCC 2112).

c. "All forms of *divination* are to be rejected: recourse to Satan or demons, conjuring up the dead or other practices falsely supposed to 'unveil' the future [cf. Deut 18:10; Jer 29:8]. Consulting horoscopes, astrology, palm reading, interpretation of omens and lots, . . . clairvoyance, and recourse to mediums all conceal a desire for power over time, history, and, in the last analysis, other human beings, as well as a wish to conciliate hidden powers. They contradict the honor, respect, and loving fear that we owe to God alone" (CCC 2116).

d. "All practices of *magic* or *sorcery*, by which one attempts to tame occult powers, so as to place them at one's service and have a supernatural power over others . . . are gravely contrary to the virtue of religion" (CCC 2117).

e. "*Tempting God* consists in putting his goodness and almighty power to the test" (CCC 2119).

f. "*Sacrilege* consists in profaning or treating unworthily the sacraments and other liturgical actions, as well as persons, things, or places consecrated to God. Sacrilege is a grave sin especially when committed against the Eucharist, for in this sacrament the true Body of Christ is made substantially present for us" [10] (CCC 2120).

g. "*Simony* is defined as the buying or selling of spiritual things [cf. Acts 8:9–24]. To Simon the magician, who wanted to buy the spiritual power he saw at work in the apostles, St. Peter responded: 'Your silver perish with you, because you thought you could obtain God's gift with money!' [Acts 8:20]" (CCC 2121).

---

[10] Cf. CIC, cann. 1367; 1376.

h. "Since it rejects or denies the existence of God, atheism is a sin against the virtue of religion [cf. Rom 1:18]. The imputability" [blameworthiness] "of this offense can be significantly diminished in virtue of the intentions and the circumstances. 'Believers can have more than a little to do with the rise of atheism. To the extent that they are careless about their . . . faith, . . . they must be said to conceal rather than to reveal the true nature of God and religion' [GS 19 § 3]" (CCC 2125).

i. "Agnosticism . . . makes no judgment about God's existence, declaring it impossible to . . . affirm or deny" (CCC 2127). "Agnosticism can sometimes include a certain search for God, but it can equally express indifferentism, a flight from the ultimate question of existence. . . . Agnosticism is all too often equivalent to practical atheism" (CCC 2128).

20. Images

"You shall not make for yourself a graven image" (Ex 20:4). "The divine injunction included the prohibition of every representation of God by the hand of man" (CCC 2129).

"Nevertheless, already in the Old Testament, God ordained or permitted the making of images that pointed symbolically toward salvation by the incarnate Word: so it was with the bronze serpent, the ark of the covenant, and the cherubim" [11] (CCC 2130).

"Basing itself on the mystery of the incarnate Word, the seventh ecumenical council at Nicaea (787) justified against the iconoclasts" [image-smashers] "the veneration of icons" [sacred images] "—of Christ, but also of the Mother of God, the angels, and all the saints. By becoming incarnate, the Son of God introduced a new 'economy' of images" (CCC 2131).

Like Jews and Muslims, Christians know the Divine Nature is purely spiritual and cannot be pictured, and they accept the first commandment's prohibition of the attempt. But unlike Jews and Muslims, Christians know that God became man. The primary "image" of God is Christ.

Protestants often accuse Catholics of "worshipping" images. This is a twofold misunderstanding of how Catholics use images.

First, Catholics give religious images veneration, or honor, not adoration, or worship. "The honor paid to sacred images is a 'respectful veneration,' not the adoration due to God alone" (CCC 2132).

Second, this honor is directed not at the image but *along* the image, as attention is directed along a pointing finger to the reality it points to. " 'Religious worship is not directed to images in themselves. . . . The movement

[11] Cf. Num 21:4–9; Wis 16:5–14; Jn 3:14–15; Ex 25:10–22; 1 Kings 6:23–28; 7:23–26.

toward the image does not terminate in it as image, but tends toward that whose image it is' [12] " (CCC 2132).

21. The second commandment

The second commandment, "You shall not take the name of the LORD your God in vain", is a corollary of the first. "Respect for his name is an expression of the respect owed to the mystery of God himself" (CCC 2144). The awe proper to God should "spill over" to his name.

People today often have a problem with this idea because they simply do not understand this fundamental religious feeling of "the sense of the holy" at all. Others do not see how it can be directed toward a name.

With regard to the first problem, the *Catechism* explains that "[t]he *sense of the sacred* is part of the virtue of religion: . . . 'feelings of fear and awe . . . are the class of feelings we *should* have—yes, have to an intense degree—if we literally had the sight of Almighty God; therefore they are the class of feelings which we shall have, *if* we realize His presence' [13] " (CCC 2144). Again, morality is a conformity to reality. (The next section deals with the second problem, the importance of names.)

22. What's in a name?

In most ancient cultures, even a human name is sacred, for a person is sacred, and a person's name is a symbol for the person, as a nation's flag is a symbol for the nation. The loss of the sense of the sacredness of names is connected with the loss of the sense of the sacredness of persons today.

But of all names, one is supremely sacred. "Among all the words of Revelation, there is one which is unique: the revealed name of God" (CCC 2143) given to Moses at the burning bush (Ex 3:14): "I AM" (JHWH). This name asserts God's (a) uniqueness, (b) infinite and indefinable mystery, and (c) ever-present reality.

a. God is not one of many gods; he is "I", the only one. When you say "I", you mean only one person, no other.

b. God does not limit himself to being *this or that*, he is just "I AM."

c. And God has no dead past ("was") or unborn future ("will be"), just living present ("AM").

No Jew will ever try to pronounce this divine name, for to utter the first-person pronoun, the name "I" (JHWH), is to claim to bear it, to be

---

[12] St. Thomas Aquinas, *STh* II-II, 81, 3 *ad* 3.

[13] John Henry Cardinal Newman, *Parochial and Plain Sermons* V, 2 (London: Longmans, Green and Co., 1907) 21–22.

it. This is why, when Jesus uttered it (Jn 8:58), the Jews who did not believe in him tried to stone him to death, for that was the penalty for blasphemy in Mosaic law.

However, so that man may speak to him and about him, God lets himself be named with many other names, not only this unutterable one. All these names are holy and come under the second commandment.

23. The positive meaning of the second commandment

"The faithful should bear witness to the Lord's name by confessing the faith" [cf. Mt 10:32; 1 Tim 6:12] (CCC 2145). Catholics should be as zealous as any of the sects (though more graceful) in "witnessing" publicly to their faith, for it is not theirs as a private and personal possession, like their good looks, but is a public divine gift. They should be proud of it, and certainly never ashamed, for this is not being proud of themselves.

To "witness" to unbelievers is to risk scorn and hostility and, in many places in the world today, even to risk death. Even in nations that have freedom of religion, to witness to the faith is to risk social ostracism and misunderstanding. But this is a small price to pay for loyalty to the Christ who paid the ultimate price for us. And it is a price Christ *requires* (see Mk 8:34–38).

24. Sins against the second commandment

a. "The second commandment *forbids the abuse of God's name*, i.e., every improper use of the names of God, Jesus Christ, but also of the Virgin Mary and all the saints" (CCC 2146), such as using their names in expletives and curses. If "profanity" must be used at all, *profane* things should be profaned, not sacred things. The name "God" or the name "Jesus" should certainly not be used where a word for excrement would be appropriate! Yet many Catholics thoughtlessly and habitually do this every day.

b. "*Promises* made to others in God's name engage the divine honor, fidelity, truthfulness, and authority. They must be respected in justice. To be unfaithful to them is to misuse God's name" (CCC 2147).

c. "*Oaths* which misuse God's name ... show lack of respect for the Lord" (CCC 2149). However, "[f]ollowing St. Paul [cf. 2 Cor 1:23; Gal 1:20], the tradition of the Church has understood Jesus' words" [Mt 5:33–34, 37; cf. Jas 5:12] "as not excluding oaths made for grave and right reasons (for example, in court)" (CCC 2154).

d. "*Blasphemy* ... consists in uttering against God—inwardly or outwardly—words of hatred, reproach, or defiance" (CCC 2148).

25. The third commandment: The two purposes
    of the sabbath

a. "The sabbath is for the Lord, holy and set apart for the praise of God"
(CCC 2171).
    b. "The sabbath was made for man, not man for the sabbath" (Mk 2:27).
"The sabbath brings everyday work to a halt and provides a respite. It is a
day of protest against the servitude of work and the worship of money" [cf.
Neh 13:15–22; 2 Chr 36:21] (CCC 2172). "[H]uman life has a rhythm of
work and rest. The institution of the Lord's Day helps everyone enjoy adequate rest and leisure" (CCC 2184).

26. The positive and negative parts of the
    third commandment

The third commandment commands the worship of God and forbids unnecessary work on the sabbath day.

27. The sabbath and public policy

Since the sabbath serves the natural good of all men, therefore "[i]n respecting religious liberty and the common good of all, Christians should seek
recognition of Sundays and the Church's holy days as legal holidays . . . and
defend their traditions as a precious contribution to the spiritual life of society" (CCC 2188).

28. Sunday or Saturday?

"Jesus rose from the dead 'on the first day of the week' [cf. Mt 28:1; Mk
16:2; Lk 24:1; Jn 20:1]. . . . For Christians it has become the first of all days,
the first of all feasts, the Lord's Day" (CCC 2174). "Sunday is expressly distinguished from the sabbath which it follows chronologically every week;
for Christians, its ceremonial observance replaces that of the sabbath. . . . Sunday fulfills the spiritual truth of the Jewish sabbath" (CCC 2175).

29. The ultimate meaning of the sabbath

The sabbath "announces man's eternal rest in God" (CCC 2175). God
designed it as a reminder and a foretaste of heaven, a glimpse of the city at
the end of the road.

Chapter 6

THE FOURTH COMMANDMENT:

FAMILY AND SOCIAL MORALITY

1. Catholic social and political morality as rooted in God and family

"Love is the fulfilling of the law" (Rom 13:10). The Ten Commandments specify how to love. The first three commandments (the first table of the law) tell us how to love God, and the last seven (the second table) how to love neighbor.

Just as the first commandment is the foundation of the first table of the law, the fourth is the foundation of the second table. "The fourth commandment opens the second table of the Decalogue. It shows us the order of charity. God has willed that, after him, we should honor our parents to whom we owe life and who have handed on to us the knowledge of God. We are obliged to honor and respect all those whom God, for our good,

213

has vested with his authority" (CCC 2197). "This commandment includes
. . . instructors, teachers, leaders, magistrates, those who govern, all who
exercise authority over others or over a community of persons" (CCC
2199).

Thus our relation to social and political authorities is rooted in our even
more basic relation to our parents, which in turn is rooted in the most basic
of all relations, to our Creator. The three are ordered hierarchically, one
derived from the other.

This fundamental principle radically distinguishes Catholic social and political morality from modern secular alternatives. Almost always, the secularist
ignoring of God and his authority is accompanied by an ignoring of the family, its authority, and its priority over the state. Secularists naturally tend to
overestimate states and underestimate families because states are made by man,
and made in many different forms, while the family is designed by God, not
man, and cannot be essentially redesigned in different forms—though secularists today often attempt to do just that, for example, by declaring the
artificial, temporary, and sterile union of two or more homosexuals to be a
"family" just as much as the natural, permanent, and procreative union of a
husband and wife.

Before outlining the details of Catholic teaching about the private family (sections 7–13) and public society (sections 14–22), we should explain a
fundamental principle governing both that is very often misunderstood today:
the meaning of "authority" and "obedience" and their compatibility with
equality (sections 2–5).

2. The meaning of authority

When St. Paul, in his epistles, summarizes God's will for man's social order,
he usually mentions four relationships: the four natural relationships that per-
sist in all times, places, cultures, and political systems: the relations between
(a) parents and children, (b) husbands and wives, (c) rulers and citizens, and
(d) masters and servants. In ancient Rome, this meant masters and slaves; in
modern terms, it means employers and employees. (You pay your plumber
for his service.)

"Authority" and "obedience" are two concepts nearly every premodern
culture uses to describe these fundamental relationships; and the Bible and
the Church use them, too, as things that are natural and proper and good.
However, these two terms are very often misunderstood and therefore
rejected today.

For one thing, the authority of parents, husbands, rulers, and masters is
not one thing but four very different things, in both nature and extent.
Rulers' authority over citizens cannot be expected to be based on unselfish

Christlike love; but this love is the only scriptural basis for a husband's authority over his wife (Eph 5:22–25), and it is also expected of parents toward children.

For another thing, while wives are told to be "subject" to their husbands, husbands are also told to be "subject" to their wives: "Be subject to one another" (Eph 5:21).

Third, if parents, husbands, rulers, and masters are in authority "over" children, wives, citizens, and servants, they are no less "under" *responsibilities* to those others. Husbands must love their wives as Christ loved the Church (see Eph 5:25), not be their "boss". God designed these human relationships to be a dance between equals playing different roles, not a power struggle between unequals for the same "top" role. It is to be like the Trinity. When God the Son became a man, he revealed to us the trinitarian nature of God as a love relationship among three equal Persons who are nevertheless related in an order of authority and obedience. The Son "obeys" the Father in all things. He thus radically changed our understanding of both authority and obedience and corrected our natural misunderstanding.

This misunderstanding is to confuse authority with power; and obedience with inferiority, weakness, or servility. The misunderstanding comes from using the world's point of view instead of God's. The world treasures power; God treasures goodness. Authority in the biblical sense is not a power word but a goodness word. It means right, not might.

Having authority over someone always presupposes being under a higher authority and transmitting it faithfully, as the Church transmits the gospel of Christ. She has no authority (that is, no right) to invent or change what she has received from God; she is God's prophet, not his critic. Your authority is your right to be obeyed based on your obeying—like the Roman centurion who said to Christ when invoking Christ's authority over his servant's life-threatening illness: "But say the word, and let my servant be healed. For I am a man set under authority, with soldiers under me: and I say to one, 'Go,' and he goes; and to another, 'Come,' and he comes" (Lk 7:7–8). Just as the centurion knew that his authority derived from his obedience to Caesar, he knew that Christ's authority derived from his obedience to the Father. Christ had authority over demons and diseases because he could truly say: "I have come down from heaven, not to do my own will, but the will of him who sent me" (Jn 6:38).

3. The meaning of obedience

This example also shows that obedience is not a mark of inferiority. No one ever obeyed the Father's will more completely than Christ, yet Christ was divine, equal to the Father in all things.

Therefore, when the fourth commandment commands children to obey
their parents, and when the New Testament tells wives to obey their husbands (Eph 5:22; Col 3:18; Tit 2:5; 1 Pet 3:1), citizens to obey their rulers
(Rom 13:1; 1 Pet 2:13–14), and servants to obey their masters (Col 3:22; Tit
2:9; 1 Pet 2:18), this does not imply a relationship between inferior and superior. Indeed, this misunderstanding is explicitly contradicted: "There is no
partiality" (Col 3:25).

4. The changing social forms of authority and obedience

Only the authority of God is absolute and unchangeable. All four forms of
human authority are culturally relative and rightly take very different forms
throughout time and place. The Church no more wishes mankind to return
to a Victorian form of the husband–wife, parent–child, or master–servant
relationship than she wishes us to return to a medieval monarchical ideal of
statehood.

However, *some* "vertical" or hierarchical dimension of authority coming
"down" and obedience responding "up" is a necessary dimension of all social
order. A "horizontal" or egalitarian dimension, of equality among all persons, is an equally necessary dimension. Without authority there is chaos;
without equality there is tyranny. How these two dimensions interact changes
with time, place, and culture. The point is simply that authority does not
contradict equality, nor does equality eliminate authority. "God instituted the
human family and endowed it with its fundamental constitution. Its members are persons equal in dignity" (CCC 2203). Yet at the same time Scripture repeatedly affirms authority and commands obedience between these
"persons equal in dignity".

This is God's design, and no man can change this fact because no man
invented it. The family's God-given constitution is the strongest possible basis
for equality as well as for the equally God-ordained fact that "[e]very human
community needs an authority to govern it"[1] (CCC 1898).

5. The rewards for obedience to the fourth commandment

St. Paul notes that "this is the first commandment with a promise" (Eph 6:2).
"Respecting this commandment provides, along with spiritual fruits, temporal fruits of peace and prosperity. Conversely, failure to observe it brings
great harm to communities and to individuals" (CCC 2200).

History verifies this promise. The three most stable, long-lasting, and internally peaceful societies in human history have been those continuing com-

[1] Cf. Leo XIII, *Immortale Dei*; *Diuturnum illud*.

munities whose basic moral foundations were laid down by Moses (more than 3,500 years ago), Confucius (more than 2,500 years ago), and Muhammad (more than 1,300 years ago). All three of them were based on a very high regard for families and on the practice of continuous moral education.

Christ did not found a new civil society but reaffirmed and fulfilled the Mosaic law, which God intended not just for Israel but for the whole world. *Any* civil society, not only Judaism, can prosper by taking the Ten Commandments as its foundation.

6. What is the family?

The *Catechism* specifies three essential features: the family's essence, origin, and end.

a. "A man and a woman united in marriage, together with their children, form a family" (CCC 2202). This is the simple and obvious definition of a family's structural parts.

b. While the ultimate origin of the family is God's design, the immediate origin of the family is a man and a woman freely choosing to create this new "body politic", this "one flesh". "The conjugal community is established upon the consent of the spouses" (CCC 2201).

c. The family has two essential ends: "Marriage and the family are ordered to the good of the spouses and to the procreation and education of children" (CCC 2201).

Thus men only, women only, unmarried people, people forced into marriage, people who marry without basic goodwill toward each other, or people who refuse ever to have children all fail to fulfill one of the essential features of a family.

7. The priority of the family over the state

a. The family is prior to the state in origin and therefore in rights. The state did not invent the family or give it its constitution or its rights. Therefore the state has no authority to un-invent or re-invent it. "This institution" [the family) "is prior to any recognition by public authority, which has an obligation to recognize it" (CCC 2202). The family does not hold its rights from the state, but from God, since it holds its existence and its "fundamental constitution" (essential structure) from God.

b. The family is prior to the state in end or purpose. The state exists to foster the good of families and individuals, not vice versa.

c. The family is prior to the state in importance, for the family is the first and foundational building block of all society, "the *original cell of social life*" (CCC 2207). Therefore "[f]ollowing the principle of subsidiarity" [see section 18 of this chapter], "larger communities should take care not to usurp the family's prerogatives or interfere in its life" (CCC 2209).

8. Specific duties of the state to the family

"The political community has a duty to honor the family, to assist it, and to ensure especially:

"—the freedom to establish a family, have children, and bring them up in keeping with the family's own moral and religious convictions" [this applies especially with regard to public schools];

"—the protection of the stability of the marriage bond . . . ;

"—the freedom to profess one's faith, to hand it on, and to raise one's children in it . . . ;

"—the right to private property, to free enterprise, to obtain work and housing, and the right to emigrate;

"—in keeping with the country's institutions, the right to medical care, assistance for the aged, and family benefits;

"—the protection of security and health, especially with respect to dangers like drugs, pornography, alcoholism, etc.;

"—the freedom to form associations with other families and so to have representation before civil authority" [cf. *FC* 46] (CCC 2211).

"As those first responsible for the education of their children, parents have the right to *choose a school for them* which corresponds to their own convictions. This right is fundamental" (CCC 2229).

9. The family and morality

"The family is the community in which, from childhood, one can learn moral values" (CCC 2207).

"The home is well suited for *education in the virtues*. This requires an apprenticeship in self-denial, sound judgment, and self-mastery—the preconditions of all true freedom. Parents should teach their children to subordinate the 'material and instinctual dimensions to interior and spiritual ones' [*CA* 36 § 2]" (CCC 2223).

10. The family and religion

"The family is the community in which, from childhood, one can . . . begin to honor God" (CCC 2207). " '[F]or this reason it can and should be called a *domestic church*' [*FC* 21; cf. *LG* 11]. It is a community of faith, hope, and charity" (CCC 2204). It is the only place most of us ever learn life's most important value: charity (*agapē*), the love that is the very nature of God (1 Jn

4:16). It is the place where children discover that this charity, and therefore this God, is not just an abstract ideal but a concrete reality. This is how most of us discover that God exists: by our parents mediating God's reality (which is charity) to us.

The family teaches children that they are loved equally and unlimitedly, whether weak or strong, healthy or ill, "normal" or "handicapped"; for they are loved not as the world loves them, for how well they can perform some task, whether of body, mind, work, entertainment, or sports, but simply for who they are: children of God and of parents who loved them into existence as God did, with a love that did not result from but, rather, caused their being and their value; a love that said: You are valuable because you are loved, rather than: You are loved because you are valuable.

Since the family is where children first meet this love that is unconditional and unlimited and unending, it is rightly called a "church", a visible "body of Christ", for this love is precisely the love of Christ, made really present, in a different form but just as really present as it is in the Eucharist.

11. The duties of children

a. *The basis of the duties of children*

"The divine fatherhood is the source of human fatherhood [cf. Eph 3:14]; this is the foundation of the honor owed to parents" (CCC 2214). "God the Father" is not a metaphor, a copy or image of human fatherhood; divine Fatherhood is the primal fact, and human fatherhood is its image or copy.

b. *Four basic duties*

(1) *Respect*: "The respect of children, whether minors or adults, for their father and mother [cf. Prov. 1:8; Tob 4:3–4] is nourished by the natural affection born of the bond uniting them. It is required by God's commandment [cf. Ex 20:12]" (CCC 2214). It is both natural and supernatural. "Filial respect promotes harmony in all of family life; it also concerns *relationships between brothers and sisters*" (CCC 2219).

(2) *Gratitude*: "Respect for parents ... derives from *gratitude* toward those who, by the gift of life, their love and their work, have brought their children into the world and enabled them to grow in stature, wisdom, and grace. ... 'Remember that through your parents you were born; what can you give back to them that equals their gift to you?' [Sir 7:27–28]" (CCC 2215).

(3) *Obedience*: "Filial respect is shown by ... *obedience*" (CCC 2216). "As long as a child lives at home with his parents, the child should obey his parents in all that they ask of him when it is for his good or that of the family. ..."

"Obedience toward parents ceases with the emancipation" [leaving home] "of the children; not so respect, which is always owed to them" (CCC 2217).

(4) *Support:* "The fourth commandment reminds grown children of their *responsibilities toward their parents.* As much as they can, they must give them material and moral support in old age and in times of illness, loneliness, or distress" (CCC 2218) [cf. Mk 7:10–12].

12. The duties of parents

a. "The fecundity of conjugal love cannot be reduced solely to the pro-creation of children, but must extend to their moral education and their spiritual formation. 'The *role of parents in education* is of such importance that it is almost impossible to provide an adequate substitute' [GE 3]" (CCC 2221).

b. "Parents must regard their children as *children of God* and respect them as *human persons*" (CCC 2222).

c. Parents should discipline but not provoke their children (see Eph 6:4).

d. "Through the grace of the sacrament of marriage, parents receive the responsibility and privilege of *evangelizing their children.* Parents should ini-tiate their children at an early age into the mysteries of the faith" (CCC 2225).

e. "Parents should be careful not to exert pressure on their children either in the choice of a profession or in that of a spouse. This necessary restraint does not prevent them—quite the contrary—from giving . . . judicious advice" (CCC 2230). Parents are by far the most important influence on a child in making the three most important choices in life: what God to wor-ship, what spouse to marry, and what career to choose.

f. "Parents have a grave responsibility to give good example to their chil-dren" (CCC 2223). This is certainly the most effective way to teach moral-ity and religion.

g. "By knowing how to acknowledge their own failings to their children, parents will be better able to guide and correct them" (CCC 2223). Chil-dren should be taught that parents, too, are under the same divine law and the same divine authority.

13. God as the source and end of community

Like the human individual, a human society is "at once visible and spiritual" (CCC 1880). A society, like a body, is visible, but its principle of unity, like a soul, is spiritual. To be a community it must have some principle of com-mon unity. "A *society* is a group of persons bound together organically by a principle of unity that goes beyond each one of them" (CCC 1880).

That principle of unity is its end: "Each community is defined by its purpose" (CCC 1881). In *The City of God*, St. Augustine defined a "city", or community, as a group of persons "bound together by a common love". "For where your treasure [your object of love] is, there will your heart [your center, your identity] be also" (Lk 12:34). Many individuals become one community by becoming present to each other through becoming present to a common goal. They identify with each other when they all identify with the same end.

Most fundamentally, this "same goal" is God. "All men are called to the same end: God himself" (CCC 1878).

14. God as the ultimate basis for equality

Because of this common end, men have a common dignity.

The same conclusion—a common dignity and worth—follows also from our common origin: "Created in the image of the one God and equally endowed with rational souls, all men have the same nature and the same origin" (CCC 1934). This is the real basis for human equality; no other basis (such as human opinion or ideology or consensus) is absolutely secure against changing human notions of "superior" races or "unwanted" groups. Only God is unchangeable.

15. God as the basis for the dignity of the human person

Nearly everyone admits human equality and human dignity and understands how important these truths are for a just society; but not everyone admits that God is the only adequate basis and guarantee of these truths.

A just society recognizes the intrinsic value of each person. But that value is "transcendent". It is not revocable by any human authority, because it is not derived from any human authority, but from God. "Social justice can be obtained only in respecting the transcendent dignity of man" (CCC 1929). "Respect for the human person entails respect for the rights that flow from his dignity as a creature" [of God]. "These rights are prior to society and must be recognized by it" (CCC 1930).

16. Duties of citizens

a. Obedience: "God's fourth commandment also enjoins us to honor all who for our good have received authority in society from God" (CCC 2234).

This does not mean that there is a "divine right of kings" or of any other particular government or form of government. It means that God designed man as a social and political creature and therefore that in obeying legitimate social authorities we are obeying God's design. We are told to "be subject for the Lord's sake to every human institution" (1 Pet 2:13; see also Rom 13:1).

b. It is also "morally obligatory to pay taxes, to exercise the right to vote, and to defend one's country" (CCC 2240).

c. There is also an obligation to be vigilant and critical: "[L]oyal collaboration includes the right, and at times the duty, to voice their just criticisms of that which seems harmful to the dignity of persons and to the good of the community" (CCC 2238). (See also chapter 7, sections 20–22.)

d. Sometimes this extends to the duty to disobey: "The citizen is obliged in conscience not to follow the directives of civil authorities when they are contrary to the demands of the moral order" (CCC 2242). "If rulers were to enact unjust laws or take measures contrary to the moral order, such arrangements would not be binding in conscience" (CCC 1903). Human social laws must be judged by a higher "natural law" (see part 2, chapter 2, section 2). In fact, *only* if there is such a higher law can any protest against human law ever be moral or just. The modern secularist who rejects a "natural law" must by his logic either accept all human law as above criticism, and be a total "status quo conservative", or else reject it for no higher moral reason, and be an outlaw, appealing only to might, not right.

e. Charity: " '[T]he often narrow path between the cowardice which gives in to evil, and the violence which under the illusion of fighting evil only makes it worse' [CA 25] . . . is the path of charity, that is, of the love of God and of neighbor. Charity is the greatest social commandment. . . . Charity inspires a life of self-giving" (CCC 1889). It is not a nice "extra" for saints but a necessity for any working family or society.

17. Duties of nations

"The more prosperous nations are obliged, to the extent they are able, to welcome the *foreigner* in search of the security and the means of livelihood which he cannot find in his country of origin" (CCC 2241).

Rich nations are also obliged in charity to aid poor nations, especially in cases of immediate need, such as famine.

Families are also expected to extend charity to other families, just as individuals and nations are. If individual and family charity did its proper work, impersonal government bureaucracies could be less extensive, less expensive, and less intrusive. "Participation" [in society] "is achieved first of all by taking charge of the areas for which one assumes *personal responsibility*: by the care taken for the education of his family, by conscientious work, and so forth [cf. *CA* 43]" (CCC 1914). These concrete, immediate duties should not be neglected for the sake of abstract, far-away causes that give one the illusion of being very idealistic and moral. Christ commanded us to love our neighbor, not "humanity".

18. Subsidiarity and socialization

On the one hand, " '*socialization*' . . . expresses the natural tendency for human beings to associate with one another for the sake of attaining objectives that exceed individual capacities" (CCC 1882).

On the other hand, "[s]ocialization also presents dangers. Excessive intervention by the state can threaten personal freedom and initiative. The teaching of the Church has elaborated the principle of *subsidiarity*, according to which 'a community of a higher' [larger] " 'order should not interfere in the internal life of a community of a lower' " [smaller] " 'order, depriving the latter of its functions, but rather should support it' [2] " (CCC 1883). This applies especially to families.

The model for the principle of subsidiarity is God's own governing of the universe. "God has not willed to reserve to himself all exercise of power. He entrusts to every creature the functions it is capable of performing, according to the capacities of its own nature. This mode of governance ought to be followed in social life. The way God acts in governing the world, which bears witness to such great regard for human freedom, should inspire the wisdom of those who govern human communities" (CCC 1884). The Creator of the universe steps back, humbly and anonymously, and lets his creatures get the glory; according to the medieval maxim, "Grace does not replace nature but perfects it." The ancient Chinese philosopher Lao Tzu, in the *Tao Te Ching*, observed the same principle in the universe, which is governed by the invisible, self-effacing "Tao" or "Way" of nature, and he also applied this principle to human governing.

Catholic teaching is two-sided, balanced, and complete here, as everywhere. On the one hand, "[t]he principle of subsidiarity is opposed to all forms of collectivism. It sets limits for state intervention" (CCC 1885). On the other hand, "socialization" is humanizing, and the state is necessary not only for law and order but also to provide a safety net of essential human needs like food, shelter, employment opportunity, and basic medical care to those not served by private initiative, individual charity, or family.

19. Personalism as the key to good politics

"The inversion of means and ends [cf. *CA* 41], which results in giving the value of ultimate end to what is only a means for attaining it, or in

---

[2] *CA* 48 § 4; cf. Pius XI, *Quadragesimo anno* I, 184–86.

viewing persons as mere means to that end, engenders unjust structures"
(CCC 1887).

"The common good is always oriented towards the progress of persons:
'The order of things must be subordinate to the order of persons, and not
the other way around' [GS 26 § 3]" (CCC 1912). The purpose of all public government, taxes, armies, and laws is the happiness of private individuals and families.

And their goodness. A very simple definition of a good society is this: "A
good society is one that makes it easy to be good" (Dorothy Day, quoting
Peter Maurin).

A good society is one in which each person recognizes, "in every human
person, a son or daughter of the One who wants to be called 'our Father.'
In this way our relationships with our neighbors are recognized as personal
in character. The neighbor is not a 'unit' in the human collective; he is
'someone' " (CCC 2212). "Human communities are *made up of persons.*
Governing them well is not limited to guaranteeing rights and fulfilling
duties such as honoring contracts. Right relations between employers and
employees, between those who govern and citizens, presuppose a natural
good will" (CCC 2213). Good people and good relationships will make
the worst society good; bad people and bad relationships will make the best
society bad.

20. Persons and institutions

On the one hand, no social justice or progress can come about merely "from
the outside in", from impersonal institutions, but only "from the inside out",
from persons, from the heart, and from free choice. "It is necessary . . . to
appeal to the spiritual and moral capacities of the human person and to the
permanent need for his *inner conversion,* so as to obtain social changes that
will really serve him" (CCC 1888). This is why the New Testament always
speaks about personal conversion and morality and not about reforming institutions. It goes to the root.

On the other hand, "[t]he acknowledged priority of the conversion of
heart in no way eliminates but on the contrary imposes the obligation of
bringing the appropriate remedies to institutions and" [external] "living conditions" (CCC 1888).

Some readers will find the principles in this book too "far left", others
too "far right". This is exactly what one would expect if they are from God
and not from man, who like a runaway train has gone off God's track in many
opposite ways. Catholic social and political morality does not conform totally
to any popular secular establishment. It is neither anarchic, individualistic
"libertarianism" nor collectivist "socialism"; neither utopian optimism nor

cynical pessimism; neither "Right" nor "Left"; neither the Republican nor the Democratic party platform. Nor is it an inconsistent compromise between them. It is a higher and more complete way, based on the essential reality of human nature, not on the changing fashions of any human ideology.

Chapter 7

THE FIFTH COMMANDMENT: MORAL ISSUES

OF LIFE AND DEATH

1. The "quality-of-life ethic"

Throughout the twentieth century, Western civilization has witnessed a titanic struggle between two radically opposed philosophies of human life: the traditional "sanctity of life ethic" and the new "quality of life ethic". This new morality judges human lives by the standard of "quality", and by this standard it declares some lives not worth living and the deliberate "termination" of these lives morally legitimate. ("Termination" is the usual euphemism for *killing*.) *Life Unworthy of Life* was the way it was described in the title of the first book to win public acceptance for this new ethic, by Ger-

226

man doctors before World War II—the basis and beginning of the Nazi medical practices.

The criteria by which a human life is most often judged in this "quality-of-life ethic" today are:

a. Whether it is wanted by another. Today this is usually applied to unborn children, to justify abortion: if the baby is "unwanted" by the mother, or predicted to be "unwanted" by "society", then it is thought morally right to take that life, in other words, to kill it. In other places and times, other "unwanted" groups have been denied the right to life, such as Jews (the Holocaust), Blacks (lynching), and people with the wrong political or religious beliefs (in totalitarian states).

b. Whether it has "too much" pain. Today this is usually applied to justify killing the old. But there is increasing pressure to justify and legalize medically assisted suicide at any age.

c. Whether it is severely handicapped, mentally or physically. Of course, there is no clear dividing line between more and less "severe" handicaps, or between "much" pain and "too much" pain. And with no objective criteria, the decision of whether it is right to kill must be based on subjective feeling and desire.

2. The "sanctity-of-life ethic"

The opposite philosophy of life is the traditional "sanctity-of-life ethic", which is taught by all the great religions of the world, is the basis of Western civilization from its Judeo-Christian roots, is presupposed in our laws, and is the basis of all Catholic teaching about the fifth commandment.

There are three reasons for the sanctity of human life: its origin, its nature, and its end.

" 'Human life is sacred because' " [a] " 'from its beginning it involves the creative action of God' " [b] " 'and it remains for ever in a special relationship with the Creator,' " [c] " 'who is its sole end' "[1] (CCC 2258).

" 'God alone is the Lord of life from its beginning until its end: no one can under any circumstance claim for himself the right directly to destroy an innocent human being' "[2] (CCC 2258).

If this is not true, then life is not sacred and God is not God. If it *is* true, then the "quality-of-life ethic" is as serious a form of idolatry as the worship of stone idols, false pagan gods, or evil spirits—all of which in ancient times also manifested themselves in the practice of human sacrifice, especially of children.

---

[1] CDF, instruction, *Donum vitae*, intro. 5.
[2] CDF, instruction, *Donum vitae*, intro. 5.

3. The sense of the sacred

Not all men throughout history have known the true reason for the sacred-ness of human life: that one God created all men. But most men and most societies have instinctively intuited that moral conclusion, even without that theological premise, and felt a strong sense of the sacredness of human life. They have often violated it—history is full of murder and bloodshed—but the sense of shame and guilt remained attached to killing, especially killing the innocent. These instinctive feelings—the sense of the sacred and the sense of shame and guilt—seem to be in crisis today.

The loss of the sense of the sacredness of human life seems closely con-nected with the loss of the sense of sacredness of three other closely connected things: motherhood, sex, and God. Of motherhood, for by far the most dangerous place in the world today in America is a mother's womb during the child's first nine months of life. Of sex, for the "sexual revolution" was a radical change not only in behavior but in vision, in philosophy. Of God, for "the fear of the Lord", which Scripture calls "the beginning of wisdom", is usually thought to be "primitive" and even harmful, even by many religious educators.

4. The basic principle of Catholic ethics
of human life

Persons are not things, objects of manipulation and control and design, to be judged by some other, higher standard than persons. There is no higher standard; God himself is personal ("I AM"). Persons are subjects, I's. They are subjects of rights. They are not to be judged as worth more or less on some abstract, impersonal scale of health, intelligence, physical power, or length of life. Each life, each individual, each human being is unique, and each is equally and infinitely precious. That is the root of Catholic morality on all issues of human life.

5. Christ and the fifth commandment

Instead of shrinking the fifth commandment, as the modern "quality-of-life ethic" does, Christ expanded it. "In the Sermon on the Mount, the Lord recalls the commandment 'You shall not kill,' [Mt 5:21] and adds to it the proscription of anger, hatred, and vengeance. Going further, Christ asks his disciples to turn the other cheek, to love their enemies [cf. Mt 5:22–39; 5:44]. He did not defend himself and told Peter to leave his sword in its sheath [cf. Mt 26:52]" (CCC 2262).

6. Self-defense

This does not mean that Christ commanded pacifism. "The legitimate defense of persons" [including oneself] "and societies" [by armed force] "is not an exception to the prohibition against the murder of the innocent that constitutes intentional killing (CCC 2263).

Self-defense is legitimate for the same reason suicide is not: because one's own life is a gift from God, a treasure we are responsible for preserving and defending. In fact, it is natural and right to feel "bound to take more care of one's own life than of another's" (St. Thomas Aquinas), just as one is bound to defend one's own family more than others.

More, "[l]egitimate defense" [by force] "can be not only a right" [morally permissible] "but a grave duty" [morally obligatory] "for one who is responsible for the lives of others. The defense of the common good requires that an unjust aggressor be rendered unable to cause harm" (CCC 2265). I am invited (though not required) by Christ's evangelical counsels to turn the other cheek even to the point of martyrdom when my *own* life is threatened; such personal "pacifism" is honorable. But it is not honorable to fail to protect others for whom I am responsible, especially my family, from life-threatening aggressors; and sometimes the only way to do this is by force, or at least the threat of it.

7. Capital punishment

"The efforts of the state to curb the spread of behavior harmful to people's rights and to the basic rules of civil society correspond to the requirement of safeguarding the common good. Legitimate public authority has the right and the duty to inflict punishment proportionate to the gravity of the offense" (CCC 2266). "Assuming that the guilty party's identity and responsibility have been fully determined, the traditional teaching of the Church does not exclude recourse to the death penalty, if this is the only possible way of effectively defending human lives against the unjust aggressor" (CCC 2267).

The morality of capital punishment follows the same principle as the morality of a just self-defense. If the execution of the murderer after he is apprehended is necessary to prevent more murders, then capital punishment is justified, for the same reason it is right to disarm a murderer by deadly force before he is apprehended, while he is in the process of committing murder. The same principle for self-defense against aggression holds for a group (a society) threatened by an individual aggressor or by an aggressive nation. "[T]hose who legitimately hold authority also have the right to use arms to repel aggressors against the civil community entrusted to their responsibility" (CCC 2265).

But the important qualifier is "*if this is the only possible way*". In most modern societies, defensive war is still necessary to repel foreign aggressors, but capital punishment is not; life imprisonment in secure prisons without parole is sufficient to protect society. "If, however, non-lethal means are sufficient to defend and protect people's safety from the aggressor, authority will limit itself to such means, as these are more in keeping with the concrete conditions of the common good and more in conformity with the dignity of the human person" (CCC 2267).

Thus the Church's prudence judges that capital punishment, though it remains a public right if necessary, is not right under today's conditions. These conditions also include unequal justice for rich and poor. It is obviously unjust to kill one man and not another because only one can afford a good lawyer or because of any kind of racial prejudice.

8. The morality of punishment

The concept of justice is essential to morality. And the concept of rewards and punishments is essential to justice. Therefore punishment is essential to morality.

But what is the justification for it? What is the purpose of punishment? The *Catechism* mentions four: order, expiation, deterrence, and rehabilitation.

a. "Punishment has the primary aim of redressing the disorder introduced by the offense" (CCC 2266). The primary purpose of punishment is justice, "just desserts". "The punishment must fit the crime." Everyone senses instinctively that it is just to require "an eye for an eye, a tooth for a tooth".

Charity does not contradict this justice; charity presupposes it in going beyond it. Individuals are required by Christ to go beyond justice to charity and forgiveness, but society must maintain a rule of law and justice to protect order. Christ did not advise public officials to forgive crimes and revoke punishments.

The *Catechism* mentions three other good reasons for punishment (CCC 2266):

b. "When it is willingly accepted by the guilty party, it assumes the value of expiation", that is, atonement, penance, "making up for" the evil, paying his debt. Christ did this for our sins, on the Cross. We do it, in some small measure, in doing penance in the Sacrament of Reconciliation.

c. Moreover, punishment has the effect of "defending public order and protecting people's safety." This is "deterrence". Deterrence cannot be the only justification for punishment, for that would justify also extreme and unjust punishments. The threat of capital punishment would surely deter drunk drivers more effectively than merely revoking their driver's license. But it would not be just.

d. Finally, punishment "has a medicinal purpose: as far as possible, it must contribute to the correction of the guilty party" (CCC 2266; cf. Lk 23:4–43). This is "rehabilitation".

9. Sins against the fifth commandment

a. *"Direct and intentional killing*. . . infanticide [cf. *GS* 51 § 3]" [killing an infant], "fratricide" [killing one's brother or sister], "parricide" [killing one's father or mother], "and the murder of a spouse are especially grave crimes by reason of the natural bonds which they break" (CCC 2268).

b. "The fifth commandment forbids doing anything with the intention of *indirectly* bringing about a person's death" (CCC 2269).

c. "The moral law prohibits exposing someone to mortal danger without grave reason, as well as refusing assistance to a person in danger" (CCC 2269).

d. Abortion, euthanasia, and suicide all demand special treatment today, since the traditional consensus against them is rapidly breaking down in so-called "civilized" and "advanced" societies in the West.

10. Abortion and the right to life

The "bottom line" first: "Human life must be respected and protected absolutely from the moment of conception. From the first moment of his existence, a human being must be recognized as having the rights of a person—among which is the inviolable right of every innocent being to life [cf. CDF, *Donum vitae* I, 1]" (CCC 2270).

The American Declaration of Independence has the same philosophy: "We hold these truths to be self-evident: that all men are created equal; that they are endowed by their Creator with certain inalienable rights; that among these rights are life, liberty, and the pursuit of happiness."

We cannot pursue our end of happiness without liberty. (Therefore slavery is a great evil.) But we can neither have liberty nor pursue happiness without having life. (Therefore murder is a greater evil.)

The State did not create us, design us, or give us life. Nor did it give us the right to life. Therefore the State cannot take away that right.

All persons, not just some, have a natural right to life simply because of their nature, because of what they are: persons. Only if someone gives up his right to life by threatening the life of another is it right to take his life, to protect the innocent other person. This is the morality of Western civilization: of Greek and Roman classicism at its best, of religious Judaism, of Islam, and of Christianity—biblical Protestantism and Eastern Orthodoxy as well as Roman Catholicism. It is the "sanctity-of-life ethic".

The other philosophy, the "quality-of-life ethic", holds that only *some*, not all, human beings have an inalienable right to life and that some human beings may draw the line for others and exclude them from the community of persons, from those who have the right to life. This same principle is at work whether those excluded persons are unwanted unborn babies, the old, the sick, the dying, those in pain, those of a certain "inferior" or unwanted race, those who have the wrong political opinions, or those who are declared "severely handicapped" because they fail to come up to a certain standard of intelligence or performance such as "significant social interaction"—which standard is always determined by the killers.

Thus the "quality-of-life ethic" denies the most basic human equality and the most basic of all human rights. No two moral philosophies could be more radically at war with each other than the philosophy of the culture Pope John Paul II has called the "culture of death" and the philosophy of the Church of the God of life.

11. The universal agreement in the Catholic tradition about abortion

"Since the first century, the Church has affirmed the moral evil of every procured abortion" [as distinct from miscarriage, or spontaneous abortion]. "This teaching has not changed and remains unchangeable" (CCC 2271).

The earliest Christian document we have, after the New Testament, the first-century Letter to Diognetus, mentions abortion as one of the things Christians never do, as a visibly distinctive feature of their faith. The latest ecumenical council, Vatican II, reaffirmed this teaching in totally uncompromising terms: " 'abortion and infanticide are abominable crimes' [GS 51 § 3]" (CCC 2271).

The presence of "dissenters" or heretics who reject some certain, essential Catholic teaching does not make that teaching uncertain or unessential. The Church's teaching did not come from human opinion, so it cannot be changed by human opinion.

12. The Church's policy on abortion

Catholic tradition distinguishes "formal" and "material" cooperation in any evil. Formal cooperation means direct, deliberate doing of the evil— for instance, a mother freely choosing to pay a doctor to abort her baby, the doctor performing the abortion, or a nurse directly helping the doctor to perform it. Material cooperation means indirect or nondeliberate aid— for instance, contributing money to a hospital that performs abortions. Material cooperation is a "gray area". Even paying taxes can be material cooperation in abortion when the government uses tax money to finance health insurance that covers abortions. It is not possible to avoid all material cooperation with evil. But it is possible, and necessary, to avoid all formal cooperation with evil, for any reason. No good reason can justify an intrinsically evil act.

"Formal cooperation in an abortion constitutes a grave offense. The Church attaches the canonical" [official Church law] "penalty of excommunication to this crime against human life. 'A person who procures a completed abortion incurs'" [automatic] "'excommunication ... [CIC, can. 1398] by the very commission of the offense' [CIC, can. 1314]" (CCC 2272) if she is aware of its penalty.

This does not mean that all who commit this sin are damned. Excommunication is not automatic damnation. But it does mean they can no longer honestly call themselves Catholics, members of the Body of Christ. For Christ cannot commit such a crime, and to be a Catholic is to be a member of his very Body, to be his hands and fingers. It is not Christ's hands that abort Christ's children. When Christ says, "This is my body", he gives his own life to us in the Eucharist. When a woman justifies abortion by saying, "This is my body", she takes a life that is not her own. No person can own another person.

"The Church does not thereby intend to restrict the scope of mercy" (CCC 2272). Forgiveness is always available for any sin, if sincerely repented; and ministries of reconciliation like "Project Rachel" deal compassionately with women who have had abortions.

Mother Teresa said: "Every abortion has two victims: the body of the baby and the soul of the mother." The first is beyond repair, but the second is not, and the Church does everything possible to repair and restore souls and lives torn by sin—which in one way or another is true of all of us. The Church does not judge the individual soul, nor should any of us. She says, as her Master did, "Let him who is without sin among you be the first to throw a stone." She is not in the business of stone-throwing. But she *is* in the business of the accurate labeling of human acts, just like her Master, who said not only "neither do I condemn you" but also "go, and do not sin again" (Jn 8:11).

13. The basic arguments for and against abortion

There are three steps, or premises, to the argument for outlawing abortion:

The first is that one of the most fundamental purposes of law is to protect human rights, especially the first and foundational right, the right to life.

The second is that all human beings have the right to life.

The third is that the already-conceived but not-yet-born children of human beings are human beings.

From these three premises it necessarily follows that the law must protect the right to life of unborn children.

There are only three possible reasons for disagreeing with this conclusion and being "pro-choice" instead of pro-life. One may deny the first, second, or third premise. For if all three are admitted, the pro-life conclusion follows.

Thus there are three different kinds of "pro-choicers":

First, there are those who admit that all persons have a right to life and that unborn children are persons but deny that this right should be protected by law (the first premise). This is a serious legal error.

"The inalienable right to life of every innocent human individual is a *constitutive element of a civil society and its legislation.*

" 'The inalienable rights of the person must be recognized and respected by civil society and the political authority. These human rights depend neither on single individuals nor on parents; nor do they represent a concession made by society and the state; they belong to human nature and are inherent in the person by virtue of the creative act from which the person took his origin. . . .[3]

" 'The moment a positive' " [human] " 'law deprives a category of human beings of the protection which civil legislation ought to accord them, the state is denying the equality of all before the law. When the state does not place its power at the service of the rights of each citizen, and in particular of the more vulnerable, the very foundations of a state based on law are undermined'[4] " (CCC 2273).

Second, there are those who admit that the law should protect the right to life and that unborn children are human beings but deny that all human beings have the right to life (the second premise). This is a very serious moral error.

It is essentially the philosophy of power, of "might makes right." Those in power—doctors, parents, legislators, adults—decree the right to kill those who lack the power to defend themselves: the smallest, most vulnerable, and most innocent of all human beings. No good reason can justify this decree; a good end does not justify an intrinsically evil means. If the babies shared the powers of the abortionists and could fight back with scalpels, there would be few abortions.

Third, there are those who admit that the law should protect the right to life and that all humans have that right, but deny that unborn children are humans (the third premise). This is a serious factual and scientific error.

Before *Roe v. Wade* legalized abortion, all science texts taught the biological truism that the life of any individual of any species begins at concep-

---

[3] CDF, *Donum vitae* III.
[4] CDF, *Donum vitae* III.

tion, when sperm and ovum unite to create a new being with its own complete and unique genetic code, distinct from both father and mother. All growth and development from then on are a matter of degree, a gradual unfolding of what is already there. There is no specific or distinct point in our development when we *become human*. (What were we before that? Birds?) Only when abortion became legal did the science textbooks change their language and cease teaching this truism—not because of any new science but because of a new politics.

Abortion is not a complex issue. Few moral issues could be clearer. As Mother Teresa said, "If abortion is not wrong, nothing is wrong."

14. Other sins against human life

a. " 'It is immoral to produce human embryos intended for exploitation as disposable biological material' [5] " (CCC 2275). This amounts to farming, killing, and selling tiny humans for their body parts!

b. "Test-tube babies", conceived without sexual union, are unnatural for the same reason artificial contraception is: both deliberately divorce what God and nature have joined: sexual union and reproduction. Test-tube babies divorce babies from sex; contraception divorces sex from babies.

c. The use of "surrogate mothers" can result in a child having three, four, or five parents. It is unnatural in itself and deeply confusing to the child.

d. " 'Certain attempts to *influence chromosomic or genetic inheritance* are not therapeutic' " [to cure genetic diseases and restore natural health] " 'but are aimed at producing human beings selected according to sex or other predetermined qualities. Such manipulations are contrary to the personal dignity of the human being and his integrity and identity' [6] which are unique and unrepeatable" (CCC 2275). "Designer genes", the demand for pre-designed genetically perfect babies, is a case of "playing God" and an insult and injustice against the human babies rejected for having the "wrong" sex, color, I.Q., and so on. Every loving parent of a handicapped child knows that there are no "wrong" children, only wrong attitudes toward them. No children are "mistakes"; the mistakes are in those who reject them and the challenges and opportunities to love them as God does.

15. Euthanasia

"Whatever its motives" [whether selfish convenience or unselfish mercy] "and means" [whether harsh or gentle], "direct euthanasia . . . is morally

[5] CDF, *Donum vitae* I, 5.
[6] CDF, *Donum vitae* I, 6.

unacceptable" (CCC 2277). For "mercy killing" is *killing*, and God's commandment says "You shall not kill." "The end does not justify the means"; a good motive (mercy) does not justify an intrinsically evil act (killing).

"Thus an act or omission which, of itself or by intention, causes death in order to eliminate suffering constitutes a murder gravely contrary to the dignity of the human person" (CCC 2277). This is how we treat a horse: we "put *it* out of *its* misery" by putting a bullet through its head, because we judge its life merely by physical, biological standards. It is only an animal. Man is not only an animal.

"Even if death is thought imminent, the ordinary care owed to a sick person cannot be legitimately interrupted" (CCC 2279). "Ordinary care" or "ordinary means" includes such things as food and water and pain relief, as distinct from intrusive and aggressive medical interventions such as respirators or feeding tubes, which are "extraordinary means" and are discretionary, or optional.

The basic principle is simple: "You shall not kill." Not anyone. Even capital punishment, defensive war, or armed self-defense is essentially the *protection* of innocent human life when threatened and has the same justification as the prohibition against murder, namely, the sacredness of human life, which must be protected against the aggressor precisely *because* it is sacred.

However, "letting die" is not the same as killing. It can be morally right under some circumstances: if there is no reasonable hope of cure. If death is inevitable and imminent, there is no moral necessity to do anything that makes dying more painful. This is sometimes misleadingly called "passive euthanasia" as distinct from "active euthanasia". "Discontinuing medical procedures" [such as chemotherapy or radiation] "that are burdensome, dangerous, extraordinary, or disproportionate to the expected outcome can be legitimate; it is the refusal of 'over-zealous' treatment. Here one does not will to cause death; one's ability to impede it is merely accepted" (CCC 2278).

Also, "[t]he use of painkillers" [such as morphine] "to alleviate the sufferings of the dying, even at the risk of shortening their days, can be morally in conformity with human dignity if death is not willed ... but only foreseen and tolerated as inevitable. Palliative care ... should be encouraged" (CCC 2279). In nearly all cases, dying today can be free from intolerable pain, though most doctors are not adequately trained in this palliative care. However, there are excellent care organizations like Hospice that are.

16. Suicide

"Physician-assisted suicide" is one of the primary "causes" defended by those who hold the "quality-of-life ethic". Though the latter are usually secularists, behind this moral philosophy that justifies suicide is a very definite religious philosophy, which is clearly expressed in the title of a movie defending euthanasia and suicide: *Whose Life Is It, Anyway?* That is indeed the question. If I am the author, owner, and lord of my life; if I am my own god, my own creator, then I have the right, the authority (the "author's rights") to do what I please with it. The same is thought to apply to "my" unborn child's life, if I think I am his or her god and lord.

Thus the fundamental question about the morality of human life is a question about fact, about truth. What ought to be depends on what is. If I am in fact God's creature, then the answer to the question "Whose life is it, anyway?" is that it is God's. My life is his gift.

Suicide is a sin not only against God but also against self. "Suicide . . . is gravely contrary to the just love of self" (CCC 2281). We are commanded to love our neighbor as ourselves; this logically entails loving ourselves as our neighbor. Killing oneself is murder just as killing another is.

"It likewise offends love of neighbor because it unjustly breaks the ties of solidarity with family, . . . and other human societies to which we continue to have obligations" (CCC 2281). It is not a victimless crime. It horribly scars the souls of all who love the one who does it.

However, "[w]e should not despair of the eternal salvation of persons who have taken their own lives. By ways known to him alone, God can provide the opportunity for salutary repentance" (CCC 2283)—perhaps at the very moment of death.

17. Scandal

"Scandal" is a technical moral term; it means "an attitude or behavior which leads another to do evil" (CCC 2284). It does not mean some tabloid newspaper reporting a famous person's sins. It certainly does not mean being unpopular or controversial or being offensive to some people—if it did, Christ would have been guilty of it!

"Scandal takes on a particular gravity by reason of the authority of those who cause it" [for example, parents, teachers, or priests] "or the weakness of those who are scandalized" [for example, children]. "It prompted our Lord to utter this curse: 'Whoever causes one of these little ones who believe in me to sin, it would be better for him to have a great millstone fastened round his neck and to be drowned in the depth of the sea' [Mt 18:6, cf. 1 Cor 8:10–13]" (CCC 2285).

To weaken the faith or hope or charity of another is a very serious evil. Teachers therefore have a very serious responsibility, especially teachers of religion to young people (see Jas 3:1).

18. Health

"Life and physical health are precious gifts entrusted to us by God. We must take reasonable care of them" (CCC 2288).

"The virtue of temperance disposes us to *avoid every kind of excess*: the abuse of food, alcohol, tobacco, or medicine" (CCC 2290). Especially "the *use of* " [illegal] "*drugs* inflicts very grave damage on human health and life" (CCC 2291).

"*Concern for the health* of its citizens requires that society help in the attainment of living-conditions that allow them to grow and reach maturity: food and clothing, housing, health care, basic education, employment, and social assistance" (CCC 2288).

19. Respect for the dead

"The dying should be given attention and care to help them live their last moments in dignity and peace. They will be helped by the prayer of their relatives, who must see to it that the sick receive at the proper time the sacraments that prepare them to meet the living God" (CCC 2299).

"The bodies of the dead must be treated with respect.... The burial of the dead is a corporal work of mercy [cf. Tob 1:16–18]" (CCC 2300).

20. War and peace

The Church is both idealistic and realistic about war.

On the one hand, "the Church insistently urges everyone to prayer and to action so that the divine Goodness may free us from the ancient bondage of war [cf. GS 81 § 4]" (CCC 2307).

On the other hand, "[i]nsofar as men are sinners, the threat of war hangs over them and will so continue until the coming of Christ" (GS 78; see Mt 24:3–8). Therefore "[a]s long as the danger of war persists and there is no international authority with the necessary competence and power, governments cannot be denied the right of lawful self-defense, once all peace efforts have failed" (GS 79).

The same moral standards apply to collective self-defense by nations as to self-defense by individuals (see section 6 of this chapter).

21. The "just war" doctrine

No war is just in itself. War is a sinful and barbaric invention. It is murder on a mass scale. But the choice to go to war can be just, if it is necessary self-defense.

The aim of a just war (that is, a just "going to war") is peace. The aim is not taking lives but saving lives: the lives of the innocent victims of aggression. The end that makes a war just can only be peace.

The "traditional elements enumerated in what is called the 'just war' doctrine" are the following "strict conditions for *legitimate defense by military force*" (CCC 2309):

a. *Defense.* As implied above, a just war cannot be aggressive, but only defensive, a response to aggression. (The Qur'an teaches the same doctrine to Muslims: "Allah hates the aggressor.")

b. *Grave damage.* "[T]he damage inflicted by the aggressor . . . must be lasting, grave, and certain" (CCC 2309).

c. *Last resort.* "[A]ll other means of putting an end to it" [this grave damage] "must have been shown to be . . . ineffective" (CCC 2309).

d. *Hope for peace.* "[T]here must be serious prospects of success" (CCC 2309) and the ultimate aim and intention must be not war but peace.

e. *Not graver evils.* "[T]he use of arms must not produce evils and disorders graver than the evil to be eliminated. The power of modern means of destruction weighs very heavily in evaluating this condition" (CCC 2309). "'Every act of war directed to the indiscriminate destruction of whole cities or vast areas with their inhabitants is a crime against God and man' [GS 80§3]. . . . A danger of modern warfare is that it provides the opportunity to those who possess modern scientific weapons—especially atomic, biological, or chemical weapons—to commit such crimes" (CCC 2314).

f. *Rules of war.* It is not true that "All's fair in love and war." "The Church and human reason both assert the permanent validity of the *moral law during armed conflict.* 'The mere fact that war has regrettably broken out does not mean that everything becomes licit between the warring parties' [cf. GS 79 § 4]" (CCC 2312). "Non-combatants, wounded soldiers, and prisoners must be respected and treated humanely. Actions deliberately contrary to . . . universal principles are crimes, as are the orders that command such actions. Blind obedience does not suffice to excuse those who carry them out. . . . One is morally bound to resist orders that command genocide" (CCC 2313).

22. Pacifism

There has been a tradition in the Church of principled Christian pacifism, as well as a tradition of "just war". Church doctrine does not pronounce in a final and authoritative way on all moral questions, leaving many up to prudential human judgment. Pacifism—the refusal to bear arms—is not a requirement for Christians, nor is it forbidden. It is an honorable option.

Therefore, "[p]ublic authorities should make equitable provision for those who for reasons of conscience refuse to bear arms; these are nonetheless obliged to serve . . . in some other way [cf. *GS* 79 § 3]" (CCC 2311).

Chapter 8

The Sixth and Ninth Commandments:
Sexual Morality

1. The contemporary situation

By its own admission, what our age finds most unacceptable in the Church's perennial wisdom is her sexual morality. Almost every controversial issue dividing "dissenters", inside the Church as well as outside, from the Church's traditional teaching today is about sexual morality: fornication (sex outside marriage), contraception, homosexuality, divorce, and, most radically of all, abortion. For abortion, too, is a sexual issue, for it is demanded as backup birth control, and birth control is the demand to have sex without having babies.

The Church has always shared her Master's holy unpopularity. But never before the "Sexual Revolution" did her (and his) unpopularity center almost exclusively on sex.

In all eras and cultures, fallen man has never been very good at obeying any of God's commandments. Man has always failed to practice what he preaches. But today he denies the preaching, the ideal itself.

But only when it concerns sex. A cross-section of popular movies and TV will reveal that most other areas of traditional morality are still assumed to be rightful and attainable ideals. But traditional sexual morality is almost always assumed to be unhealthy and unattainable, and the Church is usually portrayed as obsessed with sexual morality.

This obsession with sex is not the Church's but the world's—though the world often projects it onto the Church, its critic. There is much more to the Church's sexual morality than "just say no", much more to the Church's morality than sexual morality, and much more to the Church's teaching than morality. This book is divided into thirty-one chapters, and this chapter, on sexual morality, is only one of the thirty-one.

Each age has a different perspective. It seems incredible to most modern minds that, in the fourth century, the universal Church nearly endured a worldwide schism over the right date to celebrate Easter and *did* go into schism, in the eleventh century, over whether the Holy Spirit proceeds from the Father only or from the Father and the Son and, in the sixteenth century, over the relation between faith and works. All our Catholic ancestors, whether from the fourth, eleventh, or sixteenth century, would be just as shocked at our preoccupation with sexual morality as we are at their very different priorities.

We should not expect the Church's teachings to coincide with "the wisdom of the world" (1 Cor 1:20) in any age or culture, for her teachings do not come from this world but from heaven, not from man but from God. Man has gone off the track set for him by God—"sin" *means* separation from God—so God's track has always appeared to fallen man as "a stone that will make men stumble, a rock that will make them fall" (1 Pet 2:8), just as Christ himself did. We should expect that. G. K. Chesterton said, "I don't need a church to tell me I'm wrong where I already know I'm wrong; I need a Church to tell me I'm wrong where I think I'm right."

2. The need for sexual morality

There are three things we need—holiness, happiness, and health—because there are three levels on which we live: spirit, soul, and body; our relationships with God, with ourselves and others, and with the material world.

Living according to God's laws makes us holy, happy, and healthy. Violating them makes us unholy, unhappy, and unhealthy. This is as true of sex as of anything else.

First, sexual sin is *sin* and separates us from God.

Second, since God loves us and wants our happiness, disobedience to his plan for us will necessarily bring us unhappiness. Worldly statistics confirm this heavenly logic: every one of the sins that adulterate sexual love brings with it a catalogue of miseries. Look, for instance, at divorce, which is the suicide of the "one flesh" created by marriage. Divorce means the destruction of society's most indispensable foundation, the family, and it will inevitably stamp the same destructive marks on society at large as it already has on its immediate victims, millions of children: a hard, cynical spirit, the death of security, of trust, of faith in persons and promises and in the adventure of self-giving love.

Third, sexual sin has obvious and radical health effects: the epidemic of sexually transmitted diseases, now affecting over half of all sexually active people, the fear of AIDS, and the rising infertility rate. But the most notable physical effect of the Sexual Revolution is *death*. The human victims in just one generation of the abortion holocaust in most Western nations already vastly outnumber the victims of all the wars in their history.

It is high time to turn our attention to God's alternative.

3. The need for "the big picture": Some basic principles

Controversies have a way of narrowing our vision. They are usually resolved only by backing up and enlarging our perspective, especially by looking at foundations. The foundations of Catholic sexual morality include:

— God as the Creator and Designer of sexuality;

— the centrality of love (the very nature of God) and the need to get *that* right above all;

— the holiness of matter and the body and procreation and sexual love as an image of divine love;

— the primacy of the family;

— the Church as the extension of Christ, and her teaching authority as an extension of his;

— the divinely designed intrinsic purpose of sex as pro-creating new eternal souls for God's family;

— and above all, sex as a sign of the goodness of life. Every baby conceived is a sign that God has not given up on man. It is not a mere product of automatic nature, but a deliberate act of God. God makes a soul when we make a body. He is not forced to do this; he chooses to.

4. Sexuality is not merely physical

"*Sexuality* affects all aspects of the human person in the unity of his body and soul" (CCC 2332). It is not merely biological, as it is with animals, any more than eating and drinking are merely biological, as they are with animals. Our sexual identity extends to our souls, our personalities, our spirits. There is indeed a "feminine mind" and a "masculine mind" as well as body, for we are a psychosomatic unity (soul-body unity). To think of one's soul and mind as neither masculine nor feminine is to separate body and soul artificially, as did the ancient Gnostics, and to think of the soul as a sexless "ghost in a machine" instead of as the life and form *of the body*, and to think of masculinity and femininity as merely a material, animal thing.

5. Complementarity

It is no accident that opposites attract, sexually as well as electromagnetically. There is both "*difference* and *complementarity*" (CCC 2333) between the sexes. Men and women *are* different, by nature and divine design, not just by society's conventions. These differences are meant for union: each is *for* the other. God judged that "It is not good that man should be alone" (Gen 2:18)—for God himself is not alone, but a trinitarian society.

"Each of the two sexes is an image of the power and of the tenderness of God, with equal dignity though in a different way" (CCC 2335). Power is by nature more obvious in men, tenderness in women; yet a complete man is also tender, and a complete woman is also powerful.

6. Sexuality as an image of God

As soon as Scripture mentions "the image of God", it mentions sexuality: "So God created man in his own image, in the image of God he created him; male and female he created them" (Gen 1:27). Sexuality is an image of God by being a reflection of the Trinity: as God is one yet three, spouses are two yet one. *Relationship* "goes all the way up" into divinity.

More specifically, family relationships go all the way up. We ascend from one level of the mystery—biological and psychological complementarity—to another—the human family as "'a domestic church' [FC 21; cf. LG 11]" (CCC 2204)—to yet another—the Church as the family of God—until we reach the highest and holiest mystery of all, the nature of ultimate reality, the nature of God; and we find that this, too, is a family, the divine family of the Trinity. It is all the same mystery, on different levels.

The Church sees the mystery of sexuality in this larger context. We usually do not. That is the deepest reason why her wisdom often contradicts ours.

7. Marriage personalizes sexuality

"Sexuality, in which man's belonging to the bodily and biological world is expressed, becomes personal and truly human when it is integrated into the relationship of one person to another, in the" [a] "complete and" [b] "lifelong" [c] "mutual" [d] [free] "gift" [e] "of a man and a woman" (CCC 2337)—the five essential ingredients in a marriage. Marriage is complete "self-donation", of physical body and spiritual will. Lovers find their deepest thrill in the discovery of this intimacy: that they can actually give their very selves to each other, not just their time, possessions, work, goodwill, and pleasures.

Sexual intercourse effects this self-donation in the most intimate and complete way. For this is an intercourse of whole persons, not merely of animal bodies. " 'Sexuality, by means of which man and woman give themselves to one another through the acts which are proper and exclusive to spouses, is not something simply biological, but concerns the innermost being of the human person as such' [FC 11]" (CCC 2361). This is why " '[t]he acts in marriage by which the intimate and chaste union of the spouses takes place are noble and honorable; the truly human performance of these acts fosters the self-giving they signify' [GS 49 § 2]" (CCC 2362). Note the surprising similarity here to the Church's formula for a *sacrament*: "A sign that actually effects (or fosters) what it signifies".

8. The relationship between sex and marriage

The Church's teaching on the relationship between sex and marriage is very simple and very clear. It is the same as that of orthodox Judaism and Islam and has never changed. "The sexual act must take place exclusively within marriage. Outside of marriage it always constitutes a grave sin and excludes one from sacramental communion" (CCC 2390) until repented of and forgiven in sacramental confession.

9. Chastity

The one word that refers to all sexual virtue as opposed to all sexual vices is "chastity". It does not mean the same thing as abstinence (abstaining from sexual intercourse), for chastity includes good sexual intercourse between spouses. It means purity: pure sex, unadulterated sex, right sex, not crooked sex.

Since we are all tempted to "crooked sex", chastity requires self-control, self-mastery. This is not repression or enslavement; in fact it alone is the road to freedom. "Chastity includes an *apprenticeship in self-mastery* which is a training in human freedom. The alternative is clear: either man governs his passions and finds peace, or he lets himself be dominated by them and becomes unhappy [cf. Sir 1:22]. 'Man's dignity therefore requires him to act out of conscious and free choice; as moved and drawn in a personal way from within, and not by blind impulses in himself or by mere external constraint'" [GS 17] (CCC 2339).

Chastity is also a form of charity. "Charity is the *form*" [essence] "of all the virtues. Under its influence, chastity appears as . . . the gift of the person" (CCC 2346), or self-donation—the very heart of charity.

10. Chastity requires society's help

"Chastity represents an eminently personal task;" [but] "it also involves a *cultural effort*, for there is 'an interdependence between personal betterment and the improvement of society' [GS 25 § 1]" (CCC 2344). A good society cannot come from any other source than good persons; and one of the strongest factors that help make good persons, in turn, is a good society. If a good society is "a society that makes it easy to be good", then modern Western society is *not* a good society, especially with regard to chastity.

11. Sins against chastity

The *Catechism* lists six specific sins against chastity, in order of increasing seriousness: (a) lust, (b) masturbation, (c) fornication, (d) pornography, (e) prostitution, and (f) rape.

a. "*Lust* is disordered desire for . . . sexual pleasure. Sexual pleasure is morally disordered when sought for itself, isolated from its procreative and unitive purposes" (CCC 2351).

Lust does not mean sexual pleasure as such, nor the delight in it, nor the desire for it in its right context. Contrary to what the world thinks, the Church teaches that sexual pleasure is good, not evil. For God invented sex and its pleasure. "'The Creator himself . . . established that in the [generative] function, spouses should experience pleasure and enjoyment of body and spirit'"[1] (CCC 2362). It is natural and right that great pleasure should accompany great things, and the human sexual act is a great thing because of its two great essential ends: (1) uniting man and woman in "one flesh", body and soul, in mutual self-donation; and (2) procreating new persons who

---

[1] Pius XII, Discourse, October 29, 1951.

bear God's own image and will exist forever—the closest man ever comes to sharing God's own power of creation.

The essence of sex, like any intelligently designed thing, is in its end. Lust, like any sin, must be seen against that background. Lust divorces the two things God designed to be together; it seeks the pleasure *apart from* the purpose.

No spontaneous thoughts and feelings can be sins until they are willed or consented to by the will. Thoughts and feelings of sexual arousal are not lust; lust is *willing* the thoughts and feelings just for the pleasure, without the purposes of the marriage union (personal self-donation and procreation).

b. "By *masturbation* is to be understood the deliberate stimulation of the genital organs in order to derive sexual pleasure. 'Both the Magisterium of the Church, in the course of a constant tradition, and the moral sense of the faithful have been in no doubt and have firmly maintained that masturbation is an intrinsically and gravely disordered action.'[2] 'The deliberate use of the sexual faculty, for whatever reason, outside of marriage is essentially contrary to its purpose.' "[3] (CCC 2352). Masturbation is wrong for the same reason lust is wrong, with the physical act now added to the mental act: "For here sexual pleasure is sought outside of 'the sexual relationship . . . in which . . . mutual self-giving and human procreation . . . is achieved' "[4] (CCC 2352).

However, "[t]o form an equitable judgment about the subjects' moral responsibility . . . one must take into account the affective" [emotional] "immaturity, force of acquired habit, conditions of anxiety, or other psychological or social factors" (CCC 2352).

This sin, like lust, is very common and in *that* sense "natural". But that no more makes it right, or innocent, than selfishness is made innocent by the fact that it is common. The natural law is not derived from observing how people do in fact usually behave but from how their human nature is to be fulfilled and respected.

c. "*Fornication* is carnal union between an unmarried man and an unmarried woman. It is gravely contrary to the dignity of persons and of human sexuality which is naturally ordered to the good of spouses and the generation and education of children" (CCC 2353). Adultery is even more gravely wrong because at least one of the parties is married to another (see section 15 of this chapter).

(By the way, the use of the words "gravely" and "dignity" does not signify an attitude of humorlessness or pomposity. Good sex can be quite

[2] CDF, *Persona humana* 9.
[3] CDF, *Persona humana* 9.
[4] CDF, *Persona humana* 9.

healthily humorous. Rather, "dignity" means "greatness or high honor"; and "gravely" means "very much, not lightly".)

d. "*Pornography* consists in removing real or simulated sexual acts from the intimacy of the partners, in order to display them deliberately to third parties. . . . [I]t perverts the conjugal act, the intimate giving of spouses to each other. . . . It is a grave offense. Civil authorities should prevent the production and distribution of pornographic materials" (CCC 2354).

e. "*Prostitution* does injury to the dignity of the person who engages in it, reducing the person to an instrument of sexual pleasure. . . . Prostitution is a social scourge. It usually involves women, but also men, children, and adolescents (The latter two cases involve the added sin of scandal.). While it is always gravely sinful to engage in prostitution, the imputability of the offense can be attenuated by destitution, blackmail, or social pressure" (CCC 2355).

f. "*Rape* is the forcible violation of the sexual intimacy of another person. . . . Rape deeply wounds the respect, freedom, and physical and moral integrity to which every person has a right. It causes grave damage that can mark the victim for life. It is always an intrinsically evil act. Graver still is the rape of children committed by parents (incest) or those responsible for the education of the children entrusted to them" (CCC 2356).

12. Homosexuality

"Homosexuality" [that is, homosexual acts] "refers to" [sexual] "relations between men or between women who experience . . . sexual attraction toward persons of the same sex. It has taken a great variety of forms through the centuries and in different cultures. Its psychological genesis remains largely unexplained. Basing itself on Sacred Scripture, which presents homosexual acts as acts of grave depravity,[5] tradition has always declared that 'homosexual acts are intrinsically disordered.'[6] They are contrary to the natural law. They close the sexual act to the gift of life. They do not proceed from a genuine affective and sexual complementarity" [that is, they refuse the divinely designed "otherness" built into sexuality]. "Under no circumstances can they be approved" (CCC 2357).

There is no doubt, no gray area, and no change in the Church's teaching about the objective sinfulness of homosexual acts. However, improved psychological and biological knowledge require us to be much less judgmental about the subjective culpability of homosexual persons. "This inclination, which is objectively disordered, constitutes for most of them a trial. They

[5] Cf. Gen 19:1–29; Rom 1:24–27; 1 Cor 6:10; 1 Tim 1:10.
[6] CDF, *Persona humana* 8.

must be accepted with respect, compassion, and sensitivity. . . . [U]njust discrimination in their regard should be avoided" (CCC 2358).

It is also necessary to make a clear distinction between homosexual desires, or a homosexual orientation, and homosexual acts. We are responsible for the acts we choose to perform, but not for the desires we experience (unless we freely will them or consent to them). Homosexual desires are disordered, but they are not sins.

"Homosexual persons are called to chastity" (CCC 2359) just as heterosexual persons are. They need the virtue of self-control to conquer powerfully attractive desires for illicit pleasures just as heterosexual persons do. And they can be serious and even saintly Christians just as heterosexual persons can.

However, we must distinguish persons who experience homosexual desires from persons who choose to embrace the homosexual (or "gay") life-style. "Dignity" is an organization of "gay Catholics" who justify their homosexual acts and seek to change the Church's perennial teaching against these acts. "Courage" is an organization of homosexual Catholics who support each other in the sincere effort to live in chastity and in fidelity to Christ and his Church. The difference between them typifies the fundamental difference between two kinds of morality (on any issue, not just homosexuality): the first seeks to conform the teaching of Christ's Church to fallen human desires and sinful life-styles; the second seeks to conform human lives to the teachings of Christ's Church. The first group treats the Church as their pupil; the second treats her as their teacher.

13. Birth control

What is usually called birth *control* is really birth *prevention*. This the Church opposes.

Essentially, the Church's teaching is (a) that birth is wonderful and (b) that birth control can be legitimate, but (c) that birth prevention (contraception) is not. Each point must be understood in light of the one before it.

a. "Fecundity is a gift, an *end of marriage*, for conjugal love naturally tends to be fruitful. A child does not come from outside as something added on to the mutual love of the spouses" [or as an "accident"!] "but springs from the very heart of that mutual giving, as its fruit and fulfillment" (CCC 2366).

b. If two criteria are met, birth control is legitimate: a subjectively good intention and an objectively good means, or method, or way of regulating births. "For just reasons, spouses may wish to space the births of their children. It is their duty to make certain that their desire is not motivated by selfishness but is in conformity with the generosity appropriate to responsible parenthood. Moreover, they should conform their behavior to the objective criteria of morality." [For] " 'the morality of the behavior does not depend on sincere intention and evaluation of motives alone; but it must be determined by objective criteria, criteria drawn from the nature of the person and his acts' [GS 51 § 3]" (CCC 2368). "[M]ethods of birth regulation based on self-observation and the use of infertile periods is in conformity with the objective criteria of morality [HV 16]. These methods respect the bodies of the spouses" (CCC 2370). Natural Family Planning (NFP) is such a method. It is much more reliable than the old "rhythm method", as reliable as "the pill", has none of the pill's side effects, and fosters such great intimacy and communication among its users that they have a *1 percent* divorce rate as compared with society's 50 percent.

c. "[T]he Church, which is 'on the side of life,' [FC 30] teaches that 'it is necessary that each and every marriage act remain ordered *per se* to the procreation of human life' [HV 11]" (CCC 2366). Man may take advantage of natural infertile periods designed by God, but he many not himself try to redesign fertility and lock the door of his fertility against God's coming. Contraception is "protection" against *God*.

For every conception is an act of God, not only of a man and a woman. We only *pro*create; God creates a new immortal soul at each conception. "Let all be convinced that human life and its transmission are realities whose meaning is not limited by the horizons of this life only: their true evaluation and full meaning can only be understood in reference to man's eternal destiny" (GS 51). The sex act is like the Consecration at the Eucharist—they are like two doors through which God miraculously enters this world—and contraception is like saying the words of Consecration while deliberately preventing it from happening (for example, by using no bread). What contraception deliberately prevents is not an "accident" but an act of God.

" 'This particular doctrine, expounded on numerous occasions by the Magisterium, is based on the inseparable connection, established by God, which man on his own initiative may not break, between the unitive significance and the procreative significance which are both inherent to the marriage act' " [HV 12; cf. Pius XI, encyclical, *Casti Connubii*] (CCC 2366). The act *means* "I give you my whole self, with nothing held back" and "We hereby perform procreation." The language of the body speaks a word in the sex act, which by its own essence means both mutual self-giving union and openness to procreation. To contracept is to lie, to say one thing with the body and the opposite thing with the contraceptive instrument. The body says: "Let there be new life", while the instrument says: "Let this life be prevented."

Even if all this teaching is not fully understood by one's reason, it should be believed by faith; for being a Catholic means believing the Church teaches with divine authority given to her by Christ, her Founder, and therefore this must include believing some things on God's authority, not our own. That is one of the things "faith" *means*. And even if polls show a large percentage of Catholics disagreeing with the Church's teaching, in belief and in practice, on this or any other issue, God does not change his mind to conform to opinion polls. We did not elect him to be God, and we cannot vote him out of office.

14. Large families

Family size is rightly under the authority of parents, and responsible birth regulation by natural methods is a good thing. Not everyone can or should have many children. However, "Sacred Scripture and the Church's traditional practice see in *large families* a sign of God's blessing and the parents' generosity [cf. GS 50 § 2]" (CCC 2373). Large families are another sign of the radical difference between the outlook of the God of life and "the culture of death".

15. Sins against procreation

"Techniques that entail the dissociation of husband and wife, by the intrusion of a person other than the couple (donation of sperm or ovum, surrogate uterus), are gravely immoral. These techniques (heterologous artificial insemination and fertilization) infringe the child's right to be born of a father and mother known to him and bound to each other by marriage" [7] (CCC 2376).

"Techniques involving only the married couple (homologous artificial insemination and fertilization) are perhaps less reprehensible, yet remain morally unacceptable. They dissociate the sexual act from the procreative act. The act which brings the child into existence is no longer an act by which two persons give themselves to one another, but one that 'entrusts the life and identity of the embryo into the power of doctors and biologists and establishes the domination of technology over the origin and destiny of the human person. Such a relationship of domination is in itself contrary to the . . . equality that must be common to parents and children' " [8] (CCC 2377). Procreating begins to turn into manufacturing, and persons (children) into objects.

16. Adultery

Adultery is gravely immoral for at least three reasons:

a. "Adultery is an injustice. He who commits adultery fails in his commitment. He . . . transgresses the rights of the other spouse. . . ."

---

[7] See CDF, *Donum vitae* II, 1.

[8] CDF, *Donum vitae* II, 5.

b. "He does injury to . . . the marriage bond . . . and undermines the institution of marriage. . . ."

c. "He compromises the . . . welfare of children who need their parents' stable union" (CCC 2381).

The adulterer sins against his spouse, his society, and his children, as well as his own body and soul.

17. Divorce

The Church cannot allow divorce, as almost all Protestant churches do, because she does not have the authority to contradict Christ her Master. "The Lord Jesus insisted on the original intention of the Creator who willed that marriage be indissoluble.[9] He abrogates the accommodations" [for divorce] "that had slipped into the old" [Jewish] "Law" [cf. Mt 19:7–9] (CCC 2382). In fidelity to her Master, the Church teaches that "[b]etween the baptized, a 'ratified and consummated marriage cannot be dissolved by any human power or any reason other than death' [CIC, can. 1141]" (CCC 2382).

The Church's prohibition of divorce can be understood only in light of her teaching on marriage. The most important aspect of this teaching, and the one hardest for many today to understand and accept, is that marriage is not a human invention. It has its own unchangeable inner essence, like anything else in nature, as designed by God.

Part of its essence is its indissolubility. Once two people freely create a marriage and become "one flesh", this cannot be un-created, ever. It is like a child, like an immortal soul. Ending it is simply not a possibility offered to us by objective reality. In other words, divorce is not just bad, it is an illusion, a fantasy. The "one flesh" is as objectively real as a rhinoceros, and as non-negotiable. It may be good or bad, happy or sad, but it is real. We can disguise it or ignore it, but it will go on existing, even if we declare it dead by divorce. Its existence is not dependent on our will.

"*Divorce* is a grave offense against the natural law. It claims to break the contract, to which the spouses freely consented, to live with each other till death" (CCC 2384). It is the *prime* example of promise-breaking, as marriage is the prime example of promise-keeping and the primary human image of God's covenant with us. We are the people of a faithful God, not one who breaks faith.

"Contracting a new union, even if it is recognized by civil law, adds to the gravity of the rupture: the remarried spouse is then in a situation of public and permanent adultery" (CCC 2384).

---

[9] Cf. Mt 5:31–32; 19:3–9; Mk 10:9; Lk 16:18; 1 Cor 7:10–11.

It would *not* be "compassionate" for the Church to allow divorce. The Church forbids divorce precisely because she *is* compassionate, and knows that divorce "brings grave harm to the deserted spouse, to children traumatized by the separation of their parents and often torn between them, and because of its contagious effect which makes it truly a plague on society" (CCC 2385). Children of divorce find it much harder to have stable marriages. The Church's No to divorce gives Catholics who marry (and their children) a wonderful sense of security. In a society where half of all marriages end in divorce, the Church mercifully locks the exit door to that tragedy.

Like her teaching on contraception, the Church's teaching on divorce is rejected by many today, in belief and/or in practice, and constitutes a test of faith; for faith believes what God tells us is true and good for us because it is designed by the love and wisdom of God, even when we do not understand it. Faith gives permission to God's revelation to correct and instruct our fallible human minds and fallen human wills, realizing that God's wisdom is *bound* to contradict man's—unless man and his culture are not fallen. Catholic Christianity is always countercultural in some way. For instance, the Church's prohibition of polygamy is just as countercultural in Africa as her prohibition of divorce is in America. Each human culture, like each human being, has its blind spots. One of the reasons God gave us his Church was to correct and instruct them.

There are three things the Church does allow that are often confused with divorce:

A *separation* is not a divorce and is justified in extreme examples such as domestic violence.

An *annulment* is not a divorce. It is a finding that there never was a valid marriage to begin with because one of the essential ingredients that make a valid marriage was missing from the beginning (see section 7 of this chapter). Although annulments may have been overused and abused in practice, especially in America, they remain valid in principle—like "indulgences" (see part 3, chapter 5, section 19).

A *civil divorce* is not a Church-recognized divorce either. Therefore "[i]f civil divorce remains the only possible way of ensuring certain legal rights, the care of the children, or the protection of inheritance, it can be tolerated and does not constitute a moral offense" (CCC 2383). What marriage means to the state is a very different thing from what it means to the Church.

18. The ninth commandment

The ninth commandment ("You shall not covet your neighbor's wife") adds an internal dimension to the sixth commandment ("You shall not commit adultery"), just as the tenth commandment ("You shall not covet your neighbor's goods") adds an internal dimension to the seventh commandment ("You shall not steal"). Already in the Old Testament law God revealed that he wants not only morally good actions but also morally good hearts. For Love is not satisfied with external deeds alone.

19. The meaning of the "heart"

The ninth commandment forbids an act of the heart (coveting another's spouse). The "heart" is the scriptural term for the very center of the soul, as the physical heart is the center and source of lifeblood in the body. The heart is deeper than feelings, emotions, or sentiments. It is also deeper than thought, for it is the source of thoughts as it is the source of feelings. Solomon advises, "Keep your heart with all vigilance; for from it flow the springs of life" (Prov 4:23). "The heart is the seat of moral personality: 'Out of the heart come evil thoughts, murder, adultery, fornication' [Mt 15:19]"; as well as good thoughts, charity, purity, and honor. "The struggle against carnal covetousness entails purifying the heart" (CCC 2517). We must begin farther back than with actions; we must "take every thought captive to obey Christ" (2 Cor 10:5).

20. Concupiscence

Coveting your neighbor's wife/husband is similar to lusting after her/him (see the first point in section 11 of this chapter). We are responsible for it, for we choose to do it or not do it. (There is no sin where there is no free choice.)

Coveting is to be distinguished from concupiscence, which is not our free choice but our condition (as original sin is our condition and each actual sin is our choice). Concupiscence means "the movement of the sensitive appetite contrary to the operation of human reason" (CCC 2515). What reason says No to, concupiscence says Yes to. "Concupiscence stems from the disobedience of the first sin. It unsettles man's moral faculties and, without being in itself an offense, inclines man to commit sins" [10] (CCC 2515). No one can avoid concupiscence. But we can avoid obeying it and being dominated by it. It is like an albatross around our neck, but it need not be our master.

21. "Body" vs. "flesh"

" 'It is not a matter of despising and condemning the body' [11] " (CCC 2516). Scripture condemns "the flesh" (*sarx, sakra*), not the body (*soma*). The body

---

[10] Cf. Gen 3:11, Council of Trent: DS 1515.
[11] John Paul II, *DeV* 55; cf. Gal 5:25.

comes from God's creation; the flesh comes from man's fall. The "works of the flesh" listed in Galatians 5:19–21 include non-bodily sins such as idolatry, jealousy, and selfishness. The high ideals of Catholic sexual morality stem precisely from a high view of the body, as "a temple of the Holy Spirit" (1 Cor 6:19), not from a low one.

22. Modesty

Chastity and purity are essentially the same in every time and place. They must be distinguished from *modesty* (avoiding sexually provocative action, speech, and dress), which is culturally variable. "The forms taken by modesty vary from one culture to another. Everywhere, however, modesty exists as an intuition of the spiritual dignity proper to man" (CCC 2524) and to human sexuality. Modesty is an important *aid* to chastity.

23. The rewards of chastity

"The sixth beatitude proclaims, 'Blessed are the pure in heart, for they shall see God' [Mt 5:8]. 'Pure in heart' refers to those who have attuned their intellects and wills to the demands of God's holiness, chiefly in three areas: charity;[12] chastity or sexual rectitude;[13] love of truth and orthodoxy of faith.[14] There is a connection between purity of heart, of body, and of faith. . . . 'Pure hearts may understand what they believe' [15] " (CCC 2518).

"The 'pure in heart' are promised that they will see God face to face and be like him.[16] Purity of heart is the precondition of the vision of God. Even now it enables us to see *according to* God" (CCC 2519). "The heart has its reasons, which the reason does not know" (Pascal): it is the lover who best understands the beloved, human or divine. This is why saints are wiser than mere theologians. Pure love yields pure knowledge.

24. Some practical helps

Today, as never before, many feel that these two commandments, unlike all the others, are unrealistic: too difficult, or even impossible, for man to keep. They are indeed difficult, but not impossible. We should not be surprised that obedience is difficult for us, since each fallen human soul is a battlefield between good and evil, love and its counterfeits. But God does not ask the

---

[12] Cf. 1 Tim 4:3–9; 2 Tim 2:22.
[13] Cf. 1 Thess 4:7; Col 3:5; Eph 4:19.
[14] Cf. Titus 1:15; 1 Tim 1:3–4; 2 Tim 2:23–26.
[15] St. Augustine, *De fide et symbolo* 10, 25: PL 40, 196.
[16] Cf. 1 Cor 13:12; 1 Jn 3:2.

impossible. The saints offer some practical means, some weapons of spiritual warfare to conquer sin in any area, especially the area of sex, where modern man seems to need the most help:

a. Humility is the first requirement. We must admit that we cannot succeed by ourselves. We must confess, with St. Paul, "I know that nothing good dwells within me, that is, in my flesh" (Rom 7:18), but we must also confess that "I can do all things in him who strengthens me" (Phil 4:13). St. Thomas Aquinas says that God often withholds grace from us and lets us fall into obvious sin in order to prevent our more calamitous fall into the more subtle and more serious sin of pride and self-satisfaction.

b. We must also be uncompromising about truth and demand total honesty with ourselves, never hiding or evading the light, no matter how uncomfortable (see chapter 10).

c. The Sacrament of Reconciliation is our most powerful weapon against any sin. Satan hates and fears it and the Eucharist more than anything else in this world.

d. We can do something and not just wait for temptations to come. We can fight offensive, not just defensive, spiritual warfare and be proactive rather than reactive by voluntary penances, cheerfully chosen for love of God's honor.

e. We must resolve to give God *everything*, including our very first thoughts (2 Cor 10:5). For "sow a thought, reap an act; sow an act, reap a habit; sow a habit, reap a character; sow a character, reap a destiny."

f. Love, not fear or loathing, can overcome lust. Love of heaven, not disgust with earth, overcomes inordinate love of earth.

g. Christ gave us his Mother, the Blessed Virgin Mary, from the Cross (Jn 19:26–27) as our own mother and model. Images of holy motherhood can combat images of impurity.

h. Remember that there are no victimless crimes, that every time you weaken your soul you weaken the Body of Christ and every member of it, including those you love the most.

i. As with any long and hard struggle, take it one day at a time and one step at a time. The present problem is the only one that is real; let tomorrow and yesterday take care of themselves.

j. Remember who you are: God's child, bought with the price of Christ's blood, destined for heaven. We act out our perceived identities. "Do you not know that your bodies are members of Christ? Shall I therefore take the members of Christ and make them members of a prostitute?" (1 Cor 6:15).

k. Remember where you are going. "Look to the end." There are few sins man will commit on his deathbed. But we are on our deathbed as soon as we are born.

l.   Remember where you are: on a battlefield, not in an easy chair. If you are a Christian, you are a spiritual warrior.

m. Remember that the battle is especially urgent today, when Christ's Church faces a "culture of death".

n. Remember who the enemy is: "For we are not contending against flesh and blood, but against the principalities, against the powers, against the world rulers of this present darkness, against the spiritual hosts of wickedness in the heavenly places" (Eph 6:12).

o.   Remember that good is infinitely stronger than evil. Remember that Satan has been conquered definitively and forever by what Christ did for you on the Cross. Take refuge *there*.

The most important aspect of the whole topic of sexual morality is Jesus Christ. He is the Word (Mind) of God, who designed sex; he is the One whose love gave his blood as the price of our forgiveness for abusing his designs; and he is the one who assures us, in his very last words on earth, "Behold, I am with you always, to the close of the age" (Mt 28:20).

Chapter 9

THE SEVENTH AND TENTH COMMANDMENTS:
SOCIAL AND ECONOMIC MORALITY

1. The meaning of the seventh commandment

There is nothing mysterious or ambiguous about "You shall not steal." "The seventh commandment forbids unjustly taking or keeping the goods of one's neighbor" ["neighbor" means simply any other human being] "and wronging him in any way with respect to his goods. It commands justice and charity in the care of earthly goods" (CCC 2401).

2. The importance of the seventh commandment

The seventh commandment regulates *property*, or worldly goods—in other words, money and anything money can buy. This is one of five basic areas of human relationships in all times, places, and cultures, and every culture has some version of the Ten Commandments, some regulation of each of these five areas:

a. family (the fourth commandment)
b. life (the fifth commandment)
c. sex (the sixth and ninth commandments)
d. property (the seventh and tenth commandments)
e. communication (the eighth commandment)

Although, objectively speaking, property is not as important as life, family, sex, or communication, this commandment is important because so much of our time and energy is naturally spent on property. We live, by divine design, in a material world, and we are put here to learn how to use the things of this world as training for greater things in the next. We could think of the whole material world as the extension of our body. The goodness and importance of the body correspond to the goodness and importance of the material world of *things*. Just as these mortal bodies of ours are preliminary versions of our future immortal resurrection bodies, so this world will pass away and be replaced by "a new heaven and a new earth" (Rev 21:1). As bikes are given to young children to train them in driving skills for cars later in life, so the goods of this world, including money, are to be used as our training for the kingdom of heaven (see Christ's parable in Matthew 25:14–30).

3. Man's relationship with the earth

Catholic morality on this issue, as on others, is based on basic principles of reality. What *ought to be* is based on what *is*. Therefore, it is balanced and complete, doing justice to both the real and ideal dimensions of the human situation. This distinguishes it from ideologies, which are based not on objective reality but on fashionable and changing human ideas and desires and therefore always exaggerate some one aspect and downplay its opposite.

The principle governing the relationship of man to the earth is that "In the beginning God entrusted the earth and its resources to . . . mankind to take care of them, master them by labor, and enjoy their fruits [cf. Gen 1:26–29]" (CCC 2402). Note the balance here: we are caretakers of the earth and responsible for it, but we are also its masters. Both an irresponsible exploitation of it and a neo-pagan worship of it are extremes to be avoided. The idea that we are the "stewards" of the world avoids both of these extremes. Thus environmental and ecological conservation is part of our responsibility. This planet is supposed to be like a garden: "The LORD God took the man and put him in the garden of Eden to till it and keep it" (Gen 2:15).

4. Private property and the common good

Here, too, Catholic morality is based on fundamental principles of reality and therefore does justice to both the private and the public good.

On the one hand, "[t]he goods of creation are destined" [divinely planned and purposed] "for the whole human race" (CCC 2402). "The *right to private property* . . . does not do away with the original gift of the earth to the whole of mankind" (CCC 2403). Therefore, "'[i]n his use of things man should regard the external goods he legitimately owns not merely as exclusive to himself but common to others also'" [not in the sense that they are owned by others but], "'in the sense that they can'" [and should] "'benefit others as well as himself'" [GS 69 § 1] (CCC 2404). Private property is designed for more than private enjoyment; it is designed for the common good. "The ownership of any property makes its holder a steward of Providence, with the task of making it fruitful and communicating its benefits to others, first of all his family" (CCC 2404). Families exist partly to train us to overcome our natural "original selfishness" in this first, closest level of charity.

On the other hand, "the promotion of the common good requires respect for the right to private property" (CCC 2403). Private property is a natural need and a natural right. This is why communism is unnatural.

These two things—private property and the common good—are not by nature opposed but complementary, like man and woman. They exist for each other. The common good fosters private property, and private property fosters the common good. It is the same as the relation between individuality and society: individuality is nourished, not threatened, by social relations, and society is strengthened, not weakened, by strong individuals.

5. Government regulation of the economy

"*Political authority* has the right and duty to regulate the legitimate exercise of the right to ownership for the sake of the common good" (CCC 2406).[1] Since private property is for the common good, there is no absolute right to it or to unrestricted capitalism and a totally "free market".

6. Taking emergency needs is not theft

The right to private property may be modified not only by governments but even by private individuals in extreme cases, such as the classic example of Jean Valjean in Victor Hugo's *Les Miserables*, who "steals" a loaf of bread to feed his starving family. This is not theft. "There is no theft if . . . refusal is contrary to

[1] Cf. GS 71 § 4; SRS 42; CA 40; 48.

reason.... This is the case in obvious and urgent necessity... to provide for immediate, essential needs (food, shelter, clothing...)" (CCC 2408; cf. GS 69 § 1).

7. Business ethics

Here are some sins against the seventh commandment by both labor and management: "deliberate retention of goods lent or of objects lost; business fraud; paying unjust wages" (CCC 2409). ("A *just wage* is the legitimate fruit of work" [CCC 2434].) Also "[f]orcing up prices by taking advantage of the ignorance or hardship of another;[2]... speculation in which one contrives to manipulate the price of goods artificially in order to gain an advantage to the detriment of others; corruption in which one influences the judgment of those who must make decisions according to law; appropriation and use for private purposes of the common goods of an enterprise; work poorly done; tax evasion; forgery of checks and invoices; excessive expenses and waste. Willfully damaging private or public property..." (CCC 2409).

Notice that some of these are sins by management and some by labor. These two have different but complementary and equally important duties, like governments and citizens, husbands and wives, parents and children, and are meant to work in harmony, not opposition. When there *is* opposition, and when negotiations fail to resolve disputes between labor and management, "[r]ecourse to a *strike* is morally legitimate... when it is necessary to obtain a proportionate" [reasonable and just] "benefit" (CCC 2435).

8. Promises

"*Promises* must be kept and *contracts* strictly observed to the extent that the commitments made in them are morally just. A significant part of economic and social life depends on the honoring of contracts" (CCC 2410).

Promises bind us to each other, to our word, and to the future. Dishonoring them severs us from society, our own integrity, and history. Without trust in promises, society cannot hold together. The most important and obvious example is the marriage promise (see part 2, chapter 8, section 17).

9. Gambling

Again we have a balanced and two-sided teaching. On the one hand, "*Games of chance*... or *wagers* are not in themselves contrary to justice." [On

---

[2] Cf. Deut 25:13–16; 24:14–15; Jas 5:4; Am 8:4–6.

the other hand,] "[t]hey become morally unacceptable when they deprive someone of what is necessary to provide for his needs and those of others. The passion for gambling risks becoming an enslavement" (CCC 2413). It is like wine, which is designed by God "to gladden the heart of man" (Ps 104:15) but which is easily abused by man to "sadden" rather than "gladden". For many, gambling is harmless enjoyment, while for others it is tragically harmful. Discernment and prudence are needed in each case.

10. Animals

Once again the Church gives us a balanced and two-sided teaching, based on objective reality, on an issue that is often ideologically polarized today.

On the one hand, "[m]an's dominion over . . . other living beings granted by the Creator is not absolute; it is limited by concern for the quality of life of his neighbor, including generations to come; it requires a religious respect for the integrity of creation" [cf. *CA* 37–38] (CCC 2415). A "religious" respect because creation is the work of the Creator. Nature, God's invention, is a greater work of art than any human invention. If our vision were more like God's—that is, more true to reality—our moral duties would become quite clear, on this as on all issues.

This respect for things in nature is demanded especially by animals, the next highest material creatures after man. "*Animals* are God's creatures. . . . By their mere existence they bless him and give him glory.[3] Thus men owe them kindness. We should recall the gentleness with which saints like St. Francis of Assisi or St. Philip Neri treated animals" (CCC 2416).

On the other hand, though animals have feelings, they do not have immortal, rational, and moral souls; they are not *persons*. "Hence it is legitimate to use animals for food and clothing" (CCC 2417). And "[m]edical and scientific experimentation on animals is a morally acceptable practice if it remains within reasonable limits and contributes to caring for or saving human lives" (CCC 2417). For God created animals for man (Gen 2:18–20).

Again the Church's reasonableness avoids (and perhaps offends) both extremes. On the one hand, "It is contrary to human dignity to cause animals to suffer or die needlessly. It is likewise unworthy to spend money on them that should as a priority go to the relief of human misery. One can love animals", but "one should not direct to them the affection due only to persons" (CCC 2418).

---

[3] Cf. Mt 6:26; Dan 3: 79–81.

11. The relationship between the Church and economic and political morality

Once again Catholic teaching avoids two extremes. On the one hand, the Church's business is not economics or politics as such. "It is not the role of the Pastors of the Church to intervene directly in the political structuring and organization of social life. This task is part of the vocation of the *lay faithful*, acting on their own initiative" (CCC 2442).

There is no one absolutely best system of economics or politics. Much variety, change, and relativity characterize the economic and political dimensions of human history. "Social action can assume various concrete forms" (CCC 2442). Some people, especially in America, are quite religious about their politics and very political about their religion. They are religiously absolutistic about politically relative things and politically relativistic about religiously absolute things. The more anchored we are in the eternal principles of divine revelation, the more free we are to experiment with changing human institutions. The more we know God, the true absolute, the freer we are from the temptation to idolize any human invention.

On the other hand, the Church's business *does* include morality, including economic morality. "The Church makes a moral judgment about economic and social matters, 'when the fundamental rights of the person or the salvation of souls requires it' [GS 76 § 5]" (CCC 2420).

12. Capitalism and socialism

"The social doctrine of the Church developed in the nineteenth century when the Gospel encountered modern industrial society with its new structures for the production of consumer goods, its new concept of society, the state and authority, and its new forms of labor and ownership" (CCC 2421). In thus bringing her perennial moral principles to bear on new situations, the Church developed criteria of judgment and guidelines for action that refused to give unqualified endorsement to either "hard" capitalism or "hard" socialism.

"Any system in which social relationships are determined entirely by economic factors is contrary to the nature of the human person [cf. *CA* 24]" (CCC 2423). This "economism" is a danger of both capitalism and socialism.

Not all socialist governments are immoral. But there is a special danger in socialism: "A system that 'subordinates the basic rights of individuals and of groups to the collective organization of production' is contrary to human dignity [GS 65 § 2]" (CCC 2404). "The Church has rejected the totalitarian and atheistic ideologies associated in modern times with 'communism' or 'socialism' " (CCC 2425).

The Church does not reject capitalism as such either. But "she has . . . refused to accept, in the practice of 'capitalism,' individualism and the absolute primacy of the law of the marketplace over human labor [cf. *CA* 10; 13; 44]" (CCC 2425). There is a special danger in capitalism too: "A theory that makes profit the exclusive norm and ultimate end of economic activity is morally unacceptable" (CCC 2424). And the profit motive—a necessary virtue in capitalism—is often only another name for a capital vice, one of the "seven deadly sins", namely, greed, or avarice.

We need a balanced and reasonable attitude toward profit. On the one hand, "[t]hose *responsible for business enterprises* . . . have an obligation to consider the good of persons" [above] "the increase of *profits*. Profits are necessary, however. They make possible the investments that ensure the future of a business and they guarantee employment" (CCC 2432). Profit is to production what pleasure is to sex: right and proper and natural when associated with the intrinsic purpose of the activity, but all too easily divorced from that purpose and loved for its own sake.

We also need a balanced view toward government regulation. On the one hand, "[r]egulating the economy solely by centralized planning perverts the basis of social bonds;" [on the other hand,] "regulating it solely by the law of the marketplace fails social justice, for 'there are many human needs which cannot be satisfied by the market' [*CA* 34]" (CCC 2425).

13. Human work

One of the areas of modern life where the Church has developed and extended her principles the most today is in the area of a "theology of work".

The fundamental principle about the significance and dignity of human work is this: "*Human work* proceeds directly from persons created in the image of God and called to prolong the work of creation" (CCC 2427). Thus work is creative.

On the other hand, because of the Fall, work is also a hardship. "In the sweat of your face you shall eat bread" (Gen 3:19).

But "[i]t can also be redemptive. By enduring the hardship of work [cf. Gen 3:14–19] in union with Jesus, the carpenter of Nazareth and the one crucified on Calvary, man collaborates in a certain fashion with the Son of God in his redemptive work. . . . Work can be a means of sanctification" (CCC 2427). All human work can be an *opus Dei*, a "work of God".

14. The personalism of work

"The primordial value of labor stems from man himself, its author and its beneficiary. Work is for man, not man for work [cf. *LE* 6]" (CCC 2428).

Therefore all work must be judged by human standards—how does it benefit man?—rather than men being judged by work's standards, as if man were a mere "means of production".

15. International economics

"On the international level, inequality of resources and economic capability is such that it creates a real 'gap' between nations [cf. *SRS* 14]. On the one side there are those nations possessing and developing the means of growth, and, on the other, those accumulating debts" (CCC 2437).

"*Rich nations* have a grave moral responsibility toward those which are unable to ensure the means of their development by themselves or have been prevented from doing so by tragic historical events. It is a duty in solidarity and charity; it is also an obligation in justice" (CCC 2439). It is true both between nations and between individuals that (in the words of Pope Gregory the Great), " '[w]hen we attend to the needs of those in want, we give them what is theirs, not ours. More than performing works of mercy, we are paying a debt of justice' [4] " (CCC 2446).

16. Charity to the poor

"God blesses those who come to the aid of the poor and rebukes those who turn away from them. . . . It is by what they have done for the poor that Jesus Christ will recognize his chosen ones [cf. Mt 25:31–36]" (CCC 2443). Christ "invites us to recognize his own presence in the poor" [5] (CCC 2449) and tells us: "Truly, I say to you, as you did it to one of the least of these my brethren, you did it to me" (Mt 25:40). The phrase "Truly I say to you" means that this is no exaggeration or figure of speech. It is truth from the lips of Truth.

Riches are not evil, nor are all rich people selfish. But riches are dangerous—more dangerous than we think, if we are to take Christ's repeated warnings seriously. One indication of the danger of riches is the statistical fact that, in most cultures, the poor are much more generous than the rich to those below themselves on the economic scale. The poor can afford to give less, yet they give (proportionately) more. The rich can afford to give more, yet they give less. Generosity seems spiritually harder when it is materially easier. This shows why riches are dangerous: because they tend to be addictive. Another, more spectacular fact is that suicide is much more common among the rich (individuals *or* nations) than the poor.

Thus Christ pronounces a blessing on the "poor in spirit"—that is, those

---

[4] St. Gregory the Great, *Regula Pastoralis* 3, 21: PL 77, 87.
[5] *Am* 8:6; cf. Mt 25:40.

whose spirit is detached from riches. Thus even those who are not materially poor but who help the poor by detaching themselves from some of their wealth can be "poor in spirit" and blessed. Alms do a double good—to giver as well as to receiver—for it is even "more blessed to give than to receive" (see section 19 of this chapter).

Human "misery elicited the compassion of Christ the Savior, who willingly took it upon himself and identified himself with the least of his brethren. Hence, those who are oppressed by poverty are the object of *a preferential love* on the part of the Church" (CCC 2448). For the Church as "the extension of the Incarnation" does the very same work Christ did. The Body of Christ is directed by her Head, not as a corporation is directed from afar by its CEO, but as our bodies are directed by our own brains and nervous systems (see part 1, chapter 7).

17. The works of mercy

The Church has traditionally listed six spiritual and six corporal (bodily) works of mercy. The spiritual works of mercy are (a) instructing, (b) advising, (c) consoling, (d) comforting, (e) forgiving, and (f) bearing wrongs patiently.

The corporal works of mercy are: (a) feeding the hungry, (b) sheltering the homeless, (c) clothing the naked, (d) visiting the sick, (e) visiting the imprisoned, and (f) burying the dead.

18. The tenth commandment: "You shall not covet your neighbor's goods"

"Covetousness" means "disordered desire". This can be either desire for too much, desire for what we do not really need (this is greed), or desire for what belongs to another (this is envy, the only sin that never gives anyone any pleasure at all). Desire is in itself good and designed by God. So is pleasure. But sin distorts good things into evil things.

Greed for money is even more dangerous than greed for things, because it has no limit. We can only use or imagine using a finite number of houses or cars or meals, but the desire for money can be infinite. " 'He who loves money never has money enough' [6] " (CCC 2536). Greed for money is usually greed for power even more than greed for things, and perhaps subconsciously a fear or resentment at being less than God, vulnerable and dependent—that is, human.

---

[6] *Roman Catechism*, III, 37; cf. Sir 5:8.

19. Detachment from riches (poverty of spirit)

The first Beatitude ("Blessed are the poor in spirit"—Mt 5:3) corresponds to the tenth commandment ("You shall not covet your neighbor's goods"). Both teach detachment of spirit (desire) from riches.

"The precept of detachment from riches is obligatory for entrance into the Kingdom of heaven" (CCC 2544). "Whoever of you does not renounce [turn his heart away from] all that he has cannot be my disciple" (Lk 14:33). This apparently hard saying is really compassionate, for the detachment it commands is liberating (just as obedience to all the commandments is), like "detaching" a fly from flypaper or a prisoner from prison. The alternative is a spiritual slavery and addiction, a worshipful marriage union with money. Christ reminds us that "where your treasure is, there will your heart be also" (Mt 6:21). Detachment is liberating because we become like what we worship: dead, like money, or alive, like God. This is the principle taught in Psalm 115:

> Their idols are silver and gold,
>> the work of men's hands.
> They have mouths, but do not speak;
>> eyes, but do not see.
> They have ears, but do not hear;
>> noses, but do not smell.
> They have hands, but do not feel;
>> feet, but do not walk;
>> and they do not make a sound in their throat.
> Those who make them are like them;
>> so are all who trust in them.

20. The way to detachment

How can we be detached from covetousness?

"An evil desire can only be overcome by a stronger good desire" (St. Thomas Aquinas). Just as true love can free us from lust, so "[d]esire for true happiness frees man from his immoderate attachment to the goods of this world so that he can find his fulfillment in the vision and beatitude of God" (CCC 2548). This is not unrealistic but utterly reasonable, for " '[w]hoever sees God has obtained all the goods of which he can conceive' " [7] (CCC 2548).

---

[7] St. Gregory of Nyssa, *De beatitudinibus* 6: PG 44, 1265A.

A hymn writer, Henry Lyte, put this most practical point in these words:

> Perish every fond ambition,
> All I've thought and hoped and known,
> Yet how rich is my condition!
> God and Heaven are still my own.

For the hymn writer had pondered deeply these words of the Apostle (Paul):

> If any other man thinks he has reason for confidence in the flesh, I have more: circumcised on the eighth day, of the people of Israel, of the tribe of Benjamin, a Hebrew born of Hebrews; as to the law, a Pharisee, as to zeal a persecutor of the church, as to righteousness under the law, blameless. But whatever gain I had, I counted as loss for the sake of Christ. Indeed, I count everything as loss because of the surpassing worth of knowing Christ Jesus my Lord. For his sake I have suffered the loss of all things, and count them as refuse [KJV: "dung"!], in order that I may gain Christ, and be found in him (Phil 3:4–9).

For the Apostle, in turn, had pondered even more deeply these words of his Lord, the most practical sentence ever spoken:

> What shall it profit a man if he shall gain the whole world, and lose his own soul? (Mk 8:36, KJV).

Chapter 10

THE EIGHTH COMMANDMENT: TRUTH

1. The importance of the eighth commandment

The eighth commandment is really much more far-reaching than it seems. It forbids not only perjury, false oaths, calumny, and slander, but all kinds of falsehood, and it commands total truthfulness.

This commandment is one of the most neglected and most disobeyed of all the commandments. For like the first commandment, it is disobeyed whenever *any* commandment is disobeyed. Just as all sin is some kind of idolatry (choosing some false god), so all sin is some kind of falsehood, some kind of choice of darkness over light.

The eighth commandment does not merely tell us to speak the truth to others but also to love and live the truth in ourselves, to commit our whole hearts to truth and to live that commitment. It forbids false witness not only against our neighbor but also against ourselves, since we are to love our neighbor "as ourselves".

2. How all sin is a form of lying

Bearing false witness against our neighbor means lying to our neighbor, deceiving our neighbor. But lying to our neighbor always begins with lying to ourselves. All sin does. The pattern for all sin is shown in the first sin, in Genesis 3, the eating of the forbidden fruit. This sin began by listening to the devil's lie, sin's false advertisement, the lie that this sin would bring joy and delight while obedience to God's command would bring misery or boredom.

The first step in barring the door to sin is refusing to listen to any false witness that contradicts God's revealed truth. Faith is this bar against sin. Therefore Scripture says, "Whatever does not proceed from faith is sin" (Rom 14:23). St. Paul contrasts sin with faith, not just with virtue, and contrasts faith with sin, not just with doubt. Believing the darkness of Satan's lie rather than the light of God's commandment was the beginning of the Fall and continues to be the beginning of every fall. We eat the forbidden fruit of falsehood with our minds before we eat any other forbidden fruit with our bodies and our deeds.

3. The importance of truth for morality

Man, having both body and soul, lives in two worlds, a material world and a moral and spiritual world. God ordered man's physical world by the "days" of creation; then he ordered man's moral and spiritual world by the Ten Commandments. The source of both orders is Truth.

In all cultures, light is the natural symbol and expression of truth. No good work can be done without light. The world's best doctor in the world's best hospital with the world's best technology cannot perform the simplest operation without light. God himself did not order the universe without light; he created light first.

Created light was the first reflection of uncreated light. Light came first for God, and it must come first for us too, if we are to echo God's will and God's priorities. Our very first choice must be: "Let there be light!" We must love and seek and live and speak the truth. For if we do not *love* the truth, we will not *know* it. If we do not first seek it with our will, we will not find it with our mind.

The crucial importance of truth for morality is not generally understood today. People are rarely taught that morality is more than kindness and compassion, more than good intentions, even more than love. For love without truth is not true love.

Love and truth are equally absolute, for both are divine attributes, infinite and eternal. Truth and love are "what God is made of". These two are one in God, and the more godly we are, the more they are one in us.

4. The theological basis for the eighth commandment

"The eighth commandment forbids misrepresenting the truth. . . . This moral prescription flows from the vocation of the holy people to bear witness to their God who is the truth and wills the truth" (CCC 2464).

As with all the commandments, this one is based on reality; what ought to be follows from what is. The reality here is the ultimate reality, God—his essential nature. Repeatedly, Scripture describes God as "true". The Hebrew word used, *emeth*, means not just "objectively accurate thinking and speaking" but "personal reliability, trustability, integrity, fidelity".

We are to be people of truth because our God is truth. In him truth is perfectly personified; truth is a Person!—the One who proclaimed, "I am . . . the truth" (Jn 14:6). "Since God is 'true,' the members of his people are called to live in the truth" [1] (CCC 2465).

5. "What is truth?"

What truth means in God, its origin, determines what it means for man, God's image. And the *Catechism* mentions three aspects of truth in God: "*God is the source of all truth.* His Word is truth. His Law is truth. His 'faithfulness endures to all generations' [2] " (CCC 2465).

What do these three things mean for us?
a. The truth of God's Word is the revelation of his mind.
b. The truth of God's law is the revelation of his will.
c. The truth of God's promises is the revelation of his heart.

These three aspects of truth fulfill the needs of the three parts of the human soul:
a. God's Word fulfills the mind's search for true thought.
b. God's law fulfills the will's search for a true life.
c. God's promises fulfill the heart's search for true joy.

They also correspond to the three theological virtues:
a. God's Word (revelation) specifies what faith believes ("Your word is truth"—Jn 17:17).
b. God's law specifies what charity chooses ("If you love me, you will keep my commandments"—Jn 14:15).

---

[1] Rom 3:4; cf. Ps 119:30.
[2] Ps 119:90; cf. Prov 8:7; 2 Sam 7:28; Ps 119:142; Lk 1:50.

c. God's promises specify what hope trusts ("This is what he has promised us, eternal life"—I Jn 2:25).

The three lasting cultures of ancient times—Greek, Roman, and
Hebrew—especially emphasized these three aspects of truth, as enshrined in
their very words for "truth":

a. *Alētheia*, the Greek word for truth, means the "unhiddenness", or
revelation, of a mystery to a mind.

b. *Veritas*, the Latin word for truth, means rightness or righteousness of
thought or deed.

c. *Emeth*, the Hebrew word for truth, means faithfulness in the heart and
character.

All three are fulfilled in Christ, the "light of the world":

a. Christ is the ultimate revelation of the mystery of God to us.

b. Christ is our ultimate righteousness, or holiness.

c. Christ is the fulfillment of all God's promises to us.

6. The Christocentrism of the eighth commandment

"In Jesus Christ, the whole of God's truth has been made manifest. 'Full of
grace and truth,' he came as the 'light of the world,' he *is the Truth*" [3] (CCC
2466). Before Pilate, Christ proclaims that he "has come into the world, to
bear witness to the truth" (Jn 18:37), and Judge Pilate scornfully asked,
"What is truth?", when the most complete answer any man ever received to
that question was standing right in front of him. Pilate let Christ be crucified
in his court because he first let truth be crucified in his soul.

7. Lying is wrong because it is contrary to human nature

"Man tends by nature toward the truth" (CCC 2467). This is not a naïve
optimism that ignores original sin, the universal human tendency toward
falsehood, or the struggle between truth and falsehood. It means that man's
essence, man's God-created nature, has truth as its natural end, its spiritual
food. Man is meant for truth.

That is why lying is wrong. "By its very nature, lying is to be condemned.
It is a profanation of speech, whereas the purpose of speech is to communicate known truth to others" (CCC 2485).

(Once again the categories of "human nature" and "natural purpose"
come up as central and indispensable to Catholic morality. They are simple,
commonsense concepts, but modern sceptical philosophers have made them
unpopular for the first time in history.)

---

[3] Jn 1:14; 8:12; cf. 14:6.

8. The social necessity for truth-telling

" 'Men could not live with one another if there were not mutual confidence that they were being truthful to one another'[4]" (CCC 2469). Thus the eighth commandment is an essential part of Catholic social ethics as well as individual ethics.

9. Truth as a form of justice

"The virtue of truth gives another his just due" (CCC 2469). (Here "truth" is the virtue of truthfulness.)

The demand to be truthful and to love truth is absolute and unqualified, but the demand to communicate it is subject to justice, which must take account of the circumstances and the other person's right to know. We are not morally obligated to "tell the truth" by revealing secrets we promised to keep or to reveal all our thoughts—for instance, to say to a person we think ugly, "I think you're ugly!" "Truthfulness keeps to the just mean between what ought to be expressed and what ought to be kept secret: it entails honesty and discretion" (CCC 2469).

Honesty does not mean saying everything we feel. (That is either candor, when good, or shamelessness, when bad.) Nor is honesty opposed to keeping just secrets or withholding truth from those who have no right to know it—for instance, those who intend harm.

10. "Witnessing"

"The Christian is not to 'be ashamed . . . of testifying to our Lord' [2 Tim 1:8]. In situations that require witness to the faith, the Christian must profess it without equivocation" (CCC 2471).

"The duty of Christians to take part in the life of the Church impels them to act as *witnesses of the Gospel*" (CCC 2472). For that *is* "the life of the Church". Christ's command to "go therefore and make disciples of all nations" (Mt 28:19) did not come with a "clergy only" tag.

Witnessing should be done with prudence, grace, and sensitivity, however, rather than in the pushy way sometimes associated with the "Fundamentalist" stereotype, or in any way that harms the gospel more than it helps it. On the other hand, we must also avoid timidity (a far greater danger for most) and not tailor Christ's gospel to man's desires, omitting its unfashionable and offensive teachings. Christ warned us, "Woe to you,

---

[4] St. Thomas Aquinas, *STh* II-II, 109, 3 *ad* 1.

when all men speak well of you, for so their fathers did to the false prophets" (Lk 6:26).

11. Martyrdom

"*Martyrdom* is the supreme witness given to the truth of the faith: it means bearing witness even unto death" (CCC 2473). The Christian tradition has always put a high value on martyrdom, since this was the most important thing Christ himself did, the reason he came into the world. The word "martyr" means "witness" in New Testament Greek; a martyr is not merely one who endures wrongful death, but one who does so for truth, as a "witness" to truth.

Few things are worth more than life itself. Only what is eternal is worth more than all of time, worth more than a lifetime. But truth is eternal.

Jim Eliot, twentieth-century missionary martyr in Ecuador, explained the wisdom of martyrdom succinctly: "He is no fool who gives up what he cannot keep to win what he cannot lose."

Martyrdom is not something from some bygone era. There have been more Christian martyrs in the twentieth century than in all nineteen previous centuries combined. As history moves closer to its end and to Christ's promised Second Coming (however near or far away that may be), martyrdom will not cease but will continue to be a "sign of contradiction", a *cross*. It is a sign of the spiritual warfare between Christ and Antichrist, light and darkness, truth and falsehood, which is Scripture's persistent theme from Genesis to Revelation, because it is the central drama of human history and of each individual life.

12. Some specific sins against truth

a. "*False witness and perjury*. When it is made publicly, a statement contrary to the truth takes on a particular gravity. In court it becomes false witness [cf. Prov 19:9]. When it is under oath, it is perjury. Acts such as these contribute to condemnation of the innocent, exoneration of the guilty, or the increased punishment of the accused [cf. Prov 18:5]. They gravely compromise the exercise of justice" (CCC 2476).

b. "He becomes guilty:—of *rash judgment* who . . . assumes as true, without sufficient foundation, the moral fault of a neighbor;

"—of *detraction* who, without objectively valid reason, discloses another's faults. . . [cf. Sir 21:28];

"—of *calumny* who, by remarks contrary to the truth, harms the reputation of others and gives occasion for false judgments concerning them" (CCC 2477).

13. Lying

" 'A *lie* consists in speaking a falsehood with the intention of deceiving' [5] " (CCC 2482).

"Lying is the most direct offense against the truth. To lie is to speak or act against the truth in order to lead someone into error" (CCC 2483). Both of these elements must be present for a lie. Unintentional falsehood is not a deliberate lie. Nor is play-acting or fiction. Nor is it lying to refuse truth to one who ought not to know it. "The *right to the communication* of the truth is not unconditional. . . . [F]raternal love . . . requires us in concrete situations to judge whether or not it is" [morally] "appropriate to reveal the truth" (CCC 2488).

14. Different degrees of lying

"The *gravity of a lie* is measured against the nature of the truth it deforms, the circumstances, the intentions of the one who lies, and the harm suffered by its victims" (CCC 2484).

15. The secret of the confessional

"The *secret of the sacrament of reconciliation* is sacred, and cannot be violated under any pretext" (CCC 2490). A priest cannot and will not reveal to anyone for any reason anything he hears in sacramental confession.

16. Privacy

"Everyone should observe an appropriate reserve concerning persons' private lives. Those in charge of communications should maintain a fair balance between the requirements of the common good" [this does not include the right to hear gossip!] "and respect for individual rights" (CCC 2492).

17. Censorship and propaganda

At the opposite extreme from Western societies, in which the communications media are very free and subject to little or no moral authority or censorship, totalitarian societies sin against the truth in the opposite way, by censoring truth and broadcasting false propaganda for political purposes. "Moral judgment must condemn the plague of totalitarian states which systematically falsify the truth," [and] "exercise political control of opinion

[5] St. Augustine, *De mendacio* 4, 5: PL 40, 491.

through the media" (CCC 2499), whether this is done under communism, right-wing dictatorship, Muslim fundamentalism, or even democracy. (Is it only "totalitarian states" that falsify and try to control opinion through the media?)

18. The media

"Within modern society the communications media play a major role in information, cultural promotion, and formation" [of opinion, mind, and character]. "This role is increasing, as a result of technological progress" (CCC 2493). Since their power to mold minds is increasing, the real moral responsibility of the media is also increasing. However, modern media in the West are becoming increasingly immoral and more aggressively and uniformly secularist. As a result, modern man is becoming more docile to the secular media and less docile to God's revelation; less sceptical to the world's gospel and more sceptical to God's. The communications and entertainment media constitute one of the major battlefields in the war between truth and falsehood today and offer one of the most important opportunities for Christians to bear witness to the truth and influence their society for the good. Christians should be encouraged to be active in this field, whether professionally or privately, and hold the media to higher moral standards.

In addition to immoral *content*, there is a concern for the psychological effect of the very form and structure of modern media: The mass media "can give rise to a certain passivity among users, making them less than vigilant consumers of what is said or shown" (CCC 2496).

This is mainly due to the fact that images cannot be argued with as clearly as ideas can. This is true of all images, good or bad, naturally or supernaturally planned. According to the saints and Doctors of the Church, evil spirits cannot directly influence our minds or wills, but they can tempt us by influencing our imagination, by bringing up deceptively attractive, erotic, or confusing images that are already in our memories, many of which come from the media. Thus also good images—good movies and stories, lives of the saints, sacred art—have much more power and importance than we suspect in the spiritual warfare between truth and darkness.

19. Truth, goodness, and beauty

These three ideals of the human spirit, based on attributes of God, are by nature one. "The practice of goodness is accompanied by spontaneous spiritual joy and moral beauty. Likewise, truth carries with it the joy and splendor of spiritual beauty" (CCC 2500). Truth and goodness are beautiful. Pope

John Paul II entitled his encyclical about the foundations of moral goodness *The Splendor of Truth*, thus showing the unity of these three things.

20. The truth of natural beauty

"Truth in words, the rational expression of the knowledge of created and uncreated reality, is necessary to man, who is endowed with intellect. But truth can also find other complementary forms of human expression, above all when it is a matter of evoking what is beyond words: the depths of the human heart, the exaltations of the soul, the mystery of God. Even before revealing himself to man in words of truth, God reveals himself to him through the universal language of creation, the work of his Word, of his wisdom: the order and harmony of the cosmos—which both the child and the scientist discover—'from the greatness and beauty of created things comes a corresponding perception of their Creator' [Wis 13:5]" (CCC 2500).

21. The truth of art

"Created 'in the image of God,' [Gen 1:26] man also expresses the truth of his relationship with God the Creator by the beauty of his artistic works. Indeed, *art* is a distinctively human form of expression; beyond the search for the necessities of life which is common to all living creatures, art is a freely given superabundance of the human being's inner riches. Arising from talent given by the Creator and from man's own effort, art is a form of practical wisdom, uniting knowledge and skill, [cf. Wis 7:16–17] to give form to the truth of reality in a language accessible to sight or hearing. To the extent that it is inspired by truth and love of beings, art bears a certain likeness to God's activity in what he has created" (CCC 2501).

22. The truth of sacred art

"*Sacred art* is true and beautiful when its form corresponds to its particular vocation: evoking and glorifying, in faith and adoration, the transcendent mystery of God" (CCC 2502). We can judge sacred art by its effects, according to the principle "You will know them by their fruits" (Mt 7:16). "Genuine sacred art draws man to adoration, to prayer, and to the love of God" (CCC 2502).

If sacred art (especially sacred liturgy) fails in this, its primary purpose, it is deformed, no matter how "relevant", popular, or attractive it may be. Liturgical abuses are not just aesthetic lapses but offenses against divine truth. For the liturgy is a display, not of human taste, but of divine truth.

The greatest works of architecture were built to glorify the Architect of the universe: to house the incarnate eucharistic Christ. These were the cathedrals, miraculous "sermons in stone" that made rock and glass seem to take wing and fly like angels. Many of the world's greatest paintings and statues were made for churches, and much of the greatest music was composed for Masses. For what happens within that sacred time and place is the most beautiful work of art ever conceived: God's work of redeeming man from eternal darkness into heavenly light by enduring that hellish darkness in man's place on the Cross. The most beautiful thing man's eyes have ever seen in this world is the bloody martyrdom of God himself. There, in every Mass, where Christ becomes truly present again in an unbloody manner but in the same act of love, offering himself for our salvation, we find truth incarnate, goodness incarnate, and beauty incarnate, and their perfect union.

PART III

SACRAMENTS AND PRAYER

How Catholics Worship

Chapter 1

INTRODUCTION TO CATHOLIC LITURGY

1. Liturgy is not "soft"

We need to begin with a very general point about the whole subject of liturgy, because this will make a difference to all the specific points about liturgy, as the color of a light makes a difference to everything it shines on.

To many people, "liturgy" sounds like something "soft", something vaguely sweet and sleepy. Liturgical terms like "Paschal mystery" and "sacramental signs" sound somehow remote and removed from real life, like a fairy tale. Many dislike the subject of liturgy because it feels "soft" compared to creeds and commandments, the other two parts of the Catholic faith. Others get exactly the same feeling of "softness" but *like* it. They think it is more "creative", and like to "celebrate community", that is, themselves. They dislike "hard" creeds and commandments but like "soft" liturgy.

Both are wrong. The liturgy is not a "soft" thing, like a human experience or feeling; it is "hard", it is objectively real. It is not a humanly invented work of art, either ancient or modern; it is neither a delicate, ornate, out-of-date antique nor a practical, up-to-date piece of contemporary "relevance".

For it is not some *thing* at all but some*one*: Jesus Christ, who becomes really present and active in the liturgy. "It is the mystery of Christ that the Church proclaims and celebrates in her liturgy" (CCC 1068).

Furthermore, this person is not dead but alive. He is not only the object of our thoughts and symbols; he actually *does things to us* in his sacraments. (That is why he instituted them!) And what he does is, in one word, salvation. "[T]he Church celebrates in the liturgy above all the Paschal mystery" [Christ's death and Resurrection] "by which Christ accomplished the work of our salvation" (CCC 1067).

However, these past events are not repeated, as if they were incomplete when first done in history. Christ said on the Cross, "It is finished" (Jn 19:30). "The Paschal mystery of Christ is celebrated, not repeated. It is the celebrations that are repeated" (CCC 1104).

Finally, "Christian liturgy not only recalls the events that saved us but actualizes them, makes them present" (CCC 1104). Christ is not merely remembered, like a dead man who existed in the past, but he is encountered, as he really is, "alive and kicking" like a stallion.

"It is always shocking to meet life where we thought we were alone . . . when the [fishing] line pulls at your hand, when something breathes beside you in the darkness . . . 'Look out!' we cry, 'it's alive!' . . . There comes a moment when the children who have been playing at burglars hush suddenly: was that a real footstep in the hall? There comes a moment when people who have been dabbling in religion ('man's search for God'!) suddenly draw back. Supposing we really found Him? We never meant it to come to that! Worse still, supposing He had found us?" (C. S. Lewis, *Miracles*).

2. Liturgy as God's work

The word "liturgy" means "work". The essence of the liturgy is the actual work or deed done by God's grace in Christ, not the humanly invented ceremonies that carry it. It is not merely something we do, but something God does.

And what God does is redeem us, save us from sin, and make us holy. "Liturgy" is not a matter of ceremonies; liturgy is the work done by them. " '[I]t is in the liturgy, especially in the divine sacrifice of the Eucharist, that "the work of our redemption is accomplished" ' [SC, 2]" (CCC 1068). It is "*accomplished* "—it is really done, not just symbolized. A sacrament actually effects what it signifies (see part 3, chapter 2 on this point). "Through the liturgy Christ, our redeemer and high priest, continues the work of our redemption" (CCC 1069). In all the sacraments Christ is really present and acting on our souls, saving and sanctifying them through the material signs. In fact, all three Persons of the Trinity are present: the Father becomes "God-with-us" (*Emmanuel*) in his Son, and the Son becomes present to us in the Holy Spirit.

In addition to being a work of God, liturgy is also a work of man—not an addition to God's work, but a participation in it. "The word 'liturgy' orig- inally meant a 'public work'.... In Christian tradition it means the partici- pation of the People of God in 'the work of God' [cf. Jn 17:4]" (CCC 1069). Through the liturgy God gives us the dignity of sharing in his own work, which is the work of our redemption.

It is a work of God and man together because it is a work of the Church, which is the Body of Christ, who is God and man together. Christ, the Church's Head, is no more remote from his Body than your head is remote from your body. The Church has not been beheaded!

In the liturgy "full public worship is performed by the Mystical Body of Jesus Christ, that is, by the Head and his members. From this it follows that every liturgical celebration, because it is an action of Christ the Priest and of his Body, which is the Church, is a sacred action surpassing all others. No other action of the Church can equal its efficacy ... to the same degree" (*SC* 7).

3. The diverse and changing character of liturgy

Liturgy has more diversity and change than creed or code because it is a joint work of God and man, not only a work of God. It is less "unilateral" than creeds and codes, for the creeds summarize the truth that comes from God, not from man, and the commandments summarize the moral demands that come from God, not from man.

But though the forms of the liturgy are diverse and changeable, its sub- stance is not; it is as hard and resistant and sharp as the Cross.

When people think of Catholic liturgy, some think of Gothic cathedrals, with dark, mysterious interiors, bright stained glass, incense, and solemn organ music. Others think of monastic simplicity and inwardness. Others think of folksy enthusiasm and guitar music. Still others think of feeling bored and sleepy. But all these things are accidental, like clothing. Liturgy is not essentially a matter of aesthetic beauty or of psychological feelings. It is essen- tially the work of our salvation, accomplished by God in Christ, applied to our lives through the Church's sacramental rites.

"The mystery celebrated in the liturgy is one, but the forms of its cele- bration are diverse" (CCC 1200). For "[t]he mystery of Christ is so unfath- omably rich that it cannot be exhausted by its expression in any single liturgical tradition" (CCC 1201).

The fundamental rule for all things in the Church can be summarized in this famous threefold formula from the early Church: "In essentials, unity; in non-essentials, diversity; in all things, charity." This applies especially to liturgy.

a. "In essentials, unity." " 'In the liturgy ... there is an *immutable part*, a part that is divinely instituted and of which the Church is the guardian, and parts that *can be changed*, which the Church has the power and on occasion also the duty to adapt to the cultures of recently evangelized peoples' [1] " (CCC 1205). Adaptations are for the sake of better propagating the unchanging essence of the liturgy, not for the sake of change itself.

b. "In non-essentials, diversity." The Catholic Church has many different rites, for "catholic" means "universal", and "universal" (uni-versa) means "many in one", or "one in many"—a music that is a harmony, not a mere unison. "The Church is catholic, capable of integrating into her unity, while purifying them, all the authentic riches of cultures [cf. *LG* 23; *UR* 4]" (CCC 1202). "The celebration of the liturgy, therefore, should correspond to the genius and culture of the different peoples [cf. *SC* 37–40]. In order that the mystery of Christ be 'made known to all the nations...' [Rom 16:26], it must be proclaimed, celebrated, and lived in all cultures in such a way that they themselves are not abolished by it, but redeemed and fulfilled [cf. *CT* 53]" (CCC 1204).

"The liturgical traditions or rites presently in use in the Church are the Latin (principally the Roman rite, but also the rites of certain local churches, such as the Ambrosian rite, or those of certain religious orders) and the Byzantine, Alexandrian or Coptic, Syriac, Armenian, Maronite, and Chaldean rites.... 'Holy Mother Church holds all lawfully recognized rites to be of equal right and dignity, and ... she wishes to preserve them in the future and to foster them in every way' [*SC* 4]" (CCC 1203).

c. "In all things, charity." " 'Liturgical diversity can be a source of enrichment, but it can also provoke tensions, mutual misunderstandings, and even schisms. In this matter it is clear that diversity must not damage unity. It must express only fidelity to the common faith.... Cultural adaptation also requires a conversion of heart and even, where necessary, a breaking with ancestral customs incompatible with the Catholic faith' [2] " (CCC 1206), for example, suttee in India, or voodoo in Haiti.

4. The liturgy in history

Where did the liturgy come from?

"The Church was made manifest to the world on the day of Pentecost by the outpouring of the Holy Spirit [cf. *SC* 6; *LG* 2]. The gift of the Spirit ushers in a new era ... the age of the Church, during which Christ ... communicates his work of salvation through the liturgy of his Church, 'until he comes' [1 Cor 11:26]" (CCC 1076) at the end of time.

Like Scripture, liturgy is essentially historical. It is an event, not just an

---

[1] John Paul II, *Vicesimus quintus annus*, 16; cf. *SC* 21.
[2] John Paul II, *Vicesimus quintus annus*, 16.

idea. Christ's Incarnation, death, and Resurrection comprise "a real event that occurred in our history, but it is unique: all other historical events happen once, and then they pass away, swallowed up in the past. The Paschal mystery of Christ, by contrast, cannot remain only in the past, because . . . all that Christ is—all that he did and suffered for all men—participates in the divine eternity, and so transcends all times while being made present in them all. The event of the Cross and Resurrection *abides*" (CCC 1085).

The sacraments are historical events, like Christ. They *happen*. They are the extension of the "good news", the Gospel facts and events, made present here and now. "By his power he is present in the sacraments so that when anybody baptizes, it is really Christ himself who baptizes" (CCC 1088).

5. The relationship between the liturgies of the Old and New Covenants

"In the sacramental economy" [order] "the Holy Spirit fulfills what was prefigured in *the Old Covenant*. Since Christ's Church was 'prepared in marvellous fashion in the history of the people of Israel and in the Old Covenant,' [LG 2] the Church's liturgy has retained certain elements of the worship of the Old Covenant as integral and irreplaceable, adopting them as her own:

"—notably, reading the Old Testament;

"—praying the Psalms;

"—above all, recalling the saving events and significant realities which have found their fulfillment in the mystery of Christ (promise and covenant, Exodus and Passover, kingdom and temple, exile and return)" (CCC 1093).

Old and New Covenants complement each other, interpret each other, and explain each other. On the one hand, the Jewish Exodus and Passover, Temple and law, illumine and deepen our understanding and appreciation of Christ. Christians should become familiar with the Old Testament and with Jewish law and liturgy for this reason. "A better knowledge of the Jewish people's faith and religious life as professed and lived even now can help our better understanding of certain aspects of Christian liturgy. . . . In its characteristic structure the Liturgy of the Word originates in Jewish prayer. . . . [O]ur most venerable prayers, including the Lord's Prayer, have parallels in Jewish prayer. . . . The relationship between Jewish liturgy and Christian liturgy, but also their differences in content, are particularly evident in the great feasts of the liturgical year, such as Passover. Christians and Jews both celebrate the Passover. For Jews, it is the Passover of history . . . ; for Christians, it is . . . fulfilled in the death and Resurrection of Christ" (CCC 1096).

On the other hand, the deepest significance of these elements in the Old Covenant can be understood only in light of Christ, to whom they point. "Thus the flood and Noah's ark prefigured salvation by Baptism [cf. 1 Pet

3:21], . . . and manna in the desert prefigured the Eucharist, 'the true bread from heaven' [Jn 6:32; cf. 1 Cor 10:1–6]" (CCC 1094).

St. Thomas Aquinas explains the principle behind this symbolism: "It is befitting Holy Writ [Scripture] to put forward divine and spiritual truths by means of comparisons with material things. For God provides for everything according to the capacity of its nature. Now it is natural to man to attain to spiritual truths through sensible objects, because all our knowledge originates from sense. Hence in Holy Writ spiritual truths are fittingly taught under the likeness of material things" (*Summa theologiae*, I, 1, 9).

"The author of Holy Writ is God, in whose power it is to signify his meaning not by words only (as man also can do) but also by things themselves. [That is to say that the historical events and things pointed to by the words of Scripture are often providentially arranged by God to point to, or symbolize, other things.] So, whereas in every other science, things are signified by [human] words, in [Scripture] . . . the things signified by the words have themselves also a signification. Thus that first significance, whereby words signify things, belongs to the first sense, the historical or literal. That signification [meaning] whereby the things signified [meant] by words have themselves also a signification is called the spiritual sense, which is based on the literal and presupposes it. Now this spiritual sense has a threefold division. For (1) as the Apostle says (Heb 10:1), the Old Law is a figure [symbol] of the New Law, and . . . (2) the New Law itself is a figure of future glory. And (3) in the New Law, whatever our Head has done is a type [model] of what we ought to do" (*Summa theologiae*, I, 1, 10).

6. The Holy Spirit in the liturgy

" 'You ask how the bread becomes the Body of Christ, and the wine . . . the Blood of Christ. I shall tell you: the Holy Spirit comes upon them and accomplishes what surpasses every word and thought. . . . Let it be enough for you to understand that it is by the Holy Spirit, just as it was of the Holy Virgin and by the Holy Spirit that the Lord . . . took flesh' [3] " (CCC 1106).

It is the power of the same Spirit that changed chaos to cosmos at creation (Gen 1:2), changed the divine Word to human flesh in the Incarnation (Jn 1:14), changed water to wine at the wedding feast at Cana (Jn 2:1–11), changed bread and wine to Christ's flesh and blood in the Eucharist (Lk 22:1–20), and will change our flesh and blood to immortal "spiritual bodies" in the resurrection (1 Cor 15:35–58).

The Spirit completes the liturgy as he completes and perfects the trinitarian "economy [plan] of salvation". The Spirit reveals Christ, and Christ

---

[3] St. John Damascene, *De fide orth.* 4, 13: PG 94, 1145A.

reveals the Father. The Father sends the Son, and the Son sends the Spirit. "In the liturgy of the Church, God the Father is blessed and adored as the source of all the blessings of creation and salvation with which he has blessed us in his Son, in order to give us the Spirit" (CCC 1110).

7. Who celebrates the liturgy?

Scripture's answer to this question, as summarized in the *Catechism*, will probably surprise you.

"The book of *Revelation* of St. John, read in the Church's liturgy, first reveals to us, 'A throne stood in heaven, with one seated on the throne': 'the Lord God.' [4] It then shows the Lamb, 'standing, as though it had been slain': Christ crucified and risen, the one high priest. . . .[5] Finally it presents 'the river of the water of life . . . flowing from the throne of God and of the Lamb,' one of the most beautiful symbols of the Holy Spirit' [6] " (CCC 1137).

So the One adored in the heavenly liturgy is the Trinity. Now who are the adorers?

"These are the ones who take part in the service of the praise of God . . . : the heavenly powers" [angels], "all creation (the four living beings), the servants of the Old and New Covenants (the twenty-four elders)" [the twelve tribes of Israel plus the twelve apostles], "the new People of God (the one hundred and forty-four thousand)" [a symbolic number for totality: $12 \times 12 \times 1000$],[7] "especially the martyrs 'slain for the word of God,' and the all-holy Mother of God (the Woman), the Bride of the Lamb,[8] and finally, 'a great multitude which no one could number, from every nation, from all tribes, and peoples and tongues' [9] " (CCC 1138).

The liturgy is far greater than the universe! In it all creation adores God, fulfilling the Psalmist's last and highest aspiration: "Let everything that breathes praise the LORD" (Ps 150). And "[i]t is in this eternal liturgy that the Spirit and the Church enable us to participate" (CCC 1139)—not only after death in heaven but right now on earth, tomorrow morning, or "whenever we celebrate the mystery of salvation in the sacraments" (CCC 1139). (See Scott Hahn's *The Lamb's Supper*.)

The liturgy is not in the world, the world is in the liturgy. The heavenly liturgy surrounds the world, and the earthly liturgy participates in the heavenly, since the Church Militant (the Church on earth) and the Church

---

[4] Rev 4:2, 8; Isa 6:1; cf. Ezek 1: 26–28.
[5] Rev 5:6; *Liturgy of St. John Chrysostom*, Anaphora; cf. Jn 1:29; Heb 4:14–15; 10:19–22.
[6] Rev 22:1; cf. 21:6; Jn 4:10–14.
[7] Cf. Rev 4—5; 7:1–8; 14:1; Isa 6:2–3.
[8] Rev 6:9–11; Rev 21:9; cf. Rev 21:12.
[9] Rev 7:9.

Triumphant (the Church in heaven) are one Church. During the liturgy "we are surrounded by so great a cloud of witnesses" (Heb 12:1), like athletes surrounded by cheering fans in a stadium.

8. The roles of clergy and laity in the liturgy

It is not the clergy alone who celebrate the liturgy, but the whole Church. If the Church on earth and the Church in heaven make up one Church, certainly the clergy and the laity of the Church on earth make up one Church, not two. "It is the whole *community*, the Body of Christ united with its Head" [Christ], "that celebrates. 'Liturgical services are not private functions but are celebrations of the Church. . . . But they touch individual members of the Church in different ways, depending on their orders, their role in the liturgical services, and their actual participation in them' [SC 26]" (CCC 1140). For the Church is an organism, not just an organization; and in an organism each individual organ is unique yet also one with each other organ and with the whole body (see 1 Cor 12).

"Mother Church earnestly desires that all the faithful should be led to that full, conscious, and active participation in liturgical celebrations which is demanded by the very nature of the liturgy" (SC 14). "In liturgical celebrations each person, minister or layman who has an office to perform, should carry out all and only those parts which pertain to his office by the nature of the rite and the norms of the liturgy" (SC 28). The worshippers at the liturgy are like the cast of a play or the instruments in a symphony: each part is necessary, and each functions for the whole. We do not go to church as we go to a restaurant, to get individual meals, but as we go to fight in an army or to play on a soccer team: to perform a work in common.

In this common task there is order and leadership. "The members [of the Body] do not all have the same function" (Rom 12:4). "The ordained minister" [bishop, priest, or deacon] "is, as it were, an 'icon' of Christ the priest" (CCC 1142). And therefore the function of the clergy is to serve the laity, as Christ did (see Jn 13:3–17). "The ordained ministry or *ministerial* priesthood is at the service of the baptismal priesthood [cf. LG 10 § 2]" (CCC 1120)—that is, the priesthood of all baptized believers (see part 3, chapter 7).

The ordained priesthood is essential, for "[t]he ordained priesthood guarantees that it really is Christ who acts in the sacraments" (CCC 1120). Without priests, we would have only a human religious "club" instead of a divine agent of salvation. Priests are our link, not only to the right faith, but to the right Savior, to the historical Jesus. "The saving mission entrusted by the Father to his incarnate Son" [a mission that included the sacramental liturgy; indeed, that culminated in the sacramental liturgy] "was committed to the apostles and through them to their successors" [the bishops they ordained, and the bishops those bishops ordained, right down to our present bishops]: "they receive the Spirit of Jesus to act in his name and in his person" [cf. Jn 20:21–23; Lk 24:47; Mt 28:18–20] (CCC 1120). When Father Flanagan says "This is my Body", that is Jesus Christ who speaks, not Father Flanagan. It is not Father Flanagan's body that saves us!

The "apostolic succession" of bishops and sacramentally ordained priests bonds us to Christ. "The ordained minister is the sacramental bond that ties the liturgical action to what the apostles said and did and, through them, to the words and actions of Christ, the source and foundation of the sacraments" (CCC 1120).

9. The sources of sacred symbols

Man is a symbol maker. "In human life, signs and symbols occupy an important place. As a being at once body and spirit, man expresses and perceives spiritual realities through physical signs and symbols. As a social being, man needs signs and symbols to communicate with others, through language, gestures, and actions. The same holds true for his relationship with God" (CCC 1146).

"A sacramental celebration is woven from signs and symbols" (CCC 1145) from three main sources: nature, society, and history.

Nature as a source of symbols. "God speaks to man through the visible creation. The material cosmos is so presented to man's intelligence that he can read there traces of its Creator [cf. Wis 13:1; Rom 1:19f.; Acts 14:17]. Light and darkness, wind and fire, water and earth, the tree and its fruit speak of God and symbolize both his greatness and his nearness" (CCC 1147). "Inasmuch as they are creatures" [of God], "these perceptible realities can become means of expressing the action of God" (CCC 1148). "The great religions of mankind witness, often impressively, to this cosmic and symbolic meaning" (CCC 1149). Symbolism is the natural language of all religions, for invisible realities must be signified through visible signs.

Society as a source of symbols. "The same is true of signs and symbols taken from the social life of man: washing and anointing, breaking bread and sharing the cup can express the sanctifying presence of God" (CCC 1148).

Jewish history as a source of symbols. "The Chosen People received from God distinctive signs and symbols that marked its liturgical life. . . . Among these liturgical signs from the Old Covenant are circumcision, anointing and consecration of kings and priests, laying on of hands, sacrifices, and above all the Passover. The Church sees in these signs a prefiguring of the sacraments of the New Covenant" (CCC 1150).

The Church's use of these three sources of symbols. "The liturgy of the Church presupposes, integrates and sanctifies elements from creation and human culture, conferring on them the dignity of signs of grace, of the new creation in Jesus Christ" (CCC 1149). As an instance of the principle that "grace redeems and perfects nature"—that is, the Creator's supernatural actions use and perfect his creatures rather than setting them aside—"The sacraments of the Church do not abolish but purify and integrate all the richness of the signs and symbols of the cosmos and of social life. Further, they fulfill the types and figures of the Old Covenant, signify and make actively present the salvation wrought by Christ, and prefigure and anticipate the glory of heaven" (CCC 1152). (These last three are the three symbolic meanings of events in Scripture according to St. Thomas, indicated in section 5).

10. Four kinds of symbols in the liturgy: Acts, words, music, and images

Actions. "A sacramental celebration is a meeting of God's children with their Father . . . ; this meeting takes the form of a dialogue, through actions and words. . . . [T]he symbolic actions are already a language" (CCC 1153). Actions are a kind of word too; they point to something beyond themselves, they ,"speak" something. And often "actions speak louder than words."

Words. "The *liturgy of the Word*" [Scripture] "is an integral part of sacramental celebrations. . . . [T]he signs which accompany the Word of God should be emphasized: the book of the Word (a lectionary or a book of the Gospels), its veneration (procession, incense, candles), the place of its proclamation (lectern or ambo), its audible and intelligible reading, the minister's homily which extends its proclamation, and the responses of the assembly (acclamations, meditation psalms, litanies, and profession of faith)" (CCC 1154).

Images. "The sacred image, the liturgical icon, principally represents *Christ*" (CCC 1159). "All the signs in the liturgical celebrations are related to Christ: . . . sacred images of the holy Mother of God and of the saints as well . . . signify Christ, who is glorified in them" (CCC 1161).

An image "cannot represent the invisible and incomprehensible God, but the incarnation of the Son of God has ushered in a new 'economy' of images: 'Previously God, who has neither a body nor a face, absolutely could not be represented by an image.' " [That is why Muslims, who worship the true God but deny his incarnation, forbid all images.] " 'But now that he has made himself visible in the flesh and has lived with men, I can make an image of what I have seen of God . . . and contemplate the glory of the Lord, his face unveiled' [10] " (CCC 1159).

---

[10] St. John Damascene, *De imag.* 1, 16: PG 96, 1245–48.

Music. " 'The musical tradition of the universal Church is a treasure of ines-timable value, greater even than that of any other art' [*SC* 112]" (CCC 1156). " 'He who sings prays twice' [11] " (CCC 1156).

Angels sing. As our lives are surrounded by their guardianship, so is our liturgical music surrounded by theirs. It is part of their music, part of the song of the Church Triumphant in heaven.

"Song and music fulfill their function as signs in a manner all the more significant when they are 'more closely connected . . . with the liturgical action,' [*SC* 112 § 3] according to three principal criteria: beauty expressive of prayer, the unanimous participation of the assembly . . . , and the solemn character of the celebration" (CCC 1157)—"solemn" because the point and purpose of the liturgy is holy: the glory of God and the sanctification of man caught up into that glory.

Here is how that glory is described by the writer of the Epistle to the Hebrews, as he is contrasting the Old Covenant with the New. Keep in mind, in reading this stirring passage, that what is being described is not life after death, not heaven, but what Catholics do every Sunday morning in church:

"For you have not come to what may be touched, a blazing fire, and dark-ness, and gloom, and a tempest, and the sound of a trumpet, and a voice whose words made the hearers entreat that no further messages be spoken to them. . . . Indeed, so terrifying was the sight that Moses said, 'I tremble with fear.' But you have come to Mount Zion and to the city of the living God, the heavenly Jerusalem, and to innumerable angels in festal gathering, and to the assembly of the first-born who are enrolled in heaven, and to a judge who is God of all, and to the spirits of just men made perfect, and to Jesus, the mediator of a new covenant, and to the sprinkled blood that speaks more graciously than the blood of Abel.

"See that you do not refuse him who is speaking. For if they did not escape when they refused him who warned them on earth, much less shall we escape if we reject him who warns from heaven. His voice then shook the earth; but now he has promised, 'Yet once more I will shake not only the earth but also the heaven.' This phrase, 'Yet once more,' indicates the removal of what is shaken, as of what has been made, in order that what cannot be shaken may remain. Therefore let us be grateful for receiving a kingdom that can-not be shaken, and thus let us offer to God acceptable worship, with rever-ence and awe; for our God is a consuming fire" (Heb 12:18–29).

The "kingdom that cannot be shaken" is the same thing as the "accept-able worship". At its center is something that looks like a little round piece of bread. It is Jesus Christ.

---

[11] St. Augustine, *En. in Ps.* 72, 1: PL 36, 914; cf. Col 3:16.

11. Liturgical cycles and sacred times

Liturgy has its own times. In fact, it transforms the meaning of time. Judged by secular time standards, it "wastes" time. But this "waste" of time (and energy and even money) is the most important and joyful thing man can do in his time on earth. If people had not understood that, cathedrals would never have been built.

Liturgy not only transcends secular time, but it also transforms the times of our earthly lives. Liturgy sanctifies all times by its special sacred times.

"From the time of the Mosaic law, the People of God have observed fixed feasts" (CCC 1164) in yearly, weekly, and daily cycles. For human life naturally moves in cycles, like the seasons; in waves, like the sea.

The center of the yearly liturgical cycle is Easter. "Beginning with the Easter Triduum" [the sacred three days of Holy Thursday, Good Friday, and Easter Sunday] "as its source of light, the new age of the Resurrection fills the whole liturgical year" (CCC 1168). "*Easter* is not simply one feast among others, but the 'Feast of feasts,' the 'Solemnity of solemnities,' just as the Eucharist is the 'Sacrament of sacraments' " (CCC 1169).

The weekly cycle's center and source of movement is the same event, Christ's Resurrection, celebrated each Sunday. "Once each week, on the day which she has called the Lord's Day, she [the Church] keeps the memory of the Lord's resurrection" (*SC* 102). " 'When we ponder, O Christ, the marvels accomplished on this day, the Sunday of your holy resurrection, we say: "Blessed is Sunday, for on it began creation . . . the world's salvation" ' [12] " (CCC 1167).

The daily cycle is observed by the Liturgy of the Hours (the Divine Office) " 'so devised that the whole course of the day and night is made holy by the praise of God' [13] " (CCC 1174). It consists of seven holy times of prayer. All clergy and some members of religious institutes are obliged to pray it every day.

Recent popes have called our era "the age of the laity", and " '[t]he laity, too, are encouraged to recite the divine office, either with the priests, or among themselves, or even individually' [14] " (CCC 1175).

The divine office includes prayers, psalms, and Scripture readings. It unites Scripture and prayer and trains us in *lectio divina*, "divine reading", one of the best methods of Christian prayer, "where the Word of God is so read and meditated that it becomes prayer" (CCC 1177).

---

[12] Fanqîth, *The Syriac Office of Antioch*, vol. VI, first part of Summer, 193 B.

[13] *SC* 84; 1 Thess 5:17; Eph 6:18.

[14] *SC* 100; cf. 86; 96; 98; PO 5.

12. Sacred places

Liturgy sanctifies all places by its sacred places, as it sanctifies all times by its sacred times.

"The worship 'in Spirit and in truth' [Jn 4:24] of the New Covenant is not tied exclusively to any one place. The whole earth is sacred and entrusted to the children of men" (CCC 1179), and all men are sacred and entrusted to God: "We are the temple of the living God" (2 Cor 6:16).

This does not exclude setting apart sacred physical places, however. Without them, we forget the sacredness of all places, all creation, and all men. Thus the need for church buildings.

A church building is " 'a house of prayer in which the Eucharist is celebrated and reserved, where the faithful assemble, and where is worshipped the presence of the Son of God our Savior. . . . This house ought to be in good taste and a worthy place for prayer and sacred ceremonial.' [15]. . . [T]his 'house of God' . . . should show Christ" [cf. SC 7] (CCC 1181). That is the fundamental criterion for Christian liturgical art and architecture.

It is natural for Catholic churches to be more ornate and magnificent than Protestant churches. A Protestant church building exists primarily for man to pray and worship in, but a Catholic church exists primarily to house and glorify God in the Eucharist. *That* is why the great cathedrals are so heavenly.

13. Visible elements in the church

"The *altar* of the New Covenant is the Lord's Cross [cf. Heb 13:10], from which the sacraments of the Paschal mystery flow" (CCC 1182). That is why there is a crucifix above it. The crucifix merely symbolizes the Cross, but the altar *is* the Cross, for Christ becomes really present on it. "On the altar, which is the center of the church, the sacrifice of the Cross is made present under sacramental signs. The altar is also the table of the Lord, to which the People of God are invited" [cf. GIRM 259] (CCC 1182).

"The *tabernacle* is to be situated 'in churches in a most worthy place with the greatest honor.' [16] The dignity, placing, and security of the Eucharistic tabernacle should foster adoration before the Lord really present in the Blessed Sacrament of the altar" [cf. SC 128] (CCC 1183).

"The *chair* of the bishop (*cathedra*) or that of the priest 'should express his office of presiding over the assembly and of directing prayer' [GIRM 271]" (CCC 1184).

[15] *PO* 5; cf. *SC* 122–27.
[16] Paul VI, *Mysterium Fidei*: AAS (1965) 771.

"The *lectern* (*ambo*): 'The dignity of the Word of God requires the church to have a suitable place for announcing his message so that the attention of the people may be easily directed to that place during the liturgy of the Word' [GIRM 272]" (CCC 1184).

"The gathering of the People of God begins with Baptism; a church must have a place for the celebration of *Baptism* (baptistry) and for fostering remembrance of the baptismal promises (holy water font)" (CCC 1185).

"The renewal of the baptismal life requires *penance*. A church, then, . . . requires an appropriate place to receive penitents" (CCC 1185).

"A church must also be a space that invites us to . . . recollection and silent prayer" (CCC 1185).

"Finally, the church has an eschatological significance" ["eschatology" refers to the Last Things]. "To enter into the house of God, we must cross a *threshold*, which symbolizes passing from the world wounded by sin to the world of the new Life to which all men are called. The visible church is a symbol of the Father's house toward which the People of God is journeying and where the Father 'will wipe every tear from their eyes' [Rev 21:4]. Also for this reason, the Church is the house of *all* God's children, open and welcoming" (CCC 1186). The Church's gospel is free: "Let him who is thirsty come, let him who desires take the water of life without price" (Rev 22:17).

14. Liturgy and spirituality

Liturgy has no "practical" purpose. Its purpose is simply to adore God and to elevate man into the life of God. Its active "work" is to receive the words of God and the grace of God. Its words come from the silence in which it hears and echoes God's Word.

Liturgy trains us to hear the voice of God, by creating in us the interior silence in which that voice can be heard in the soul. For God's voice is not loud and obvious, but more like a subtle whisper—as Elijah discovered long ago: "And a great and strong wind rent the mountains and broke in pieces the rocks . . . but the LORD was not in the wind; and after the wind an earthquake, but the LORD was not in the earthquake; and after the earthquake a fire, but the LORD was not in the fire; and after the fire a still, small voice. And when Elijah heard it, he wrapped his face in his mantle" (1 Kings 19:11–13).

The point of the words and music of the liturgy is to create the silence in which we hear God, to protect and surround the silence as a frame surrounds a picture. Liturgy helps us develop the art of listening throughout our lives. For we can hear God (and the deepest hearts of our fellow men too) only in the spaces between the louder passions, in subtle and shy whispers. For love is both subtle and shy, and God is love.

The criterion for good liturgy is, then: Does it create silence?—the silence of joy-full love, worship-full wonder, and awe-full adoration?

This is one reason our ancestors' faith was often stronger than ours. Their souls were ravished to heaven by the music of Bach and Mozart and Palestrina and Handel in churches whose "sermons in stones" spoke of the bright color and passion and joy of the saints, for they were built by saints, out of the pennies and sweat and blood of poor and oppressed but proud and grateful immigrants who would die for their faith. Who would die for (or live for) a faith whose heartbeat was echoed in the erotic pulses of secular music played to embarrassedly mumbling congregations in ugly, utilitarian buildings and by chatty "presiders" who sound like DJs?

It is said that Luther won the heart of Germany by his hymns more than by his theology. We cannot give our whole selves to a faith even when our minds find it true and our consciences find it good if our hearts find it ugly, shallow, and joyless. We cannot wholeheartedly embrace a faith without beauty any more than a faith without goodness or truth.

For the beauty of the liturgy is not an extra "decoration", but an index of the truth and the goodness of the Catholic faith. Thus, a shallow and ugly liturgy is almost always an indication of doctrinal shallowness and moral laxity as well. For liturgy is not something added on to doctrine and morality, creed and code, from without; it is that very creed and code, faith and works, truth and goodness, made visible.

The *Catechism* begins its section on the liturgy with this indispensable and essential vision of all three dimensions of the Catholic faith as one and the same mystery: "It is this mystery of Christ that the Church proclaims and celebrates in her liturgy" (CCC 1068). The three are one at their center because Christ is that center. The Christ who said "I am the truth", the Christ who is the final revelation of the God whose very essence is love and goodness, is also the Christ who "became flesh and dwelt among us, full of grace and truth; we have beheld his glory" (Jn 1:14).

Chapter 2

INTRODUCTION TO THE SACRAMENTS

1. What is a sacrament?

A sacrament is (a) *a sacred sign* (b) *instituted by Christ* (c) *to give grace.*

2. Sacraments as signs

First, a sacrament is a *sign*. A sign always *signifies* something, points to something real beyond itself. Like Christ's miracles in the Gospels (which Scripture also calls "signs"), sacraments teach by "sign language". Sacrament means sacred sign. " 'Because they are signs they also instruct' [*SC* 59]" (CCC 1123). This instruction is an essential part of their purpose. Specifically, their purpose is to be *sacred* signs, to teach sacredness, holiness, sanctity.

3. Sacraments give grace *ex opere operato*

Sacraments sanctify men not merely by teaching, however, but also by actually giving the grace they signify. Thus another definition of a sacrament is "a sacred sign that actually effects what it signifies". Sacraments "really work", really give grace.

"Grace" (see section 8 of this chapter) means the undeserved gift of God. It is the work of God himself. In fact, it is the very life of God, which he shares with us. In the sacraments we participate in God's own life and work. "As fire transforms into itself everything it touches, so the Holy Spirit transforms into the divine life whatever is subjected to his power" (CCC 1127).

The sacraments give grace *ex opere operato*, which means "from the performance of the act itself", rather than from the individual human souls, the feelings or experiences or spiritual energies of the person receiving the sacrament (or from the person administering it). It works from the outside in rather than from the inside out. It is objective, not subjective.

This also means that it is not usually subjectively felt or experienced. God remains an object of faith rather than of feeling or experience. The sacraments do not usually *feel* miraculous. (For God's reason for remaining hidden, see part 3, chapter 4, section 3.)

Though the sacraments give grace *ex opere operato*, from God rather than from our own souls, yet God works in ways appropriate to the human soul. He plants seeds of grace, which grow gradually, rather than all at once.

4. Christ's presence in the sacraments

Christ was not only present at the origin of the sacraments, two thousand years ago, but he is really present and active in them now. Christ is not passive but active. He is not merely signified, but acts. He does not sit still, like an artist's model, but works, like the artist.

That is why the sacraments do not merely signify grace but actually give grace. As the *Catechism* explains, the sacraments are "efficacious" (that is, they actually work) only "because in them Christ himself is at work: it is he who baptizes, he who acts in his sacraments in order to communicate the grace that each sacrament signifies" (CCC 1127).

5. The consequences of Christ's presence *ex opere operato*

This doctrine is not only true, it is also powerful: it makes a great difference to our lives, in at least six ways:

a. Since in each sacrament Christ is really present—the same Christ in different ways and different actions—we are not alone in any sacrament; we are with Christ.

b. We are also with the whole Church, his Body. For where he is, his Body is. Though the recipient of each sacrament is always the individual person, each sacrament is public and communal, since it is administered by the

Catholic (universal) Church as a whole, by the authority of Christ her Head. In each of the sacraments, "the whole Christ" acts, Head and Body.

c. "[T]he sacraments act *ex opere operato* . . . i.e., by virtue of the saving work of Christ, accomplished once for all. It follows that 'the sacrament is not wrought by the righteousness of either the celebrant or the recipient but by the power of God.' [1] From the moment that a sacrament is celebrated in accordance with the intention of the Church, the power of Christ and his Spirit acts in and through it, independently of the personal holiness of the minister" (CCC 1128). So when we look at the priest we should see the perfect Christ, not the imperfect minister.

d. Because the sacraments work from God, not from us, we are free to focus all our attention on God, not on ourselves, and to invest all our faith and hope in him, not in ourselves.

The sacraments are invitations to forget our own limitations and problems, to lose ourselves in God (and thus find ourselves: see Matthew 10:39). This is rehearsal for heaven, where we will be in eternal joy precisely because we will be looking at God, not at ourselves. Even here, our moments of greatest joy are always when we are "taken out of ourselves", our needs and plans and worries, by some truth or goodness or beauty that is a tiny appetizer of God.

e. We can thus be freed from concern with our imperfections: those in ourselves, in our worship, and in our fellow worshippers. Since Jesus Christ is really present in the sacraments, in celebrating them we are celebrating him, not ourselves, not even our human community. Though all sacraments are communal and public rather than individual and private, their focus is no more on the human community than on the human individual. Our focus should not be on what we are doing for Christ but on what Christ is doing for us. So it should be irrelevant to us whether our fellow worshipper is wearing ugly clothes, carrying a crying baby, or singing off-key—or even whether we think he is a great sinner or even a hypocrite. When in the presence of God, we do not judge or criticize, we simply adore and love.

f. Because Christ is really present in the sacraments, they are a "highway to heaven", a meeting place between earth and heaven, time and eternity. They are "eschatological"; they are a foretaste and veiled preview of our eternal destiny. They are like an engagement gift from our divine Lover. If we understand this, we will not complain that Church is "boring".

6. How sacraments are not like magic

A sacrament is indeed supernatural, and indeed efficacious (that is, "really works"). In those two ways it *is* like magic. But in at least one essential way,

---

[1] St. Thomas Aquinas, *STh* III, 68, 8.

a sacrament is just the opposite of magic: it is a free gift, and therefore must be freely accepted in order to be received. It is not automatic or impersonal. Though it does not come from the soul of the recipient, yet it can be blocked by the soul of the recipient, wholly or partly; and the degree of grace we receive depends on the degree of our faith, hope, and love.

Receiving a sacrament is like turning on a water faucet whose supply is the whole ocean but whose handle can open more or less. The power and grace of the sacraments is infinite, since its source is God, but "the fruits of the sacraments also depend on the disposition of the one who receives them" (CCC 1128). It is like the fruits of a rain depending on the softness of the soil. Or like sunlight: though we receive it rather than generate it, yet we can receive more or less of it as we open our eyes more or less. The theological formula for this is that the sacraments work *ex opere operantis* as well as *ex opere operato*.

7. The relation between the sacraments, faith, and tradition

Though we receive grace from the sacraments in proportion to our individual faith, even that private and individual faith in turn depends on the Church's public and collective Tradition, that is, what Christ "handed over" or "handed down" (the literal meaning of "tradition") to her. Thus St. Paul's formula in defining the Eucharist in 1 Corinthians 11:23: "I received from the Lord what I also delivered to you." "The Church's faith precedes the faith of the believer who is invited to adhere to it. When the Church celebrates the sacraments, she confesses the faith received from the apostles. . . . Liturgy is a constitutive element of the holy and living Tradition" [cf. *DV* 8] (CCC 1124). "For this reason no sacramental rite may be modified or manipulated at the will of the minister or the community" (CCC 1125).

8. What is "grace"?

The sacraments "give grace". But what is grace?

Grace has been defined as "an undeserved gift of God". It is undeserved for two reasons: first, because God is our Creator and therefore can owe us nothing; all good things we receive, beginning with our very existence, are gifts from God's generosity, not owed to us in justice. Second, God's grace is doubly undeserved because we are sinners; we have broken our covenant relationship with him and disobeyed his law.

Yet our disobedience cannot change God's nature. "God is love", and therefore God continues to give grace. Sin stops us from receiving it but not God from giving it.

For grace is not some "thing" God gives, as if grace were like gasoline and the sacraments were like filling stations. Rather, God's grace is God himself, God's own life in our souls. For God is love, and the lover's primary gift to the beloved is the gift of himself. That is what a lover wants above all else: to give himself to his beloved. Therefore God's grace is God's gift of himself.

Why does the lover always want to give himself to the beloved? Because the essential aim of love is intimacy, closer union. Therefore grace is essentially a love-relationship of intimacy between Christ and the Christian, Christ and his Body (see CCC 2003). An increase in grace means an increase in intimacy with Christ.

9. The freedom of God's grace

Because love is necessarily free—freely given and freely received—therefore we obtain grace by freely cooperating with God (see CCC 2002), not by automatic "deposits" to our accounts. We cannot be passive like piggy banks. God demands we act and choose. God will take the initiative and seduce our souls, but he will not force himself on us. When he accomplished the most tremendous deed in history, the Incarnation, he first asked permission of Mary before giving himself to her! She *cooperated* in the redemption. And so must we.

The sacraments work in the same way. First, God takes the initiative in making the free offer of grace to us in the sacraments, *ex opere operato* (see CCC 1128). But then we must freely accept God and open our souls to his grace *ex opere operantis*. Thus all the initiative is God's, yet the sacraments are not magical or automatic or impersonal. They work *ex opere operato* because, as Christ assured us, "apart from me you can do nothing" (Jn 15:5). They work *ex opere operantis* because, as St. Augustine reminded us, "God created us without us: but he did not will to save us without us." We cannot do it without him and he will not do it without us.

10. Sin and the need for sacraments

Man needed no sacraments in Eden, for he knew God with face-to-face intimacy. And we will need no sacraments in heaven, for the same reason. But our weak and fallen human nature needs them now. Doubt about the need for sacraments often comes from the loss of the sense of sin. For each of the sacraments is designed in some way to heal our sin and bring us closer to our lost innocence and our future perfection. It is pride that refuses to use the humble material means God so graciously stoops to give us in the sacraments. (See the story of Naaman the leper in 2 Kings 5:1–14.) God tells us we need sacraments; who are we to say we do not?

We need sacraments also because we are not purely spiritual beings. Bowing the knees of our bodies helps us to bow the knees of our souls, because body and soul are not two things, like a ghost and a house, but two dimensions of the same thing, like the meaning and the words of a poem. That "same" thing is ourselves. Each of us is a single self. For this reason, receiving the Eucharist into our mouths is the visible dimension of receiving Christ into our hearts, not some magical physical cause of it. Our mouths (bodies) and our hearts (souls) are not separate, like two bodily organs.

God designed our bodies as an essential part of our nature, and he designed the Catholic religion for the embodied souls he designed. Our goal is not "spirituality" but holiness; not freedom from bodies but freedom from sin.

11. Why does the Church have seven sacraments?

Because Christ instituted seven sacraments. A sacrament must be "instituted by Christ". The Church did not invent them; she only defined and defended them.

"There are seven sacraments in the Church: Baptism, Confirmation ... , Eucharist, Penance, Anointing of the Sick, Holy Orders, and Matrimony" [2] (CCC 1113).

This is defined doctrine: " 'Adhering to the teaching of the Holy Scriptures, to the apostolic traditions, and to the consensus ... of the Fathers,' we profess that 'the sacraments of the new law were ... all instituted by Jesus Christ our Lord' [Council of Trent (1547): DS 1600–1601]" (CCC 1114).

How does the Church know this to be true, and why did it take her fifteen hundred years to define it?

As with the other dogmas of the faith, it is God who revealed this truth, but he revealed it gradually, in accordance with humanity's way of learning. We learn to understand and appreciate great truths only gradually, and divine grace uses human nature and its learning style rather than setting it aside.

All important doctrines took time to be defined, including the canon of the Bible, the two natures of Christ, and the Trinity. "As she has done for the canon of Sacred Scripture and for the doctrine of the faith, the Church, by the power of the Spirit who guides her 'into all truth' [Jn 16:13], has gradually recognized this treasure received from Christ. . . . Thus the Church has discerned over the centuries that among liturgical celebrations there are seven that are, in the strict sense of the term, sacraments instituted by the Lord" (CCC 1117).

The Church never adds new doctrines to the original "deposit of faith"

---

[2] Cf. Council of Lyons II (1274): DS 860; Council of Florence (1439): DS 1310; Council of Trent (1547): DS 1601.

received from Christ, but she is led by the Holy Spirit gradually and increasingly to understand that deposit of faith better.

12. Why did Christ institute seven sacraments?

"The seven sacraments touch all the stages and all the important moments of the Christian life" [3] (CCC 1210): birth (Baptism), maturing (Confirmation), strengthening by food and drink (Eucharist), repair and restoration (Penance), service of others (Matrimony and Holy Orders), and strengthening in serious illness and preparation for death (Anointing of the Sick). "There is thus a certain resemblance between the stages of natural life and the stages of the spiritual life" (CCC 1210). Every important transition, from birth to death, is sanctified; for the spiritual life is built on the basis of our natural life, since nature is a kind of training program for our supernatural destiny.

a. "The sacraments of Christian initiation—Baptism, Confirmation, and the Eucharist—lay the *foundations* of every Christian life. 'The sharing in the divine nature given to men through the grace of Christ bears a certain likeness to the origin, development, and nourishing of natural life. The faithful are born anew by Baptism, strengthened by the sacrament of Confirmation, and receive in the Eucharist the food of eternal life' [4] " (CCC 1212), as birth, maturing, and strengthening by food and drink are at the foundation of our bodily life.

b. Holy Orders and Matrimony prepare us for lifelong service. The two are similar, for the priesthood is a form of marriage—marriage to the Church—and marriage, too, is a form of priesthood—the "priesthood of all believers", which the sacramental priesthood serves (see part 3, chapter 7, section 9).

c. Finally, there are two sacraments of repair. Penance and the Anointing of the Sick repair and strengthen souls and bodies. The last is also our preparation for our final journey of death, our *viaticum* (*via-te-cum*, "go-with-you").

13. What is required for a valid sacrament?

Four things:

First, valid matter, or "the right stuff". For instance, the Eucharist must be made of wheat bread and grape wine, and Baptism must be in water.

Second, valid form. The essential words cannot be changed: for instance,

---

[3] Cf. St. Thomas Aquinas, *STh* III, 65, 1.

[4] Paul VI, apostolic constitution, *Divinae consortium naturae*: AAS 63 (1971) 657; cf. RCIA Introduction 1–2.

"This is my body . . . this is my blood", and "I baptize you in the name of the Father, and of the Son, and of the Holy Spirit."

Third, valid intention, the intention to do what the Church does.

Fourth, a valid mind, that is, faith and understanding on the part of the recipient. The recipient must be a Christian (have faith in Christ) to receive Christian sacraments. He should also understand what is being done. (In the case of infant Baptism, it is the parents' faith and understanding that stand in for the infant's.)

This fourth requirement is not to be taken for granted. Many Catholics have been "sacramentalized" without having been evangelized or catechized; that is, the minimal faith in Christ and understanding of his sacraments are missing. Those who receive the sacraments of Christ should surely be able to say "I know whom I have believed" (2 Tim 1:12).

14. Who administers the sacraments?

Baptism can be validly administered by anyone in case of necessity, as long as there is the intention to baptize according to the will of the Church; but a bishop, priest, or deacon is the usual minister. (Deacons also are ordained clergy, but they cannot administer the Eucharist, Penance, the Anointing of the Sick, Confirmation, or Holy Orders.)

In the Western Church the bishop is the ordinary minister of Confirmation, although in some circumstances priests also may confirm.

Holy Orders are administered by a bishop.

In the Western Church, Matrimony is administered by the man and the woman, to each other. The priest is the official witness. (See also CCC 1623.)

The Eucharist is celebrated only by a bishop or a priest.

Penance and the Anointing of the Sick are administered by a bishop or a priest.

15. How often can we receive the sacraments?

"The three sacraments of Baptism, Confirmation, and Holy Orders confer, in addition to grace, a sacramental *character* or 'seal' by which the Christian . . . is made a member of the Church according to different states and functions. This . . . is indelible;[5] it remains for ever in the Christian. . . . Therefore these sacraments can never be repeated" (CCC 1121).

Matrimony also confers a permanent sacramental mark on the soul and also cannot be repeated while both spouses of a valid sacramental marriage are alive.

The Anointing of the Sick used to be called "Extreme Unction" because of the expectation that it would be administered before death, as a preparation

---

[5] Cf. Council of Trent (1547): DS 1609.

for the crossing over into eternity. There has been a change in emphasis to remind us that the sacrament is given in hope of healing and recovery from a life-threatening illness. It can be given as many times as needed.

The Eucharist and Penance are the two ongoing and oft-repeated sacraments. They are to the soul as eating and washing to the body. The Church highly recommends daily reception of the Eucharist, but she mandates weekly Mass attendance and reception of the Eucharist at the very least once every year during the Easter season for all adult Catholics. The Church mandates Penance at least once a year but also tells us to confess "regularly". What is regularly? Probably more frequently than most of us do. For anyone serious about spiritual growth and a relationship with God, once a month would be appropriate.

16. Sacramentals

Sacramentals are " 'sacred signs which bear a resemblance to the sacraments' [6] " (CCC 1667) but are not sacraments in the strict sense for two reasons. First, they were not instituted by Christ but by the Church (" 'Holy Mother Church has . . . instituted sacramentals' "—CCC 1667).[7] Second, they do not work *ex opere operato* to produce the effects they signify but only " 'signify effects . . . which are obtained through the intercession of the Church' " [8] (CCC 1667). "Sacramentals do not confer the grace of the Holy Spirit in the way that the sacraments do, but by the Church's prayer, they prepare us to receive grace and dispose us to cooperate with it" (CCC 1670). Also, sacramentals vary much more with time and place than sacraments do. They "respond to the needs, culture, and special history of the Christian people of a particular region or time" (CCC 1668).

17. The purpose of sacramentals

" 'By them . . . various occasions in life are rendered holy' " [9] (CCC 1667). "[S]acramentals sanctif[y] almost every event of [the] lives [of the faithful] with the divine grace which flows from the paschal mystery of the Passion, Death and Resurrection of Christ. From this source all sacraments and sacramentals draw their power" (SC 61). "This is why the Church imparts blessings by invoking the name of Jesus, usually while making the holy sign of the cross of Christ" (CCC 1671).

"There is scarcely any proper use of material things which cannot thus be directed toward the sanctification of men and the praise of God" (SC 61).

---

[6] SC 60; cf. CIC, can. 1166; CCEO, can. 867.
[7] SC 60; cf. CIC, can. 1166; CCEO, can. 867.
[8] SC 60; cf. CIC, can. 1166; CCEO, can. 867.
[9] SC 60; cf. CIC, can. 1166; CCEO, can. 867.

This is not just a matter of interior or spiritual intentions; the spiritual power of the Church's prayer flows into material things like waves onto a beach. In the Catholic tradition, much more than in the Protestant, there is a "sacramental sense" that unites, rather than divides, matter and spirit, secular and sacred. Thus sacramentals "sanctify" or make holy material things, times, and places, such as relics, holy days, church buildings, altars, statues, holy water, rosaries, medals, processions, religious dances, and pilgrimages, and even "secular" things, such as houses and fishing boats.

18. Church authority regarding sacramentals

Sacramentals often arise from "grass-roots" popular traditions. "Pastoral discernment is needed to sustain and support popular piety and, if necessary, to purify and correct the religious sense which underlies these devotions" [10] (CCC 1676). But the Church is much more prone to approve than to correct these popular devotions. For she believes that " '[a]t its core the piety of the people is a storehouse of values that offers answers of Christian wisdom to the great questions of life. The Catholic wisdom of the people is . . . a Christian humanism that radically affirms the dignity of every person as a child of God, establishes a basic fraternity' " [sense of brotherhood], " 'teaches people to encounter nature and understand work, provides reasons for joy and humor even in the midst of a very hard life' [11] " (CCC 1676).

19. Exorcism

Its meaning: "When the Church asks publicly and authoritatively in the name of Jesus Christ that a person or object be protected against the power of the Evil One and withdrawn from his dominion, it is called *exorcism*. . . . Exorcism is directed at the expulsion of demons or to the liberation from demonic possession through the spiritual authority which Jesus entrusted to his Church" [cf. CIC, can. 1172] (CCC 1673).

Its power: "Jesus performed exorcisms and from him the Church has received the power and office of exorcising [cf. Mk 1:25–26; 3:15; 6:7, 6:13; 16:17]" (CCC 1673).

Its forms: "In a simple form, exorcism is performed at the celebration of Baptism. The solemn exorcism, called 'a major exorcism,' can be performed only by a priest and with the permission of the bishop. The priest must

---

[10] Cf. John Paul II, *CT* 54.

[11] CELAM, Third General Conference (Puebla, 1979), final Document, § 448 (trans. NCCB, 1979); cf. Paul VI, *EN* 48.

proceed with prudence, strictly observing the rules established by the Church. . . . Illness, especially psychological illness, is a very different matter; treating this is the concern of medical science. Therefore, before an exorcism is performed, it is important to ascertain that one is dealing with the presence of the Evil One, and not an illness" [cf. CIC, can. 1172] (CCC 1673).

20. Funerals

Funerals are by nature sacramental and even a kind of consummation of all the sacraments, for "[a]ll the sacraments . . . have as their goal the last Passover of the child of God which, through death, leads him into the life of the Kingdom" (CCC 1680). They are the Church's business because they are "family business": "The Church who, as Mother, has borne the Christian sacramentally in her womb during his earthly pilgrimage, accompanies him at his journey's end, in order to surrender him 'into the Father's hands'" (CCC 1683).

Funerals center on the eucharistic sacrifice because "[i]n the Eucharist, the Church expresses her efficacious communion with the departed. . . . It is by the Eucharist thus celebrated that the community of the faithful, especially the family of the deceased, learn to live in communion with the one who 'has fallen asleep in the Lord,' by communicating in the Body of Christ of which he is a living member" (CCC 1689).

Thus, Christian funerals are positive expressions of faith. "'For even dead, we are not at all separated from one another, because . . . we will find one another again in the same place. We shall never be separated, for we live for Christ' [12]" (CCC 1690).

---

[12] St. Simeon of Thessalonica, *De ordine sepulturæ*. 336: PG 155, 684.

Chapter 3

BAPTISM AND CONFIRMATION

BAPTISM

1. The importance of Baptism

"Holy Baptism is ... the gateway to life in the Spirit ... ,[1] and the door which gives access to the other sacraments" (CCC 1213). It is like birth—indeed, Christ calls it being "born anew" (Jn 3:7), being born from above. The most radical, life-changing event in your natural life was your birth, for it was the beginning of your whole life on earth; all subsequent changes were only the beginning of parts of your life. Similarly, the most radical, life-changing event in your supernatural life was its beginning: your Baptism.

---

[1] Cf. Council of Florence: DS 1314: *vitae spiritualis ianua*.

2. The effects of Baptism

Baptism has two effects, one negative and one positive. "Through Baptism we are freed from sin and reborn as sons of God" (CCC 1213).

a. The first, negative effect is a total cleansing from original sin, symbolized by washing with water. "This sacrament is also called '*the washing of regeneration*' [Titus 3:5; Jn 3:5]" (CCC 1215). "Regeneration" means "new beginning". "By Baptism *all sins* are forgiven, original sin and all personal sins . . . [cf. Council of Florence (1439): DS 1316]" (CCC 1263).

"Yet certain temporal" [not eternal] "consequences of sin remain in the baptized, such as suffering, illness, death, and such frailties inherent in life as weaknesses of character, and so on, as well as an inclination to sin that Tradition calls *concupiscence*" (CCC 1264).

b. The second, positive effect of Baptism is a real spiritual transformation, the beginning of our sharing in the very life of God himself, which is the fundamental end and purpose of the whole Catholic religion (and of life itself!). This mystery is called by many different names, such as "supernatural life", "eternal life", "divine life", "sanctifying grace", "the kingdom of heaven", "the kingdom of God", "justification", "sanctification", and "salvation". This all begins in Baptism, in which we die to our old self and are "born anew" to this new identity. "Baptism not only purifies from all sins, but also makes the neophyte 'a new creature,' an adopted son of God, who has become a 'partaker in the divine nature,' [2] member of Christ and co-heir with him,[3] and a temple of the Holy Spirit" [4] (CCC 1265). He is given "sanctifying grace, the grace of *justification*" (CCC 1266), and the assistance of the theological virtues and the gifts of the Holy Spirit. "Thus the whole organism of the Christian's supernatural life has its roots in Baptism" (CCC 1266).

"Baptism seals the Christian with an indelible spiritual mark (*character*) of his belonging to Christ. No sin can erase this mark, even if sin prevents Baptism from bearing the fruits of salvation" [5] (CCC 1272). " 'Baptism indeed is the seal of eternal life.' [6] The faithful Christian who has 'kept the seal' until the end, remaining faithful to the demands of his Baptism, will be able to depart this life 'with the sign of faith,' [7] with his baptismal faith, in expectation of the blessed vision of God—the consummation of faith" (CCC 1274).

---

[2] 2 Cor 5:17, 2 Pet 1:4; cf. Gal 4:5–7.
[3] Cf. 1 Cor 6:15; 12:27; Rom 8:17.
[4] Cf. 1 Cor 6:19.
[5] Cf. Rom 8:29; Council of Trent (1547): DS 1609–19.
[6] St. Irenaeus, *Dem ap.* 3: SCh 62, 32.
[7] *Roman Missal*, EP I (Roman Canon) 97.

3. Immersion and sprinkling as alternative forms of Baptism

The two aspects of Baptism, negative and positive, are a death and resurrection. This double event is symbolized by the water: "This sacrament is called *Baptism*, after the central rite by which it is carried out: to baptize (Greek *baptizein*) means to 'plunge' or 'immerse'; the 'plunge' into the water symbolizes the catechumen's burial into Christ's death, from which he rises up by resurrection with him, as 'a new creature'[8]" (CCC 1214).

For this reason, "Baptism is performed in the most expressive way by triple immersion in the baptismal water. However, from ancient times it has also been able to be conferred by pouring the water three times over the candidate's head" (CCC 1239). "In the Latin Church this triple infusion is accompanied by the minister's words: 'N., I baptize you in the name of the Father, and of the Son, and of the Holy Spirit.' In the Eastern liturgies the catechumen turns toward the East and the priest says: 'The servant of God, N., is baptized in the name of the Father, and of the Son, and of the Holy Spirit.' At the invocation of each person of the Most Holy Trinity, the priest immerses the candidate in the water and raises him up again" (CCC 1240).

4. The water symbolism in Baptism

Few things in nature are as necessary to us as water, and few things are more beautiful and wonderful. Our hearts are naturally drawn to oceans, rivers, and lakes, and our souls are as refreshed by the rain as is the earth itself. St. Teresa of Avila said that she loved to sit by water for hours and let it teach her. For water is the first material creation of God mentioned in the Genesis story, and God has used this element in a unique way throughout the various stages of salvation history. All of these ways point forward to and are completed in Baptism, as the *Catechism* explains:

a. "Since the beginning of the world, water, so humble and wonderful a creature, has been the source of life and fruitfulness. Sacred Scripture sees it as 'overshadowed' by the Spirit of God [cf. Gen 1:2]: 'O God, whose Spirit / in the first moments of the world's creation / hovered over the waters'[9]" (CCC 1218). The water that is necessary for natural life symbolizes supernatural life.

b. "The Church has seen in Noah's ark a prefiguring of salvation by Baptism, for by it 'a few, that is, eight persons, were saved through water' [1 Pet 3:20]" (CCC 1219).

[8] 2 Cor 5:17; Gal 6:15; cf. Rom 6:3–4; Col 2:12.
[9] *Roman Missal*, Easter Vigil 42: Blessing of Water.

c. "[T]he water of the sea is a symbol of death and so can represent the mystery of the cross. By this symbolism, Baptism signifies communion with Christ's death" (CCC 1220). Thus in the early Church, in Eastern liturgies, and in Protestant Baptist baptisms, the person is baptized by being plunged into—"drowned in"—the water.

d. "But above all, the crossing of the Red Sea, literally the liberation of Israel from the slavery of Egypt, announces the liberation wrought by Baptism: 'O God, who caused the children of Abraham to pass dry-shod through the Red Sea, so that the chosen people, set free from slavery to Pharaoh, would prefigure the people of the baptized' [10] " (CCC 1221). In the Exodus, the same waters brought death to the Egyptians and life to the Jews; in Baptism, the same waters bring death to sin and new life in Christ.

e. "Finally, Baptism is prefigured in the crossing of the Jordan River by which the People of God received the gift of the land promised to Abraham's descendents, an image of eternal life" (CCC 1222).

f. "All the Old Covenant prefigurations find their fulfillment in Christ Jesus. He begins his public life after having himself baptized by St. John the Baptist in the Jordan [cf. Mt 3:13]. After his resurrection Christ gives this mission to his apostles: 'Go therefore and make disciples of all nations, baptizing them in the name of the Father and of the Son and of the Holy Spirit' [Mt 28:19–20; cf. Mk 16:15–16]" (CCC 1223).

5. The relationship between Baptism and Christ

First, we are baptized "*into* Christ" (Rom 6:3, emphasis added).

Second, Christ instituted and commanded Baptism (Mt 28:19–20).

Third, Christ also provided the power for Baptism. He is the source of its supernatural power to remove original sin and instill divine life into the soul of the baptized, so that Baptism actually saves us (1 Pet 3:21).

Many Protestants argue that Baptism cannot save us because it is Christ's death on the Cross that has already saved us. Christ's death does save us, but this is communicated to us through Baptism (Rom 6:3).

This communication is not just a legal transaction, God crediting to our "account" Christ's righteousness and crediting to his "account" our sins. It is more like an organic "grafting" than a external legal relationship (see Rom 11:17–24 and Jn 15:1–6). Christ's death two thousand years ago causes our salvation today by God *putting us into* Christ's death, burial, and Resurrection through Baptism (Rom 6:3–4; Col 2:12).

---

[10] *Roman Missal*, Easter Vigil 42: Blessing of Water: "Abrahæ filios per mare Rubrum sicco vestigio transire fecisti, ut plebs, a Pharaonis servitute liberata, populum baptizatorum præfiguraret."

The water into which we are plunged in Baptism is not just a universal natural symbol but also points to a specific historical fact: "The blood and water that flowed from the pierced side of the crucified Jesus are types of Baptism and the Eucharist, the sacraments of new life [cf. Jn 19:34; 1 Jn 5:6–8]" (CCC 1225). Baptism is not just a symbolic remembering of that; that is a symbol foreshadowing Baptism. " 'Baptism comes from . . . the cross of Christ, from his death. There is the whole mystery: he died for you. In him you are redeemed, in him you are saved' [11] " (CCC 1225).

Baptism does what Christ does because Baptism *is* what Christ does: it gives us a new birth and makes us children of God. "The newly baptized is now, in the only Son, a child of God entitled to say the prayer of the children of God: 'Our Father' " (CCC 1243). We do not become children of God by natural birth; we become children of our natural parents by natural birth. We become children of God by being "born again", and this happens in Baptism (Jn 3:3–6).

6. Is Baptism necessary for salvation?

a. *The Baptism of water*: "The Lord himself affirms that Baptism is necessary for salvation [cf. Jn 3:5]" (CCC 1257). However, this does not mean that all the unbaptized are unsaved. *"God has bound salvation to the sacrament of Baptism, but he himself is not bound by his sacraments"* (CCC 1257). For sacramental Baptism, or water Baptism, is not the only kind of Baptism.

b. *The Baptism of blood*: "The Church has always held the firm conviction that those who suffer death for the sake of the faith without having received Baptism are baptized by their death for and with Christ. This *Baptism of blood*, like the *desire for Baptism*" [the "Baptism of desire"; see next paragraph], "brings about the fruits of Baptism without being a sacrament" (CCC 1258).

c. *The Baptism of desire*: "For *catechumens* who die before their Baptism, their explicit desire to receive it, together with repentance for their sins, and charity, assures them the salvation that they were not able to receive through the sacrament" (CCC 1259).

d. *The Baptism of implicit desire*: "Every man who is ignorant of the Gospel of Christ and of his Church, but seeks the truth and does the will of God in accordance with his understanding of it, can be saved. It may be supposed that such persons would have *desired Baptism explicitly* if they had known its necessity" (CCC 1260).

e. *Unbaptized infants*: "As regards *children who have died without Baptism*, the Church can only entrust them to the mercy of God, as she does in her funeral rites for them. Indeed, the great mercy of God who desires that all men

---

[11] St. Ambrose, *De sacr.* 2, 2, 6: PL 16, 444; cf. Jn 3:5.

should be saved, and Jesus' tenderness toward children which caused him to say: 'Let the children come to me, do not hinder them' [Mk 10:14; cf. 1 Tim 2:4], allow us to hope that there is a way of salvation for children who have died without Baptism" (CCC 1261).

f. *Limbo*: Many Catholic theologians in the past have reasoned that children who die unbaptized go to a place of eternal peace but without the vision of God, since these infants have committed no actual sins and therefore have not chosen or deserved hell, but they are born with original sin and therefore cannot enter heaven. They named the place "Limbo". The Church has never officially approved or disapproved this idea; it is neither a dogma nor a heresy. But most theologians now believe God will somehow get his innocent little ones into heaven. We cannot limit God's love or his cleverness in arranging for his loving will to be done. God is not limited to any one means.

7. Adult and infant Baptism

"Since the beginning of the Church, adult Baptism is the common practice where the proclamation of the Gospel is still new" (CCC 1247). But also "[t]he practice of infant Baptism is an immemorial tradition of the Church. There is explicit testimony to this practice from the second century on, and it is quite possible that, from the beginning of the apostolic preaching, when whole 'households' received baptism, infants may also have been baptized [cf. Acts 16:15, 33; 18:8; 1 Cor 1:16]" (CCC 1252).

The reasons for infant Baptism are as follows:

a. "Born with a fallen human nature and tainted by original sin, children also have need of the new birth in Baptism" (CCC 1250).

b. Infant Baptism shows our faith in God's initiative. "The sheer gratuitousness of the grace of salvation is particularly manifest in infant Baptism" (CCC 1250). Infant Baptism fits the nature of God's love: God loves us before we love him. Even our desire for him is his gift.

c. Infant Baptism shows the wideness of God's grace. God withholds his love from no one. Intelligence is not a qualification, only openness. And who is more open than an infant? There is no actual sin, no guilt, no refusal.

d. Loving parents want to give their children the very best of everything, and nothing is better than God's grace, nothing is more necessary for a good life. "The Church and the parents would deny a child the priceless grace of becoming a child of God were they not to confer Baptism shortly after birth" [12] (CCC 1250).

e. Christ told his apostles to let the children come to him (Mk 10:14–16).

---

[12] Cf. CIC, can. 867; CCEO, cann. 681; 686, 1.

f. God deals with us not only as individuals but also as families. Throughout Scripture, covenant (marriage) and kinship (family) are central.

g. Infant Baptism is scriptural (see Acts 16:15).

h. Finally, since we simply cannot understand how God's grace works, we cannot limit it.

8. How Baptism fits into the liturgical order

Baptism manifests much historical variation, depending on times, places, and rites; but also an invariable essential structure:

"From the time of the apostles, becoming a Christian has been accompanied by a journey and initiation in several stages. This journey can be covered rapidly or slowly, but certain essential elements will always have to be present: proclamation of the Word, acceptance of the Gospel entailing conversion" [change of mind, heart, and life], "profession of faith, Baptism itself, the outpouring of the Holy Spirit" [given in Confirmation], "and admission to Eucharistic communion" (CCC 1229). These last three steps are the three "sacraments of initiation".

"This initiation has varied greatly through the centuries according to circumstances" (CCC 1230). "Today in all the rites, Latin and Eastern, the Christian initiation of adults begins with their entry into the catechumenate and reaches its culmination in a single celebration of the three sacraments of initiation: Baptism, Confirmation, and the Eucharist" [13] (CCC 1233).

9. After Baptism

"For the grace of Baptism to unfold, the parents' help is important. So too is the role of the *godfather* and *godmother*, who must be firm believers, able and ready to help the newly baptized—child or adult—on the road of Christian life" [14] (CCC 1255). The Church's "new rite [of Baptism] . . . places the parents at the very heart of things—where they belong. . . . They renounce sin and profess faith; it is their responsibility to see to it that their lives give testimony to the faith they have professed, for they will be the first Christian influence on this child. But parents also need help. The godparents can be looked upon as a kind of link to the extended family of the Church" (Fr. Peter Stravinskas, *Understanding the Sacraments*).

The Catechism says that the task of a godparent is a truly ecclesial function (see CCC 1255). Therefore godparents should be chosen, not just to honor friends or relatives, but to represent the Church by their words and

---

[13] Cf. *AG* 14: CIC, cann. 851; 865–66.
[14] Cf. CIC, cann. 872–74.

example. Baptized non-Catholic Christians can also fulfill this task, provided one godparent is Catholic.

"For all the baptized, children or adults, faith must grow *after* Baptism. For this reason the Church celebrates each year at the Easter Vigil the renewal of baptismal promises" (CCC 1254).

10. Who can baptize?

"The ordinary ministers of Baptism are the bishop and priest and, in the Latin Church, also the deacon.[15] In case of necessity, anyone, even a non-baptized person, with the required intention, can baptize,[16] by using the Trinitarian baptismal formula. The intention required is to will to do what the Church does when she baptizes. The Church finds the reason for this possibility in the universal saving will of God and the necessity of Baptism for salvation" [17] (CCC 1256).

11. Who can be baptized?

Anyone who is willing (Rev 22:17).

But not anyone who is unwilling. Though it is God's grace and does not depend on our worthiness, Baptism is not magic; so it cannot be applied indiscriminately. To baptize an unwilling adult or a child against the will of the parents is a kind of spiritual kidnapping; it is unjust and illicit by Church law (see CIC, can. 865, 868).

For God's grace does not violate nature, and the nature of man is to be free. "Ask and it will be given to you" (Mt 7:7) implies that God will not give grace if we do not ask.

This does not mean it is wrong to baptize infants who are orphaned or victims of abortion or who are in danger of death, even if Baptism is not asked for; for it is not refused either.

CONFIRMATION

1. What is Confirmation and why is it needed?

The "point" of Confirmation is that it is the sacrament of the Holy Spirit.

Why is it needed? Because of the difference it makes. And what difference does it make? If you read the first five books of the New Testament,

---

[15] Cf. CIC, can. 861 § 1; CCEO, can. 677 § 1.
[16] CIC, can. 861 § 2.
[17] Cf. 1 Tim 2:4.

you can see the answer for yourself, just as the world did: the Sacrament of Confirmation's need and purpose is to make the same difference to the individual Catholic that the descent of the Holy Spirit at Pentecost made to the Church. "[T]he effect of the sacrament of Confirmation is the special outpouring of the Holy Spirit as once granted to the apostles on the day of Pentecost" (CCC 1302).

Why is the Holy Spirit needed? Is Christ not enough? Yes, but the Holy Spirit is needed to bring Christ closer. Christ told his disciples that it would be better for them if he went away physically so that he could send his Spirit to them (Jn 16:7). For the Spirit would be *in* them, even more intimately than Jesus was with them in the flesh. For love always seeks maximum intimacy, and God is Love.

2. The effects of Confirmation

The effects of this intimacy can be seen by contrasting the disciples (especially Peter, who is mentioned the most) "before and after" the coming of the Spirit—that is, in the four Gospels and then in the Acts of the Apostles. Christ told them they would not be ready to preach and testify and evangelize and suffer for him until the Spirit had come (Acts 1:4–5).

The reason for the Sacrament of Confirmation is the same as the reason for Pentecost. Confirmation "confirms", that is, "firms up" or strengthens, the supernatural life within us that we received in Baptism; it strengthens us to be mature, adult witnesses for Christ. The old formula stated that Confirmation made us into "soldiers of Christ". Though we may no longer prefer the military imagery today, the point remains valid that Confirmation prepares us for spiritual warfare, for an active mission.

And it does this by "baptizing" (immersing) us in the Holy Spirit. This is a crucial change. For Christ, our "objective" or "external" Lord and Savior and ideal, now becomes also our "subjective" or internal source of power by sending us his Spirit. Just as children become adult when they internalize the laws and values of their parents instead of just reacting to their parents' external authority, so Christians become adult when the Spirit adds this internal source of motivation and power.

The need for Confirmation is most obvious when considering infant Baptism. Since an infant, who has not reached the age of the exercise of reason and free choice, cannot personally put forth an act of faith, the faith of the parents and of the Church substitutes, or stands in for, the faith of the infant. This was designed as a temporary, not a permanent, substitute. The child will later have to accept freely, by his own will, the grace of God he has received at the will of his parents in infant Baptism. This is done in Confirmation.

For this reason, careful education and preparation of the candidates for

Confirmation are essential. The sacrament cannot be an "automatic" social occasion but must be clearly understood and freely chosen—like marriage, or like enlisting in the army.

And—also like marriage or enlistment—Confirmation is not an end but a beginning. Unfortunately, many Catholics treat Confirmation as the end of their religious education instead of as the end only of its childhood phase and as the beginning of its adult phase. A personal relationship with God in "spiritual marriage", like a personal relationship with a spouse in natural marriage, cannot be static; it either grows, or it shrinks.

3. Confirmation completes Baptism

Confirmation is the completion of Baptism. It is the sealing of the baptismal covenant relationship, or spiritual marriage, between the Christian and Christ.

Because of this close link between the two sacraments, it is desirable (though not strictly required) that the same person who was the godparent in Baptism be the sponsor in Confirmation.

The link between the two sacraments is expressed more strongly in the Church's Eastern rites: "In the East, ordinarily the priest who baptizes also immediately confers Confirmation in one and the same celebration. But he does so with sacred chrism" [oil] "consecrated by the patriarch or the bishop, thus expressing the apostolic unity of the Church" (CCC 1312).

4. The powers received in Confirmation

Those who are confirmed receive two powers, one for themselves and one for others:

a. They receive, first of all, the power to live a life of personal holiness in an unholy world, especially the courage to sacrifice and suffer for Christ. Christians are always described in the New Testament as a people set apart. (Indeed, the very word "holy" means "set apart".) Christians are always called to be "countercultural". Their guide is not their society but their Lord.

b. They also receive the power to spread that faith by word and example, that is, to be witnesses. " '[B]y the sacrament of Confirmation, [the baptized] are . . . enriched with a special strength of the Holy Spirit. Hence they are, as true witnesses of Christ, more strictly obliged to spread and defend the faith by word and deed' [18] " (CCC 1285). Confirmation "gives us a special strength of the Holy Spirit to spread and defend the faith by word and action

[18] *LG* 11; cf. *OC*, Introduction 2.

as true witnesses of Christ, to confess the name of Christ boldly, and never to be ashamed of the Cross" [19] (CCC 1303).

5. Charismatic gifts

In addition to these two graces (section 4), the outpouring of the Holy Spirit, whether in Confirmation or at any other time, often includes the grace of "charismatic gifts" (cf. 1 Cor 12–14; CCC 799–801; 1830–32). These are special supernatural gifts, different gifts for different Christians, all of them to be used for the work of the Church as a whole (1 Cor 12). One "gift" that is given to all by the outpouring of the Holy Spirit is the gift of understanding, especially the understanding of Scripture, which can "light up" from within when the same Spirit that inspired its ancient authors to write it now inspires the present-day Christian to read it.

6. The historical origin of Confirmation

a. "In the Old Testament the prophets announced that the Spirit of the Lord would rest on the hoped-for Messiah [cf. Isa 11:2; 61:1; Lk 4:16–22]" (CCC 1286).

b. When he came, "He was conceived of the Holy Spirit; his whole life and his whole mission are carried out in total communion with the Holy Spirit" (CCC 1286).

c. "Christ promised this outpouring of the Spirit [cf. Lk 12:12; Jn 3:5–8, 7:37–39; 16:7–15; Acts 1:8], a promise which he fulfilled ... at Pentecost [cf. Jn 20:22; Acts 2:1–4]" (CCC 1287).

d. " 'From that time on the apostles, in fulfillment of Christ's will, imparted to the newly baptized by the laying on of hands the gift of the Spirit' [20] " (CCC 1288).

e. " '[T]he sacrament of Confirmation ... perpetuates the grace of Pentecost in the Church' [21] " (CCC 1288).

7. The liturgical rite of Confirmation

In the early Church, the sacraments of Baptism, Confirmation, and Eucharist were all received together, forming a unified rite of Christian initiation (see CCC 1212, 1290, 1298, 1306). This is still done today in the Eastern churches, where infants are baptized, chrismated (confirmed), and communicated, and for adult converts in the Roman rite.

[19] Cf. Council of Florence (1439): DS 1319; LG 11; 12.
[20] Paul VI, *Divinae consortium naturae*, 659; cf. Acts 8:15–17; 19:5–6; Heb 6:2.
[21] Paul VI, *Divinae consortium naturae*, 659; cf. Acts 8:15–17; 19:5–6; Heb 6:2.

"In the first centuries Confirmation generally comprised one single celebration with Baptism, forming with it a 'double sacrament,' according to the expression of St. Cyprian. Among other reasons, the multiplication of infant baptisms all through the year . . . often prevented the bishop from being present at all baptismal celebrations. In the West the desire to reserve the completion of Baptism" [that is, Confirmation] "to the bishop caused the temporal separation of the two sacraments. The East has kept them united, so that Confirmation is conferred by the priest who baptizes. But he can do so only with the 'myron'" [oil] "consecrated by a bishop" [22] (CCC 1290).

8. The "mark" received in Confirmation

"By this anointing the confirmand receives the 'mark,' the *seal* of the Holy Spirit. A seal is a symbol of a person, a sign of personal authority, or ownership of an object.[23] Hence soldiers were marked with their leader's seal and slaves with their master's" (CCC 1295). "This seal of the Holy Spirit marks our total belonging to Christ, our enrollment in his service for ever" (CCC 1296).

Therefore, "[l]ike Baptism which it completes, Confirmation is given only once, for it too imprints on the soul an *indelible spiritual mark*" [24] (CCC 1304).

9. Who can receive Confirmation?

"Every baptized person not yet confirmed can and should receive the sacrament of Confirmation.[25] . . . Baptism, Confirmation, and Eucharist form a unity. . . . [W]ithout Confirmation and Eucharist, Baptism is certainly valid and efficacious, but Christian initiation remains incomplete" (CCC 1306).

"For centuries Latin custom has indicated 'the age of discretion' as the reference point for receiving Confirmation" (CCC 1307). All cultures have had some "coming of age" rite of passage to mark personal adulthood.

But "[a]lthough Confirmation is sometimes called the 'sacrament of Christian maturity,' we must not confuse adult faith with the adult age of natural growth. . . . St. Thomas reminds us of this: 'Age of body does not determine age of soul. Even in childhood man can attain spiritual maturity. . . . Many children, through the strength of the Holy Spirit they have received, have bravely fought for Christ even to the shedding of their blood' [26]" (CCC 1308).

[22] Cf. CCEO, can. 695 § 1; 696 § 1.
[23] Cf. Gen 38:18; 41:42; Deut 32:34; CT 8:6.
[24] Cf. Council of Trent (1547): DS 1609; Lk 24:48–49.
[25] Cf. CIC, can. 889 § 1.
[26] St. Thomas Aquinas, *STh* III, 72, 8, *ad* 2; cf. Wis 4:8.

10. Preparation for Confirmation

"*Preparation* for Confirmation should aim at leading the Christian toward a more intimate union with Christ and a more lively familiarity with the Holy Spirit—his actions, his gifts, and his biddings" (CCC 1309). God speaks in a "still small voice" (1 Kings 19:12), and if we are to hear it, we need to develop the lifelong habit of listening to this voice—in our personal prayer, in reading Scripture, in our participation in the Church's liturgy, and in all of life's occasions and relationships. This should be seriously undertaken both in preparation for and in application of Confirmation.

11. Who administers Confirmation?

"*In the Latin Rite*, the ordinary minister of Confirmation is the bishop.[27] If the need arises, the bishop may grant the faculty of administering Confirmation [28] to priests, although it is fitting that he confer it himself. . . . Bishops are the successors of the apostles. . . . The administration of this sacrament by them demonstrates clearly that its effect is to unite those who receive it more closely to the Church, to her apostolic origins, and to her mission of bearing witness to Christ" (CCC 1313).

"If a Christian is in danger of death, any priest can give him Confirmation.[29] Indeed the Church desires that none of her children, even the youngest, should depart this world without having been perfected by the Holy Spirit" (CCC 1314).

In the truest sense, it is only Jesus Christ who can administer the sacrament of Confirmation, for it is only Christ who can give the Holy Spirit.

12. The "gifts of the Holy Spirit" and the "fruits of the Holy Spirit"

"The seven *gifts* of the Holy Spirit are wisdom, understanding, counsel, fortitude, knowledge, piety, and fear of the Lord. They belong in their fullness to Christ" [cf. Isa 11:1–2] (CCC 1831).

"The *fruits* of the Spirit are perfections that the Holy Spirit forms in us as the first fruits of eternal glory. The tradition of the Church lists twelve of them: 'charity, joy, peace, patience, kindness, goodness, generosity, gentleness, faithfulness, modesty, self-control, chastity' [Gal 5:22–23 (Vulg.)]" (CCC 1832).

---

[27] Cf. CIC, can. 882.
[28] Cf. CIC, can. 884 § 2.
[29] Cf. CIC, can. 883 § 3.

Chapter 4

THE EUCHARIST

1. Its importance

The sacraments are the crown of the Catholic faith, and the Eucharist is the crown of the sacraments. Why are the sacraments the crown of the faith? Because the God we believe in the Creeds and obey in the Commandments, we meet and receive in the sacraments. Why is the Eucharist the greatest of the sacraments? Because " 'in the blessed Eucharist is contained the whole spiritual good of the Church, namely Christ himself' " [PO 5] (CCC 1324).

The *Catechism* says that "[t]he Eucharist is 'the source and summit of the Christian life' [LG 11]" (CCC 1324). Why? Because the Eucharist is both the origin and the end of that supernatural reality which is the point of everything in the Catholic religion. That reality, called by many different names, such as "salvation", "eternal life", "sanctifying grace", "the Kingdom of God", and "the Christian life", consists in participating in the very life of God.

The Eucharist is the origin of that because it does more than merely symbolize it: the Eucharist actually gives us that.

And the Eucharist is the culmination of the Christian life, of man's life in relation to God, because it is the culmination of God's life in relation to man, at least while we are on this earth. It is both the greatest thing God does to man and the greatest thing man does to God. " 'The Eucharist . . . is the culmination both of God's action sanctifying the world in Christ and of the worship men offer to Christ and through him to the Father in the Holy Spirit' [1] " (CCC 1325).

2. Its relationship to the creation of the universe

Let us look at the Eucharist in its most fundamental context. Why did God institute it? To answer this question, we must begin where the whole *Catechism* begins, which is where all reality begins:

"God, infinitely perfect and blessed in himself, in a plan of sheer goodness freely created man to make him share in his own blessed life. For this reason, . . . God draws close to man" (CCC 1). Out of the pure and unselfish love that is his very essence, God created the universe so that we could exist and enjoy his love forever. To this end, he revealed himself to the whole world through a "chosen people", established a covenant of love with them, revealed his law to them, sent them prophets, and finally fulfilled his covenant by sending his eternal Son, who was born, lived, died, resurrected, and ascended so that we could be saved from sin and united to God. Jesus Christ the Son of God continued his presence and work among us by appointing apostles and establishing the Church, his "Mystical Body". God did all this for one reason: for the love-union with us that is achieved most perfectly in this life in the Eucharist.

The universe is a gigantic cathedral. We can understand the point and purpose of the universe by looking at a cathedral. Every detail in the great medieval cathedrals was for the Eucharist. They were built primarily for the Eucharist, to house the Eucharist. Similarly, the whole Church on earth is the "House of Bread" (the meaning of "Bethlehem") that Christ established for the Eucharist. This is his love's ultimate aim, for love's aim is union, and the Eucharist is the most intimate union between us and Christ that exists in this world. God created the universe for this love-union. He made the universe to house the Church; and he made the Church to house the Eucharist; so it is true to say that the ultimate reason, in this life, for the creation of the universe is the Eucharist.

---

[1] Congregation of Rites, instruction, *Eucharisticum mysterium*, 6.

3. Its hiddenness

In the Eucharist God is both truly present and hidden. Not only in the Eucharist but in all of life, God both reveals himself and at the same time conceals himself. Why?

To elicit our free response of faith and trust. Even human lovers do not give or demand proofs or guarantees. God gives just enough light for lovers, who can find him when they seek him, but not so much as to compel non-lovers and non-seekers to find him against their will. The lover respects the beloved's freedom.

The greatness of the Eucharist is known only to faith, not to the feelings or the senses or the sciences. Its being (reality) is far greater than its seeming (appearances). "The presence of Christ's true body and blood in this sacrament cannot be detected by sense, nor understanding, but by faith alone, which rests upon Divine authority" (St. Thomas Aquinas, *Summa theologiae* III, 75, 1), not on human experience.

Many "once in a lifetime" experiences in this world feel more heavenly to us than what happens every Sunday: our reception of the Eucharist. Many experiences move us to tears of joy and remain in our memory throughout our lives: births, deaths, weddings, honeymoons, reunions, sunsets, even sports triumphs. In contrast, most of us usually feel very little when we receive the very Body of God incarnate, even though this reality is infinitely greater than anything else in our lives.

This is normal, and God-ordained, for a reason. God does not give us heavenly feelings when we receive the Eucharist for the same reason he does not give us heavenly sights. We neither feel nor see Christ as he really is so that faith, not feelings or sight, can be exercised, trained, and emerge triumphant.

The Eucharist does not look like Christ; thus, it tests, not our sight, but our faith: Do we believe God's word or our human senses?

> Sight, taste, and touch in Thee are each deceived;
> The ear alone most safely is believed:
> I believe all the Son of God has spoken:
> Than Truth's own word there is no truer token.
> —St. Thomas Aquinas

Just as the Eucharist does not look like Christ to our outer senses, it does not feel like Christ to our emotions. Here again it tests our faith. A faith that does not go beyond human feelings is not faith at all, just as a faith that does not go beyond seeing—a faith that says "Seeing is believing"—is no faith at all.

Sometimes God sends us special graces that can be felt when we receive the Eucharist. But he usually does not—not because he is stingy and unloving, but because he knows exactly what each of us needs, and most of us need to exercise more faith, not to "hanker after sensible consolations", as the saints put it. Feelings are like sweets. They are not our food. Christ himself is our food. Feelings are our jam; Christ is our bread. We must learn continually to turn our faith around and focus, not on ourselves and our own feelings, but on Christ, who is faith's proper object.

4. Its names

"The inexhaustible richness of this sacrament is expressed in the different names we give it. Each name evokes certain aspects of it. It is called:

a. "Eucharist" ['thanksgiving'] "because it is an action of thanksgiving to God" (CCC 1328), "a sacrifice of praise in thanksgiving for the work of creation. In the Eucharistic sacrifice the whole of creation loved by God is presented to the Father . . . in thanksgiving for all that God has made good, beautiful, and just in creation and in humanity" (CCC 1359). In the little round Host is offered up the entire universe.

b. "The Lord's Supper, because of its connection with the supper which the Lord took with his disciples on the eve of his Passion" [when he instituted the Eucharist] "and because it anticipates the wedding feast of the Lamb in the heavenly Jerusalem" [2] (CCC 1329).

c. "The *Breaking of Bread*, because . . . it is this expression that the first Christians will use; [3] . . . by doing so they signified that all who eat the one broken bread, Christ, enter into communion with him and form but one body in him" [4] (CCC 1329).

d. "The *Eucharistic assembly (synaxis)*, because the Eucharist is celebrated amid the assembly of the faithful, the visible expression of the Church" [5] (CCC 1329).

e. "The *memorial* of the Lord's Passion and Resurrection" (CCC 1330).

f. "The *Holy Sacrifice*, because it makes present the one sacrifice of Christ" (CCC 1330).

g. The "*Divine Liturgy*" (CCC 1330).

h. The "*Sacred Mysteries*" (CCC 1330).

i. The "*Most Blessed Sacrament*" (CCC 1330).

---

[2] Cf. 1 Cor 11:20; Rev 19:9.
[3] Cf. Acts 2:42, 46; 20:7, 11.
[4] Cf. 1 Cor 10:16–17.
[5] Cf. 1 Cor 11:17–34.

j. *"Holy Communion"* (CCC 1331).
k. *"[T]he bread of angels"* (CCC 1331).
l. *"[B]read from heaven"* (CCC 1331).
m. *"[M]edicine of immortality"* [6] (CCC 1331).
n. *"[V]iaticum"* (CCC 1331).
o. *"Holy Mass"* (CCC 1332).

5. Its origin

The Eucharist rests on the authority of Christ, who instituted it (Lk 22:14–20). "Faithful to the Lord's command the Church continues to do ... what he did" (CCC 1333). Those who reject what the Church teaches and does, whether they know it or not, really reject what Christ teaches and does; for the Church's creed, code, and cult—her theology, morality, and liturgy—are all in his name, who said to the apostles, "He who hears you hears me" (Lk 10:16).

The Eucharist has always been controversial and divisive, as was Christ. This is supremely ironic, for the Eucharist is the sacrament of *unity* with Christ and, through him (the "one bread"), with his whole Body the Church (the "one body"). Yet, like Christ himself, the Eucharist divided and offended men from the beginning. "The first announcement of the Eucharist divided the disciples, just as the announcement of the Passion scandalized them: 'This is a hard saying; who can listen to it?' [Jn 6:60]. The Eucharist and the Cross are stumbling blocks. It is the same mystery and it never ceases to be an occasion of division. 'Will you also go away?' [Jn 6:67]: the Lord's question echoes through the ages, as a loving invitation to discover that only he has 'the words of eternal life' [Jn 6:68] *and that to receive in faith the gift of his Eucharist is to receive the Lord himself"* (CCC 1336).

6. Its history

"From the beginning the Church has been faithful to the Lord's command. Of the Church of Jerusalem it is written: 'They devoted themselves to the apostles' teaching and fellowship, to the breaking of bread and the prayers' [Acts 2:42, 46]" (CCC 1342).

"From that time on down to our own day the celebration of the Eucharist has been continued so that today we encounter it everywhere in the Church with the same fundamental structure. It remains the center of the Church's life" (CCC 1343).

---

[6] St. Ignatius of Antioch, *Ad Eph.* 20, 2: SCh 10,76.

7. Its essential elements

"The liturgy of the Eucharist unfolds according to a fundamental structure which has been preserved throughout the centuries down to our own day. It displays two great parts that form a fundamental unity:

"—. . . the liturgy of the Word . . . ;

"—the liturgy of the Eucharist" (CCC 1346).

Within these two, the *Catechism* more specifically mentions four parts: "The Eucharistic celebration always includes:" [a] "the proclamation of the Word of God;" [b] "thanksgiving to God the Father for all his benefits, above all the gift of his Son;" [c] "the consecration of bread and wine; and" [d] "participation in the liturgical banquet by receiving the Lord's body and blood. These elements constitute one single act of worship" (CCC 1408).

8. Its participants: Who celebrates the Eucharist?

a. God the Father, to whom the sacrifice of Christ the Son is offered and who accepts it.

b. At the Eucharistic assembly's "head is Christ himself, the principal agent of the Eucharist" (CCC 1348). Christ gave the Eucharist (himself) to us for our salvation so that we could offer it with him to God the Father for our salvation.

c. The Holy Spirit, who energizes it.

d. Christ's whole Body, the Church. *"The whole Church is united with the offering"* (CCC 1369).

"To the offering of Christ are united not only the members still here on earth, but also those already *in the glory of heaven"* (CCC 1370). And "[t]he Eucharistic sacrifice is also offered for *the faithful departed* who 'have died in Christ but are not yet wholly purified' [7] " (CCC 1371). So in the Eucharist are united: the Church Militant, on earth; the Church Triumphant, in heaven; and the Church Suffering, in purgatory.

And the Church on earth includes both clergy and laity, who are equally necessary but with different roles: "It is in representing him" [Christ] "that the bishop or priest acting *in the person of Christ the head* (*in persona Christi capitis*) presides over the assembly" (CCC 1348). But "[a]ll have their own active parts to play . . . : readers, those who bring up the offerings, those who give communion, and the whole people whose 'Amen' manifests their participation" (CCC 1348).

e. In the Eucharist the whole creation is presented to God through man, the mediator and priest of all creation, just as all mankind is presented to God through Christ, the mediator and High Priest of man. As Christ is priest

---

[7] Council of Trent (1562): DS 1743.

for all men, man is priest for all creation. Christ restores man to his priestly role given to Adam by God and perverted by sin. "In the Eucharistic sacrifice the whole of creation loved by God is presented to the Father" (CCC 1359). The Eucharist is cosmic.

Everything in the universe and everything in our lives can be offered and transformed in the Eucharist. We can bring our whole selves to the Eucharist and lay them down on the altar—all of them, nothing held back. For the Eucharist is Christ, and whatever we give to Christ, we get back perfected and transformed. To the extent that we give ourselves up, to that extent we get our true, Christ-transformed selves back. Nothing in our lives should remain outside the Eucharist. "The lives of the faithful, their praise, sufferings, prayer, and work, are united with those of Christ and with his total offering, and so acquire a new value" (CCC 1368).

9. Its identity: Christ really present

As a sacrament, the Eucharist has a double aspect: it is both a sign and the reality signified by it, both a remembering of the past and a making really *present*: "When the Church celebrates the Eucharist, she commemorates Christ's Passover, and it is made present: the sacrifice Christ offered once for all on the cross remains ever present" [cf. Heb 7:25–27] (CCC 1364).

Here the three meanings of "present" come together: Christ in the Eucharist is (a) present, not absent, but really here; (b) present, not past, but happening now; and (c) presented as a gift (a "present"), really given; offered, not withheld.

Christ " 'is present in many ways to his Church' [8] " (CCC 1373) but "[t]he mode of Christ's presence under the Eucharistic species" [forms, appearances] "is unique. It raises the Eucharist above all the sacraments as 'the perfection of the spiritual life and the end to which all the sacraments tend.' [9] In the most blessed sacrament of the Eucharist 'the body and blood, together with the soul and divinity, of our Lord Jesus Christ and, therefore, *the whole Christ is truly, really, and substantially contained.*' [10] 'This presence . . . is presence in the fullest sense' [11] " (CCC 1374).

10. Its relationship to the Cross

Christ offered himself once for all on the Cross. He said, "It is finished" (Jn 19:30). The Eucharist does not repeat this sacrifice, but re-presents it to the Father. The sacrifice that was accomplished on Calvary is offered again in

[8] Rom 8:34; cf. LG 48.
[9] St. Thomas Aquinas, *STh* III, 73, 3c.
[10] Council of Trent (1551): DS 1651.
[11] Paul VI, *MF* 39.

each Mass. It can be offered now only *because* "it is finished", perfected, "a perfect offering".

"In the Eucharist Christ gives us the very body which he gave up for us on the cross, the very blood which he 'poured out for many for the forgiveness of sins' [Mt 26:28]" (CCC 1365). We know this is true because Christ said so: "This is my body which is given for you" and "This cup which is poured out for you is the new covenant in my blood" (Lk 22:19–20).

The Eucharist is not merely an image or symbol of Christ's sacrifice; it is Christ's sacrifice. "The sacrifice of Christ and the sacrifice of the Eucharist are *one single sacrifice*: 'The victim is one and the same: the same' " [Christ] " 'now offers through the ministry of priests, who then offered himself on the cross; only the manner of offering is different.' . . . '[I]n the Mass, the same Christ who offered himself once in a bloody manner on the altar of the cross is contained and offered in an unbloody manner' [12] " (CCC 1367).

Christ on the Cross of Calvary two thousand years ago and Christ on the altar of your local Catholic church today are *the same person*. The Christ we meet today in the Mass is the Christ of history, for "Jesus Christ is the same yesterday and today and for ever" (Heb 13:8). Christ is not divided by time.

Christ is also not divided by space. "Christ is present whole and entire in each of the species" [consecrated bread and wine] "and whole and entire in each of their parts, in such a way that the breaking of the bread does not divide Christ" [13] (CCC 1377).

The practical consequence of this fact is that we can and should have the same attitude to the Eucharist as we would have to Christ himself if he were visibly present as he was to his apostles: the same attitude we would have had if we were standing under the Cross as he was offering his lifeblood for our salvation.

And what attitude is that? It is accurately summed up by Hans Urs von Balthasar: "Everything that I am (insofar as I am anything more on this earth than a fugitive figure without hope, all of whose illusions are rendered worthless by death), I am solely by virtue of Christ's death, which opens up to me the possibility of fulfillment in God. I blossom on the grave of God who died for me" (*The Moment of Christian Witness*, pp. 26–27).

11. Transubstantiation

God performs a miracle in each Mass. In fact, there has never been a miracle as great as this anywhere on earth for almost two thousand years. And it happens in every Catholic church every day!

---

[12] Council of Trent (1562): *Doctrina de ss. Missae sacrificio*, c. 2: DS 1743; cf. Heb 9:14, 27.
[13] Cf. Council of Trent (1551): DS 1641.

" 'It is not man that causes the things offered to become the Body and Blood of Christ, but he who was crucified for us, Christ himself. The priest, in the role of Christ, pronounces these words, but their power and grace are God's. This is my body, he says. This word transforms the things offered' [14] " (CCC 1375). "This change is not like natural changes, but is entirely supernatural, and effected by God's power alone" (St. Thomas Aquinas, *Summa theologiae* III, 75, 4).

Such a miracle is beyond the power of man, but not beyond the power of God. " 'Could not Christ's word, which can make from nothing what did not exist, change existing things into what they were not before?' [15] " (CCC 1375).

Reason says it is possible. But faith says it is actual. Faith prays, with St. Thomas Aquinas:

> Godhead here in hiding, whom I do adore
> Masked by these bare shadows, shape and nothing more,
> See, Lord, at thy service low lies here a heart
> Lost, all lost in wonder at the God thou art.
>
> Seeing, touching, tasting are in thee deceived;
> How says trusty hearing? that shall be believed;
> What God's Son has told me, take for truth I do;
> Truth himself speaks truly or there's nothing true [16] (CCC 1381).

Why do Catholics believe this astonishing idea—that what seems to all human perception to be ordinary bread and wine is in fact the body and blood of God incarnate? Because Christ said so! " 'Because Christ our Redeemer said that it was truly his body that he was offering under the species of bread, it has always been the conviction of the Church of God, and this holy Council now declares again, that by the consecration of the bread and wine there takes place a change of the whole substance' " [being, essence] " 'of the bread into the substance of the body of Christ our Lord and of the whole substance of the wine into the substance of his blood. This change the holy Catholic Church has fittingly and properly called transubstantiation' [17] " (CCC 1376).

"The Eucharistic presence of Christ begins at the moment of the consecration and endures as long as the Eucharistic species subsist" [18] (CCC 1377).

---

[14] St. John Chrysostom, *prod. Jud.* 1:6: PG 49, 380.

[15] St. Ambrose, *De myst.* 9, 50; 52: LP 16, 405–7.

[16] St. Thomas Aquinas (attr.), *Adoro te devote*; trans. Gerard Manley Hopkins.

[17] Council of Trent (1551): DS 1642; cf. Mt 26:26 ff.; Mk 14:22 ff.; Lk 22:19 ff.; 1 Cor 11:24 ff.

[18] Cf. Council of Trent (1551): DS 1641.

Since this remains for about fifteen minutes when in the human body after being swallowed, we should spend this time in prayer, thanksgiving, and adoration, and not quickly turn to worldly occupations.

12. Worship of the Eucharist

" 'The Catholic Church has always offered and still offers to the sacrament of the Eucharist . . . adoration, not only during Mass, but also outside of it, reserving the consecrated hosts with the utmost care, exposing them to the solemn veneration of the faithful, and carrying them in procession' [19] " (CCC 1378).

If the doctrine of the Real Presence of Christ in the Eucharist were not true, this adoration would be the most monstrous idolatry: bowing to bread and worshipping wine! And if it *is* true, then to refuse to adore is equally monstrous.

Eucharistic adoration has transformed many lives and parishes. Pope John Paul II has said, " 'The Church and the world have a great need for Eucharistic worship. Jesus awaits us in this sacrament of love. Let us not refuse the time to go to meet him in adoration, in contemplation full of faith, and open to making amends for the serious offenses and crimes of the world. Let our adoration never cease' [20] " (CCC 1380).

13. The tabernacle

The most sacred object in the history of the chosen people was the Ark of the Covenant, kept in the "holy of holies" in the Temple. It was a golden box containing the actual stone tablets on which the finger of God wrote the Ten Commandments, the heart of the Old Covenant. The Ark was a foreshadowing of the tabernacle—the golden box behind the altar in which the consecrated Host is kept—for this now contains the eucharistic Christ, the heart of the New Covenant.

"The tabernacle was first intended for the reservation of the Eucharist in a worthy place so that it could be brought to the sick and those absent, outside of Mass. As faith in the real presence of Christ in his Eucharist deepened, the Church became conscious of the meaning of silent adoration of the Lord present under the Eucharistic species. It is for this reason that the tabernacle should be located in an especially worthy place in the church and should be constructed in such a way that it emphasizes and manifests the truth of the real presence of Christ in the Blessed Sacrament" (CCC 1379). It is

[19] Paul VI, *MF* 56.
[20] John Paul II, *Dominicae cenae*, 3.

the Church's "holy of holies" but now open to all since Christ's death tore apart the Temple veil that separated man from God (Mt 27:51).

Now, through our receiving Holy Communion, Christ actually lives in another tabernacle: our souls, and even our bodies, which Scripture calls God's tabernacles, or temples (1 Cor 3:16–17; 6:19–20).

14. Eucharist as sacrifice and Eucharist as meal

We are said to "offer" the Eucharist, for it is a sacrifice: the sacrifice Christ made of himself on the Cross. We are also said to "partake" of the Eucharist, for it is our spiritual food. St. Thomas explains: "The Church's sacraments are ordained for helping man in the spiritual life. But the spiritual life is analogous to the corporeal, since corporeal things bear a resemblance to the spiritual. Now it is clear that just as generation is required for corporeal life, since thereby man receives life; and growth, whereby man is brought to maturity: so likewise food is required for the preservation of life. Consequently, just as for the spiritual life there had to be Baptism, which is spiritual generation; and Confirmation, which is spiritual growth: so there needed to be the sacrament of the Eucharist, which is spiritual food" (*Summa theologiae* III, 73, 1).

These two aspects of the Eucharist are inseparable. And since it is a banquet meal as well as a sacrifice, the place it is celebrated is a table as well as an altar. "*The altar*, around which the Church is gathered in the celebration of the Eucharist, represents the two aspects of the same mystery: the altar of the sacrifice and the table of the Lord" (CCC 1383).

The two aspects depend on each other: (a) it is a sacrifice so that it can be a banquet, and (b) it is a banquet only because it is a sacrifice:

a. "The Mass is at the same time, and inseparably, the sacrificial memorial in which the sacrifice of the cross is perpetuated and the sacred banquet of communion with the Lord's body and blood. But the celebration of the Eucharistic sacrifice is wholly directed toward the intimate union of the faithful with Christ through communion" (CCC 1382).

b. But it is a banquet because it is a sacrifice, just as any earthly food can be eaten only because it is first killed and "offered" to eat. Whether animal or vegetable, its natural life is ended, given up to nourish the life of the one who eats it. "My life for yours"—this is the law of nature and of grace. It is even the life of glory. Self-donation, the ecstatic coming out of the self and giving of the self in love, is the essence of our eternal life in heaven, because that is our sharing in the very inner life of the Trinity.

The "banquet" aspect of the Eucharist is not merely human comradeship or "fellowship" or "community", good as those things are. It is intimate personal union with Jesus Christ, and thus—only because of that, through him—

with all Christians, not merely on a human level now but on a divine level (see 2 Cor 5:16–17), as members of his Mystical Body, the body that is made by our common union (comm-union) in his eucharistic Body.

15. Who may receive the Eucharist?

Christ intended this holy banquet for everyone, but not everyone is ready (see Christ's parables of the wise and foolish virgins and the man with no wedding garment in Mt 25:1–13 and 22:1–14). The *Catechism* specifies four qualifications:

a. We must be prepared. There are certainly occasions when one should not receive the Eucharist, and Catholics should not be encouraged to receive it as a matter of course, without faith, understanding, or examination of conscience. "[W]e must *prepare ourselves* for so great and so holy a moment" (CCC 1385), as we would prepare ourselves deeply and seriously for a wedding (see 1 Cor 11:23–29). It is not to be treated trivially, like any other moment. "Bodily demeanor (gestures, clothing) ought to convey the respect, solemnity, and joy of this moment" (CCC 1387). The sense of the sacred is expressed by distinctions, by differences: This is not *ordinary*, in fact this is not like anything else in the world.

This does not mean we must judge ourselves to be holy before we can receive. Just the opposite: the precondition is not worthiness but unworthiness and humble acknowledgement of it: "Before so great a sacrament, the faithful can only echo humbly and with ardent faith the words of the Centurion: ... 'Lord, I am not worthy that you should enter under my roof, but only say the word and my soul shall be healed' [21] " (CCC 1386). The Church's liturgy tells us to say (and to mean) those words before we receive Communion.

b. We must be in a state of grace. "Anyone conscious of a grave sin must receive the sacrament of Reconciliation before coming to communion" (CCC 1385).

c. We must fast. "To prepare for worthy reception of this sacrament, the faithful should observe the fast required in their Church" [22] (CCC 1387). In the United States this is fasting from all food and drink except medications and water for at least one hour before receiving communion.

d. We must be in communion with the Catholic Church to receive her Eucharist. At present, intercommunion with all non-Catholic Christians in the Eucharist is not possible because union in doctrine and authority is, sadly, lacking. For the Church to offer communion to those who do not believe

[21] *Roman Missal*, response to the invitation to communion; cf. Mt 8:8.
[22] Cf. *CIC*, can. 919.

what she teaches or accept her authority would be a false sign, a lie of "body language". For this sacrament signifies oneness: union with Christ and with his Church (St. Paul says we are "one body" because we all partake of this "one bread"). We may not signify Church unity when it does not exist; that would make the sign a countersign.

This does not mean that all other churches' celebrations of the Eucharist are invalid. The Eastern Orthodox churches, " 'although separated from us, yet possess true sacraments' [23] " (CCC 1399). A certain communion with them, " 'given suitable circumstances and the approval of Church authority' " [both Catholic and Orthodox], " 'is not merely possible but is encouraged' [24] " (CCC 1399).

"Ecclesial communities derived from the Reformation and separated from the Catholic Church 'have not preserved the proper reality of the Eucharistic mystery in its fullness, especially because of the absence of the sacrament of Holy Orders.' [25] It is for this reason that, for the Catholic Church, Eucharistic intercommunion with these communities is not possible" (CCC 1400). "Only validly ordained priests can preside at the Eucharist and consecrate the bread and the wine so that they become the Body and Blood of the Lord" (CCC 1411). Protestants do not have priests who can consecrate the Eucharist, therefore they do not have the Eucharist—though they have Christ and salvation through faith, hope, and charity.

"The more painful the experience of the divisions in the Church which break the common participation in the table of the Lord, the more urgent are our prayers to the Lord that the time of complete unity among all who believe in him may return" (CCC 1398). Catholics have been commanded by every pope since Vatican II (and with great passion) to pray and work for reunion, especially the Eastern Orthodox. Pope John Paul II has often called the two Churches, Western and Eastern, the two "lungs" of the one Church.

16. How often?

"The Church obliges the faithful to take part in the Divine Liturgy on Sundays and feast days and, prepared by the sacrament of Reconciliation, to receive the Eucharist at least once a year, if possible during the Easter season.[26] But the Church strongly encourages the faithful to receive the holy Eucharist on Sundays and feast days, or more often still, even daily" (CCC 1389).

---

[23] *UR* 15 § 2; cf. CIC, can 844 § 3.
[24] *UR* 15 § 2; cf. CIC, can 844 § 3.
[25] *UR* 22 § 3.
[26] Cf. *OE* 15; CIC, can. 920.

"It is in keeping with the very meaning of the Eucharist that the faithful, if they have the required dispositions,[27] *receive communion when* they participate in the Mass" [28] (CCC 1388).

For "[w]hat material food produces in our bodily life, Holy Communion wonderfully achieves in our spiritual life" (CCC 1392). "As bodily nourishment restores lost strength, so the Eucharist strengthens our charity, which tends to be weakened in daily life; and this living charity *wipes away venial sins*" [29] (CCC 1394). " 'If, as often as his blood is poured out, it is poured for the forgiveness of sins, I should always receive it, so that it may always forgive my sins. Because I always sin, I should always have a remedy' [30] " (CCC 1393).

17. Communion under the species [appearance] of bread alone?

"Since Christ is sacramentally present under each of the species, communion under the species of bread alone makes it possible to receive all the fruit of Eucharistic grace. For pastoral" [practical] "reasons this manner of receiving communion has been legitimately established as the most common form in the Latin rite. But 'the sign of communion is more complete when given under both kinds' " [bread and wine], " 'since in that form the sign of the Eucharistic meal appears more clearly [GIRM 240].' This is the usual form of receiving communion in the Eastern rites" (CCC 1390).

18. Who can consecrate the Eucharist?

"Consecration" is what the priest does; "transubstantiation" is what God does. It is the same event, the same miracle. God is its cause; the priest is his instrument

Only validly ordained priests can validly consecrate. This is the chief glory of Holy Orders: ordination gives a mere man the (instrumental) power to change bread and wine into the body and blood of Christ!

"In the other sacraments the consecration of the matter consists only in a blessing. . . . But in this sacrament the consecration of the matter consists in the miraculous change of the substance, which can be done only by God; hence the minister in performing this sacrament has no other act save the pronouncing of the words. . . . The forms of the other sacraments are

[27] Cf. CIC, can. 916.
[28] Cf. CIC, can. 917; *The faithful may receive the Holy Eucharist only a second time on the same day* [cf. Pontificia Commissio Codici Iuris Canonici Authentice Intrepretando, *Responsa ad proposita dubia*, 1: AAS 76 (1984) 746].
[29] Cf. Council of Trent (1551): DS 1638.
[30] St. Ambrose, *De Sacr.* 4, 6, 28: PL 16, 446; cf. 1 Cor 11:26.

pronounced in the person of the minister . . . as when it is said, 'I baptize thee,' or 'I confirm thee' . . . , but the form of this sacrament is pronounced as if Christ were speaking in person, so that it is given to be understood that the minister does nothing in perfecting this sacrament except to pronounce the words of Christ" (St. Thomas Aquinas, *Summa theologiae* III, 78, 1).

Therefore the Consecration does not depend on the priest's piety. For "the priest consecrates this sacrament not by his own power but as minister of Christ, in whose person he consecrates this sacrament. But from the fact of being wicked he does not cease to be Christ's minister" (*Summa theologiae* III, 82, 5).

19. The effects of Communion

a. "*Holy Communion augments our union with Christ.* The principal fruit of receiving the Eucharist in Holy Communion is an intimate union with Christ Jesus. Indeed, the Lord said: 'He who eats my flesh and drinks my blood abides in me, and I in him' [Jn 6:56]. Life in Christ has its foundation in the Eucharistic banquet" (CCC 1391).

b. "*Communion separates us from sin.* . . . [T]he Eucharist cannot unite us to Christ without at the same time cleansing us from past sins and preserving us from future sins" (CCC 1393). "The more we share the life of Christ and progress in his friendship, the more difficult it is to break away from him by mortal sin" (CCC 1395).

c. "[*T*]*he Eucharist makes the Church.* . . . Communion renews, strengthens, and deepens this incorporation into the Church, already achieved by Baptism" (CCC 1396).

20. The Eucharist and heaven

Though there will be no need for sacraments in heaven, "the Eucharist is also an anticipation of the heavenly glory" (CCC 1402). For "[a]t the Last Supper the Lord himself directed his disciples' attention toward the fulfillment of the Passover in the kingdom of God: 'I tell you I shall not drink again of this fruit of the vine until that day when I drink it new with you in my Father's kingdom' [Mt 26:29; cf. Lk 22:18; Mk 14:25]" (CCC 1403).

St. Ignatius of Antioch called the Eucharist " 'the one bread that provides the medicine of immortality, the antidote for death, and the food that makes us live for ever in Jesus Christ' [31] " (CCC 1405). Christ himself said: "I am the living bread which came down from heaven; if any one eats of this bread,

---

[31] *LG* 3; St. Ignatius of Antioch, *Ad Eph.* 20, 2: SCh 10, 76.

he will live for ever; and the bread which I shall give for the life of the world is my flesh" (Jn 6:51). Let your spirit sink like a diver into the bottomless depths of this saying—in fact, the whole sixth chapter of John's Gospel—and you will begin to understand the Eucharist.

Chapter 5

THE SACRAMENT OF PENANCE

1. Its presupposition: Sin

The sacrament of the forgiveness of sins presupposes sins to be forgiven. What is sin? The meaning is quite simple.

Sin is not something vague like "forgetting God's love" or "not appreciating God's gifts". Sin means something specific and concrete: disobedience to God's commandments. It is not a lapse of feeling, like unappreciativeness, or a mental lapse, like forgetfulness; it is a moral lapse, a free choice of the will.

Sin must be admitted if it is to be forgiven. We cannot be forgiven for sins we do not confess and repent of:

" 'When Christ's faithful strive to confess all the sins that they can remember, they undoubtedly place all of them before the divine mercy for pardon. But those who fail to do so and knowingly withhold some, place nothing before the divine goodness for remission . . . "for if the sick person is too

ashamed to show his wound to the doctor, the medicine cannot heal" ' [1] "
(CCC 1456).

Sin is in the soul what disease is in the body. A healing operation, on body or soul, requires light. Forgiveness is a healing operation, a real spiritual change. It requires the light of truth to shine on it, by confession. Only then can we find peace. There is no other way to peace. For we cannot be at war and at peace at the same time, and sin is like being at war with God, while repentance, confession, and penance bring peace with God.

The "good news" of our reconciliation with God presupposes the "bad news" of our separation from God; the very idea of "salvation" presupposes the idea of sin, for that is what we are saved *from*.

This is not "gloom and doom". As C. S. Lewis noted, "Humility, after the first shock is a *cheerful* virtue." The greatest saints have always had the greatest joy—indeed, one of the things the Church looks for in canonizing saints is heroic joy in their lives, for joy is one of the fruits of the Holy Spirit (Gal 5:22). Yet these same saints also are the most emphatic about their being sinners. The greatest saints see themselves as the greatest sinners. And the greatest saints are not the greatest fools.

Or are they? Either they are wrong or they are right. If they are wrong, then sanctity is the way to self-deception, not self-knowledge; and if that is so, then the human heart is so divided against itself that its two deepest demands—for goodness and for truth, for sanctity and for knowledge—contradict each other. On the other hand, if they are right, then we who are less saintly must have less knowledge of ourselves and of our sins.

Pascal said that there are only two kinds of people: saints, who know they are sinners, and sinners, who think they are saints. Socrates said something similar: that the wise are those who know they are fools and the fools are those who think they are wise.

2. Our society's denial of sin

We frequently hear of the value of positive self-esteem and confessing our worth today but hardly ever of the value of confessing our *sins*. In fact, there has been a radical decline in the sense of sin and even in the understanding of the meaning of the very concept of sin. There has also been a radical decline in the use of the Sacrament of Penance among Catholics. Obviously these two phenomena are related as cause and effect. Those who think they are well do not go to the doctor (see Mt 9:12–13).

There are two extremes here: we can be overscrupulous or unscrupulous. If previous eras were often oversensitive to sin, this era is insensitive to it as

---

[1] Council of Trent (1551): DS 1680 (ND 1626); cf. St. Jerome, *In Eccl.* 10, 11: PL 23, 1096.

few times or cultures have ever been. One extreme does not justify the opposite.

We are wholly good in our *being*, our God-created essence. But we are
not wholly good in our lives and choices and actions. We are made in God's
image, but we have marred that image. We are ontologically good—"good
stuff"—but not morally good. In fact, we are far better than we think ontologically and worse than we think morally. If we take God's Word as our index
of truth rather than our fallen human nature and feelings, we find a double
surprise: we are so good that God thought us worth dying for and so bad
that God had to die to save us.

We usually think we are morally pretty good because we measure ourselves, not against the standards of our Lord, but against the standards of our
society—a society that is fallen not only from Eden and innocence but also
from religious faith and the admission of guilt. Modern Western society is
not even pagan, that is, pre-Christian; it is secular, or post-Christian. The
difference between the two is like the difference between a virgin and a
divorcee.

Many people today are suspicious of talk about sin because of negative
stereotypes from the secular media. But even if these were wholly true,
although the sense of sin and guilt may have been badly overemphasized and
misused in the past, the error of the present is more dangerous: it is living
in denial. Rejecting one extreme does not justify embracing the other.

One powerful antidote to denial is the realization that we must die. (Dr.
Johnson says; "I know no thought that more wonderfully clarifies a man's
mind than the thought that he will hang tomorrow morning.") "In this
sacrament" [Penance], "the sinner, placing himself before the merciful judgment of God, *anticipates* in a certain way *the judgment* to which he will be
subjected at the end of his earthly life" (CCC 1470).

Satan tempts us to deny responsibility for our sins. Our only defense is to
take responsibility for them. The only weapon that can defeat the Prince of
Darkness is light. That is the purpose of the Sacrament of Penance. The priest
in the confessional is a more formidable foe to the devil than an exorcist.

3. The deeper meaning of sin

Sin means disobedience to God's law. But it has a deeper meaning. For God's
law (the Commandments) expresses and defines his *covenant* with man—the
marriage-like relationship of personal intimacy that is his goal for us and the
ultimate meaning of our lives. When we sin against God's law, we sin against
God's love and against our own final end and happiness. We also harm all
others who are organically united with us in Christ's Body, by weakening
that Body. Thus "[t]he sinner wounds God's honor and love, his own human

dignity as a man called to be a son of God, and the spiritual well-being of the Church" (CCC 1487).

4. The communal dimension of sin

"Sin is before all else an offense against God, a rupture of communion with him. At the same time it damages communion with the Church. For this reason conversion" [repentance from sin] "entails both God's forgiveness and reconciliation with the Church, which are expressed and accomplished liturgically by the sacrament of Penance" [cf. *LG* 11] (CCC 1440).

Even when our sins do not directly and visibly harm our neighbor, they do so indirectly and invisibly. All sins harm all men. For "no man is an island": we are connected with each other not only visibly, for instance, by physical gravity, but also invisibly, by a kind of spiritual gravity. For the Church is not just an organization but a living organism. We are "members" of the Body of Christ, not as individual workers are "members" of a trade union, but as our individual organs are "members" of our bodies. In a body, "if one member suffers, all suffer" (1 Cor 12:26; read the whole chapter!). When one part of a body is wounded, the whole body suffers. We cannot sin without harming all, including those we love the most.

5. The horror of sin

"Horror" is not too strong a word. All the saints teach that "no evil is graver than sin" (CCC 1488). That is why saints choose torture and death rather than even small compromises with sin. For saints see things as they really are, and what saints see above all is that which is above all: the love of God. "It is in discovering the greatness of God's love that our heart is shaken by the horror and weight of sin and begins to fear offending God by sin and being separated from him. The human heart is converted by looking upon him whom our sins have pierced" [cf. Jn 19:37; Zech 12:10] (CCC 1432).

6. How to regain the lost sense of sin

The answer to this question is very simple and concrete: Contemplate a crucifix. To know Christ on the Cross is to know two things: the depth of God's love and the depth of our sin. When, after seeing Christ perform a miracle, Peter realized who Christ was, his natural reaction was to confess to him: "I am a sinful man, O Lord" (Lk 5:8).

Only God can convict and convert the human heart; we cannot. David prayed, "Create in me a clean heart, O God" (Ps 51:10), using the unique Hebrew verb *bara'* for "create"—something only God can do. "God must give man a new heart [cf. Ezek 36:26–27]. Conversion is first of all a work of the grace of God who makes our hearts return to him" (CCC 1432). And he does this, not by force or power, but by truth: by revealing his Son (see the previous paragraph).

Who needs conversion? All do, beginning with ourselves.

7. The meaning of conversion and repentance

"Conversion" and "repentance" mean essentially the same thing. "Conversion" does not mean merely changing religious affiliations. It means literally a "turn-around"—turning one's heart and will and life over to God. And "repentance" does not mean merely feeling sorry or remorseful. "Interior repentance is a radical reorientation of our whole life, a return, a conversion to God. . . , a turning away from evil, . . . the desire and resolution to change one's life, with hope in God's mercy and trust in . . . his grace" (CCC 1431).

8. The continuing need for conversion

Jesus' message is summarized in two words: Repent and believe (Mk 1:15). These are the two parts of conversion, the negative and the positive.

Conversion begins in Baptism. "Baptism is the principal place for the first and fundamental conversion. It is . . . by Baptism [cf. Acts 2:28] that one renounces evil and gains salvation, that is, the forgiveness of all sins and the gift of new life" (CCC 1427).

But conversion does not end with Baptism. It is an ongoing process because it is an ongoing need. "Christ's call to conversion continues to resound in the lives of Christians. This *second conversion* is an uninterrupted task for the whole Church who, 'clasping sinners to her bosom, [is] at once holy and always in need of purification' [*LG* 8 § 3]" (CCC 1428). "St. Ambrose says of the two conversions that, in the Church, 'there are water and tears: the water of Baptism and the tears of repentance' [2]" (CCC 1429).

9. The psychological need for confession

"The confession . . . of sins, even from a simply human point of view, frees us and facilitates our reconciliation with others. Through such an admission man looks squarely at the sins he is guilty of, takes responsibility for them, and thereby opens himself again to God and to the communion of the Church" (CCC 1455).

---

[2] St. Ambrose, *Ep.* 41, 12: PL 16, 1116.

Many Protestants are increasingly realizing the need for confession. For not only is it needed objectively—to live in the truth—but also subjectively, on the level of human psychology. Everyone needs to "let it out", to "unload". Even more, everyone needs to hear and know that they are forgiven—ideally, by the authoritative word of the priest of the Church of the Christ against whom they have sinned.

The healing words are not "forget it" but "forgive it". We need our sins forgiven, not just forgotten; admitted, not denied. Pardon and peace come from confession.

10. The names of this sacrament

There are at least five names for this sacrament, each of which corresponds to an essential aspect of it:

a. "It is called the *sacrament of conversion* because it makes sacramentally present Jesus' call to conversion, the first step in returning to the Father [cf. Mk 1:15; Lk 15:18] from whom one has strayed by sin" (CCC 1423).

b. "It is called the *sacrament of confession*, since the disclosure or confession of sins to a priest is an essential element of this sacrament" (CCC 1424).

c. "It is called the *sacrament of Reconciliation*" (CCC 1424) because penitents "'obtain pardon from God's mercy for the offense committed against him, and are, at the same time, reconciled with the Church which they have wounded by their sins' [LG 11 § 2]" (CCC 1422).

"'[T]his reconciliation with God leads, as it were, to other reconciliations, which repair the other breaches caused by sin. The forgiven penitent is reconciled with himself in his inmost being, where he regains his innermost truth. He is reconciled with his brethren whom he has in some way offended and wounded. He is reconciled with the Church. He is reconciled with all creation' [3]" (CCC 1469).

d. "It is called the *sacrament of Penance*" (CCC 1423) because we must not only internally turn from our sins but also externally do something to repair the damage our sins have done.

"Many sins wrong" [or harm] "our neighbor. One must do what is possible in order to repair the harm (e.g., return stolen goods, restore the reputation of someone slandered, pay compensation for injuries). Simple justice requires as much. But sin also injures and weakens the sinner himself.... Absolution takes away sin, but it does not remedy all the disorders sin has caused.[4] Raised up from sin, the sinner must still ... make amends for the

---

[3] John Paul II, *RP* 31, 5.
[4] Cf. Council of Trent (1551): DS 1712.

sin: he must 'make satisfaction for' or 'expiate' his sins. This satisfaction is also called 'penance' " (CCC 1459).

"The interior penance of the Christian can be expressed in many and various ways. Scripture and the Fathers insist above all on three forms, *fasting, prayer,* and *almsgiving* [cf. Tob 12:8; Mt 6:1–18], which express conversion in relation to oneself, to God, and to others" (CCC 1434). All three are forms of self-denial, movements against the selfishness or egotism that is the heart of all sin.

"[P]enances help configure us to Christ, who alone expiated our sins once for all.... 'The satisfaction that we make for our sins...is not...ours as though it were not done through Jesus Christ. We who can do nothing ourselves, as if just by ourselves, can do all things with...him' [5] " (CCC 1460).

e. "It is called the *sacrament of forgiveness,* since by the priest's sacramental absolution God grants the penitent 'pardon and peace' [6] " (CCC 1424).

"For those who receive the sacrament of Penance with contrite heart.. ., reconciliation 'is usually followed by peace and serenity of conscience with strong spiritual consolation' [7] " (CCC 1468). This is the peace Jesus Christ gives, "not as the world gives" (Jn 14:27). It is *shalom*—a concept too rich to be translated by a single word. It is a "peace" that includes wholeness, oneness, harmony, and right relationships with God, self, and others. It is an echo from Eden and a foretaste of heaven.

11. Perfect and imperfect contrition

"Contrition" is another term for "repentance". "Contrition is 'sorrow of the soul and detestation for the sin committed, together with the resolution not to sin again' [8] " (CCC 1451).

"When it arises from a love by which God is loved above all else, contrition is called 'perfect' (contrition of charity). Such contrition remits venial sins; it also obtains forgiveness of mortal sins if it includes the firm resolution to have recourse to sacramental confession as soon as possible" [9] (CCC 1452).

"The contrition called 'imperfect'...is also a gift of God, a prompting of the Holy Spirit. It is born of the consideration of sin's ugliness or the fear of eternal damnation and the other penalties threatening the sinner (contrition of fear).... [I]mperfect contrition cannot obtain the forgiveness of grave

---

[5] Council of Trent (1551): DS 1691; cf. Phil 4:13; 1 Cor 1:31; 2 Cor 10:17; Gal 6:14; Lk 3:8.

[6] OP 46: formula of absolution.

[7] Council of Trent (1551): DS 1674.

[8] Council of Trent (1551): DS 1676.

[9] Cf. Council of Trent (1551): DS 1677.

sins, but it disposes one to obtain forgiveness in the sacrament of Penance" [10] (CCC 1453).

12. The need to confess sins to a priest

The question is often asked by Protestants: Why must we confess to a priest and not just to God? What is questioned here is not so much the Sacrament of Penance as the Sacrament of Holy Orders. And the answer is that throughout Scripture, God's forgiveness is always mediated. In the Old Testament God's forgiveness was mediated by the high priest and the scapegoat in the Hebrew feast of Yom Kippur, the Day of Atonement. In the New Testament it was mediated by Christ on the Cross (the fulfillment of all these Old Testament symbols), and then it was mediated by his commission to his apostles: "If you forgive the sins of any, they are forgiven; if you retain the sins of any, they are retained" (Jn 20:23). "Since Christ entrusted to his apostles the ministry of reconciliation [cf. Jn 20:23; 2 Cor 5:18], bishops who are their successors, and priests, the bishops' collaborators, continue to exercise this ministry. Indeed bishops and priests, by virtue of the sacrament of Holy Orders, have the power to forgive all sins 'in the name of the Father, and of the Son, and of the Holy Spirit'" (CCC 1461).

The fact that Christ made forgiveness available to us so concretely through confession to a priest is a sacramental sign of his concrete presence. He—the one who alone forgives sins—is just as really present as his priest is.

And the privacy and individuality of the one-to-one encounter between priest and penitent is a sacramental sign of Christ's love for each of us as individuals.

We should never fear going to confession, for when we do we are not going to a mere man, but to Christ. The priest is only his instrument. "The confessor is not the master of God's forgiveness, but its servant" (CCC 1466).

13. The authority of the priest to forgive sins

"Only God forgives sins [cf. Mk 2:7]. Since he is the Son of God, Jesus . . . exercises this divine power. . . . Further, by virtue of his divine authority he gives this power to men to exercise in his name [cf. Jn 20:21–23]" (CCC 1441).

"In imparting to his apostles his own power to forgive sins the Lord also gives them the authority to reconcile sinners with the Church. This ecclesial dimension of their task is expressed most notably in Christ's solemn words to Simon Peter: 'I will give you the keys of the kingdom of heaven, and

---

[10] Cf. Council of Trent (1551): DS 1678; 1705.

whatever you bind on earth shall be bound in heaven, and whatever you loose on earth shall be loosed in heaven' [11] " (CCC 1444). "The words *bind and loose* mean: whomever you exclude from your communion, will be excluded from communion with God; whomever you receive anew into your communion, God will welcome back into his. *Reconciliation with the Church is inseparable from reconciliation with God* " (CCC 1445).

14. How this sacrament has changed

"Over the centuries the concrete form in which the Church has exercised this power" [to forgive sins] "received from the Lord has varied considerably. During the first centuries the reconciliation of Christians who had committed particularly grave sins after their Baptism (for example, idolatry, murder, or adultery) was tied to a very rigorous discipline, according to which penitents had to do public penance for their sins, often for years, before receiving reconciliation. To this 'order of penitents' (which concerned only certain grave sins), one was only rarely admitted and in certain regions only once in a lifetime. During the seventh century Irish missionaries, inspired by the Eastern monastic tradition, took to continental Europe the 'private' practice of penance, which does not require public and prolonged completion of penitential works before reconciliation with the Church. From that time on, the sacrament has been performed in secret between penitent and priest" (CCC 1447).

15. How this sacrament has not changed

"Beneath the changes in discipline and celebration that this sacrament has undergone over the centuries, the same *fundamental structure* is to be discerned. It comprises two equally essential elements: on the one hand, the acts of . . . contrition, confession, and satisfaction" [penance]; "on the other, God's action through the intervention of the Church" (CCC 1448).

Today, "[t]he elements of the celebration are ordinarily these:" [1] "a greeting and blessing from the priest," [2] "reading the word of God to illuminate the conscience and elicit contrition, and an exhortation to repentance;" [3] "the confession, which acknowledges sins and makes them known to the priest;" [4] "the imposition and acceptance of a penance;" [5] "the priest's absolution;" [6] "a prayer of thanksgiving and praise and dismissal with the blessing of the priest" (CCC 1480).

The penitent usually begins: "Bless me, Father, for I have sinned", tells the priest how long it has been since his last confession, and then simply and

[11] Mt 16:19; cf. Mt 18:18; 28:16–20.

directly confesses any sins he is aware of having committed during that time, including all grave sins. When the priest asks him to say an "act of contrition", he may use his own words or use a traditional formula such as the following:

"O my God, I am heartily sorry for having offended you. I detest all my sins, because I fear your just punishments, but most of all because my sins offend you, who are all good and worthy of all my love. I firmly resolve, with the aid of your grace, to sin no more and to avoid the near occasions of sin."

16. Who must confess?

a. "According to the Church's command, 'after having attained the age of discretion, each of the faithful is bound by an obligation faithfully to confess serious sins at least once a year' [12] " (CCC 1457).

This is the bare and absolute minimum, not the norm. "Without being strictly necessary," [the regular] "confession of everyday faults (venial sins) is nevertheless strongly recommended by the Church" [13] (CCC 1458). "Priests must encourage the faithful to come to the sacrament of Penance and must make themselves available to celebrate this sacrament each time Christians reasonably ask for it" [14] (CCC 1464). For there is simply nothing that more quickly and effectively strengthens the average Catholic's moral and spiritual life than frequent and regular confession.

b. "Anyone who is aware of having committed a mortal sin must not receive Holy Communion, even if he experiences deep contrition, without having first received sacramental absolution, unless he has a grave reason for receiving Communion and there is no possibility of going to confession" [15] (CCC 1457).

c. "Children must go to the sacrament of Penance before receiving Holy Communion for the first time" [16] (CCC 1457).

17. General absolution

"In case of grave necessity recourse may be had to a *communal celebration of reconciliation with general confession and general absolution*. Grave necessity of this sort can arise when there is imminent danger of death without sufficient time for the priest or priests to hear each penitent's confession. Grave necessity

[12] Cf. CIC, can. 989; Council of Trent (1551): DS 1683; DS 1708.
[13] Cf. Council of Trent: DS 1680; CIC, can. 988 § 2.
[14] Cf. CIC, can. 986; CCEO, can. 735, PO 13.
[15] Cf. Council of Trent (1551): DS 1647; 1661; CIC, can. 916; CCEO, can. 711.
[16] Cf. CIC, can. 914.

can also exist when, given the number of penitents, there are not enough confessors to hear individual confessions properly in a reasonable time, so that the penitents through no fault of their own would be deprived of sacramental grace or Holy Communion for a long time. In this case, for the absolution to be valid the faithful must have the intention of individually confessing their grave sins in the time required" [17] (CCC 1483). General absolution is not designed as something normal, an alternative to private confession, but for emergencies ("grave necessities"), such as battlefield combat situations.

18. The seal of the confessional

"Given the delicacy and greatness of this ministry and the respect due to persons, the Church declares that every priest who hears confessions is bound under very severe penalties to keep absolute secrecy regarding the sins that his penitents have confessed to him. He can make no use of knowledge that confession gives him about penitents' lives.[18] This secret, which admits of no exceptions, is called the 'sacramental seal,' because what the penitent has made known to the priest remains 'sealed' by the sacrament" (CCC 1467).

19. Indulgences

The scandalous *sale* of indulgences for money was the abuse that sparked the Protestant Reformation. But the theology behind the Church's practice of *granting* indulgences is beautiful and profound.

What is an indulgence? It is not a permission to sin but a forgiveness of punishment. " 'An indulgence is a remission before God of the temporal punishment due to sins whose guilt has already been forgiven' [19] " (CCC 1471).

"To understand this doctrine and practice of the Church, it is necessary to understand that sin has a *double consequence*. Grave sin deprives us of communion with God and therefore makes us incapable of eternal life, the privation of which is called the 'eternal punishment' of sin. On the other hand every sin, even venial, . . . must be purified either here on earth, or after death in the state called Purgatory. This purification frees one from what is called the 'temporal punishment' of sin" [because Purgatory, unlike hell, is only temporary]. "These two punishments must not be conceived of as a kind of vengeance inflicted by God from without, but as following from the very

---

[17] Cf. CIC, can. 962 § 1.

[18] Cf. CIC, can. 1388 § 1; CCEO, can. 1456.

[19] Paul VI, apostolic constitution, *Indulgentiarum doctrina*, Norm 1.

nature of sin" [20] (CCC 1472)—as a stomachache naturally follows from overeating or broken bones from a fall.

The doctrine of indulgences is based on the doctrine of the communion of saints: "The Christian who seeks to purify himself of his sin and to become holy with the help of God's grace is not alone. 'The life of each of God's children is joined in Christ and through Christ in a wonderful way to the life of all the other Christian brethren in the supernatural unity of the Mystical Body of Christ' [21] " (CCC 1474).

"In the communion of saints, 'a perennial link of charity exists between the faithful who have already reached their heavenly home, those who are expiating their sins in purgatory and those who are still pilgrims on earth. Between them there is, too, an abundant exchange of all good things.' [22] In this wonderful exchange, the holiness of one profits others, well beyond the harm that the sin of one could cause others" [good is far stronger than evil!]. "Thus recourse to the communion of saints lets the contrite sinner be more promptly and efficaciously purified of the punishments for sin" (CCC 1475).

"We also call these spiritual goods of the communion of saints the *Church's treasury*. . . . '[T]he "treasury of the Church" is the infinite value, which can never be exhausted, which Christ's merits have before God' [23] " (CCC 1476). " 'This treasury includes as well the prayers and good works of the Blessed Virgin Mary. They are truly immense. . . . In the treasury, too, are the prayers and good works of all the saints, all those who have . . . attained their own salvation and at the same time cooperated in saving their brothers in the unity of the Mystical Body' [24] " (CCC 1477).

God—the God who is a trinitarian society of charity—has arranged for even our forgiveness and salvation to be communal and social, not isolated and individual. We "bear one another's burdens, and so fulfil the law of Christ" (Gal 6:2), even to the extent of aiding one another's sanctification, after death as well as before it.

---

[20] Cf. Council of Trent (1551): DS 1712–13; (1563): 1820.
[21] Paul VI, apostolic constitution, *Indulgentiarum doctrina*, 5.
[22] Paul VI, apostolic constitution, *Indulgentiarum doctrina*, 5.
[23] Paul VI, apostolic constitution, *Indulgentiarum doctrina*, 5.
[24] Paul VI, apostolic constitution, *Indulgentiarum doctrina*, 5.

Chapter 6

MATRIMONY

1. Its importance today

The institution of marriage, and the family that results from it, is the single most indispensable foundation for happiness in all societies and in most individual lives. It is the fundamental building block for all other human relationships. Therefore "[t]he well-being of the individual person and of both human [natural] and Christian [supernatural] society is closely bound up with the healthy state of conjugal and family life" (GS 47). If there is a single cause for most of today's malaise, both religious and secular, it is the weakening of marriages and families.

In today's "culture of death", only a "countercultural" marriage can succeed. For the message we hear from most modern culture and modern psychology is profoundly destructive of marriage. It is the "gospel" that the happiness of me the individual comes first, before the good of my spouse, my marriage, my family, or my children. It is "the gospel of respectable

348

selfishness". Nothing is further from the gospel of Christ, in which the way to save your life is to lose it, to give it up.

Christians are called to be countercultural, above all regarding marriage and family today. "From the beginning, the core of the Church was often constituted by those who had become believers 'together with all [their] household' [cf. Acts 18:8]. When they were converted, they desired that 'their whole household' should also be saved [cf. Acts 16:31; 11:14]. These families who became believers were islands of Christian life in an unbelieving world" (CCC 1655).

"In our own time, in a world often alien and even hostile to faith, believing families are of primary importance" (CCC 1656).

2. Marriage and God

Most marriages will not succeed today without God. There will be tension about "who's the boss" unless God is the "boss". The instruments in an orchestra play in harmony only if they obey the same conductor's baton.

"Why do you have to bring God into it?" To ask that about marriage is like asking why you have to bring Shakespeare into *Romeo and Juliet*. In the words of Archbishop Fulton Sheen's classic title, it takes *Three to Get Married*. God is the author and designer of marriage and the Creator of the man's and the woman's life and the life of their children. The spouses are only his "procreators". Sex is a "mystery" because in it we share in God's power of creation. That is why sex is naturally connected to religion.

3. Two radically different views of marriage

There are two fundamentally opposed views of marriage: the religious view (which is not limited to Christianity alone) and the non-religious view. There are at least four fundamental differences between them:

a. The Church bases all her laws and teachings about marriage on the fundamental fact that " 'the married state has been established by the Creator and endowed by him with its own proper laws. . . . God himself is the author of marriage' [GS 48 § 1]. The vocation to marriage is written in the very nature of man and woman as they came from the hand of the Creator. Marriage is not a purely human institution despite the many variations it may have undergone through the centuries in different cultures, social structures, and spiritual attitudes. These differences should not cause us to forget its common and permanent characteristics" (CCC 1603).

The religious view claims that marriage is an objective reality, which man discovers rather than invents. It is a real thing, a big thing, like an elephant. If two people choose to ride on it, they must conform to its terms.

It has an unchangeable essence, or nature, and a "natural law" written into it. Human attitudes about it are to be judged by it, not vice versa.

The non-religious view, which has become popular in the modern secular West, is that marriage is man-made, not God-made, and therefore it is whatever we want it to be. We can change it. It conforms to us, not we to it. Thus secularists can speak of "open marriage" (a euphemism for adultery), polygamous, polyandrous, or even group "marriages", homosexual "marriages", temporary "marriages", or even "marriage" between a man and an animal, if they wish. Marriage to them is a "whatever"—whatever they make it. Marriage to us is a "this"—this reality God has made.

b. A second fundamental difference between the secular and the religious views is that the religious view interprets sex and marriage in terms of man, while the secular view (in our society, at least) interprets man and marriage in terms of sex. Religion interprets sex in terms of marriage, marriage in terms of man, and man in terms of God. Religion personalizes sex; materialism depersonalizes it. Religion sees sex as an image of the divine; materialism sees it as an image of the animal. For materialism, love is a human excuse for sex; for religion, sex is a human echo of divine love.

In the Christian view (contrary to the Victorian), sex is a *good*, but (contrary to the Freudian) it is not a *god*. It is not only good but is remarkably good, almost magically good. Here is why:

Love's aim is unity, but matter by its own nature prevents unity: one stone cannot become one with another stone without losing its identity. Things made of matter cannot be shared without being diminished: the more money I give you, the less I have myself. But things made of spirit can be given without being lost: I lose no love or knowledge when I share them. Now sex enables even the flesh to share in love's unity because sex is closely bound up with the soul in man. God invented sex to enrich love in souls, as he invented the senses to enrich knowledge in minds. Neither is a mere "accident" of evolution. "Explaining" human sex by biology is like "explaining" this book by the physics of ink and paper.

c. A third difference between the secular and religious views concerns *hope*. The secular view leads to despair because according to this view, the greatest joy comes at the beginning and gradually degenerates and dies, with the body. In the religious view, the greatest joy comes at the end, in heaven (and as love increasingly matures on earth). The flesh grows older, but the spirit grows younger. Mere sex always seems to get shallower with age, while the mystery of love gets deeper.

d. Most fundamentally, married love is perfected only when grounded in God because otherwise there are only the two persons, while with God there are three—an image of the Trinity. Only when Love is something "bigger than both of us" can the two humans be united in this Third, as two plants in one soil. It is the Holy Spirit who, hovering over the waters of love's flesh as he did over the matter of the universe at creation, turns "you and I" into "we".

When "you" and "I" are not united in Love itself, there is always the danger of one of them being absorbed into the other. When the true God is not present and active, there is always the danger of treating the other human person (or yourself) as God, as the source of all your joy and hope and happiness. And that is the sure recipe for disaster. Whenever divine burdens are placed on human shoulders, they break.

4. The history of marriage

Marriage has a history, in the plan of God (history is "his story").

a. It begins in the eternal essence of God himself, for God's institution of marriage manifests its Creator. And God is a society of mutual self-giving love among the three Persons of the Trinity.

b. "Sacred Scripture begins with the creation of man and woman in the image and likeness of God [cf. Gen 1:26–27]" (CCC 1602) and therefore in the image of love. God's very first command to them was to marry, to "be fruitful and multiply" (Gen 1:22).

c. Like everything else in life, marriage is now fallen from innocence and infected with sin.

d. "Moral conscience concerning . . . marriage developed under the pedagogy of the old law" (CCC 1610).

e. Christ revealed the deepest meaning of marriage by "marrying" and saving the human race by his Incarnation and sacrificial death.

f. In the New Law, marriage was " 'raised by Christ the Lord to the dignity of a sacrament' [1] " (CCC 1601).

g. Finally, Scripture "concludes with a vision of 'the wedding-feast of the Lamb' [2] " (CCC 1602). Marriage is an image of our ultimate destiny and heavenly joy.

5. God's reason for instituting marriage

God instituted marriage because God is love.

"God who created man out of love also calls him to love—the fundamental and innate vocation of every human being. For man is created in the image and likeness of God who is himself love [cf. Gen 1:27; 1 Jn 4:8, 16]. Since God created him man and woman, their mutual love becomes

---

[1] CIC, can. 1055 § 1; cf. GS 48 § 1.
[2] Rev 19:7, 9.

an image of the absolute and unfailing love with which God loves man" (CCC 1604).

That is why marriage must be both "absolute and unfailing", both a gift of one's whole life and for the whole of one's life. There are many forms of love in human life, and all of them in some way mirror the God who is love, but only conjugal love has this twofold privilege of totality and indissolubility. " 'Conjugal love involves a totality, in which all the elements of the person enter—appeal of the body and instinct, power of feeling and affectivity, aspiration of the spirit and of will. It aims at a deeply personal unity, a unity that, beyond union in one flesh, leads to forming one heart and soul; it demands *indissolubility* and *faithfulness* in definitive mutual giving' [*FC* 13]" (CCC 1643). Spouses say to each other what God says to us in Christ: "I give you my *all*."

6. Complementarity

According to Scripture the "image of God" is "male and female" (Gen 1:27).

"Holy Scripture affirms that man and woman were created for one another: 'It is not good that the man should be alone' [Gen 2:18]" (CCC 1605). Man is *for* woman, and woman is *for* man. They are "complementary": each exists for the other, not for self, thus imaging the nature of God's trinitarian love.

Man and woman are *equal in value, different in nature, and complementary in purpose.* This divinely revealed truth about the nature of man and woman fundamentally contradicts all three popular secular alternatives found in our society: chauvinism, which denies their natural equality; unisexism, which denies their natural differences; and individualism, which denies their natural complementarity.

7. Marriage in a sinful world

This vision of the unchangeable essence of marriage as designed by God could be called "marriage essential". But marriage as fallen into sin and selfishness could be called "marriage existential" (Frank Sheed, *Society and Sanity*).

"Every man experiences evil around him and within himself. This experience makes itself felt in the relationships between man and woman. Their union has always been threatened by discord, a spirit of domination, infidelity, jealousy, and conflicts that can escalate into hatred and separation. This disorder can manifest itself more or less acutely, and can be more or less overcome according to the circumstances of cultures, eras, and individuals, but it does seem to have a universal character" (CCC 1606).

"[T]he disorder we notice so painfully does not stem from the *nature* of man and woman, nor from the nature of their relations, but from *sin*. As a break with God, the first sin had for its first consequence the rupture of the original communion between man and woman. Their relations were distorted by mutual recriminations [cf. Gen 3:12] . . . domination and lust [cf. Gen 2:22; 3:16b]" (CCC 1607).

"Nevertheless, the order of creation persists, though seriously disturbed" (CCC 1608). Marriage, like human nature itself, could not change in its essence, which God created and declared "very good" (Gen 1:31; Heb 13:4).

But "[t]o heal the wounds of sin, man and woman need the help of . . . God. . . . Without his help man and woman cannot achieve the union of their lives for which God created them" (CCC 1608), for "marriage helps to overcome self-absorption, egoism, pursuit of one's own pleasure, and to open oneself to the other, to mutual aid and to self-giving" (CCC 1609). Marriage is a school of saint-making.

If you are married, you probably spontaneously applied that last sentence to yourself (you are learning to be saintly by sacrificing and putting up with your spouse's faults) rather than to your spouse (he or she is learning to be saintly by having to deal with *your* faults and by sacrificing for *you*). Your spontaneous reaction tells you why you need to go to a saint-making school.

8. Marriage in Christ

Marriage is the primary example of a "covenant"—a binding relationship based neither on mere feeling nor on external human law but on a freely chosen commitment. Throughout Scripture, God's relationship with us has always been described as a "nuptial" or marriage-like "covenant". "The nuptial covenant between God and his people Israel had prepared the way for the new and everlasting covenant in which the Son of God, by becoming incarnate and giving his life, has united to himself in a certain way all mankind saved by him" [for 'uniting' is the aim of marriage], "thus preparing for 'the wedding-feast of the Lamb' [Rev 19:7, 9; cf. GS 22]" (CCC 1612). The ultimate aim of God's whole plan of creation and redemption, of the whole Christian religion, and of our whole lives, is a spiritual marriage with God. Human marriage is an image, sign, and sacrament of that.

"The entire Christian life bears the mark of the spousal love of Christ and the Church. Already Baptism, the entry into the People of God, is a nuptial mystery; it is so to speak the nuptial bath [3] which precedes the wedding feast, the Eucharist" (CCC 1617).

In all sacraments, we supply the matter while God supplies the mystery,

---

[3] Cf. Eph 5:26–27.

the supernatural grace. In the Eucharist we supply the bread, the wine, and the words, while God supplies the transubstantiation. In marriage, a man and a woman supply the flesh, and God supplies the immortal soul—both the soul of the new "two become one flesh" organism created by the marriage *and* the soul of each child conceived in it.

9. The effects of the Sacrament of Matrimony

What difference does it make that " 'this covenant between baptized persons has been raised by Christ the Lord to the dignity of a sacrament' [4] " (CCC 1601)?

The Sacrament of Matrimony, like all sacraments, gives to its recipients (the spouses) actual grace—that is, the real presence of Christ, in fact the very life of Christ in our souls. "Christ dwells with them, gives them the strength to take up their crosses and so follow him, to rise again after they have fallen, to forgive one another, to bear one another's burdens, to 'be subject to one another out of reverence for Christ' [Eph 5:21; cf. Gal 6:2], and to love one another with supernatural, tender, and fruitful love" (CCC 1642).

10. The need for sacrifice

The truest test of love is giving—that is, sacrifice. Almost all marriages that fail, fail because they fail this test, because the spouses refuse to make sacrifices. The old marriage rite taught couples this wisdom: "Sacrifice is usually difficult and irksome. Only love can make it easy; only perfect love can make it a joy."

"Justice", "rights", and "freedom" are three words that lovers never use. Lovers do not want to be free; they want to be bound to each other. Lovers do not seek their rights but the rights of the beloved. And justice sets limits, while love knows no limits (1 Cor 13:7). When we love a person as *person*, not object, we do not say, "I will love you until . . ." or "I will love you unless . . .", but simply "I will love you always", with no qualifications whatsoever. Not even "if you reciprocate", for that would be only justice.

The wise words of the old rite taught us to vow to love "for better or for worse, for richer or for poorer, in sickness and in health, till death do us part". This is realism; for there *will* be "worse" as well as "better", sickness as well as health. And there will be death. Life cannot avoid the need for sacrifice, and love does not avoid sacrifice. Love also forgives all things, because it knows God's forgiveness.

Like everything in our religion, it is all there in the crucifix.

[4] CIC, can. 1055 § 1; cf. GS 48 § 1.

11. The indissolubility of marriage

"Indissolubility" means permanence, or "foreverness". The human marriage covenant can no more be dissolved than God's covenant, for God designed it to be the image of that covenant (see section 5 of this chapter and CCC 1643).

Christ clearly taught the permanence and indissolubility of marriage (Mt 5:31–32; 19:3–12; Mk 10:2–9). "In his preaching Jesus unequivocally taught the original meaning of the union of man and woman as the Creator willed it from the beginning: permission given by Moses to divorce one's wife was a concession to the hardness of hearts [cf. Mt 19:8]. The matrimonial union of man and woman is indissoluble: God himself has determined it: 'what therefore God has joined together, let no man put asunder' [Mt 19:6]" (CCC 1614). In quoting Genesis 2:24 ("they become one flesh"), "[t]he Lord himself shows that this signifies an unbreakable union" (CCC 1605), for "one flesh" means "one living body", and a living body is broken only by death.

Divorce is a kind of suicide: an attempt to kill the "one flesh" created by marriage. In fact, since marriage is an image of trinitarian love, human divorce is impossible because it images an impossible "divine divorce": if the Father and the Son could ever divorce, the Spirit would die, for the Spirit is the love between them.

"Thus *the marriage bond* has been established by God himself" [not by the Church] "in such a way that a marriage concluded and consummated between baptized persons can never be dissolved. This bond, which results from the free human act of the spouses and their consummation of the marriage, is a reality" [not just an ideal or an intention], "henceforth irrevocable. . . . The Church does not have the power to contravene this disposition of divine wisdom" [5] (CCC 1640). One should not say "I disagree with the Church about divorce", but "I disagree with Christ about divorce."

Churches that permit divorce claim far more authority than the Catholic Church claims for herself: the authority to contradict her Lord. In the sixteenth century, the Catholic Church lost England (or rather, England lost her) because of her fidelity to Christ her King when England's King Henry VIII demanded the Church's infidelity to Christ to justify his own infidelity to his barren wife.

There are even compelling reasons for the indissolubility of marriage from a purely secular point of view, both from the interest of individuals and from the interest of society. Lovers themselves, throughout history, insist on

[5] Cf. CIC, can. 1141.

taking vows that speak the language of eternity. Shakespeare wrote, "Love is not love / Which alters when it alteration finds. . . . Love's not Time's fool." Euripides said, "He is not a lover who does not love forever." And even John Denver echoes, "If love never lasts forever, what's forever for?" Indissolubility is also necessary for society, for no society can endure without loyalty and promise-keeping; and the marriage vow is the first and foundational promise. When half our married citizens break their promise to the person they love the most, why should society trust them to keep their promises to anyone else?

"Today there are numerous Catholics in many countries who have recourse to civil *divorce* and contract new civil unions. In fidelity to the words of Jesus Christ—'Whoever divorces his wife and marries another, commits adultery against her; and if she divorces her husband and marries another, she commits adultery' [Mk 10:11–12]—the Church maintains that a new union cannot be recognized as valid, if the first marriage was. If the divorced are remarried civilly, they find themselves in a situation that objectively contravenes God's law. Consequently, they cannot receive Eucharistic communion as long as this situation persists" (CCC 1650).

"Toward Christians who live in this situation, and who often keep the faith and desire to bring up their children in a Christian manner, priests and the whole community must manifest an attentive solicitude, so that they do not consider themselves separated from the Church" (CCC 1651). Catholics are not excommunicated for obtaining a civil divorce and remarriage, but they cannot receive the Eucharist because they are living in adultery, according to the clear teaching of Christ (Mk 10:3–10).

"Reconciliation through the sacrament of Penance can be granted only to those who have repented for having violated the sign of the covenant and of fidelity to Christ, and who are committed to living in complete continence" (CCC 1650). On his part, God forgives all sins, but on our part we must confess and repent in order to receive that forgiveness, and we do not repent of a sin if we keep living in it. Like all God's laws, this works for our happiness, not our misery, since it comes from divine love and wisdom. If we do not immediately feel this fact, it remains a fact, and faith still affirms it, for faith does not depend on feeling.

12. Fidelity

"By its very nature conjugal love requires the inviolable fidelity of the spouses. This is the consequence of the gift of themselves which they make to each other. Love seeks to be definitive; it cannot be an arrangement 'until further notice' " (CCC 1646).

The need for fidelity follows from the essence of marriage as "mutual self-donation": that is, spouses give their whole selves to each other, especially their most intimate, sexual, procreative selves (and future children!)—not only a part of that self to one person and a part to someone else.

The two reasons marriage requires fidelity are the same two reasons it requires indissolubility: [a] "The 'intimate union of marriage, as a mutual giving of two persons, and'" [b] "'the good of the children, demand total fidelity from the spouses and require an unbreakable union between them' [GS 48 § 1]" (CCC 1646).

A third reason is that marriage is an image of the union between Christ and his Bride, the Church (us!), and Christ is not an adulterer. He is faithful forever.

13. Why no sex outside marriage?

The Catholic Church, along with most other religions and even many pagan traditions, teaches that marriage is the only right place for sex. This is not as a concession, as if sex were somehow bad ("If you must smoke, please do it in this room"), but as a formula for its triumphant fulfillment. The Church's commandment (that is, *Christ's* commandment) *against* sexual promiscuity is *for* sexual fulfillment. And it is against contraceptive sex for the same reason: because it is *for* "total sex", with nothing held back. The positive vision is the only reason for the negative strictures; the big Yes is the basis for the little No's.

The deepest cause of sexual promiscuity is that our spirits, made in God's image, long for the infinite. Promiscuity is a false infinite, the substitution of a succession of finite loves for infinite Love. St. Thomas Aquinas says, "No man can live without joy. That is why one deprived of spiritual joys must turn to carnal pleasures." The process works as follows. The beginning of the problem is that we do not "know" God (with personal, not just impersonal, knowledge); we are not "married" to God. Thus we tend to expect from another human being what only God can give. And then we are inevitably disappointed. And this is why we seek another. But all others eventually prove disappointing, too. Soon we may conclude that love is a delusion, that it promises what it cannot deliver. It promised ecstasy and turned into a routine.

The mistake here is to confuse the appetizer with the meal. What we felt when we first fell in love was no delusion; the delusion was to think that human love alone had the power to fulfill its own promises. It was God's prophet, not God. It takes "three to get married". It takes *agapē* (charity and fidelity) to fulfill the hopes of *eros* (romantic love). It takes the love that comes from God (*agapē*) to fulfill the love that comes from man (*eros*). See C. S. Lewis, *The Four Loves*.

14. Openness to fertility

The same reason that demands fidelity demands openness to fertility. That reason is the essential nature of marriage itself. " 'By its very nature the institution of marriage and married love is ordered to the procreation and education of the offspring and it is in them that it finds its crowning glory.' [6] . . . '[W]ishing to associate them in a special way in his own creative work, God blessed man and woman with the words: "Be fruitful and multiply" ' [7] " (CCC 1652). The Church affirms that the "unitive" and "procreative" aspects of married love may not be artificially separated, either by artificial contraception or by test-tube babies. Love and life must not be divorced from each other. "What God has joined together, let no man put asunder."

"The fruitfulness of conjugal love extends to the . . . moral, spiritual, and supernatural life that parents hand on to their children by education" [cf. GE 3] (CCC 1653).

All this—indissolubility, fidelity, fertility, education—is based on the same fundamental fact of marriage's essential nature and purpose: "[T]he fundamental task of marriage and family is to be at the service of life" [cf. FC 28] (CCC 1653). Marriage is a "task"—a vocation, a calling, fully as much as the priesthood is. It will not "work" if we do not "work at it". It is like writing a song, not like hearing a song.

15. Marriage and the vow of consecrated virginity

"From the very beginning of the Church there have been men and women who have renounced the great good of marriage to . . . be intent on the things of the Lord [1 Cor 7:32]" (CCC 1618), like priests, nuns, monks, and religious brothers today.

"Both the sacrament of Matrimony and virginity for the Kingdom of God come from the Lord himself" (CCC 1620) and are honorable and holy states of life.

" 'Whoever denigrates marriage also diminishes the glory of virginity' [8] " (CCC 1620) and vice versa. Only if marriage is very good can it be offered up in sacrifice as a worthy offering to God.

16. The wedding ceremony

a. "[T]he celebration of marriage between two Catholic faithful normally takes place during Holy Mass, because of the connection of all the sacra-

---

[6] GS 48 § 1; 50.
[7] GS 50 § 1; cf. Gen 2:18; Mt 19:4; Gen 1:28.
[8] St. John Chrysostom, De virg. 10, 1: PG 48, 540; cf. John Paul II, FC 16.

ments with the Paschal mystery of Christ [cf. *SC* 61]" (CCC 1621). The Eucharist should be at the heart of a Catholic wedding celebration because it is the consummation of the "New Covenant", or marriage between Christ and his Bride, the Church.

b. "According to the Latin tradition, the spouses ... mutually confer upon each other the sacrament of Matrimony by expressing their consent before the Church. In the traditions of the Eastern Churches, the priests (bishops or presbyters) are witnesses to the mutual consent given by the spouses,[9] but for the validity of the sacrament their blessing is also necessary" [10] (CCC 1623).

c. "The priest (or deacon) who assists at the celebration of a marriage receives the consent of the spouses in the name of the Church and gives the blessing of the Church. The presence of the Church's minister ... visibly expresses the fact that marriage is an ecclesial reality" (CCC 1630). "Sacramental marriage is a liturgical act. It is therefore appropriate that it should be celebrated in the public liturgy of the Church" (CCC 1631).

d. "Since marriage is a state of life in the Church, certainty about it is necessary (hence the obligation to have witnesses)" (CCC 1631).

e. "The public character of the consent protects the 'I do' once given and helps the spouses remain faithful to it" (CCC 1631).

17. Who can marry?

"The parties to a marriage covenant are a baptized man and woman, free to contract marriage, who freely express their consent" (CCC 1625).

"So that the 'I do' of the spouses may be a free and responsible act and so that the marriage covenant may have solid and lasting human and Christian foundations, preparation for marriage is of prime importance. ...

"The role of pastors and of the Christian community as the 'family of God' is indispensable for the transmission of the human and Christian values of marriage and family,[11] and much more so in our era when many young people experience broken homes which no longer sufficiently assure this initiation" (CCC 1632).

The Church's regulations for this initiation, or instruction, may vary with time and place. But the Church always requires basic instruction before marriage just as before adult Baptism, Confirmation, or admission to the Eucharist, as a kind of "truth in labeling" service. Everyone has a right (and a duty) to know what anything is before he chooses it. This is certainly no less true of marriage than of buying a house or adopting a child.

---

[9] Cf. CCEO, can. 817.
[10] Cf. CCEO, can. 828.
[11] Cf. CIC, can. 1063.

18. Annulments

"[T]he Church, after an examination of the situation by the competent eccle-siastical tribunal, can declare the nullity of a marriage, i.e., that the marriage never existed" [12] (CCC 1629) because one of its essential preconditions was missing (see CCC 1625–32)—for instance, free consent.

An annulment is not a "Catholic divorce". The Church cannot end any real marriage; she can only find that some apparent marriages were not real ones. The practice of granting annulments may have been misused and abused, especially in America in the last generation, but the principle is valid: if one was not really married, one is free to marry.

19. Separations

Just as annulments are not divorces, neither are separations. "[T]here are some situations in which living together becomes practically impossible for a variety of reasons" [such as violence and abuse]. "In such cases the Church permits the physical *separation* of the couple and their living apart. The spouses do not cease to be husband and wife before God and so are not free to contract a new union. In this difficult situation, the best solution would be, if possi-ble, reconciliation" [13] (CCC 1649).

20. Mixed marriages

In the strict, technical sense of the word a "mixed marriage" is a marriage between a Catholic and a baptized non-Catholic—that is, between two Christians. A marriage "with disparity of cult" is one between a Catholic and a non-baptized person.

a. Mixed marriages, or "[d]ifference of confession between the spouses does not constitute an insurmountable obstacle for marriage, when they . . . learn from each other the way in which each lives in fidelity to Christ" (CCC 1634) "and encourage the flowering of what is common to them in faith and respect for what separates them" (CCC 1636). "But the difficulties of mixed marriages must not be underestimated. They arise from the fact that the separation of Christians has not yet been overcome. The spouses risk experiencing the tragedy of Christian disunity even in the heart of their own home" (CCC 1634).

b. "Disparity of cult can further aggravate these difficulties. Differences about faith and the very notion of marriage . . . can become sources of

[12] Cf. CIC, cann. 1095–1107.
[13] Cf. *FC* 83; CIC, cann. 1151–55.

tension in marriage, especially as regards the education of children. The temptation to religious indifference can then arise" (CCC 1634). "In case of disparity of cult an *express dispensation* from this impediment is required for the validity of the marriage.[14] This permission or dispensation presupposes that both parties know and do not exclude" [reject] "the essential ends and properties of marriage; and furthermore that the Catholic party confirms the obligations, which have been made known to the non-Catholic party, of preserving his or her own faith, and ensuring the baptism and education of the children in the Catholic Church" (CCC 1635). All Catholic parents are obligated by their faith to baptize and educate their children in the Church, even if only one parent is Catholic.

[14] Cf. CIC, can. 1086.

Chapter 7

HOLY ORDERS

1. Its purpose

"Holy Orders is the sacrament through which the mission entrusted by Christ to his apostles continues to be exercised in the Church until the end of time: thus it is the sacrament of apostolic ministry" (CCC 1536).

2. Its degrees

"It includes three degrees: episcopate" [bishops], "presbyterate" [priests], "and diaconate" [deacons] (CCC 1536). " 'The divinely instituted ecclesiastical ministry is exercised in different degrees by those who even from ancient times have been called bishops, priests, and deacons' [LG 28]" (CCC 1554). These orders "are all three conferred by a sacramental act called 'ordination,' that is, by the sacrament of Holy Orders" (CCC 1554).

3. Its effect

"[I]t confers a gift of the Holy Spirit that permits the exercise of a 'sacred power' ... [cf. LG 10] which can come only from Christ himself" (CCC 1538). After ordination, a priest has the power to turn bread and wine into the Body and Blood of Christ. Such a supernatural power can come only from a supernatural source.

"As in the case of Baptism and Confirmation . . . [t]he sacrament of Holy Orders . . . confers an *indelible spiritual character* and cannot be repeated"[1] (CCC 1582).

"It is true that someone validly ordained can, for grave reasons, be discharged from the obligations and functions linked to ordination, or can be forbidden to exercise them; but he cannot become a layman again in the strict sense,[2] because the character imprinted by ordination is for ever" (CCC 1583).

4. Its material sign

"The *laying on of hands* by the bishop, with the consecratory prayer, constitutes the visible sign of this ordination" (CCC 1538). "The *essential rite* of the sacrament of Holy Orders for all three degrees consists in the bishop's imposition of hands on the head" (CCC 1573).

5. Bishops

Bishops are the successors to the apostles, in an " 'unbroken succession going back to the beginning' [*LG* 20]" (CCC 1555); for the apostles " 'passed on to their auxiliaries the gift of the Spirit which is transmitted down to our day through episcopal consecration' [*LG* 21; cf. Acts 1:8; 2:4; Jn 20:22–23; 1 Tim 4:14; and 2 Tim 1:6–7]" (CCC 1556).

" 'Episcopal consecration confers . . . also the offices of teaching and ruling' [*LG* 21]" (CCC 1558).

"Apostolic succession" is a historical fact. Scripture shows that Christ chose apostles and commissioned them to continue his work with his authority and that they in turn ordained successors. Apostolic succession is the link that connects the Church today to the Christ who walked the earth two thousand years ago. Many converts from Protestantism, both great (such as Cardinal Newman) and small (such as the present writer), found their way into the Church through confronting this simple historical fact.

Christ did not tell the apostles how to choose successors, and the "politics" of choosing bishops has varied through Church history. "In our day, the lawful ordination of a bishop requires a special intervention of the Bishop of Rome" [the pope], "because he is the supreme visible bond of the communion of the particular Churches in the one Church" (CCC 1559).

---

[1] Cf. Council of Trent (1563): DS 1767; *LG* 21; 28; 29; *PO* 2.
[2] Cf. CCC cann. 290–93; 1336 § 1 3°, 5°; 1338 § 2; Council of Trent (1563): DS 1774.

6. Priests

a. *Their relation to bishops.* Priests are " '*co-workers of the episcopal order* for the proper fulfillment of the apostolic mission' [*PO* 2 § 2]" (CCC 1562). "Priests can exercise their ministry only in dependence on the bishop and in communion with him" [and, indeed, make a] "promise of obedience . . . to the bishop at the moment of ordination" (CCC 1567). Priests, in turn, as "presbyters", share in the priestly office of the bishop. (This is why all priests who are present also lay hands on the man being ordained a priest.)

b. *Their relation to the Eucharist.* The priesthood exists for the Eucharist. It is in the Eucharist that " 'they exercise in a supreme degree their sacred office; there, acting in the person of Christ . . . and in the sacrifice of the Mass they make present again . . . the unique sacrifice of . . . Christ offering himself. . . .'³ From this unique sacrifice their whole priestly ministry draws its strength [cf. *PO* 2]" (CCC 1566). When the priest pronounces Christ's words "This is my Body" and "This is my Blood", it is Christ who speaks and acts. Only Christ has such miraculous power.

That is why the saintly Curé of Ars said, " 'The priest continues the work of redemption on earth. . . . If we really understood the priest on earth, we would die not of fright but of love'⁴ " (CCC 1589). Saints have seen angels bowing before priests—not because the priests were especially holy as human beings but because the power Christ gave them in the Eucharist infinitely exceeds the greatest powers of the greatest angel.

c. *Their relation to the laity.* The title "Father" should show that love of which the Curé of Ars speaks. It is a reminder that the relationship between priest and people is *familial*, since it expresses the relationship between God and his people, which is also familial and "fatherly". "Father" was the word Christ used the most for God, and we cannot be better taught than by him.

7. Deacons

Deacons' ordination is " 'not unto the priesthood, but unto the ministry'⁵ " (CCC 1569). Deacons assist the bishops in the service of the poor and in some liturgical functions. They are clergy, and as such they can preside at weddings and funerals. They also "assist the bishop and priests in the celebration of the divine mysteries, above all the Eucharist, in the distribution of Holy Communion, . . . in the proclamation of the Gospel and preaching,

---

³ *LG* 28; cf. 1 Cor 11: 26.
⁴ St. John Vianney, quoted in B. Nodet, *Jean-Marie Vianney, Curé d'Ars*, 100.
⁵ *LG* 29; cf. *CD* 15.

... and in dedicating themselves to the various ministries of charity [cf. *LG* 29; *SC* 35 § 4; *AG* 16]" (CCC 1570).

"Since the Second Vatican Council the Latin Church has restored the diaconate 'as a proper and permanent rank of the hierarchy' [*LG* 29 § 2], while the Churches of the East had always maintained it. This *permanent diaconate* . . . can be conferred on married men" (CCC 1571).

8. Christ as fulfillment of the Old Covenant priesthood

A priest is a mediator between God and man. "Everything that the priesthood of the Old Covenant prefigured finds its fulfillment in Christ Jesus, the 'one mediator between God and men' [1 Tim 2:5]" (CCC 1544).

Israel was God's "chosen people"—chosen not for their own sake but for service to the whole world. As Israel was God's collective prophet to the whole world, Israel was also the collective priest for the whole world. "The chosen people was constituted by God as 'a kingdom of priests and a holy nation' [6] " (CCC 1539). And "within the people of Israel, God chose one of the twelve tribes, that of Levi, and set it apart for liturgical service. . . .[7] The priests are 'appointed to act on behalf of men in relation to God, to offer gifts and sacrifices for sins' [8] " (CCC 1539).

Even earlier there was also the priesthood of Melchizedek (Gen 14:18). "The Christian tradition considers Melchizedek, 'priest of God Most High,' as a prefiguration of the priesthood of Christ, the unique 'high priest after the order of Melchizedek';[9] . . . 'by a single offering he has perfected for all time those who are sanctified' [Heb 10:14], that is, by the unique sacrifice of the cross" (CCC 1544).

Christ fulfilled the Old Covenant priesthood on the Cross and extended that work through all time by the ordained priesthood of his Catholic Church, which God designed, like Israel, not for herself but for the whole world ("catholic" means "universal"). The Catholic priesthood today is the extension of Christ. It is not a third step, so to speak, after the Old Covenant priests and then Christ. Priests are Christ's own hands and lips. " 'Christ is the source of all priesthood: the priest of the old law was a figure of Christ, and the priest of the new law acts in the person of Christ' [10] " (CCC 1548).

What Christ did on the Cross was the most important thing he came to earth to do: to save us from sin and reconcile us to the Father. This was his "priestly" work; and this incomparably important work—the work of

---

[6] Ex 19:6; cf. Isa 61:6.
[7] Cf. Num 1:48–53; Josh 13:33.
[8] Heb 5:1; cf. Ex 29:1–30; Lev 8.
[9] Heb 5:10; cf. 6:20; Gen 14:18.
[10] St. Thomas Aquinas, *STh* III, 22, 4c.

salvation—he now performs through the ordained priesthood of his Church, for her priests are the ones he appointed as successors to the apostles to communicate his salvation through his sacraments. Thus the fundamental purpose of the Sacrament of Holy Orders is the salvation of the world.

"The redemptive sacrifice of Christ is unique, accomplished once for all" (see Heb 10:10); "yet it is made present in the Eucharistic sacrifice of the Church. The same is true of the one priesthood of Christ; it is made present through the ministerial priesthood without diminishing the uniqueness of Christ's priesthood: 'Only Christ is the true priest, the others being only his ministers' [11] " (CCC 1545).

9. The priesthood of all believers

All Christians are priests. "The ministerial or hierarchical priesthood of bishops and priests, and the common priesthood of all the faithful participate, 'each in its own proper way, in the one priesthood of Christ.' . . ." [They are] " 'ordered one to another' . . . [LG 10 § 2]. [T]he ministerial priesthood is at the service of the common priesthood" (CCC 1547).

Christ instituted the sacramental priesthood to serve the larger priesthood of all Christians, and he instituted the priesthood of all Christians to serve and save the world. If ordained priests fulfill their mission well, the laity in turn will be effective priests of Christ to the world. The priesthood is a missionary task.

10. The relationship between Christ and his priests

"In the ecclesial service of the ordained minister, it is Christ himself who is present to his Church as Head of his Body. . . . This is what the Church means by saying that the priest, by virtue of the sacrament of Holy Orders, acts *in persona Christi Capitis*" [12] [in the person of Christ the Head] " 'and possesses the authority to act in the power and place of the person of Christ himself' [13] " (CCC 1548) when he acts not as a private individual but as a minister of Christ's Church.

"This presence of Christ in the minister is not to be understood as if the latter were preserved from all human weaknesses, the spirit of domination, error, even sin. The power of the Holy Spirit does not guarantee all acts of ministers in the same way. . . ." [Yet] "this guarantee extends to the sacra-

[11] St. Thomas Aquinas, *Hebr.* 8, 4.
[12] Cf. *LG* 10; 28; *SC* 33; *CD* 11; *PO* 2; 6.
[13] Pius XII, encyclical, *Mediator Dei*: AAS, 39 (1947) 548.

ments, so that even the minister's sin cannot impede the fruit of grace"
(CCC 1550).

11. Who can ordain?

a. "Christ himself chose the apostles. . . . Thus, it is Christ whose gift it is
that some be apostles, others pastors. He continues to act through the bishops [cf. *LG* 21; Eph 4:11]" (CCC 1575). It is the bishops whom his apostles ordained as their successors.

   b. "Validly ordained bishops, i.e., those who are in the line of apostolic succession, validly confer the three degrees of the sacrament of Holy Orders" [14]
(CCC 1576).

12. Who can be ordained?

For bishops or priests, as distinct from deacons, " '[o]nly a baptized man (*vir*)
validly receives sacred ordination [CIC, can. 1024].' The Lord Jesus chose
men (*viri*) to form the college of the twelve apostles, and the apostles did
the same when they chose collaborators to succeed them in their ministry.[15].
. . The Church recognizes herself to be bound by this choice made by the
Lord himself. For this reason the ordination of women is not possible" [16]
(CCC 1577). It is not arrogance but humility that makes the Church insist
that she has no authority to correct her Lord.

   One compelling reason against the ordination of women is that a religion
with priestesses would be a different *religion* and would implicitly signify a
different *God*. To see this point, we must begin with data, with facts. One
such fact is that the true God, the God who revealed himself to the Jews,
the God of Jesus Christ, is never called "she" but always "he" throughout
the Scriptures. As C. S. Lewis put it, "Christians believe God Himself has
taught us how to speak of Him." Jesus himself always called him "Father",
never "Mother". His mother was Mary. It is also a fact that the Jews, alone
of ancient peoples, had no priestesses. For priestesses represent goddesses,
and priests represent gods. God chose to incarnate himself in a man. This is
also a fact; this we know. What God's reason was we do not know with certainty—though we do know what that reason *was not*: it was not because
women are inferior or less holy, for Scripture declares "the image of God"
to be "male *and female*" (Gen 1:27; emphasis added).

---

[14] Cf. DS 794 and cf. DS 802; CIC, can. 1012; CCEO, can 744; 747.
   [15] Cf. Mk 3:14–19; Lk 6:12–16; 1 Tim 3:1–13; 2 Tim 1:6; Titus 1: 5–9; St. Clement of
Rome, *Ad Cor.* 42, 4; 44, 3: PG 1, 292–93; 300.
   [16] Cf. John Paul II, *MD* 26–27; CDF, declaration, *Inter insigniores*: AAS 69 (1977): 98–116.

Three more strong reasons against the demand for priestesses are that this demand is very recent, very local, and very secular.

a. The demand is very recent. Women have never been ordained. Throughout all of Jewish and Christian history, only men have been ordained to represent the God of Scripture.

The reason most of the saints give for this is that "he" symbolizes the divine transcendence. God is other than and more than nature and human souls; and God comes into nature and into human souls from without, from himself, from heaven. He is not within us automatically, by nature. He is not a part of human nature, like thoughts and feelings, and he is not a part of the natural universe, as planets are or as the pagan gods were supposed to be. All human souls are feminine to God; he impregnates them with new life, as he performs miracles in nature; for this God is not "Mother Nature" but is "other" than nature, as a man is other than a woman. There is surely a connection between the two historical facts that throughout the ancient world (1) all Gentile religions, polytheistic or pantheistic, had goddesses and priestesses and that (2) these religions did *not* have the knowledge of the divine transcendence or the doctrine of creation in the proper sense of the word (see part 1, chapter 3, sections 1–2).

b. The demand is also very local. It is limited to Western Europe and North America. It is almost as limited in space as it is in historical time.

c. And the demand is very secular. It is derived from secular feminism, with its language of "demands" and "rights". Anyone who demands ordination for "empowerment" shows a radical misunderstanding of the priesthood. Christ's priesthood, like Christ, is for service, not power (see Jn 13:12–15; Mt 20:20–28). And anyone who demands it as a "right" is also using a radically different set of categories—legal and political ones—from those of Christ. "No one has a *right* to receive the sacrament of Holy Orders. Indeed no one claims this office for himself; he is called to it by God [cf. Heb 5:4]. Anyone who thinks he recognizes the signs of God's call to the ordained ministry must humbly submit his desire to the authority of the Church. . . . Like every grace this sacrament can be *received* only as an unmerited gift" (CCC 1578).

God ordained two sexes, not one, to be equal in value, different in nature, and complementary in function. He created women to be a kind of priest that men cannot be; for motherhood is a kind of priesthood and mediation between God and the world. Every mother brings a new image of God into this world as the Blessed Mother brought God himself into this world.

13. Priestly celibacy

"All the ordained ministers of the Latin Church, with the exception of permanent deacons, are normally chosen from among men of faith who live a celibate life and who intend to remain *celibate* 'for the sake of the kingdom of heaven' [Mt 19:12].'' They are "[c]alled to consecrate themselves with undivided heart to the Lord and to 'the affairs of the Lord' [1 Cor 7:32]" (CCC 1579).

"In the Eastern Churches a different discipline has been in force for many centuries: while bishops are chosen solely from among celibates, married men can be ordained as deacons and priests. . . ." [However,] "priestly celibacy is held in great honor in the Eastern Churches and many priests have freely chosen it for the sake of the Kingdom of God. In the East as in the West a man who has already received the sacrament of Holy Orders can no longer marry" (CCC 1580).

The Church's *disciplines* can and have changed through time, for serious reasons arrived at through long experience and reflection; for Christ put this authority into her hands. Her *doctrines*, however, are unchanged and unchangeable, for she did not originate them. Priestly celibacy, like rules of fasting and how bishops and popes are chosen, are matters of Church discipline. The sacrament of Holy Orders itself is a matter of doctrine.

14. Are priests holier than laity?

There are two answers: (a) No, not necessarily. And (b) Yes, they should be.

a. "Since it is ultimately Christ who acts and effects salvation through the ordained minister, the unworthiness of the latter does not prevent Christ from acting.[17]. . . 'The spiritual power of the sacrament is indeed comparable to light: those to be enlightened receive it in its purity, and if it should pass through defiled beings, it is not itself defiled'[18]" (CCC 1584).

b. "St. Gregory of Nazianzus, as a very young priest, exclaimed: 'We must begin by purifying ourselves before purifying others; we must be instructed to be able to instruct, become light to illuminate, draw close to God to bring him close to others, be sanctified to sanctify'[19]" (CCC 1589).

---

[17] Cf. Council of Trent (1547): DS 1612; DS 1154.
[18] St. Augustine, *In Jo. ev.* 5, 15: PL 35, 1422.
[19] St. Gregory of Nazianzus, *Oratio* 2, 71, 74, 73: PG 35, 480–81.

Chapter 8

ANOINTING OF THE SICK

1. The importance of illness and suffering

This sacrament, like all sacraments, addresses one of the basic aspects of life. "Illness and suffering have always been among the gravest problems confronted in human life" (CCC 1500).

Many religions and philosophies sharply separate body and soul, matter and spirit, and cultivate "spirituality" instead of sanctity, detachment from the material world instead of involvement in it. But Christianity, like Christ, takes matter and the body, and therefore physical illness, very seriously. God created the angels as pure spirits, but he designed us to be a unity of body and soul. Part of Christ's ministry was the healing of bodies, and the Church continues this ministry.

Sickness, suffering, and death are also important for a spiritual reason: because they are an effect of sin—not of one's individual, personal sin ("actual sin") but of the "original sin" of the whole human race. Sin is the disease of the soul, and the body is not insulated from the soul. "The wages of sin is death" (Rom 6:23; cf. Gen 2:17).

2. Two choices regarding illness

It may seem that illness removes our choices and makes us passive. But even in illness, and even as we are dying, we are able to choose between two attitudes.

a. "Illness can lead to anguish, self-absorption, sometimes even despair and revolt against God" (CCC 1501). Pain can make it very difficult to avoid self-absorption and to turn from self to God.

b. Difficult, but not impossible: the man of faith "lives his sickness in the presence of God. It is before God that he laments his illness, and it is of God, Master of life and death, that he implores healing [cf. Pss 6:3; 38; Isa 38]" (CCC 1502).

3. Why does God allow sickness and suffering?

God did not invent illness; he is the God of life, not of death. The activity that flows from his nature is not to bring illness but to cure it. But he allows it, for the sake of some greater good. Some of its possible good effects are:

a. "It can ... make a person more mature, helping him to discern in his life what is not essential so that he can turn toward that which is" (CCC 1501).

b. Illness can be a teacher; it makes us wise by showing us what our pride naturally ignores: "In illness, man experiences his powerlessness, his limitations, and his finitude. Every illness can make us glimpse death" (CCC 1500).

c. "Very often illness provokes a search for God and a return to him" (CCC 1501).

d. "[S]uffering can also have a redemptive meaning for the sins of others [cf. Isa 53:11]" (CCC 1502), and we can "offer it up" for them. We may make a more powerful contribution to the good of other souls on our sickbed, and even our deathbed, than at any other time in our lives. Illness does not destroy or even lessen our active participation in the Mystical Body of Christ and the communion of saints, if we use our suffering by uniting it to Christ's. Suffering is a *task*, and God often sends the greatest crosses to those he loves the most, those who can use them most effectively.

Offering up our suffering for others also helps us to focus on a reality outside ourselves and overcome the temptation to self-absorption that is one of the worst effects of illness.

4. Christ's attitude toward sickness

Christ did not ignore or downplay physical illness. In fact, he took it more seriously than any other religious figure in history:

a. According to all four Gospels, much of his ministry on earth consisted in physical healings. We can continue this work of his. The fact that we use natural rather than supernatural powers does not make our work any less an extension of his.

b. "But he did not heal all the sick. His healings were signs of the coming of the Kingdom of God. They announced a more radical healing: the victory over sin and death.... By his passion and death on the cross Christ has given a new meaning to suffering: it can henceforth configure us to him and unite us with his redemptive Passion" (CCC 1505). Christ came, not to make all our sufferings disappear, but to give them all a new meaning, to unite them to his own.

c. The most important thing he did for the sick is something we can do too: he loved them and associated himself with them. "Moved by so much suffering Christ not only allows himself to be touched by the sick, but he makes their miseries his own: 'He took our infirmities and bore our diseases' [Mt 8:17; cf. Isa 53:4]" (CCC 1505). Most often, the best and most Christlike thing we can do for the suffering, the sick, and the dying is simply to be present to them, as God made himself present to us and our sorrows in Christ.

When your car is stuck in the snow, your friend who comes to be with you in the car is doing a more important and intimate work than the tow truck that gets you out. *Sharing* the problem can be more precious than *solving* the problem. Christ does both, but one at a time.

d. Our ministry to the sick is not only *from* Christ, inspired by his Spirit, but also *for* Christ. He makes himself present to us "in the distressing guise of the poor and suffering" (Mother Teresa) and tells us that in the Last Judgment we will hear these words from his mouth: "I was sick and you visited me.... Truly, I say to you, as you did it to one of the least of these my brethren, you did it to me" (Mt 25:36, 40).

5. The Church's work of healing

Christ commanded his disciples to "heal the sick" (Mt 10:8). "The Church has received this charge from the Lord and strives to carry it out" [by both natural and supernatural means] "by taking care of the sick as well as by accompanying them with her prayer of intercession" (CCC 1509).

Christ not only commanded this, he promised that his Church would do it: " 'In my name ... they will lay their hands on the sick, and they will recover' [Mk 16:17–18]" (CCC 1507). The hands of the doctor or surgeon and the hands of the one who prays for divine intervention both fulfill this promise.

6. When the sick are not healed

When we or our loved ones are not healed, we should not attribute this to a lack of faith any more than to personal sin. We simply do not know why God heals some and not others.

"The Holy Spirit gives to some a special charism" [supernatural gift] "of healing [cf. 1 Cor 12:9, 28, 30], so as to make manifest the power of the grace of the risen Lord. But even the most intense prayers do not always obtain the healing of all illnesses. Thus St. Paul must learn from the Lord that 'my grace is sufficient for you, for my power is made perfect in weakness,' and that the sufferings to be endured can mean that 'in my flesh I complete what is lacking in Christ's afflictions for the sake of his Body, that is, the Church' [2 Cor 12:9; Col 1:24]" (CCC 1508).

7. The sacramental rite of healing

"[T]he apostolic Church has its own rite for the sick, attested to by St. James: 'Is any among you sick? Let him call for the elders [presbyters] of the Church and let them pray over him, anointing him with oil in the name of the Lord; and the prayer of faith will save the sick man, and the Lord will raise him up; and if he has committed sins, he will be forgiven' [Jas 5:14–15]. Tradition has recognized in this rite one of the seven sacraments" [1] (CCC 1510).

"From ancient times in the liturgical traditions of both East and West, we have testimonies to the practice of anointings of the sick with blessed oil. Over the centuries the Anointing of the Sick was conferred more and more exclusively on those at the point of death. Because of this it received the name 'Extreme Unction' " (CCC 1512), and it was expected to be given only once in a person's life, as a preparation for one's final crossing to eternity. This is still done, but the sacrament is also given in hope of healing and recovery from a serious illness, and so it can be given as many times as needed.

8. Who receives this sacrament?

"The Anointing of the Sick 'is not a sacrament for those only who are at the point of death. Hence, as soon as anyone of the faithful begins to be in danger of death from sickness or old age, the fitting time for him to receive this sacrament has certainly already arrived' [2] " (CCC 1514).

"If a sick person who received this anointing recovers his health, he can in the case of another grave illness receive this sacrament again. If during the same illness the person's condition becomes more serious, the sacrament may be repeated. It is fitting to receive the Anointing of the Sick just prior to a serious operation" (CCC 1515).

---

[1] Cf. Council of Constantinople II (553): DS 216; Council of Florence (1439): 1324–25; Council of Trent (1551) 1695–96; 1716–17.

[2] SC 73; cf. CIC, cann. 1004 § 1; 1005; 1007; CCEO, can. 738.

9. Its connection with the Eucharist

Since it prepares us for our meeting with God, "the sacrament can be preceded by the sacrament of Penance and followed by the sacrament of the Eucharist. As the sacrament of Christ's Passover the Eucharist should always be the last sacrament of the earthly journey, the 'viaticum' for 'passing over' to eternal life" (CCC 1517) because the Eucharist is Christ himself, and for the Christian, death as well as life is "Christocentric". If "to live is Christ", then "to die is gain" (Phil 1:21).

10. Its effects

a. "The first grace of this sacrament is one of strengthening, peace and courage to overcome the difficulties that go with the condition of serious illness or the frailty of old age. This grace is a gift of the Holy Spirit, who renews trust and faith in God and strengthens against the temptations of the evil one, the temptation to discouragement and anguish in the face of death [cf. Heb 2:15]" (CCC 1520). It "fortifies the end of our earthly life like a solid rampart for the final struggles before entering the Father's house" [3] (CCC 1523).

b. "This assistance from the Lord by the power of his Spirit is meant to lead the sick person to healing of the soul, but also of the body if such is God's will" [4] (CCC 1520).

c. "Furthermore, 'if he has committed sins, he will be forgiven' [5] " (CCC 1520).

d. "By the grace of this sacrament the sick person receives . . . the gift of uniting himself more closely to Christ's Passion. . . . Suffering, a consequence of original sin, acquires a new meaning; it becomes a participation in the saving work of Jesus" (CCC 1521). We are never closer to Christ and Christ's essential work, done on the Cross, than when we are dying.

"The Anointing of the Sick completes our conformity to the death and Resurrection of Christ, just as Baptism began it. It completes the holy anointings that mark the whole Christian life: that of Baptism which sealed the new life in us, and that of Confirmation which strengthened us for the combat of this life" (CCC 1523). "[J]ust as the sacraments of Baptism, Confirmation, and the Eucharist form a unity called 'the sacraments of Christian initiation,' so too it can be said that Penance, the Anointing of the Sick and the Eucharist as viaticum constitute at the end of Christian life 'the sacraments that prepare for our heavenly homeland' " (CCC 1525).

[3] Council of Trent (1551): DS 1694.
[4] Cf. Council of Florence (1439): DS 1325.
[5] Jas 5:15; cf. Council of Trent (1551): DS 1717.

Chapter 9

PRAYER

1. What is prayer?

Prayer is extremely simple: it is just communication with God, conversation with God, communing with God.

Prayer can be either private or public, individual or communal. We need both kinds.

Prayer can be either informal or formal, in our own words or in the words of the saints from the many centuries of the Church's tradition. We need both kinds.

Prayer can be either vocal or silent, with words or without words. We need both kinds.

Prayer can be either active or receptive, speaking to God or listening to God (just being in his presence, waiting in love, open to his will). We need both kinds.

2. The most important thing about prayer

The most important thing about prayer is not *how* we do it but *that* we do it. The single most important answer to the question "How to pray?" is: "Begin!" "Just do it." We learn to do it by doing it, not by merely reading or thinking about doing it.

Prayer is work: a "cooperative" work of ourselves and God. We cannot do it without God, and God will not do it without us. "Prayer is both a gift of grace and a determined response on our part. It always presupposes effort" (CCC 2725).

"[P]rayer is a battle. Against whom? Against ourselves and against the wiles of the tempter who does all he can to turn man away from prayer, away from union with God" (CCC 2725). The battle of prayer is therefore more important—infinitely more important—than any battle in military history.

3. Is prayer necessary?

Yes. One simply cannot be a Christian without prayer, any more than one can be a Christian without faith or good works. What communication is to our marriage relationship with our spouse, prayer is to our relationship with God. If we say we love God but do not pray, we lie. For love is intimacy, and intimacy is communication, and communication with God is prayer.

If God is necessary, prayer is necessary, for prayer is our spiritual lifeline to God. In prayer, we "plug in to God", the source of all good; we "charge our spiritual batteries", we feed our souls. Without prayer our souls starve.

4. Prayer and heaven

Prayer is preparation for heaven, as courtship is preparation for marriage. If Christ had to define eternal life in one word, he would probably say "prayer". For what he actually said was: "This is eternal life, that they know you the only true God" (Jn 17:3). And we know God best by prayer.

We know God better by one moment of prayer—of praise or thanks or contrition—than by a thousand books. When we only talk about him, we only know about him; when we talk *to* him, we get to know *him*.

Job got a foretaste of heaven, seeing God "face to face", because he spoke *to* God, while his three friends only spoke *about* him. Though God gave Job no explanations for his mysterious trials, Job was satisfied because he had something infinitely better than any answer: the Answerer. He said to God: "I had heard of you by the hearing of the ear [secondhand], but now my eye sees you" (Job 42:5). This is what heaven is: seeing God. Prayer is its appetizer.

5. The first prerequisite for prayer: Humility

The *Catechism* speaks of three necessary prerequisites for prayer. These do not include experience or wisdom or saintliness. Prayer is for beginners and fools and sinners. But not for those devoid of humility, of love, or of faith. These are the prerequisites for prayer.

The *Catechism* speaks of humility as "the foundation of prayer" (CCC 2559). The greatest master of prayer in the Old Testament was probably Moses. God said of Moses, " 'With him I speak face to face, clearly, not in riddles,' for 'Moses was very humble, more so than anyone else on the face of the earth' [Num 12:3, 7–8]" (CCC 2576).

The human reason for humility in prayer is simply the truth that " '[m]an is a beggar before God' [1] " (CCC 2559). We should not be reluctant to confess this truth in all its force, for unless our hands are empty, God finds no place to put his gifts. When we are nothing before him, we can become everything through him.

The divine reason for humility in prayer is the truth that all our prayers, as well as their answers, are God's gifts. "*God calls man first.* . . . God's initiative of love always comes first; our own first step is always a response" (CCC 2567). God is the First Cause of every good prayer and even of our very desire to pray. Our feeble desire for him is a tiny tongue of flame kindled by the infinite bonfire of his burning desire for us. We cannot imagine "the depths of God's desire for us. Whether we realize it or not, prayer is the encounter of God's thirst with ours. God thirsts that we may thirst for him" [2] (CCC 2560).

So our *motive* for praying, our right answer to the question "Why should I pray?" is first of all: "Because God wants it." We need it, but that is why God wants it. Even when we are conscious of no desire in us for God, we should pray to satisfy God's desire for us. Baby should eat her spinach because she needs it, but above all because Mommy wants her to. Even if Baby does not feel she needs it, she should do what Mommy says because she loves and trusts her Mommy.

Is this comparison demeaning and insulting? No, it is far too flattering.

---

[1] St. Augustine, *Sermo* 56, 6, 9: PL 38, 381.
[2] Cf. St. Augustine, *De diversis quæstionibus octoginta tribus* 64, 4: PL 40, 56.

The gap between Baby's wisdom and Mommy's, which requires this blind faith and trust, is nothing compared with the gap between our wisdom and God's. That is why prayer demands humility.

6. The second prerequisite for prayer: Love

"Love is the source of prayer" (CCC 2658). The attitude of "trust and obey" described in the preceding section is what love does.

Abraham is the Old Testament model of this obedient, trusting love. "When God calls him, Abraham goes forth 'as the Lord had told him' [Gen 12:4]; Abraham's heart is entirely submissive to the Word and so he obeys. Such attentiveness of the heart, whose decisions are made according to God's will, is essential to prayer, while the words used count only in relation to it. Abraham's prayer is expressed first by deeds" (CCC 2570).

The New Testament models of this love that submits and obeys are Christ and his Mother. "His exclamation, 'Yes, Father!' expresses the depth of his heart, his adherence to the Father's 'good pleasure,' echoing his mother's *Fiat*" ['Yes', 'Let it be to me according to your word'—Lk 1:38] "at the time of his conception" (CCC 2603). In this single word "Yes" to God is the heart of Christian prayer and the secret of sanctity.

The surest test of love is sacrifice. To love someone is to put the beloved's good before our own. To pray is always a sacrifice—of our time, at least, and of all the other things we could be doing during the time we pray. A sure test of your love for your spouse, your child, or your God is how much you give them of your time—that is, your lifetime, your life.

7. Prayer from the heart

"Where does prayer come from? Whether prayer is expressed in words or gestures, it is the whole man who prays. But in naming the source of prayer, Scripture speaks sometimes of the soul or the spirit, but most often of the heart (more than a thousand times)" (CCC 2562). "Heart" means something far deeper than feeling or sentiment. It means the center of my identity. "The heart is the dwelling-place where I am, where I live. . . . The heart is our hidden center, beyond the grasp of our reason and of others; only the Spirit of God can fathom the human heart and know it fully. The heart is the place of decision . . . where we choose life or death" (CCC 2563).

Prayer comes from our heart and God's heart, our spirit and God's Spirit: "Christian prayer . . . is the action of God and of man, springing forth from both the Holy Spirit and ourselves" (CCC 2564).

God moving us to pray does not take away our freedom because God moves us from within ourselves, not from without; by his Spirit within us, at the heart of our own heart. He acts on us to *perfect* our freedom (for he created it!), not to remove it.

8. The third prerequisite for prayer: Faith and hope

"One enters into prayer . . . by the narrow gate of *faith* . . . and . . . *hope*" (CCC 2656–57).

But how could finite, mortal, sinful man dare to hope that the infinite, eternal, perfect God should pay attention to his prayers? It would seem far stranger than some great king caring about the lives of lice or the wishes of fishes. Yet prayer is " 'the union of the entire holy and royal Trinity . . . with the whole human spirit.' [3] Thus, the life of prayer is . . . being in the presence of the thrice-holy God and in communion with him" (CCC 2565). It is truly "amazing grace".

Who let us into that divine throne room? Christ. "This communion of life is always possible because, through Baptism, we have already been united with Christ [cf. Rom 6:5]" (CCC 2565). Christ's death on the Cross tore apart the curtain (Mt 27:51) that had closed off the "Holy of holies". This was the holiest part of the Temple and symbolized God's own dwelling place. No man was allowed to enter it except the High Priest once a year to make atonement for sin with the blood of the sacrificial lamb. Christ's death gave each one of us complete access to the highest throne room of the Trinity. He thus opened up *a radically new reality* for us and for our prayer. We could always pray, of course, and God had always loved and heard us, but sin separated us from God until Christ's death made atonement ("at-one-ment"). This "gospel" or "good news" means something good and something new about prayer, too. "What is new is to 'ask *in his name*' [Jn 14:13]. . . . Jesus is 'the way.' [Jn 14:6]" (CCC 2614).

Not *a* way but *the* way. "There is no other way of Christian prayer than Christ. Whether our prayer is communal or personal, vocal or interior, it has access to the Father only if we pray 'in the name' of Jesus" (CCC 2664), by his authority, by the right his death has given us to enter God's presence.

Prayer is thrice Christocentric, for Christ " 'prays for us as our priest, prays in us as our Head, and is prayed to by us as our God' [4] " (CCC 2616).

9. The five purposes of prayer

But what should we say to God, now that we have full access to him in Christ? The Church's tradition, based on her Jewish roots, the revealed

---

[3] St. Gregory of Nazianzus, *Oratio*, 16, 9: PG 35, 945.
[4] St. Augustine, *En. in Ps.* 85, 1: PL 37, 1081; cf. GILH 7.

examples of masters of prayer in Scripture, and two millennia of the wisdom of the saints, gives us five themes or purposes of prayer:

a. adoration
b. thanksgiving
c. repentance
d. intercession
e. petition

The beginner can remember them by the acronym A TRIP. Prayer is the greatest of all trips we can take: a trip to heaven. Our spirit is already present in heaven before God when we pray. There is no distance, no separation.

10. Adoration and praise

"*Adoration* is the first attitude of man acknowledging that he is a creature before his Creator" (CCC 2628). To adore is to acknowledge what truly is, to live in reality. We do not know God truly until we adore him. For if we know the true God, we *will* adore him and humble ourselves. Throughout Scripture, whenever man meets God—the real God—he describes it in words like these: "I fell at his feet as though dead" (Rev 1:17). He does not "chat" with God; he adores. For, as Rabbi Abraham Heschel says, "God is not an uncle; God is an earthquake."

This does not contradict what was said before about intimacy and access through Christ. We *are* intimate with God, but we are intimate with *God*. It is precisely God's greatness and holiness that make our intimacy with him so staggering. Christ's Incarnation and death did not take away God's holiness; it took away our sin. It did not make God less adorable, but us more adoring.

Adoration is a permanent psychological need. It lets us transcend ourselves, and this self-forgetfulness produces the purest joy. It enables us to turn away from ourselves and our problems, to turn all our attention to the God who is perfect beauty, letting his light shine into our darkness. For in adoration we stand with our face turned toward God, toward the light, and our backs turned toward ourselves and our darkness. The alternative is standing with our backs toward the light and our faces toward our own darkness, that is, standing in our own shadow. Even the small moon can eclipse the great sun because it is so close to the earth. Even a little problem can distract us from God because it is so close, so subjective, so much ours.

Although adoration is a psychological need, our motive for it must not be that we need it but that God deserves it. We worship not to play psychological games with ourselves but to make an honest response to reality. Only when we do this do we find joy; only when we forget ourselves do we find ourselves.

We must begin with God rather than self because "that's the way it is", that is the way reality is ordered. God is first, and to treat him as second or as a means to our ends is to reverse reality's order and to have a false God, an idol; and all idols break.

11. Thanksgiving

"The evangelists have preserved . . . explicit prayers offered by Christ during his public ministry" [Mt 11:25–27 and Lk 10:21–23]. "Each begins with thanksgiving" (CCC 2603). The same is true of the prayer given in Jn 11:41–42.

It is always healing to our spirits to "count our blessings" and thank God for everything that is good. It is also realistic, or honest to reality. For whatever means he uses—nature, family, friends, our own talents—it is God who is the First Cause of all life and goodness (and *not* of death and sin). In the poorest life there are always immeasurable riches to thank God for. Everyone's "blessing list" should include at least:

a. Life itself and time and family and friends and our own mental and spiritual powers and the many little pleasures that are always available in this world;

b. our very existence; for the birth of each one of us was designed and willed from eternity by the Creator (our parents were only our "pro-creators");

c. salvation from sin and the hope of heaven; that is, infinite and unimaginable joy in intimate union with God forever;

d. God's patient, daily grace in making us holy and good and able to enjoy him more in eternity. Even when we have few earthly gifts, we have God (sometimes, only then!). "The Giver is more precious than the gift" (CCC 2604).

Our gratitude, too, should be Christocentric. If we do not feel grateful, we should turn again to the crucifix. *That* is what God did for us. We should practice giving thanks especially when we do not feel thankful, for that is when we need to most. "Give thanks in all circumstances; for this is the will of God in Christ Jesus for you" (1 Thess 5:18).

12. Repentance

"Asking forgiveness is the prerequisite for both the Eucharistic liturgy and personal prayer" (CCC 2631). We can come into God's presence only on our knees.

We should examine our conscience and confess our sins privately each day, as well as sacramentally at least each month if possible, for the same reason we adore and give thanks: a just and proper admission of reality, of truth. In the presence of other sinful men, we may seem to be "O.K."; but in the presence of the all-holy God, honesty compels repentance, a continual "conversion" or "turning" of heart and life from our habitual self-centeredness.

We should not linger here, in contemplating our sin, or let our spirit sink into despondency or despair, but we should turn again and again to Christ and his Blood as the more-than-sufficient divine answer to our sins. "Where sin increased, grace abounded all the more" (Rom 5:20).

13. Intercession

"Since Abraham, intercession—asking on behalf of another—has been characteristic of a heart attuned to God's mercy. In the age of the Church, Christian intercession participates in Christ's, as an expression of the communion of saints" (CCC 2635).

It is good to keep a "prayer list" of people to intercede for daily. In addition to praying for others, we should ask others to pray for us. All men on earth need each other's help, spiritually as well as materially, especially those in authority in the Church, state, and families.

The saints in heaven no longer need our intercession, but we need theirs, and God loves to answer our prayers by glorifying his intermediaries. "We can and should ask them to intercede for us and for the whole world" (CCC 2683). Their bodies are gone from the earth *but not their love*. They are the great "cloud of witnesses" (Heb 12:1) who surround us like spectators in a stadium. The Church Triumphant in heaven, the Church Suffering in purgatory, and the Church Militant on earth are one Body in three places, united in prayer through the communion of saints.

14. Petition

Petition (asking) should not be the whole of our prayer; there are four other essential purposes. Nor should it habitually be first in time; for if it is prefaced and surrounded by adoration, thanksgiving, repentance, and intercession, it finds a place and perspective more in tune with reality.

Nevertheless, we should not try to be "high-minded" and scorn this obvious and popular purpose of prayer; for we do need many things, and God does want us to ask for them. In fact, he often withholds good things from us until we pray (petition) for them, because he sees that what we need first and most is to pray. We need to petition for the same reason we need to adore, to thank, to repent, and to intercede: to be honest to reality, to live in the truth of humility instead of the illusion of pride. For to petition is to admit what we are: beggars. "[B]y prayer of petition we express awareness of our relationship with God. We are creatures who are not our own beginning, not the masters of adversity, not our own last end. We are sinners who as Christians know that we have turned away from our Father" (CCC 2629). Petition is not the highest kind of prayer, but precisely because it is not, it is humble and honest and thus pleasing to God.

In all five kinds of prayer, including petition, we should ask the Holy Spirit to help us to pray, for Scripture says that he " 'helps us in our weakness; for we do not know how to pray as we ought, but the Spirit himself intercedes for us with sighs too deep for words' [Rom 8:26]" (CCC 2630).

"[E]very need can become the object of petition" (CCC 2633), for "my God will supply every need of yours according to his riches in glory in Christ Jesus" (Phil 4:19). St. Francis of Assisi asks: "Which do you think is the more ready: God to give or we to ask?"

"To pray" means in ordinary language primarily "to petition", to ask. Thus, when Catholics "pray to" saints, they do not adore or worship them, as Protestants often charge, but merely petition them to intercede with God for us as we would petition any living friend on earth to do the same.

15. When to pray?

There are four answers: at important times, at all times, at special times, and at this time.

a. We should pray before the important things we do—usual things (such as getting up, sleeping, eating, and receiving the sacraments) as well as unusual things. In the Gospels, "Jesus prays before the decisive moments of his mission" (CCC 2600). For example, the Evangelists record his praying in Luke 3:21, 9:28, and 22:41–44.

b. We should pray at all times. St. Paul writes, "Pray constantly" (1 Thess 5:17—one of the shortest verses in the Bible, only two words). "It is always possible to pray. . . . 'It is possible to offer fervent prayer even while walking in public or strolling alone, or seated in your shop, . . . while buying or selling, . . . or even while cooking' 5 " (CCC 2743). All of one's daily work can be offered as a prayer. Ora et labora, "pray and work", is the maxim of the Benedictines. Work is a prayer, and prayer is a work—in fact, the most important and lasting work we do on this earth.

c. But if we do not also make special times for prayer, we will not remember to pray at all times. Our lives require rhythms, structures, schedules. "Prayer . . . ought to animate us at every moment. But we tend to forget him who is our life and our all. . . . 'We must remember God more often than

---

5 St. John Chrysostom, Ecloga de oratione 2: PG 63, 585.

we draw breath.'[6] But we cannot pray 'at all times' if we do not pray at specific times, consciously willing it" (CCC 2697).

Since our lives have daily, weekly, and yearly rhythms, so does our prayer. "The Tradition of the Church proposes to the faithful certain rhythms of praying intended to nourish continual prayer. Some are daily, such as morning and evening prayer, grace before and after meals, the Liturgy of the Hours. Sundays, centered on the Eucharist, are kept holy primarily by prayer. The cycle of the liturgical year and its great feasts are also basic rhythms of the Christian's life of prayer" (CCC 2698).

All Muslims pray five times a day. Most Christians pray less than that. Perhaps that is why Islam is growing faster than Christianity in many places.

d. The very best answer to "When to pray?" is: Now. "Behold, now is the acceptable time; behold, now is the day of salvation" (2 Cor 6:2). The present is the only time there is, for the past is the time that is no longer, and the future is the time that is not yet.

We should learn to pray "in the events of *each day*" . . . [for] "it is in the present that we encounter him, not yesterday nor tomorrow, but today: 'O that *today* you would hearken to his voice!' [Ps 95:7–8]" (CCC 2659). "Pay later" may be wise, but "pray later" is not.

And we should pray here as well as now, and about the here and now, not only about large, faraway, abstract things. "It is right and good to pray so that the coming of the kingdom of justice and peace may influence the march of history, but it is just as important to bring the help of prayer into humble, everyday situations" (CCC 2660). Not one of the saints fell into what Charles Dickens (in *Bleak House*) called "telescopic philanthropy": ignoring nearby needs to focus on those far away. God is no specialist in big, faraway abstractions. We meet him, as we meet our family, mostly in concrete little things.

16. Using formal prayers

Do we need set prayers at all? Should we not just be spontaneous and use our own words instead of words composed by others?

We should do both. As we need other people's works, we need their words—as in music and in literature, so in prayer. It is as natural to pray others' prayers as to sing others' songs. For when we do, we make them our own. We should not merely recite these prayers; we *pray* them. We do not "say our prayers"; we *pray*.

We need others' prayers for the same reason we needed the help of walkers when we were infants learning to walk. We are only spiritual infants.

---

[6] St. Gregory of Nazianzus, *Orat. theo.*, 27, 1, 4: PG 36, 16.

"Religion is a crutch" indeed, and we need it because we are cripples. Others' beautiful prayers are beautiful crutches to help us walk.

17. Praying the Psalms

The Psalms are our first and foremost treasure-house of prayers. They are the only whole book of prayers in Scripture, the only book of prayers we know are inspired by the Spirit of God and given to us by the providence of God. There are psalms for every person, every mood, every situation, every time, and every need. Jews and Christians have used them continuously since David's time, more than three thousand years ago, and will continue to use them until the end of time.

The Psalms, too, are Christocentric because they are both "[p]rayed by Christ and fulfilled in him" [since they include many Messianic prophecies] (CCC 2586).

18. Praying Scripture

Lectio divina, "divine reading", is a method of private prayer used and recommended by the Church since ancient times. It is simply reading Scripture as prayer, reading Scripture in God's presence, praying verse by verse, sentence by sentence, or word by word, slowly and thoughtfully, letting the words of Scripture suggest themes of prayer. This is both one of the best ways of praying and one of the best ways of reading Scripture, especially the Psalms and the Gospels. "The Church 'forcefully and specially exhorts all the Christian faithful . . . to learn "the surpassing knowledge of Jesus Christ" (Phil 3:8) by frequent reading of the divine Scriptures. . . . Let them remember, however, that prayer should accompany the reading of Sacred Scripture, so that a dialogue takes place between God and man' [7]" (CCC 2653).

19. Christocentric prayer

What is the best way to pray? Christianity gives fewer detailed methods of prayer than most other religions do, because it shows us instead something far better: the final and definitive answer to the question of the way to pray. The way is not a "what" but a "who": the One who said, "I am the way . . . ; no one comes to the Father, but by me" (Jn 14:6). "There is no other way of Christian prayer than Christ. Whether our prayer is communal or personal, vocal or interior, it has access to the Father only if we pray 'in the name' of Jesus" (CCC 2664).

---

[7] *DV* 25; cf. Phil 3:8; St. Ambrose, *De officiis ministrorum* 1, 20, 88: PL 16, 50.

"The name 'Jesus' contains all: God and man and the whole economy of creation and salvation. To pray 'Jesus' is to invoke him and to call him within us" (CCC 2666). The simplest of all Christian prayers is this one word. "The invocation of the holy name of Jesus is the simplest way of praying always" (CCC 2668).

"This simple invocation of faith developed in the tradition of prayer under many forms in East and West. The most usual formulation, transmitted by the spiritual writers of the Sinai, Syria, and Mt. Athos, is the invocation, 'Lord Jesus Christ, Son of God, have mercy on us sinners' " (CCC 2667).

20. Vocal prayer

"Christian Tradition has retained three major expressions of prayer: vocal" [aloud], "meditative" [silent], "and contemplative" [wordless] (CCC 2699).

Vocal prayer is the most obvious and the most popular. It is also the easiest, for words reinforce thought and keep us from distraction.

"Vocal prayer is an essential element of the Christian life" (CCC 2701). Jesus, the Word made flesh, fittingly taught us a vocal prayer, the Our Father, for "[b]y words, mental or vocal, our prayer takes flesh" (CCC 2700). "The need to involve the senses in ... prayer corresponds to a requirement of our human nature. We are body and spirit, and we ... must pray with our whole being" (CCC 2702).

21. Meditation

Meditation is silent prayer, without external words but with "internal words" or themes that serve the same purpose as external words: to help keep the mind on target. It is also called "mental prayer", but it is not only intellectual: "Meditation engages thought, imagination, emotion, and desire" (CCC 2708).

Christian meditation does not consist in emptying the mind of all objects, as in Buddhism. "Christian prayer tries above all to meditate on the mysteries of Christ" (CCC 2708).

"[A]ttentiveness is difficult to sustain. We are usually helped by books, and Christians do not want for them: the Sacred Scriptures, particularly the Gospels, holy icons, liturgical texts of the day or season, writings of the spiritual fathers, works of spirituality, the great book of creation" [the sea, the stars, the sun, mountains, rivers, gardens—no substitute for Church but very powerful aids], "and that of history—the page on which the 'today' of God is written" (CCC 2705).

Each event in our lives can become a thing to pray about, vocally or silently; for each event is a "lesson", a sign deliberately planned by God for our greatest good (Rom 8:28). In Christ we have a perfect spiritual master, who never sleeps, never errs, and who meets us in every thing and event in our lives, as he promised: "Behold, I am with you always" (Mt 28:20).

22. Contemplation

Of the three kinds of prayer (vocal, meditative, contemplative) this is the most interior. It is wordless. However, it is not objectless. "In this inner prayer . . . our attention is fixed on the Lord himself" (CCC 2709).

Contemplative prayer is difficult precisely because it is so simple. "Contemplation is a *gaze* of faith, fixed on Jesus. 'I look at him and he looks at me': this is what a certain peasant of Ars in the time of his holy curé used to say while praying before the tabernacle" (CCC 2715). This simple and childlike "method" is really the highest form of Christian contemplative prayer. "Contemplative prayer is . . . 'silent love' [8] " (CCC 2717).

A form of contemplative prayer that has brought deep and lasting transformation to parishes and individuals that have initiated it is Eucharistic adoration.

In contemplative prayer there is a forgetting of self-awareness and a renunciation of self-will. What replaces self is not nothingness but Jesus. "This focus on Jesus is a renunciation of self" (CCC 2715)—not of the reality of the self (it is not an illusion) or the value of the self (it is the image of God), but of its habitual turning-in-on-itself, a renunciation of self-consciousness and self-will. It is a training for and a foretaste of our future heavenly "ecstasy" (the word means "standing-outside-yourself"), for it is a sharing in the very life of God. Each Person of the Trinity is in eternal ecstasy precisely because he loves and focuses on the Others.

Contemplative prayer is not an "elitist" form of prayer for monks and mystics. Everyone can do it, and everyone should. But most Christians refuse God's invitation to this heavenly kind of prayer because they feel it "wastes time"—nothing seems to *happen*: we simply rest lovingly in his presence. It is foolish to measure this contact with eternity by earthly time standards. Therefore "[o]ne does not undertake contemplative prayer only when one has the time: one makes time for the Lord, with the firm determination not to give up, no matter what trials and dryness one may encounter" (CCC 2710). The secret of succeeding at contemplative prayer is not technique or natural gifts but Churchillian determination. (The shortest commencement

---

[8] St. John of the Cross, *Maxims and Counsels*, 53 in *The Collected Works of St. John of the Cross*, trans. K. Kavanaugh, O.C.D., and O. Rodriguez, O.C.D. (Washington, D.C.: Institute of Carmelite Studies, 1979), 678.

speech in history was Churchill's: "Never, never, never, never, never, never, never, never, never give up!") For Satan fears this prayer so much that he will always find an excuse for us to avoid it.

Paradoxically, although contemplative prayer requires greater effort of will on our part, it cannot be done by our will. God does it. "It is a *gift*, a grace; it can be accepted only in humility and poverty" (CCC 2713). The words of John the Baptist about Christ describe this prayer: "He must increase, but I must decrease" (Jn 3:30).

23. Some mistaken ideas about prayer

The *Catechism* mentions some typical "*erroneous notions of prayer*" (CCC 2726; see also CCC 2727) that harm not only our understanding of prayer but also our practice of it.

a. "Some people view prayer as a simple psychological activity" (CCC 2726). Psychology can help, but prayer is not psychology. Prayer is a miracle. Prayer is supernatural. "[S]ome would have it that only that is true which can be verified by reason and science; yet prayer is a mystery that overflows both our conscious and unconscious lives" (CCC 2727).

b. "Others" [see prayer] "as an effort of concentration to reach a mental void" (CCC 2726). This may be Zen or yoga but not Christian prayer, which is essentially dialogue with God in Christ. One is not alone, not is prayer subjective; the Great Other is present.

c. "Still others reduce prayer to ritual words and postures" (CCC 2726). But prayer is not impersonal or automatic, like magic or technology. Prayer is not a *technique*, like auto repair.

d. "Many Christians unconsciously regard prayer as an occupation that is incompatible with all the other things they have to do: they 'don't have the time'" (CCC 2726)—as if only people of leisure could pray, or as if one could not pray and work at the same time. This error is like a parent thinking he has too many things to do in the house to have time to talk to his children. "[S]ome see prayer as a flight from the world . . . ; but in fact, Christian prayer is neither an escape from reality nor a divorce from life" (CCC 2727). Exactly the opposite: it is a "plug-in" to the Source of reality and the Heart of life.

If every Christian spent even ten minutes each day—not even fifteen, just ten—"doing" nothing but being open to God, in mind and will, letting God love him, then the world would be changed. If *one* person started doing it every day for the rest of his life, his life would be changed.

e. "Others overly prize production and profit; thus prayer, being unproductive, is useless" (CCC 2727). By this standard, beauty and love and joy are also useless.

f. "Still others exalt sensuality and comfort", seeking joy's earthly rivulets and ignoring its divine fountainhead.

24. Practical obstacles to prayer

The *Catechism* also mentions some inner attitudes of heart that may be obstacles to prayer and must be fought and overcome:

a. "[D]isappointment over not being heard according to our own will" (CCC 2728)—but the purpose of prayer, like that of life, is not to bend God's will to ours but ours to God's;

b. "[W]ounded pride, stiffened by the indignity that is ours as sinners" (CCC 2728)—but we *are* sinners; we must kill our pride, or we will kill our souls;

c. "[O]ur resistance to the idea that prayer is a free and unmerited gift" (CCC 2728)—which is also from pride and the desire to control, to "play God" with God.

These are all obstacles of pride, for "[t]he humble are not surprised by their distress" (CCC 2733).

d. "The habitual difficulty in prayer is *distraction*. . . . To set about hunting down distractions would be to fall into their trap, when all that is necessary is to turn back to our heart: for a distraction reveals to us what we are attached to, and this humble awareness before the Lord" [that we love our distractions so much and God so little] "should . . . lead us resolutely to offer him our heart to be purified" (CCC 2729). Distractions are an opportunity for us to practice the essence of prayer: offering God our selves again and again in love. "Therein lies the battle, the choice of which master to serve [cf. Mt 6:21, 24]" (CCC 2729).

St. Columba writes: "Shame on my thoughts, how they stray . . . they run, they distract, they misbehave before the eyes of the great God. . . . One moment they follow ways of loveliness, and the next, ways of riotous shame—no lie! . . . Rule this heart of mine, O swift God . . . that you may be my love and that I may do your will!"

e. "Another difficulty, especially for those who sincerely want to pray, is *dryness* . . . . This is the moment of sheer faith clinging faithfully to Jesus in his agony" (CCC 2731), when he too, on the Cross, felt no "sensible consolations" and cried out, "My God, my God, why have you forsaken me?" (Mt 27:46). If we offer up our dryness to God, it can become a participation in Christ's "dark night of the soul". Dryness is a test: Do we choose Christ without comfort or comfort without Christ?

f. The simplest obstacle is the most obvious, yet it is the last one we usually think of. "The most common yet most hidden temptation is our *lack of faith*" (CCC 2732). This lack of faith manifests itself in simply giving up. For "trust is tested—it proves itself—in tribulation" (CCC 2734).

25. Why don't we get what we pray for?

The question is often asked: Why didn't God answer my prayer? (This concerns prayers of petition.)

a. All prayers are answered, but often the answer is No because what we ask for is not what we really want, only what we think we want. " 'Do not be troubled if you do not immediately receive from God what you ask him; for he desires to do something even greater for you, while you cling to him in prayer' [9] " (CCC 2737).

b. Sometimes the answer is "Wait", because God's timing is wiser than ours. God does not follow our timetable. He is a lover, not a train.

c. Jesus tells us, "Your Father knows what you need before you ask him" (Mt 6:8), but "[H]e awaits our petition because the dignity of his children lies in their freedom" (CCC 2736)—or, as Pascal said, "God instituted prayer to communicate to his creatures the dignity of being causes."

d. He also waits for our prayer before he gives us what we pray for because he sees that what we need most of all is prayer, patience, and conformity of our will to his. In fact, that is the very purpose of prayer: "Transformation of the praying heart is the first response to our petition" (CCC 2739). Humility would answer the question "Why don't we get what we pray for?" with another question: "Are we convinced that 'we do not know how to pray as we ought' [Rom 8:26]?" (CCC 2736).

e. Finally, God waits with his answer in order to make us "pray without ceasing." "This tireless fervor can come only from love" (CCC 2742). It is to elicit our love that God does everything he does. He does not need us to love him, but we do. So he plunges us into the fire of battle in order to plunge us more deeply into the fire of love. The battle is within us, not between us and God, it is a battle of love against its enemies. "Against our dullness and laziness, the battle of prayer is that of humble, trusting, and persevering *love*" (CCC 2742). Love with these three qualities is a gift of God and the most precious gift in life.

[9] Evagrius Ponticus, *De oratione* 34: PG 79, 1173.

Chapter 10

THE LORD'S PRAYER

1. The perfect prayer

" 'The Lord's Prayer is the most perfect of prayers. . . . In it we ask, not only for all the things we can rightly desire, but also in the sequence that they should be desired' [1] " (CCC 2763). " 'Run through all the words of the holy prayers [in Scripture], and I do not think that you will find anything in them that is not contained and included in the Lord's Prayer' [2] " (CCC 2762).

This is the prayer that is Christ's answer to his disciples' plea, "Teach us to pray" (Lk 11:1). That is why it is called "the Lord's Prayer". It is the perfect prayer because it comes from the perfect Pray-er. We learn to pray by going to Jesus' school of prayer. And in that school the single teacher wrote the single textbook, one with just fifty-five words.

Instead of giving us psychological techniques, Christ gives us the actual words of a prayer. "But Jesus does not give us a formula to repeat mechanically [cf. Mt 6:7; 1 Kings 18:26–29]. . . . Jesus not only gives us the words of our filial prayer; at the same time he gives us the Spirit by whom these words become in us 'spirit and life' [Jn 6:63]" (CCC 2766). Christ gives us these words, not like a book, to read, but like a piece of sheet music, to sing.

We must pray this prayer not just with our words but with our minds, and not just with our minds but with our hearts. In fact, we will understand it

---

[1] St. Thomas Aquinas, *STh* II-II, 83, 9.
[2] St. Augustine, *Ep.* 130, 12, 22: PL 33, 503.

with our minds only when we will it with our hearts. We will understand what God reveals only when we will what God wills. (That is what Jesus says in John 7:17 and in Matthew 5:8.)

2. "Our"

When St. Teresa of Avila prayed the Our Father, she found it almost impossible to get beyond the first two words, for they were like a beautiful country that she wanted to dwell in forever. Until we feel that way, we have not understood these two words.

One of life's greatest mysteries is contained in the first little word, "our". It is the mystery of solidarity. Each individual who prays is instructed to call God, not just "*my* Father", but "*our* Father". Each individual is to pray in the name of the whole Church, for each Christian is a cell in the one Body of Christ, a member of God's family, a child of the same Father. " 'Our' . . . does not express possession" [who could *possess* God?], "but an entirely new relationship with God" (CCC 2786).

"The *Church* is this new communion of God and men" (CCC 2790). "In praying 'our' Father, each of the baptized is praying in this communion" (CCC 2790), the communion of saints. We pray with all the saints and angels, surrounded by the great "cloud of witnesses" (Heb 12:1).

"[I]n spite of the divisions among Christians, this prayer to 'our' Father remains our common patrimony" (CCC 2791). "If we are to say it truthfully, our divisions and oppositions have to be overcome [cf. Mt 5:23–24; 6:14–15]" (CCC 2792).

Because of the mystery of solidarity in this Body, all prayers *echo*. My prayers will have effects on my great-grandchildren, on strangers I have never met, on the most abandoned soul in purgatory. My prayers, ascending like mist today, will descend like rain at another time and place, wherever God directs it, where thirsty soil needs it. My prayers can help feed souls far removed from me in space and time, just as truly as my work or my money can help feed bodies. Spiritual transportation systems are as real as physical ones, for the spiritual universe is as real as the physical universe, and just as unified; and its gravity is as strong as physical gravity. It is called love.

3. "Father"

Before Jesus taught it, " '[t]he expression God the Father had never been revealed to anyone. When Moses himself asked God who he was, he heard another name. The Father's name has been revealed to us in the Son' [3] "

---

[3] Tertullian, *De orat.* 3: PL 1, 1155.

(CCC 2779). We cannot improve on this word for God, for "Father" is the name Jesus used consistently, and Jesus the "Word of God" knew the right word for God!

Jesus *called* God our Father because he *made* God our Father. Without him, God is not our Father. He radically changed our relationship with God: he made us children of God and thus made God our Father. (Of course, he did not change God, he changed us.)

And the word is not just "Father" but "Abba"—the intimate word "Daddy". Jesus restored the intimacy we had lost in Eden.

We can appreciate how incredible this intimacy is only if we have first appreciated the opposite truth, God's awesome holiness and inaccessible transcendence. Only after we know God in awe and adoration can we know him truly in intimacy. "The fear of the LORD is the beginning of wisdom" (Prov 9:10), but filial intimacy is its end. Jesus has made it possible for us truly to address the infinite abyss of eternal perfection as our Daddy!

"Father" means "giver of life". Animal fathers give animal life, human fathers give human life, and God gives divine life. At the very heart of our religion is the astonishing "good news" that we are called to share in the divine life, the divine nature, without losing our human nature; to become like Jesus our brother: both human and divine.

The fact that man can conceive this astonishing transformation is evidence that it has been given. No one could be expected to conceive the transition from non-being to being except one who has been born. So no one could call God "Father" and conceive the transition of the "new birth" except one who had been "born anew" (Jn 3:3) into God's family. " 'When would a mortal dare call God "Father," if man's innermost being were not animated by power from on high?' [4] " (CCC 2777). "We can adore the Father because he has caused us to be reborn to his life by *adopting* us as his children in his only Son: by Baptism, he incorporates us into the Body of his Christ; through the anointing of his Spirit who flows from the head to the members, he makes us other 'Christs' " (CCC 2782). "Thus the Lord's Prayer *reveals us to ourselves* at the same time that it reveals the Father to us [cf. GS 22 § 1]" (CCC 2783).

If we really believe this, our lives are transformed. " 'We must remember ... and know that when we call God "our Father" we ought to behave as sons of God' [5] " (CCC 2784). We act out our perceived identities. " 'We must contemplate the beauty of the Father without ceasing and adorn our own souls accordingly' [6] " (CCC 2784). An infinitely more powerful reason for "self-esteem" than any secular psychology can give us!

---

[4] St. Peter Chrysologus, *Sermo* 71, 3: PL 52, 401CD; cf. Gal 4:6.

[5] St. Cyprian, *De Dom. orat.* 11: PL 4, 526B.

[6] St. Gregory of Nyssa, *De orat. Dom.* 2: PG 44, 1148B.

There are many instructive aspects of this analogy between God and a good human father. One of them is that God, like a good human father, is "easy to please but hard to satisfy", pleased with the first faltering steps of his spiritual toddlers yet not satisfied even with the heroics of his saints until they reach perfection, "the measure of the stature of the fulness of Christ" (Eph 4:13; cf. Mt 5:48). Jesus, the perfect mirror of the Father ("like father, like son"), manifests both of these attitudes in greater strength and greater union than any man who ever lived: he is terribly tender and terribly tough, infinitely patient and infinitely demanding. He is what we find it so hard to be: gentle without being weak and strong without being harsh.

It is harder to know and love God as our heavenly Father if we do not first know and love our earthly fathers, God's own chosen image and analogy. If "father" is no longer a word that is loved, understood, and revered in our society, the solution is to make it so, not to change divinely revealed language. We should not bend God's Word to conform to our brokenness, but straighten out our brokenness to conform to God's Word.

To call God "Father" is certainly not "male chauvinism". For if it is, then Jesus Christ was a chauvinist and the One who was able to transcend all other sins in his culture was unable to transcend just one sin, the "sin of sexism".

Another reason why "God the Father" is not male chauvinism is that the image of God's "masculinity" entails the "femininity" of all mankind in relation to him. The Church is his Bride.

4. "Who art in heaven"

What is "heaven"? "This biblical expression does not mean . . . that God is distant, but majestic. Our Father is not 'elsewhere': he transcends everything we can conceive" (CCC 2794).

What difference does God's transcendence make? For one thing, it prevents idolatry, the worship of any finite and graspable creature instead of the infinite and ungraspable Creator. It also elicits humility and awe, worship and adoration.

Heaven is a real place but not a spatial place: it is not anywhere in this universe. God's revelation tells us much more about how to get there than about what it is, for it tells us what we most need to know. There will be time enough to understand it once we get there. One thing we do know about heaven is that it is our home, our destiny, our happiness; and that even now Jesus is preparing a place there especially for us (Jn 14:2–3).

5. The structure of the seven petitions of the Our Father

"The first series of petitions carries us toward him, for his own sake: *thy* name, *thy* kingdom, *thy* will! It is characteristic of love to think first of the one whom we love. In none of the three petitions do we mention ourselves" (CCC 2804).

"The second series of petitions . . . go up from us and concern us . . . : 'give us . . . forgive *us* . . . lead *us* not . . . deliver *us*' " (CCC 2805).

The structure of this prayer is parallel to the structure of the Ten Commandments, because both follow the structure of reality. Both are divided into two parts: God first, man second. And both are concerned above all with love. The first three commandments tell us how to love God, and the last seven how to love our neighbor. The first three petitions of the Lord's Prayer also tell us how to love God: how to adore and worship and praise him. The other four tell us how to love our neighbor, since they tell us to pray for "our" primary needs, not just "my" needs. Intercessory prayer has no separate petition here because the whole second half of the prayer is equally for neighbor and self.

6. "Hallowed be thy name"

"Hallow" is an old word. We have forgotten much of its meaning. It means "make holy", and "holy" means "set-apart", sacred, special, superior, worthy of worship. "The holiness of God is the inaccessible center of his eternal mystery. What is revealed of it in creation and history, Scripture calls 'glory' [cf. Ps 8; Isa 6:3]" (CCC 2809).

"The term 'to hallow' is to be understood here not primarily in its causative sense (only God hallows, makes holy), but above all in an evaluative sense: to recognize as holy" (CCC 2807). It confesses that God *is* holy and asks that all men recognize it and adore him. We do not make him holy; but we do make his "name", his "reputation", his being-known on earth, holy. We do this by being saints. Saints are the unanswerable argument for Christianity. And sinners are the strongest argument against it. We make God's name holy or unholy.

" '[W]e ask that this name of God should be hallowed in us through our actions. For God's name is blessed when we live well, but is blasphemed when we live wickedly' [7] " (CCC 2814).

This petition is training for heaven. There is only a difference of degree between the worship of any ordinary believer and the greatest mystic's highest flight of ecstasy; between the tiny spark of joy kindled in our soul by our act of adoration and the fire that will eternally consume us in heaven when we "enter into the joy of your master" (Mt 25:21). Heaven's music is a "Hallowed Be Thy Name" sung by every creature, from angels down to atoms. Jesus says that if we do not praise God, the very stones

---

[7] St. Peter Chrysologus, *Sermo* 71, 4: PL 52, 402A; cf. Rom 2:24; Ezek 36:20–22.

will take our place (Lk 19:40). The only place where there is no praise is hell.

The desire to hallow God's name by adoration and praise is "an acquired taste", a habit our fallen nature needs training in, especially today. We modern egalitarians find it hard to bow. We have little earthly training for heaven's life. In any era, our "original selfishness" does not want to get out of the way and put God first. We need to work at it.

7. "Thy kingdom come"

"In the New Testament the word *basileia* can be translated by 'kingship' (abstract noun), 'kingdom' (concrete noun) or 'reign' (action noun)" (CCC 2816).

God's "kingship" is his nature: he *is* the King of all creation.

God's kingdom is the Church, his Bride, his people.

God's reign is first of all in our hearts and then in our lives.

"In the Lord's Prayer, 'thy kingdom come' refers primarily to the final coming of the reign of God through Christ's return [cf. Titus 2:13]. But, far from distracting the Church from her mission in this present world, this desire commits her to it all the more strongly" (CCC 2818).

On the other hand, "Christians have to distinguish between the growth of the Reign of God and the progress of the culture and society in which they are involved. This distinction is not a separation. Man's vocation to eternal life does not suppress, but actually reinforces, his duty to put into action in this world the energies and means received from the Creator to serve justice and peace"[8] (CCC 2820).

The major obstacle to "Thy kingdom come" is "My kingdom come." Every person who has ever lived has one absolute choice: "Thy kingdom come" or "My kingdom come", letting God be God or playing God. "My kingdom come" is doomed to death and futility. "Thy kingdom come" is guaranteed immortality and success. This petition is always answered.

8. "Thy will be done on earth as it is in heaven"

The key to the fulfillment of the petition "Thy kingdom come" is the fulfillment of the next one, "Thy will be done." The way for God's kingdom to come is the easiest thing in the world to understand and the hardest thing in the world to accomplish: simply turning over all our will to God. We can begin to do this, even if we do not do it completely. To choose to begin is our "fundamental option", our most absolute choice. As C. S. Lewis

[8] Cf. *GS* 22; 32; 39; 45; *EN* 31.

said, "There are only two kinds of people in the end: those who say to God, 'Thy will be done'; and those to whom God says, in the end, '*Thy* will be done.'"

Sin means that my will is in rebellion against God. By saying (and meaning) "Thy will be done", I declare my will to end this rebellion and make peace with God by submitting my will to his, by willing what he wills.

But what does God will? Two answers are certain:

a. "His commandment is 'that you love one another; even as I have loved you' [Jn 13:34; cf. 1 Jn 3; 4; Lk 10:25–37].... This commandment... expresses his entire will" (CCC 2822).

b. "Our Father 'desires all men to be saved and to come to the knowledge of the truth' [1 Tim 2:3–4]. He 'is forebearing toward you, not wishing that any should perish' [2 Pet 3:9; cf. Mt 18:14]" (CCC 2822). " '[H]e did not say "thy will be done in me or in us," but "on earth," the whole earth, so that error may be banished from it, truth take root in it, all vice be destroyed on it, virtue flourish on it, and earth no longer differ from heaven' [9] " (CCC 2825). When God's will is done perfectly on earth as it is in heaven, earth will become heaven.

Do we truly will "Thy will be done" when we submit to God or when we act in the world? "Thy will be done" is both submissive and active. For his kingdom comes by our submitting to his will and by our working to carry it out. It must be both, for any work that is not submitted to God's will is not his kingdom but ours; and any submission to a God who does not send us out to work for our neighbor is not submission to the God of Jesus Christ but to a figment of our own fancy.

9. "Give us this day our daily bread"

This petition expresses "[t]he trust of children who look to their Father for everything" (CCC 2828). It gives God a "blank check"—"our daily bread" means "whatever you see we really need".

There is a solid basis for such total trust: God has become our Father. Christ shows us how reasonable this total trust is when he argues, "What man of you, if his son asks him for bread, will give him a stone?" (Mt 7:9). Does God love us less than our earthly fathers? Or does he have less power to give us what we need? Or less wisdom to know what that is? Put these three non-negotiable dogmas of God's love, God's power, and God's wisdom together with the fact that Christ has made God our Father, and you get a totally realistic, reasonable, and non-sentimental basis for the total trust that this petition expresses.

---

[9] St. John Chrysostom, *Hom. in Mt.* 19, 5: PG 57, 280.

But this total trust is not passive. "He is not inviting us to idleness [cf. 2 Thess 3:6–13], but wants to relieve us from nagging worry" (CCC 2830). We must trust, but we must also "pray and work" (*ora et labora*: the motto of St. Benedict) for our daily bread; and " 'Pray as if everything depended on God and work as if everything depended on you' [10] " (CCC 2834). When we submit our will to God in trust, that does not make us flabby, but strong; for God is not our rival but our Father, and fathers want their children to grow to maturity. "Grace perfects nature." The more submissive to God's grace we are, the more free and strong our human will becomes. Our will's strength and courage and freedom are the effect of our trust and submission to God, for God is the first cause of all good things, including those.

The petition "Give us this day our daily bread" is to be prayed in the total certainty that it will be answered. For Christ promised to answer every prayer we ask in his name (Jn 14:13), and his own prayer is certainly in his name. So when we do not get what we ask for, we know that that is not our "daily bread", not what we need this day. Either God or we are mistaken about what we need. Which is more likely?

Our needs and our wants are not identical. We need some things we do not want (for example, to pray more, to fast, to relax, to trust, to be tested, to suffer), and we want some things we do not need (luxuries, creature comforts, indulgences). We really need only one thing: "One thing is needful" (Lk 10:42). That is why God offers us only one thing: himself, in Christ (see Phil 4:19).

"[T]he presence of those who hunger because they lack bread opens up another . . . meaning of this petition. . . . This petition . . . cannot be isolated from the parables of the poor man Lazarus and of the Last Judgment [cf. Lk 16:19–31; Mt 25:31–46]" (CCC 2831).

"This petition . . . also applies to another hunger from which men are perishing: 'Man does not live by bread alone, but . . . by every word that proceeds from the mouth of God' [Deut 8:3; Mt 4:4]. . . . There is a famine on earth, 'not a famine of bread, nor a thirst for water, but of hearing the words of the LORD' [Amos 8:11]" (CCC 2835).

The petition tells us only to pray for today's bread, for Christ tells us, "Do not be anxious about tomorrow. . . . Let today's own trouble be sufficient for the day" (Mt 6:34). Pray for today's bread today; pray for tomorrow's tomorrow—that is, when tomorrow becomes today. Christ lived in the present, and we are to do the same. Otherwise, if we are always planning to be happy or good, we never *are*. For "tomorrow is always a day

---

[10] Attributed to St. Ignatius Loyola, cf. Joseph de Guibert, S.J., *The Jesuits: Their Spiritual Doctrine and Practice* (Chicago: Loyola University Press, 1964), 148, n. 55.

away." Christ warns us with striking frequency against worry and fear, for that is a most powerful enemy of faith, of hope, and of love.

The Greek word here for " '[d]aily' (*epiousios*) occurs nowhere else in the New Testament.... Taken literally (*epi-ousios*: 'super-essential'), it refers directly to the Bread of Life, the Body of Christ.... 'The Eucharist is our daily bread ... so that, ... made members of him, we may become what we receive' [11] " (CCC 2837). We are thus to pray for the gift God has already given us. As we pray "give", we must take heed to receive what has been given.

10. "And forgive us our trespasses, as we forgive those who trespass against us"

"This petition is astonishing ... for the two parts are joined by the single word 'as' " (CCC 2838). If we think carefully about it, we realize that Christ is commanding us to pray for our own damnation if we do not forgive all the sins of all who sin against us.

All sins. "There is no limit or measure to this essentially divine forgiveness [cf. Mt 18:21–22; Lk 17:3–4]" (CCC 2845).

Never did Jesus emphasize a point more dramatically. "This petition is so important that it is the only one to which the Lord returns and which he develops explicitly in the Sermon on the Mount" [12] (CCC 2841).

The reason for his insistence is that "this outpouring of mercy" [God's forgiveness] "cannot penetrate our hearts as long as we have not forgiven those who have trespassed against us.... In refusing to forgive our brothers and sisters, our hearts are closed and their hardness makes them impervious to the Father's merciful love" (CCC 2840). Put plainly, Jesus Christ guarantees us that if we do not forgive our neighbors, we cannot go to heaven.

It is not that God arbitrarily decided to make our forgiving others the prerequisite for his forgiving us. Rather, it is intrinsically impossible for us to receive God's forgiveness if we do not forgive others, as it is impossible for someone with a closed fist to receive a gift.

What is it to "forgive"? It is not a feeling or a thought but a *choice*. "It is not in our power not to feel or to forget an offense; but the heart ... turns ... the hurt into intercession" (CCC 2843). To forgive is to will good to those who do not deserve it, as God does to us.

And even before they repent, as God also does to us. Forgiveness "takes" only when its recipient accepts it, that is, confesses the wrong and repents of it. But just as God gives forgiveness even before we accept it, we are to

[11] St. Augustine, *Sermo* 57, 7: PL 38, 389.
[12] Cf. Mt 6:14–15; 5:23–24; Mk 11:25.

do the same to those who wrong us. That is the clear implication of the formula "Forgive us ... *as* we forgive."

But what if we do not think we need forgiveness? We may think that only if we do not know God. That is why the petitions are arranged in the order they are: the way to come to know this necessary truth about ourselves—that we are sinners in need of forgiveness—is to get to know the all-holy God by adoring him, thus understanding ourselves in his light rather than trying to understand him in ours. For by human standards, most of us seem pretty good, and God's demands seem much too high. If we use human standards, we naturally wonder "why bad things happen to good people", but when we come to know God, we come to know ourselves better, and then we wonder instead why good things happen to bad people! For we do not deserve God's forgiveness. It is simply a wonderful and baffling mystery why he forgives so much. It is "just the way he is". And we must treat each other in the light of this mystery.

Besides making our salvation possible, our giving "[f]orgiveness also bears witness that, in our world, love is stronger than sin" (CCC 2844). It triumphs over evil. It may seem like weakness, but it is the greatest power in the world. To fools it seems like foolishness, but to the wise it is divine wisdom (1 Cor 1:18–25).

11. "Lead us not into temptation"

"This petition goes to the root of the preceding one, for our sins" [which need to be forgiven] "result from our consenting to temptation; we therefore ask our Father not to 'lead' us into temptation" (CCC 2846).

But God never actively leads anyone into temptation; that is the work of the Evil One. " 'God cannot be tempted by evil and he himself tempts no one' [Jas 1:13]; on the contrary, he wants to set us free from evil" (CCC 2846). The Greek word for "lead" here "means both 'do not allow us to enter into temptation' and 'do not let us yield to temptation' [cf. Mt 26:41]" (CCC 2846).

"Temptation" could also be interpreted as "trials", so that this petition means we humbly confess our weakness and ask God to be gentle to us, as promised: "A bruised reed he will not break" (Is 42:3). It would be arrogant to ask God for trials, thinking we were strong enough to endure them. It is God's business, not ours, to decide each person's quantity of trials. It is our business to avoid them when possible and endure them in faith when it is not. Even Christ asked, "Father, if it be possible, let this cup [of suffering] pass from me." Only then did he add, "If this cannot pass unless I drink it, your will be done" (Mt 26:39, 42). We are not to pretend to be stronger or holier than Christ!

But we are to believe that "God is faithful, and he will not let you be tempted beyond your strength, but with the temptation will also provide the way of escape, that you may be able to endure it" (1 Cor 10:13).

"The Holy Spirit makes us *discern* between trials, which are necessary for the growth of the inner man,[13] and temptation, which leads to sin and death.[14] We must also discern between being tempted and consenting to temptation. Finally, discernment unmasks the lie of temptation, whose object appears to be good, a 'delight to the eyes' and desirable [cf. Gen 3:6], when in reality its fruit is death" (CCC 2847). Satan is a fisherman; inside his bait is his hook.

12. "But deliver us from evil"

Every religion in the world promises deliverance. Not all religions believe in a God, a divine law, a life after death, or even a soul (Buddhism, for example). But all offer deliverance.

In Christianity, deliverance is not an abstraction, an ideal, or a state of mind, but a relationship with a Person: the Deliverer, the Savior. And evil is a relationship with his enemy. "In this petition, evil is not an abstraction, but refers to a person, Satan, the Evil One, the angel who opposes God" (CCC 2851). " '[A] liar and the father of lies,' Satan is 'the deceiver of the whole world' [Jn 8:44; Rev 12:9]. Through him sin and death entered the world and by his definitive defeat all creation will be 'freed from the corruption of sin and death' [15] " (CCC 2852). "Therefore the Spirit and the Church pray: 'Come, Lord Jesus' [Rev 22:17, 20], since his coming will deliver us from the Evil One" (CCC 2853).

"When we ask to be delivered from the Evil One, we pray as well to be freed from all evils, present, past, and future, of which he is the author or instigator. In this final petition, the Church brings before the Father all the distress of the world" (CCC 2854), confident that "earth has no sorrows that heaven cannot heal."

Christ puts this petition last. We tend to put it first. The child puts it first; his first prayer is usually: "God, help me!" This is a perfectly good prayer, and the greatest saints never outgrow it; but they outgrow putting it first. Instructed by the Lord's Prayer, they wrap it in adoration. For the God we petition without adoring and loving and trusting can be treated not as a person but as a machine; not an end but a means. When we do not get what we want from a machine, we abandon it. When we don't get what we want from a person whom we love and trust, we do not abandon him. Much less with God.

---

[13] Cf. Lk 8:13–15; Acts 14:22; Rom 5:3–5; 2 Tim 3:12.
[14] Cf. Jas 1:14–15.
[15] *Roman Missal*, Eucharistic Prayer IV, 125.

Adoration changes not only the place of our petition but also its quality; changes it from demanding or cajoling or complaining (all of which are self-centered) into trusting (which is God-centered). We are honestly to confront and acknowledge our needs and then place them all in God's hands and leave them there, turning our attention away from ourselves and our problems and back to him.

We are promised deliverance, but not instant deliverance. Our deliverance is not instantaneous because our being is not instantaneous. If a machine does not work immediately, it is defective. Persons, and love, however, take time to grow. Religion is about love and persons, not machines. Therefore deliverance takes time. It took God thousands of years to prepare the Cross.

For that is where deliverance takes place. It is a bloody business, deliverance. The Lord's Prayer ends with the Cross, with the gospel, with Christ. It is the "Lord's Prayer" not only because Christ is its author but also because he is its fulfillment.

13. "For thine is the kingdom, the power, and the glory, now and forever. Amen"

This doxology ("word of praise") is not in Scripture, but the Church added it very early in her history. It is right to end the prayer as it began—with adoration and praise—because our lives and the life of the universe will do the same. God is the Alpha and the Omega, the First and the Last. The prayer conforms to the very structure of reality.

"Amen" does not mean simply "I'm finished now", but "So be it!" It is not a mere wish but a word of command. When a great king says "So be it", it is done. The King of the universe has made us princes (Ps 45:16), and prayer is our staff of power. "More things are wrought by prayer than this world dreams of." If God let us see all the difference every one of our prayers made, throughout all of history and all of humanity, we probably would be unable ever to get up off our knees again.

"By the final 'Amen' we express our 'fiat' concerning the seven petitions: 'So be it'" (CCC 2865).

The Lord's prayer is not a mere thought or wish but an *act* (an "act of prayer"). In fact, each petition of the Lord's Prayer, if honestly meant, is sacramental: it effects what it signifies. When we say "Our Father", this faith ratifies our sonship (Rom 8:15–16). When we pray "Hallowed be thy name", we are by that act actually hallowing it. When we pray "Thy kingdom come", we are making it come, since the kingdom exists first of all in the praying heart. When we pray "Thy will be done", the very desire is its own fulfillment, for that *is* his will: that we pray and mean "Thy will be done." When we pray, "Give us this day our daily bread", we are already receiving our daily bread, the food of our souls, which is prayer. When we pray "Forgive us our trespasses as we forgive those who trespass against us", we are forgiving others, for we are praying for our own damnation if we are not. When we pray, "Lead us not into temptation", we are escaping temptation by placing ourselves in the presence of God. And when we pray "Deliver us from evil", we are effecting that deliverance by holding up our sins and our needs into the burning light of God, against which no darkness can stand.

Chapter 11

MARY

1. The high place of Mary in Catholicism

It is fitting to conclude this book on the whole of the Catholic religion with a chapter on Mary, because everything in the Catholic religion exists for the single purpose that was most clearly and perfectly fulfilled in her: to conform us to the image of her Son, to make humanity Christlike. Mary shows us the summit of God's success in his saint-making business and also the summit of *humanity's* success, how high humanity can rise under God's grace.

She thus shows us ourselves; for what he did for Mary, he wants to do for us. He announced his plan for us: "You . . . must be perfect, as your heavenly Father is perfect" (Mt 5:48). If we cannot fulfill this divine demand in this life, as Mary did, he will not rest until we have fulfilled it in heaven. He will not lower his ideal for us, only postpone its fulfillment. We are all "called to be saints" (Rom 1:7).

Saints are made by love (*agapē*, charity; see part 2, chapter 4, section 13). That is why Mary is the greatest saint: she was full of the most perfect love: both God's love to Mary and Mary's love to God:

—of God's love to Mary, because in Mary God exalted a creature as much as any creature could be exalted. He gave "to the maximum". To give her maximum glory, he gave her maximum grace. Mary was literally "full of grace". She was "wholly borne by God's grace" (CCC 490), like a perfect surfer on a perfect wave.

—of Mary's love to God, because she also gave "to the maximum"; she obeyed "the first and greatest commandment", to love God with her whole heart and mind and soul and strength, with perfect charity, simply and purely. As God withheld nothing from her, she withheld nothing from him.

We will show how Mary fits into each of the three main parts of the Catholic faith. (a) First, we will explain the Church's main Marian *doctrines* as expressed in her main titles: the "New Eve", the "Virgin Mother", the "Mother of God", her "Immaculate Conception", her Assumption into heaven, and her role as "Advocate", "Mediatrix of All Graces", and "Co-redemptrix" (sections 3–8). (b) Next, we will summarize Marian *morality*: her faith, her submission, and its fruit, her fearless joy (section 9). (c) Finally, we will look at Marian *prayer*: both prayers by her and prayers to her; and the spiritual importance of Mary today in relation to the Church in the next millennium, especially with regard to Marian prophetic apparitions and with regard to ecumenical unity (sections 10–16).

2. The primary objection to Catholic teaching about Mary

Most devout Protestants find the Church's teachings about and devotions to Mary the single most objectionable thing about the Catholic religion. On the other hand, most devout Catholics find them the crowning glory of their religion, as Mary is the crowning glory of the human race, "our tainted nature's solitary boast". For the most beautiful thing in the universe is a saint; and Mary is the most perfect saint; therefore Mary is the most beautiful thing in the universe. Why would Protestants object to this?

Because they worry that the Catholic Church, in raising Mary so high, obscures the uniqueness and all-sufficiency of Christ. Catholics find this objection strange, for Mary can no more rival Christ than the reflection of a face in a mirror can rival that face. How could Mary obscure Christ? All her beauty is his. She is only his obedient, humble handmaid: that is precisely why she is so highly revered. Mary's greatness, and Catholics' devotion to her, is completely dependent on her total dependence on him, beginning at the Annunciation, when her submission to the Word of God made his Incarnation and our salvation possible. And her whole effort now, in interceding with him for us in heaven, and also whenever she appears to anyone on earth, is to point beyond herself to Christ.

In the fundamental formula for Mary—"Mother of God"—is contained the fundamental formula for Christ: true God and true man, that is, God truly born from this human mother.

Mary is "full of grace", as the angel announced and as the Hail Mary confesses, for this reason: she was filled with grace because she was filled with *Christ*. "To become the mother of the Savior, Mary 'was enriched by God with gifts appropriate to such a role' [*LG* 56]" (CCC 490), beginning with her Immaculate Conception. She was the perfect door for the perfect God to enter this imperfect world.

It is no accident that Catholic art, like Scripture, almost always portrays Mary in relation to Christ rather than alone. She is about to conceive Christ (at the Annunciation), has just given birth to him (at the Nativity), surrounds his infancy (as the Madonna), stands at his Cross (at the Crucifixion), or receives his dead body (in the Pietà). Her Assumption is to him; when she is crowned Queen of Heaven, it is by him; and when she appears on earth (as at Fatima or Guadalupe), it is to do his work.

Mary's light is like that of the moon, totally reflected from the sun, the Son of God. This is true in all three dimensions of the Catholic religion: theology, morality, and liturgy. (a) All the Marian dogmas are Christocentric; "What the Catholic faith believes about Mary is based on what it believes about Christ, and what it teaches about Mary illumines in turn its faith in Christ" (CCC 487). (b) Mary is also the perfect moral ideal precisely because of her perfect submission to Christ. And (c) "Mary's role in the Church is inseparable from her union with Christ and flows directly from it" (CCC 964).

3. Mary as the "New Eve"

This is the earliest of her titles, going back to the first Church Fathers, who see both her and her Son foretold in Genesis 3:15. After Adam and Eve have fallen, God says to the serpent: "I will put enmity between you and the woman, and between your seed and her seed; he shall bruise your head, and you shall bruise his heel."

"At the very beginning there was Eve; despite her disobedience, she receives the promise of a posterity that will be victorious over the evil one" (CCC 489). "This passage in Genesis" [3:15] "is called the *Protoevangelium* ('first gospel'): the first announcement of the Messiah and Redeemer, of a battle between the serpent and the Woman" (CCC 410). "[M]any Fathers and Doctors of the Church have seen the woman announced in the *Protoevangelium* as Mary, the mother of Christ, the 'new Eve' " (CCC 411). For Mary reverses Eve's disobedience with her obedience, in cooperation with Christ, the New Adam (1 Cor 15:21–22, 45), who reverses Adam's disobedience by his obedience "unto death, even death on a cross" (Phil 2:8).

Where Eve said No, Mary said Yes. Where Eve's faith failed, Mary's stood firm. "At the announcement that she would give birth to 'the Son of the

Most High' without knowing man, by the power of the Holy Spirit, Mary responded with the obedience of faith . . . : 'Behold, I am the handmaid of the Lord; let it be [done] to me according to your word' [Lk 1:28–38; cf. Rom 1:5]. . . . As St. Irenaeus says, 'Being obedient she became the cause of salvation . . . for the whole human race.' [1] Hence not a few of the early Fathers gladly assert . . . : 'The knot of Eve's disobedience was untied by Mary's obedience: what the virgin Eve bound through her disbelief, Mary loosened by her faith.' [2] Comparing her with Eve, they . . . frequently claim: 'Death through Eve, life through Mary' [3] " (CCC 494).

4. Mary as Virgin Mother

Mary is "the Blessed Virgin". She makes virginity blessed. This does not lessen the value of sex and marriage; it raises their value. For only a good thing can be worthily offered to God in sacrifice. (God invented sex and marriage, after all!)

The point of the Virgin Birth is not something negative but something positive: Christ's divinity. "The Fathers see in the virginal conception the sign that it truly was the Son of God who came in a humanity like our own" (CCC 496). "The gospel accounts understand the virginal conception of Jesus as a divine work [cf. Mt 1:18–25; Lk 1:26–28]" (CCC 497). He was conceived by the Holy Spirit, spiritually and supernaturally, instead of by Joseph, physically and naturally. Christ had no human father because he has a divine Father, and he has his divine nature from his Father in eternity. He received his human nature from his mother Mary in time, and from her alone.

The Church has always taught that Mary is *Aeiparthenos*—"ever-virgin"—before, during, and after Christ's birth. "Against this doctrine the objection is sometimes raised that the Bible mentions brothers and sisters of Jesus [cf. Mk 3:31–35; 6:3; 1 Cor 9:5; Gal 1:19]". . . . [But] "[i]n fact James and Joseph, 'brothers of Jesus,' are the sons of another Mary, a disciple of Christ, whom St. Matthew significantly calls 'the other Mary' [Mt 13:55; 28:1; cf. Mt 27:56]. They are close relations of Jesus, according to an Old Testament expression" [4] (CCC 500). The Hebrew expression can mean "cousins" as well as "brothers".

The *Catechism* mentions four "reasons why God in his saving plan wanted his Son to be born of a virgin" (CCC 502):

[1] St. Irenaeus, *Adv. haeres.* 3, 22, 4: PG 7/1, 959A.
[2] St. Irenaeus, *Adv. haeres.* 3, 22, 4: PG 7/1, 959A.
[3] *LG* 56; Epiphanius, *Haer.* 78, 18: PG 42, 728CD–729AB; St. Jerome, *Ep.* 22, 21: PL 22, 408.
[4] Cf. Gen 13:8; 14:16; 29:15; etc.

a. "Mary's virginity manifests God's absolute initiative in the Incarnation. Jesus has only God as Father" (CCC 503).

b. "Jesus is conceived by the Holy Spirit in the Virgin Mary's womb because he is the New Adam, who inaugurates the new creation: 'The first man was from the earth, a man of dust; the second man is from heaven' [1 Cor 15:45, 47]" (CCC 504). "By his virginal conception, Jesus, the New Adam, ushers in *the new birth* . . . 'not of blood nor of the will of the flesh nor of the will of man, but of God' [Jn 1:13]" (CCC 505).

c. "Mary is a virgin because her virginity is *the sign of her faith*.[5] . . . 'Mary is more blessed because she embraces faith in Christ than because she conceives the flesh of Christ'[6]" (CCC 506).

d. Mary is not just virgin but "virgin *mother*"; and not just the mother of Jesus, but also "her spiritual motherhood extends to all men whom indeed he came to save" (CCC 501). "At once virgin and mother, Mary is the symbol and the most perfect realization of the Church: 'the Church indeed . . . by receiving the word of God in faith becomes herself a mother. By preaching and Baptism she'" [the Church] "'brings forth sons, who are conceived by the Holy Spirit and born of God, to a new and immortal life. She herself is a virgin, who keeps in its entirety and purity the faith she pledged to her spouse' [*LG* 64; cf. 63]" (CCC 507).

5. Mary as "Mother of God"

As the Ecumenical Council of Ephesus declared in A.D. 431, "Mary is truly 'Mother of God' since she is the mother of the eternal Son of God made man, who is God himself" (CCC 509). "In fact, the One whom she conceived as man by the Holy Spirit, who truly became her Son according to the flesh, was none other than the Father's eternal Son, the second person of the Holy Trinity. Hence the Church confesses that Mary is truly 'Mother of God' (*Theo-tokos*)"[7] (CCC 495).

Mary's title "Mother of God" is inseparable from Christ's two essential titles, "Son of God" and "Son of Man"; to deny Mary her title is to deny Christ his. To deny that Mary is the Mother of God is either to deny Christ's divinity (that is, to deny that Mary's Son is God) or to deny his Incarnation (that is, to deny that God really became Mary's Son). And these two doctrines, of Christ's divinity and Incarnation, are two of the earliest and most central of all Christian dogmas. They were formulated in the two earliest and shortest Christian creeds in the New Testament: "Jesus is Lord" (*Kyrios*,

[5] *LG* 63; cf. 1 Cor 7:34–35.
[6] St. Augustine, *De virg.*, 3: PL 40, 398.
[7] Council of Ephesus (431): DS 251.

God) (1 Cor 12:3; Phil 2:11) and "Jesus Christ has come in the flesh" (1 Jn 4:2). If we believe that Jesus is God and that Mary is Jesus' mother "in the flesh", then we must believe that Mary is the Mother of God "in the flesh". Mary and Jesus are creedally inseparable.

Since Mary is the Mother of Christ, Mary is also the Mother of the Church, for the Church and Christ are inseparable. They are one Body. Thus Mary is "the mother of the 'whole Christ' [cf. Jn 19:25–27]" [Head and Body]. "As such, she was present with the Twelve . . . [Acts 1:14] at the dawn of the 'end time' which the Spirit was to inaugurate on the morning of Pentecost with the manifestation of the Church" (CCC 726).

Mary is therefore *our* mother, if we are Catholics, for "We *are* the Church." Christ gave her to us and us to her from the Cross: "When Jesus saw his mother, and the disciple whom he loved [John, representing all disciples] standing near, he said to his mother, 'Woman, behold your son!' Then he said to the disciple, 'Behold, your mother!' And from that hour the disciple took her to his own home" (Jn 19:26–27). And the Church did what John did: heard Christ's command and obeyed it; beheld Mary and took her into our homes and hearts.

6. Mary's Immaculate Conception

Non-Catholics (and even Catholics) often confuse the Immaculate Conception with the Virgin Birth. But the Virgin Birth refers to *Christ* being conceived in his mother Mary's womb without sexual intercourse from a human father, while the Immaculate Conception refers to *Mary* being conceived in *her* mother Anna's womb without *original sin*. (It is the world, not the Church, that confuses sex with sin here!)

"Through the centuries the Church has become ever more aware that Mary, 'full of grace' through God [Lk 1:28], was redeemed from the moment of her conception. That is what the dogma of the Immaculate Conception confesses . . . : 'The most Blessed Virgin Mary was, from the first moment of her conception, by a singular grace and privilege of almighty God and by virtue of the merits of Jesus Christ, Savior of the human race, preserved immune from all stain of original sin' [8] " (CCC 491).

The dogma was not officially defined until 1854, for it took time for the Church to understand it properly and define it; but its substance had been known and believed from the beginning, since it was present from the beginning in the original "deposit of faith"—like all dogmas, including the Trinity, the Incarnation, and the canon of the New Testament, all of which took centuries before they were understood and defined infallibly. The

---

[8] Pius IX, *Ineffabilis Deus*, 1854: DS 2803.

truth did not change with time; the Church's awareness and understanding of it did.

By God's grace Mary was not only immaculately conceived without original sin (natural sinfulness), but also preserved from all actual sin (committed sins) during her life. This total sinlessness of Mary, far from detracting in any way from Christ, was (a) wholly *for* Christ's sake and (b) wholly *from* Christ's power.

a. Mary's glory was wholly for Christ, for his Incarnation: "To become the mother of the Savior, Mary 'was enriched by God with gifts appropriate to such a role' [LG 56]. The angel Gabriel at the moment of the annunciation salutes her as 'full of grace' [Lk 1:28]" (CCC 490). Because of her vocation to be Mother of God, "it was necessary that she be wholly borne by God's grace" (CCC 490). "It was fitting that the mother of him in whom 'the whole fullness of deity dwells bodily' [Col 2:9] should herself be 'full of grace' " (CCC 722). It was for Christ's glory that Mary was glorified.

The simplest answer to the Protestant objection to the doctrine of Mary's sinlessness is this: Suppose God had not made Mary "full of grace" and immaculate; would Christ have had more glory if Mary had thus had less? The objection has three hidden errors: Mary and Jesus are never rivals, glory is not a divisible quantity like money, and God is not a miser with his grace.

b. Mary's glory is wholly *from* Christ, too, as the moon's glory is wholly from the sun. "The 'splendor of an entirely unique holiness' by which Mary is 'enriched from the first instant of her conception' comes wholly from Christ: she is 'redeemed . . . by reason of the merits of her Son' [LG 53, 56]" (CCC 492).

Mary, too, needed Christ for her salvation, just as we do, but she was saved before she sinned, while we were saved after we sinned. It is like one person being saved from a disease by an inoculation to prevent it, and another person being saved from the same disease by an operation to cure it—by the same doctor.

7. Mary's Assumption into heaven

Mary, " 'when the course of her earthly life was finished, was taken up body and soul into heavenly glory' [9] " (CCC 966). This dogma, too, is Christocentric. Like the Immaculate Conception, it is both from Christ and for Christ. It is from Christ because "[t]he Assumption of the Blessed Virgin is a singular participation in her Son's Resurrection and an anticipation of the resurrection of other Christians" (CCC 966). And it is *for*

[9] LG 59; cf. Pius XII, *Munificentissimus Deus* (1950): DS 3903; cf. Rev 19:16.

Christ because God did this for her " 'so that she might be the more fully conformed to her Son, the ... conqueror of sin and death' [10] " (CCC 966). Death is the consequence of sin, and it was fitting that sinless Mary be spared sin's consequence.

There are grave sites, or reported grave sites, and relics, or reported relics, of the bodies of all the other important early saints and apostles, but there is none at all for Mary.

What of Mary after her Assumption? The last glorious mystery of the Rosary is the Coronation of Mary as "Queen of Heaven"—the fulfillment of her humility, as prophesied in her Magnificat: "All generations shall call me blessed.... He has put down the mighty from their thrones, and exalted those of low degree" (Lk 1:48, 52). Like everything about her, it points to Christ; for the reason we call her blessed is his grace: "For he who is mighty has done great things for me, And holy is his name" (Lk 1:49). And it verifies what Christ said, that "the last will be first, and the first last" (Mt 20:16).

8. The titles "Advocate", "Mediatrix of All Graces", and "Co-redemptrix"

What is Mary doing now? Praying for us, interceding with her Son, with more wisdom and power than any other creature. We are invited to invoke her intercession. Thus, she is our "Advocate".

There is no kind of grace she cannot ask God for and mediate; and in so doing she is the "Mediatrix of All Graces".

Finally, by her faith and submission, she cooperates still, as she did on earth, with God's will and work of redemption. "To cooperate" means "to work with". Mary cooperates with God by her faith and submission. She says her *Fiat*, her "Let it be done", still, in praying to her Son to come to us with his saving grace, and in this way she is "Co-redemptrix". The "co" here does not mean "equal" but "helping", as a humble handmaid helps a great Lord— a Lord who exalts his handmaids rather than keeping them passive and inactive.

The Church has not dogmatically defined these three titles, but, properly understood, they are in line with everything else the Church has already defined about Mary. The reluctance some feel toward applying these titles to Mary is usually based on the fear that using them is to confuse Mary with Christ, to exalt her too much, or to compromise Christ's uniqueness. But as we have seen before, every facet of Mary's greatness, from her Immaculate Conception to her present role as advocate and intercessor in heaven,

[10] *LG* 59; cf. Pius XII, *Munificentissimus Deus* (1950): DS 3903; cf. Rev 19:16.

consists precisely in her transparency to Christ, like a clear window. *That* is why she is associated so closely with his work. " 'Mary's function . . . in no way obscures or diminishes this unique mediation of Christ, but rather shows its power. But the Blessed Virgin's salutary influence on men . . . flows forth from the superabundance of the merits of Christ, rests on his mediation, depends entirely on it, and draws all its power from it' [LG 60]. 'No creature could ever be counted along with the Incarnate Word and Redeemer; but just as the priesthood of Christ is shared in various ways both by his ministers and the faithful, and as the one goodness of God is radiated in different ways among his creatures, so also the unique mediation of the Redeemer does not exclude but rather gives rise to a manifold cooperation which is but a sharing in this one source' [LG 62]" (CCC 970).

St. Paul says "there is one mediator between God and men, the man Christ Jesus" (1 Tim 2:5); but "one" here (*eis*) means "first", not "only". Just as we share Christ's sonship by participation (Jn 1:12), we share his work (cooperation) of our salvation (Phil 2:12). Mary does this too, in a preeminent way.

"Share" is the key word. Unlike pagan gods and bad fathers, God is not in competition with his children. He withholds his gifts from us only when necessary for our own good because of our sins—which he did not need to do with Mary. A key Catholic principle is that grace does not rival, demean, or suppress nature but perfects it. God perfects the natural instruments he uses, especially Mary. And in fact, not only Mary but all Christians share in the work of cooperating with God (1 Cor 3:9), mediating his grace, being instruments in his work of salvation, and being advocates for others by effective intercessory prayer (Jas 5:16). If Mary cannot do these things, we certainly cannot; if we can, she certainly can. For "She uttered her 'yes' 'in the name of all human nature' " (St. Thomas Aquinas, *Summa theologiae* III, 30, 1).

This is how she is our spiritual "mother". The title "mother" is not something subjective and sentimental, but a real analogy to physical childbearing: " '[S]he cooperated by her obedience, faith, hope, and burning charity in the Savior's work of restoring supernatural life to souls. For this reason she is a mother to us in the order of grace' [LG 61]" (CCC 968). " 'This motherhood of Mary in the order of grace continues uninterruptedly from the consent which she loyally gave at the Annunciation and which she sustained without wavering beneath the cross, until the eternal fulfillment of all the elect. Taken up to heaven she did not lay aside this saving office but by her manifold intercession continues to bring us the gifts of eternal salvation. . . . Therefore the Blessed Virgin is invoked in the Church under the titles of Advocate, Helper, Benefactress, and Mediatrix [LG 62]" (CCC 969).

9. Mary as moral ideal

Her perfection. In Mary alone among all the merely human beings who have ever lived on earth, there is no gap between the real and the ideal, between what she was and what she should have been, between her will and God's will, between her actual life in time and God's eternal plan for her. That is why the Church applies to her, in the liturgy of her feast days, the scriptural words about divine Wisdom, eternally in God's presence: because Mary's actual earthly life was no different from God's eternal plan for her. She alone perfectly realized God's perfect will; she is the greatest Artist's greatest masterpiece.

Her charity. Mary's holiness is not just negative (sinlessness) but positive (charity). Her freedom *from* all sin, both original and actual, is only a means to the greater end of her freedom—*for* perfect charity. Goodness is not primarily purity but plenitude, as perfect gold is not primarily its lack of imperfections but its perfection. Purity is essential to gold only because gold is something worthy to be purified.

Her hope. Hope is faith directed to the future, to God's promises. That Mary is blessed because she has perfect faith and hope is the prophetic point of Elizabeth's words that prompted Mary's Magnificat (Lk 1:45): "Blessed is she who believed that there would be a fulfilment of what was spoken to her from the Lord."

The prayer Hail, Holy Queen also addresses Mary as "*our* hope". Our hope of what? Of moral perfection, for one thing. If no merely human being were ever sinless, like Mary, we would think avoiding sin was impossible; we would limit sinlessness to divinity and despair of humanity. Mary gives humanity hope, a hope for perfection that will be fulfilled for each of us in heaven. Mary is a sign that God still has high hopes for us.

Her joy. Mary's moral perfection also shows us the secret of joy. The first five mysteries of the Rosary, which center around events in her life recorded in the Gospels, are the "joyful mysteries". The secret of her joy is her self-surrender. She is "too self-renounced for fears". Fear is perhaps the most common obstacle to joy because it is the most common obstacle to sanctity. Many sins stem from fear: thieves fear poverty, the violent fear weakness, liars fears truth, cowards fear suffering, adulterers fear loneliness. But Mary's "perfect love casts out fear" (1 Jn 4:18). Mary is so in love with Christ and with us that she forgets herself, and her fears, and so is liberated from fear into joy. There is no reason to keep her secret secret!

Her faith. Faith also casts out fear, and Mary's faith is perfect because it is simple: her "faith is to submit freely to the word that has been heard" [from God], "because its truth is guaranteed by God, who is Truth itself.... The Virgin Mary is its most perfect embodiment" (CCC 144). "The Virgin Mary most perfectly embodies the obedience of faith. By faith Mary welcomes the tidings and promise brought by the angel Gabriel, believing that 'with God nothing will be impossible.' [Lk 1:37–38; cf. Gen 18:14] . . . It is for this faith that all generations have called Mary blessed [cf. Lk 1:48]" (CCC 148). " 'Nothing is more apt to confirm our faith and hope than holding it fixed in our minds that nothing is impossible with God. Once our reason has grasped the idea of God's almighty power, it will easily and without any hesitation admit everything that [the Creed] will afterwards propose for us to believe—even if they be great and marvellous things, far above the ordinary laws of nature' [11] " (CCC 274).

Her simplicity. It is hard to be as saintly as Mary only because it is hard to be as simple as Mary, simply to say (and live) Yes to God and nothing more, no qualifications, no "ifs, ands, or buts". The secret of all the saints is in Mary's single word: her *Fiat*, her Yes, her Amen. The word *islam*, which means "submission", or "the peace that comes from submission to God", expresses that simplicity. (In the religion of Islam, by the way, Mary is also held in very high esteem as its exemplar and embodiment.)

There is nothing more to be said about Mary as the perfect moral example. She is the perfect example precisely because there is nothing more to be said.

10. Devotion to Mary

" 'The Church's devotion to the Blessed Virgin is intrinsic to Christian worship' [12] " (CCC 971). It is "home-grown", not an alien addition, an imitation of paganism. It is authentically Christian and incarnational.

"The Church rightly honors 'the Blessed Virgin with special devotion. From the most ancient times the Blessed Virgin has been honored with the title of "Mother of God," to whose protection the faithful fly in all their dangers and needs. . . . This very special devotion . . . differs essentially from the adoration which is given to the incarnate Word and equally to the Father and the Holy Spirit' [LG 66]" (CCC 971).

We revere all saints with *dulia* (human reverence and devotion) and Mary with *hyperdulia* (the greatest human reverence and devotion), but worship and adoration (*latria*) are given to God alone. There is only a difference in degree between Mary and us but a difference in kind between Mary and Christ. Therefore there is also a difference in degree between the reverence paid to Mary (*hyperdulia*, supreme human respect) and the reverence paid to other saints (*dulia*), but there is a difference in kind between our reverence given

---

[11] *Roman Catechism*, I, 2, 13.
[12] Lk 1:48; Paul VI, *MC* 56.

to Mary and our *worship* (*latria*) of Christ. The same is true of their work: her intercession, the saints' intercession, and the intercession of our friends who pray for us on earth are different only in degree; but there is a difference in kind between Christ's unique intercession and any human's. Ours—and Mary's—is totally dependent on him.

Devotion to Mary fosters and purifies our adoration of God rather than polluting it. Devotion to idols does not foster adoration of God, but devotion to his saints does. For a saint is like a stained-glass window that makes us more aware and appreciative of the divine light. And the holier the saint, the better the window, the more our devotion to that saint fosters our adoration of God. Thus devotion to Mary " 'greatly fosters this adoration' [*LG* 66]" (CCC 971).

11. The prayers of Mary

a. Mary's most essential prayer is her simple response to the angel. "She whom the Almighty made 'full of grace' responds by offering her whole being: 'Behold I am the handmaid of the Lord; let it be [done] to me according to your word.' '*Fiat*': this is Christian prayer: to be wholly God's" (CCC 2617).

b. "The Gospel reveals to us how Mary prays and intercedes in faith. At Cana [cf. Jn 2:1–12], the mother of Jesus asks her son for the needs of a wedding feast; this is the sign of another feast—that of the wedding of the Lamb where he gives his body and blood at the request of the Church, his Bride" (CCC 2618).

c. "[T]he Canticle of Mary [cf. Lk 1:46–55], the *Magnificat* . . . is the song both of the Mother of God and of the Church" (CCC 2619). It is truly "magnificent" because it "magnifies" the Lord, who has magnified his lowly saints, who magnify not themselves but him.

12. The prayer to Mary: The Ave Maria (Hail Mary)

The Church has addressed Mary trillions of times with the most repeated prayer in human history, the Hail Mary and its "string of roses" in the Rosary.

"*Hail Mary.*" "[T]he greeting of the angel Gabriel opens this prayer. It is God himself who, through his angel as intermediary, greets Mary. Our prayer dares to take up this greeting" [13] (CCC 2676) and, by standing with the angel, becomes angelic. We say, not "hello" (or "hi!"), but "hail"; our speech is high and holy as we hail her, meek and lowly.

"*Full of grace, the Lord is with thee.*" She is not just "graced", but "*full of*

[13] Cf. Lk 1:48; Zeph 3:17b.

grace", 100 percent, up to the brim, to the creature's limit. Why? Because Christ the Lord himself is with her, wholly in her soul and wholly in her womb. "These two phrases of the angel's greeting shed light on one another. Mary is full of grace because the Lord is with her. The grace with which she is filled is the presence of him who is the source of all grace. 'Rejoice. . . O Daughter of Jerusalem . . . the Lord your God is in your midst' [Zeph 3:14, 17a]. Mary, in whom the Lord himself has just made his dwelling, is the daughter of Zion in person, the ark of the covenant, the place where the glory of the Lord dwells" (CCC 2676).

"Blessed art thou among women and blessed is the fruit of thy womb, Jesus." "After the angel's greeting, we make Elizabeth's greeting our own" (CCC 2676). Not a word of the prayer so far is our invention, only Scripture's. When we say to Mary "blessed are *you*", we bless *God*, for he is the one who blessed her. And then, as soon as we bless her, we immediately turn to Christ: " . . . and blessed is the fruit of your womb, Jesus." Musically, the movement of the prayer stops only here. This is its floor, its bottom, its weight. "The name of Jesus is at the heart of Christian prayer. . . . The *Hail Mary* reaches its high point in the words 'blessed is the fruit of thy womb, Jesus' " (CCC 435).

"Holy Mary, Mother of God, pray for us. . . ." As with the Our Father, the first half of the prayer has been all self-forgetful praise. Only when we are transformed by this praise from fearful self-regard to joyful God-regard, do we now ask for our own needs, through her intercession. Our petition thus becomes trusting, not fretful or wheedling, for "[b]y entrusting ourselves to her prayer, we abandon ourselves to the will of God together with her" (CCC 2677). Her prayer is simply "Be it done to me according to thy will." When we ask her to pray for us, that is what we ask her to pray, for that is all she ever did pray on earth and all she ever will pray in heaven. We ask her intercession because she is *"holy* Mary", spiritually closest to God; and because she is *"Mother* of God", physically closest to God. She carried God in her womb!

"Sinners". Our petition is that of the publican, not the Pharisee; for mercy, not justice. The very act of asking Mary to pray for us expresses our humble acknowledgment that we are weak pray-ers, in need of her stronger help, like infants in need of a big sister. We further express this by confessing who we are: sinners, though not despairing but hoping and trusting God's mercy. In choosing Mary, the humblest of saints, as our intercessor, we express our humble realization that we lack her humility.

"Now and at the hour of our death". We ask for her help at the two most important moments in our lives: the two times when time intersects eternity. "[O]ur trust broadens further, already at the present moment, to surrender 'the hour of our death' wholly to her care. May she be there as she was at her son's death on the cross. May she welcome us as our mother at

the hour of our passing [cf. Jn 19:27] to lead us to her son, Jesus, in paradise" (CCC 2677). We ask this also in the prayer Hail, Holy Queen: "And
after this our exile, show unto us the blessed fruit of thy womb, Jesus." There
is nothing she will do more willingly than that.

No one can comfort us more at the hour of our death than our Mother.
No one can be a better "matchmaker" between ourselves and Christ, for no
one else is closer to Christ and no one else is closer to us, or loves us more,
than our Mother. Because she is Christ's Mother as well as ours, she makes
him brother to us. Like all mothers, she longs for her children to be close to
each other.

13. Mary as symbol of the Church

Since the times of the Church Fathers, Mary has been seen as both a symbol and an embodiment of "Holy Mother Church" for two reasons: because
she is mother and because she is holy.

a. Like *Mother Church*, she is the place where Christ comes to the
world. She mothers Christ, gives birth to Christ, gives Christ to the world.
She is something like a sacrament, effecting what she signifies, actually sharing with us, by her intercession, the grace of the Christ she constantly
points to.

b. She is also *holy*. Holiness is one of the "four marks of the Church" (see
part 1, chapter 7). " '[I]n the most Blessed Virgin the Church has already
reached that perfection whereby she exists without spot or wrinkle," [but]
"the faithful still strive to conquer sin and increase in holiness. And so they
turn their eyes to Mary': [14] in her, the Church is already the 'all-holy' " (CCC
829).

Holiness is the Church's primary business. Everything else in her is a means
to that end. Even the Magisterium (teaching authority) of the Church, however essential, is but a means to the greater end of her holiness (that is, her
members' holiness); and therefore the *Catechism* says that "the 'Marian'
dimension of the Church precedes the 'Petrine' [15] " (CCC 773), that is, Peter's
and succeeding popes' apostolic teaching authority. For "Mary goes before
us all in the holiness that is the Church's mystery" (CCC 773).

14. Mary and the sins of Catholics

If "Mary goes before us all" in holiness, we all go behind her in holiness.
We ask her to "pray for us sinners." The Church is a hospital for sinners.

---

[14] *LG* 65; cf. Eph 5:26–27.
[15] Cf. John Paul II, *MD* 27

Christ promised to keep his Church on earth free from error (infallible), but not her members free from sin. Her doctrine is pure, but her members' lives are not. Pope John Paul II has publicly confessed and apologized for past sins of Catholics. And whenever Catholics have failed, throughout history, it has been by being unholy not just generically or in any way, but in a specifically un-Marian way. All their sins have had a specifically anti-Marian character and could have been avoided if they had looked to Mary as their model. For example:

a. Pride instead of Marian humility made many seek earthly glory and empire for the Church when she acquired great political power.

b. Some within the Church at times sought to attain a heavenly end by worldly means: to save souls by power and control rather than by Marian humble, submissive love; thus the scandal of the torture of heretics and the Inquisition.

c. They sometimes encouraged worldly war and violence, as in the Crusades. But Mary defeats Satan (Gen 3:15; Rev 12:1–6) by her Christlike non-violence; she suffers evil rather than inflicts it.

d. They have often succumbed to greed for wealth, resulting in such corruption as provoked the Reformation. In contrast, when Catholics embrace the poverty of Mary's stable, the Church thrives, even when persecuted and martyred, whether in ancient Rome or under totalitarian dictatorships today.

e. Catholics in the past have been guilty of anti-Semitism. But Mary is the flower of Israel, and in the *Magnificat* she exalts Israel as a holy vessel prepared for God's Incarnation. God chose this people so that out of them he could choose this one person to be his own Mother. Through Mary all Israel shares in being God's Mother. To hate Jews is to hate God's Mother.

f. Mary, and woman in general, is a peacemaker; but the Church, through the faults of her own members, was rent by division in 1054 and in 1517. Mary, like her Son, longs to heal these divisions.

g. Churchmen have sometimes been intellectually arrogant, claiming authority outside the Church's God-given realm of faith and morals, as in the case of Galileo. When instead Catholics have had the patience to "ponder in their heart" the "deposit of faith", as Mary did (Lk 2:19), the Church has given birth to profound and beautiful teachings, such as her Marian doctrines.

h. Catholics have sometimes (especially in the late Middle Ages) substituted cleverness and complexity for intuitive wisdom and simplicity and have developed theology in a direction away from rather than back to Christ, like a tree whose complex system of branches grew too far from its roots. Vatican II turned us back to our roots in Christ, the Bible, and the apostolic Fathers, as Mary always turns us back to Christ and simplicity.

i. Overcomplexity has also produced elaborate legalism, such as that of the Pharisees. This was another reason for the Reformation: the law of love had been obscured by the love of law. Women instinctively perceive the primacy of love, especially when they are mothers, like Mary.

j. Pope John Paul II apologized to all women in the name of the Church, for churchmen have often shared society's prejudices against women and treated them as inferior (contrary to the Church's own teachings), even though a woman (Mary) is her only sinless saint and many of her greatest saints and Doctors of the Church have been women.

k. Most men and women in the Church today are infected with our secular society's obsession with lust. Lust among the clergy has caused great scandal and stumbling; and lust among the laity makes Catholics act (and sometimes even think) no differently from non-Catholics on issues of sexual morality: abortion, contraception, adultery, divorce, fornication, homosexual sex. Mary as Virgin Mother is a radically countercultural figure to a culture that worships sex and denigrates motherhood.

It is no coincidence that the Church has deepened her appreciation of Marian theology at the same time as she has deepened her understanding of Marian morality and has repudiated these anti-Marian sins. Mary is no exception to the rule that doctrine and holiness are inseparable and interdependent.

15. Catholic wisdom is Marian wisdom

Just as the Church has suffered whenever Catholics have displayed an un-Marian character, she has won the world (and will continue to do so) when Catholics have displayed specifically Marian characteristics, which are typically and distinctively Catholic wisdom. In fact, they are the themes that have run through all parts of this book, because they run through all parts of the Catholic faith. Five in particular stand out:

a. *Charity.* No one can argue with love. "Everybody loves a lover." God's love in Christ is Christianity's greatest selling point. It was the saints and martyrs—that is, the greatest lovers—who won the world for the Church. Saints are the irrefutable argument for Christianity. All morally sane human beings know the value of unselfish love. Among human institutions, religion emphasizes it the most. Among religions, Christianity emphasizes it the most. Within the Church, the saints exemplify it the most. And among the saints, Mary exemplifies it the most.

b. *Grace perfects nature.* Since charity "goes all the way up" into the divine nature, since God is unselfish and self-giving, that is why his grace always exalts, redeems, and perfects nature rather than depressing its value, bypassing it, or despairing of it. For he is a Father, and a good father trains his children to be mature co-workers with him, even though he does not need them and could do everything himself. This is why God gives us free will; why he allows evil and suffering; why he uses miracles very rarely; why he makes us "our brother's keeper"; and also why he arranges for Mary to be such a powerful cooperator. He gives *maximally*; he exalts Mary as much as any human being can be exalted.

c. *"Both-and" rather than "either-or"*. The Catholic instinct is to say Yes, like Mary, rather than No; to unite rather than divide; to make peace rather than war. The Church's gospel is a "full gospel", which always tends to a "both-and" instead of an "either-or" on potentially divisive issues like nature and grace, God and man, doctrine and morality, head and heart, truth and love, free will and predestination, individual and community, justice and mercy. Mary united these things perfectly, instinctively; and the Church has the same instinct.

d. *Optimism.* The Church's seriousness about evil scandalizes a world that has ceased to believe in sin; yet there is always a radical underlying optimism in her philosophy. The natural moral law can never be abolished from the heart of man (St. Thomas Aquinas, *Summa theologiae* I–II, 94, 6). Good is stronger than evil. God always wins. And he always surprises us and prepares something better than we could ever have imagined—as he did with Mary.

e. *Christocentrism.* This has been a recurring theme in every single chapter in this book, and it is Mary's supreme work: being totally centered in Christ. She is *for him*, and thus shows us ourselves and the meaning of our lives and who we are for.

16. Mary and the future

Marian apparitions. Apparitions (apparently miraculous appearances) of Mary have multiplied throughout the modern era, especially in the later decades of the twentieth century. Some of these the Church has declared inauthentic (such as those at Bayside, Long Island); some of them, after long and careful investigation, she has declared "worthy of belief" (such as those at Lourdes, France, in 1854, and at Fatima, Portugal, in 1917). Many of them are still under investigation (such as those at Garabandal, Spain; Akita, Japan; Medjugorge, Yugoslavia; Scottsdale, Arizona; Cairo, Egypt). These are private revelations, not Church dogma, and Catholics are not bound to believe in them (see CCC 67). But we cannot help asking, What is the significance of so many apparent apparitions of Mary today? What is their message?

Mary's messages usually have a prophetic tone: the need for repentance and conversion of heart to avoid disaster. This does not necessarily mean that the "end of the world" is near (though it may be, at any time: see Christ's parables in Matthew 24 and 25), but perhaps that the "end of the age", the end of the era of secularism and selfishness, is upon us.

Mary reveals no new secrets. All authentic apparitions and prophecies throughout Christian history repeat the message of Christ. All true prophets in Old Testament times, too, reminded God's people, when they had forgotten, what they had been told from the beginning. Mary's message, too, is not new; what she points to is still Christ and the need for conversion of heart to him.

Ecumenism. Mary's is an ecumenical message, a message of unity and peace. One of the most frequent and passionate themes of Marian apparitions is her desire for peace. For it is one of today's most obvious needs, both within the Church and within the world. But how can Mary be an agent for ecumenical unity? Protestants see Mary as a major *obstacle* to unity in the Church, since they object to the Catholic Church's Marian teachings. However, Protestants must agree that Mary's message is the key to unity, for her message is—today as always—simply to point to Christ. "Do whatever he tells you", she told the waiters at the wedding feast at Cana; and their obedience was rewarded with Christ's first miracle, turning water into wine. Christ has not stopped performing this miracle—he does it at every Eucharist—and Mary has not changed her formula. The formula is difficult only because it is so simple: "Do whatever he tells you." This is the key to unity because insofar as Christ is the Lord of all Christians, he is like the conductor of a single orchestra, and insofar as Christians believe and obey Mary's message of conversion to Christ, they will play in harmony, like the diverse instrument artists of an orchestra, because they follow a single baton. And we know his will is unity (Jn 17); therefore Mary's message, simply to follow him, as she did, is the key to unity.

Mary is also the key to unity between men and women. In an age of many "feminisms", Mary is the true "feminist", "blessed among women". Just as Christ reveals to us not only God but also ourselves, since he shows us what is a true and perfect and complete man—the only perfect man in history— so Mary shows us what a true and complete and perfect woman is, not just in words but in the flesh. In her we have something more than a set of abstract principles or ideals to argue about. We have instead the perfect "finished product", the living model.

And she is not a *passive* model, like a picture, but active, like a mother. She does not just "sit there" to be imitated, letting us do all the work. Rather, she acts, humbly and invisibly, as powerfully and as subtly as water wears away rock. She will not rest until she and her Son have finished his work of softening our hearts of stone by endless waves of prayer. For a mother's work is never done.

CONCLUSION

This is the Catholic faith. It is the "greatest story ever told"—either the greatest lie or the greatest truth. It is the incredible story of the Creator's proposal of spiritual marriage to the creature. You can accept or reject this proposal. You can believe it or not, as you choose. But if you do believe it, you should be prepared; you should know that this is no ordinary thing. You are embarking on life's greatest adventure, and you will never be the same again.

ABBREVIATIONS

AA	Vatican II, *Apostolicam actuositatem*
AAS	*Acta Apostolicae Sedes*
AG	Vatican II, *Ad gentes divinitus*, December 7, 1965
CA	John Paul II, Encyclical, *Centesimus annus*, May 1, 1991
CCEO	Corpus Canonum Ecclesiarum Orientalium
CD	Vatican II, *Christus Dominus*, October 28, 1965
CELAM	Consejo Episcopal Latinoamericano
CIC	Codex Iuris Canonici
CPG	Paul VI. *Credo of the People of God: Solemn Profession of Faith*, June 30, 1968
CT	John Paul II, Apostolic Exhortation, *Catechesi tradendae*, October 16, 1979
DCN	Apostolic Constitution *Divinae consortium naturae*, August 15, 1971
DeV	John Paul II, Encyclical, *Dominum et Vivificanum*, May 18, 1986
DH	Vatican II, *Dignitatis humanae*, December 7, 1965
DS	*Enchiridion Symbolorum Definitionum Enchiridion Symbolorum Definitionum et Declarationum de rebus fidei et morum*
DV	Vatican II, *Dei verbum*, November 18, 1965
EN	Paul VI, Apostolic Exhortation, *Evangelii nuntiandi*, December 8, 1975
FC	John Paul II, Apostolic Exhortation, *Familiaris consortio*, November 22, 1981
GE	Vatican II, *Gravissimum educationis*, October 28, 1965
GILH	General Introduction to the Liturgy of the Hours
GIRM	General Instruction to the Roman Missal
GS	Vatican II, *Gaudium et spes*, December 7, 1965
HV	Encyclical, *Humanae vitae*, July 25, 1968
Ide	Pius IX, Bull, *Ineffabilis Deus*, December 8, 1854
IM	Vatican II, *Inter mirifica*, December 4, 1963
LG	Vatican II, *Lumen gentium*, November 21, 1964
MC	Paul VI, Apostolic Exhortation, *Marialis cultus*, February 2, 1974
MD	John Paul II, Apostolic Letter, *Mulieris dignitatem*, August 15, 1988
MF	Paul VI, Encyclical, *Mysterium fidei*, September 3, 1965

NA Vatican I, *Nostra aetate*, 28 October 1965
OE Vatican II, *Orientalium ecclesiarum*, November 21, 1964
OP *Ordo paenitentiae* (Order of Penance)
OT Vatican II, *Optatam totius*, October 28, 1964
PC Vatican II, *Perfectae caritatis*, October 28, 1964
PG J. P. Migne, ed., *Patrologia Graeca*
PL J. P. Migne, ed., *Patrologia Latina*
PO Vatican II, *Presbyterorum ordinis*, December 7, 1965
RP John Paul II, Apostolic Exhortation, *Reconciliatio et pænitentia*, December 2, 1984
SC Vatican II, *Sacrosanctum concilium*, December 4, 1963
SS John Paul II, Encyclical, *Sollicitudo rei socialis*, December 30, 1987
UR Vatican II, *Unitatis redintegratio*, November 21, 1964
VQA John Paul II, Apostolic Letter, *Vicesimus quintus annus*, December 4, 1988